Ethnographic Research
A Reader

Ethnographic Research: A Reader

This Reader provides some of the set readings for a 16-week course (D844 Ethnography) which is offered by The Open University Masters programme in the Social Sciences.

The Open University Masters programme

Students can select from a wide range of courses to create a personal study programme or follow one of the named study lines to obtain a Masters degree. These include:

- an MSc in Social Research Methods
- an MSc in Psychological Research Methods
- an MSc in Psychology
- an MA in Social Policy and Criminology
- an MA in Cultural and Media Studies.

OU Supported Learning

The Open University's unique, supported open ('distance') learning Masters programme in the Social Sciences is designed to introduce the concepts, approaches, theories and techniques associated with a number of academic areas of study. The programme offers great flexibility. Students study in their own environments, in their own time, anywhere in the European Union. They receive specially prepared course materials and structured tutorial support throughout their coursework and assessment assignments.

How to apply

If you would like to register for this programme, or simply to find out more information, please write for the Masters in Social Sciences prospectus to The Open University, Course Reservations Centre, PO Box 625, MK7 6AA, UK (Telephone +44(0)1908 653 231 E-mail:ces-gen©nen.ac.uk) Details can also be viewed on our web page http://www.open.ac.uk

Ethnographic Research

A Reader

Edited by

Stephanie Taylor

SAGE Publications

London • Thousand Oaks • New Delhi

In association with

The Open
University

SAGE Publications Ltd
6 Bonhill Street
London EC2A 4PU

SAGE Publications Inc.
2455 Teller Road
Thousand Oaks, California 91320

SAGE Publications India Pvt Ltd
32, M-Block Market
Greater Kailash – I
New Delhi 110 048

British Library Cataloguing in Publication data

A catalogue record for this book is available from the British Library

ISBN 0 7619 7392 3
ISBN 0 7619 7393 1 (pbk)

Library of Congress Control Number available

Typeset by Photoprint, Torquay, Devon
Printed in Great Britain by The Cromwell Press Ltd,
Trowbridge, Wiltshire

Contents

Acknowledgements

The authors and publishers wish to thank the following for permission to use copyright material.

Chapter 1
Cambridge University Press for *In Search of Respect: Selling Crack in El Barrio* by Philippe Bourgois, 1995.

Chapter 2
Oxford University Press for 'Policing and Public Health: Law Enforcement and Harm Minimisation in a Street-level Drug Market' by L. Maher and D. Dixon, *British Journal of Criminology*, vol. 39, no. 4, pp. 488–512, 1999.

Chapter 3
Open University Press for *The Company She Keeps: An Ethnography of Girls' Friendship* by Valerie Hey, 1997.

Chapter 4
Clarendon Press for *The Art of Being Black: The Creation of Black British Youth Identities* by Claire E. Alexander, 1996.

Chapter 5
Sage Publications for 'Manufacturing sexual subjects, "harassment", desire and discipline on a Maquiladora shopfloor' by L. Salzinger, *Ethnography*, vol. 1, no. 1, July 2000, pp. 67–92.

Chapter 6
Cambridge University Press for 'Distributed cognition in an airline cockpit' by E. Hutchins and T. Klausen in Engestrom, Y. and Middleton, D. (eds), *Cognition and Communication at Work*, 1996.

Chapter 7
Routledge for *Tourists at the Taj: Performance and Meaning at a Symbolic Site* by Tim Edensor, 1998.

Chapter 8
National Communications Association 'The Global, the Local and the Hybrid: A Native Ethnography of Glocalization' by M.M. Kraidy, *Critical Studies in Mass Communication*, vol. 16, pp. 456–76, 1999.

Chapter 9
Blackwell for 'Humour as resistance to professional dominance in community mental health teams' by L. Griffiths, *Sociology of Health and Illness*, vol. 20, no. 6, pp. 874–95, 1998.

Chapter 10
Blackwell for 'Openness and specialisation: dealing with patients in a hospital emergency service' by N. Dodier and A. Camus, *Sociology of Health and Illness*, vol. 20, no. 4, pp. 413–44, 1998.

Researching the social: an introduction to ethnographic research

The aim of this Reader is to illustrate the innovation and variety within recent ethnographic research. It will be of interest to academics and students across the social sciences but is particularly directed towards novice researchers. It includes work from a range of disciplines and different social and national contexts, including Britain, the USA, Australia, India, France and Lebanon. The studies collected here provide an introduction to ethnographic research through example, demonstrating multiple approaches to data collection, analysis and project design. They range from a conventional ethnography, for which a researcher makes the enormous personal investment of moving into a different community for an extended period, to a tightly scheduled team project which employs several discrete methods of formal data collection (the first two studies in the collection exemplify these extremes) to, in a further contrast, a relatively small-scale project in which the principal form of data is audio-recorded talk (for instance, in the second to last reading). Despite their differences, these are all examples of ethnographic research, as are the other seven studies in the Reader.

What, then, characterizes ethnography? The term is wide ranging, with different associations and traditions within different disciplines. Some common features which are often identified are that it involves empirical work, especially observation in order to study people's lives, defined broadly ('human activities', Baszanger and Dodier, 1997: 8; 'ways of life', Denzin, 1997: xi; 'human experience', Willis and Trondman, 2000: 5). Recent theoretical texts also emphasize the centrality of writing (e.g. Denzin, 1997; Van Maanen, 1995). The studies in this collection conform to these points. More precisely, they have in common, first, that the researchers set out to study people and aspects of their lives and social worlds, and to produce a research text; secondly, that the text aims to be full, nuanced and non-reductive, incorporating change and process without resorting to simplistic aetiological models; and, thirdly, that the researchers consciously locate their work within the cross-currents of ongoing debates about ethnography and qualitative research. I use the term 'ethnographic tradition' to refer to these debates and their background and I will attempt to outline them in the next section, although it is impossible to explore them thoroughly in the space available. Some readers may therefore want to read the studies in conjunction with a text on ethnographic and qualitative research.[1] The exercises at the end of this book provide additional support. They are designed to draw readers' attention to the key features of each chapter. If the collection is to be used as a teaching text, these exercises could also provide a basis for seminar or tutorial discussion.

The ethnographic tradition

A historical overview of ethnographic research generally refers to European colonizers' accounts of 'other' peoples, the development of Western anthropological fieldwork in pre-industrial societies, and various studies of migrant and ethnic minorities and urban populations within the USA, particularly from the middle decades of the twentieth century.[2] This complexity is sometimes given chronological order as a succession of phases or 'moments' (Denzin, 1997: xi), characterized by differences in the relationships between the researcher and those being studied, and also in the researcher's aims and assumptions about the knowledge which such a study can produce. However, these phases can also be said to persist and co-exist across the contemporary field of academic social research (Denzin and Lincoln, 1998b: 12–13). An alternative way in which they can be summarized is therefore in terms of competing ideas, as a collection of challenges and counter-challenges around the central concern of social research, to understand people and their lives.

One major issue for social researchers has been a contest to achieve the same status as their counterparts in the natural and physical sciences. This has led some social scientists to advocate the use of quantitative methods which resemble those used to study the physical world. On the other hand, certain kinds of qualitative analysis (such as grounded theory) have been defended on the grounds that they too are rigorous and scientific. A third position has been the rejection of so-called 'scientific' methods and their premises as inappropriate for social research. One argument against such methods is that they deny social complexity in order to produce (over-) simple cause-and-effect models. Another related criticism is that they deny human agency and creativity in order to identify social laws as a basis for prediction. 'Scientific' approaches have also been criticized for producing an empty universalism by abstracting from the complexity of particular societies and their historically and culturally specific circumstances.[3]

Ethnography has been mainly associated with qualitative research but can also employ a combination of qualitative and quantitative methods.

Ethnographers may refer to these debates to make an argument for employing this form of research. They may present an ethnographic approach as a practical choice from one out of several alternatives; for instance, Maher and Dixon, the authors of the second study, suggest their ethnographic project produced a 'more accurate representation' of a street-level drug-using population than could have been achieved through survey research. Alternatively, ethnography may be associated with a rejection of the theoretical principles underlying scientific/quantitative research; this is the position taken by the first author, Bourgois. Several arguments have been presented to support the claim that ethnography is more appropriate to the study of the social world than scientific/quantitative methods. The ethnographic researcher is said to obtain an insider's view of a society and so to understand other people's own worldview, instead of taking the outsider's perspective of the conventional scientist. Ethnographic research is said to produce situated knowledge rather than universals and to capture the detail of social life (e.g., through 'thick description', Geertz, 1973, cited in Vidich and Lyman, 1998: 78; and 'slice of life' accounts, Denzin and Lincoln, 1998b: 15) rather than abstracting from this detail to produce reductive models.

The distinction between insider and outsider perspectives is implicated in several other issues. One of these is the extent to which research findings can be objective. The notion of objectivity suggests that a researcher is *able* to obtain knowledge of an external world as it exists independently of the research process (see Hammersley and Atkinson, 1995; Silverman, 1985). If this is accepted, then the aim of research is to maximize accurate observation and reduce distortion and bias to a minimum. (The term 'rigour' is often employed to suggest that research findings derive more from the data than from the researcher's interpretation, as if these can be separated, which is itself a part of the same realist/naturalist premise.) These assumptions are strongly, though not exclusively, associated with quantitative research methods (see Seale, 1999). Similar claims have also been made for conversation analysis.[4]

However, the notion of objectivity has been challenged by the reflexive turn in the social sciences. This draws attention to the researcher as a part of the world being studied and to the ways in which the research process constitutes what it investigates. It considers the identity of the researcher and the relationship between researcher and researched, which is seldom one of equals. Any form of research involves issues of power and these are particularly relevant to ethnographic research as it has so often been about people who are positioned as 'other' within large-scale relationships of domination and subordination. Examples would be the colonizer studying the colonized, a white person studying people of colour, or an established citizen studying an immigrant population.[5]

A somewhat different but related argument is that objectivity is not attainable because people's perceptions and interpretations are inevitably selective and are shaped by the understandings they bring to any situation; it is not possible to perceive the world as a separate step prior to attaching meaning to it. As Denzin says: 'Humans are always already tangled up . . . in a secondhand world of meanings and have no direct access to reality' (1997: 246). Accepting that people always experience the world through what Vidich and Lyman call 'a mediated framework . . . of symbols and cultural meanings' (1998: 44) has led some researchers to explore these meanings rather than attempt to investigate reality as if it were separate. This kind of exploration appears in the studies in this collection, for example, in accounts of the intersection of the social and the personal, and of discourses (e.g., in the chapters by Hey and Alexander). It is also part of the project of symbolic interactionist researchers (see Rock, 1979; Silverman, 1985). However, it is important to note that a researcher who is conducting such a project still does so from within the meanings in which she or he is already tangled.

It follows logically from this position that any account of a research project is also an interpretation rather than an objective description. This has led to a new focus in ethnography on writing and the research text. Classic texts have been re-examined as artful and selective constructions with similar features to writing which is referred to as literature or fiction.[6] For example, a 'realistic' piece of writing does not necessarily have a special relation to any reality but rather is characterized by a certain style which is *accepted* as realistic. Some postmodern ethnographers have experimented with producing new forms of text, for example, by including very extended passages of quotation in order to undermine the authority of a single authorial voice, or using poetic language in order to convey an emotional truth (such as pain) (see Denzin, 1997: chapter 7).

These developments have led some researchers to what Denzin and Lincoln have described as a 'double crisis of representation and legitimation' (1998b: 21). The crisis of representation arises when the research text is no longer assumed to capture the world which was studied; instead, the world presented in the text is accepted as the construction of the author. Does this mean that an ethnographer is unable to say anything about the social world which she or he set out to study? The crisis of legitimation arises when it is no longer assumed that research can be evaluated by checking it against the reality which it supposedly represents; this undermines conventional criteria for evaluation such as validity (see Seale, 1999 for a fuller discussion). Does this mean that there is no way of distinguishing good research from bad, or ethnography from, say, journalism or fiction? Denzin also identifies a third crisis, of 'praxis' (1997: 3), which concerns the application of findings. Together these might suggest that ethnography has reached an impasse in which ethnographic researchers can no longer trust themselves to collect and interpret data, write about other people or produce findings which have useful applications.

Fortunately, however, as this collection shows, the ethnographic tradition has not led to such a point of paralysis. Significant work continues. The writer who is perhaps most strongly associated with identifying the crises outlined above, Denzin (1997), does consider that the nature of ethnography and, especially, the ethnographic text should change. He suggests that there are other possibilities beyond conventional ethnography: for example, 'A feminist, communitarian, public ethnography, working hand in hand with public journalism, is one way to forward this project' (1997: 287). Other writers have suggested that the crisis of representation is exaggerated and more established approaches can still be employed. For instance, Hammersley (1998) argues that it is possible to accept that our perceptions and understandings of the world are mediated but still to operate with knowledge which is less than certain: in other words, 'knowledge claims can be judged in terms of their likely truth.' (Hammersley, 1998: 66).

Similarly, Willis and Trondman (2000) reject the idea that societies can be understood without reference to mediating ideas and culture, but they also consider it fruitless for a researcher to analyse culture as if it were free-floating. They call for 'the ethnographic recording of lived experience within the social' (Willis and Trondman, 2000: 10), suggesting that through such experience a researcher *can* obtain knowledge which has a wider reference. They also call for 'theoretically informed' ethnography and I would suggest that the studies collected here all fit into this category. The researchers proceed with an awareness of the issues and debates which I have outlined, acknowledging the limits to their claims and the situated nature of their findings, but still successfully conform to Willis and Trondman's description of ethnography as 'the disciplined and deliberate witness-cum-recording of human events' (2000: 5). The studies are not necessarily new classics (although this may be because they are so recent and some may well be on their way way to becoming so) but all are of high quality and all are texts which I found exciting and satisfying to read because of their complexity, elegance, commitment and energy.

The chapters

The first two chapters, in Part I, 'At society's margins', present studies of drug takers in inner-city areas. Bourgois's research was conducted in the area of New York City known as El Barrio, Maher and Dixon's in Cabramatta in Sydney, Australia. Both readings present an argument for the appropriateness of ethnographic methods to their concerns, although they differ markedly in their research approaches and style of writing.

The first chapter, by Bourgois, is based on an immersion study in the anthropological tradition. Bourgois moved into the area he was studying and tried to become a part of its community. His data are therefore his observations and his own experiences over an extended period as well as the transcribed talk which is presented in the text. His aim was to describe a phenomenon, social marginalization, and also, in doing so, to challenge an earlier, highly influential study of the same population, 'Nuyoricans' (New Yorkers of Puerto Rican descent). That study, by Oscar Lewis, gave rise to the theory of the 'culture of poverty', according to which successive generations within poor families become locked in a cycle of failure and crime. Bourgois is committed to a (by his account) less deterministic view of society which takes account of individual freedom to act, or agency, while also showing how 'history, culture and political-economic structures constrain the lives of individuals' (p. 17). The extracts which are included here from his book-length study concern the difficulties faced by 'Ray's network', a group of 'Nuyoricans' involved in the drug trade, when they try to move into 'legit' work. In response to the debates around writing referred to above, Bourgois discusses his selection of material and the process of creating the research text, and also the different impressions which readers may take from it.

The focus of Bourgois's study is broad. He is interested in the experiences and worldview of the group he is studying and how this shared culture impacts on their social position and prospects for the future. In contrast, the authors of the second study, Maher and Dixon, have more immediately pragmatic concerns, about the effect of certain policing practices on street-level drug use and public health. In addition, they aim, as they state at the end of this chapter, to demonstrate empirically how a problem can be solved, so as to develop new theory and change practices about policing through negative example, that is, by showing what does *not* work. They also aim to challenge preconceptions, in their case about the effectiveness of policing drug use. This is a team study involving observation of behaviours in public urban areas and interviews with drug users. Maher and Dixon present tables summarizing relevant characteristics of their sample, in a similar style to that of statistical studies, and they compare their research favourably to survey research. Both the style and the claim may be connected to their broader aims and the audience they wish to address, since it is widely accepted that quantitative research has often been more influential than qualitative in influencing policy-makers.[7]

Part II, 'Gendered identities', contains two British studies which investigate the social processes through which identities are constructed and lived out. Both researchers studied young people (though rather different age groups) and their peer relationships. Hey investigated teenage girls' friendships, suggesting that such friendships are of unacknowledged importance and intensity, and showing how in the interactions and negotiations around them girls' gender identities are reinforced. The research was conducted in two British city schools and the data include the notes girls pass to each other during class. This is therefore an example of observation within a school context, considered as a site for socialization. The chapter includes Hey's discussion of her role as a feminist ethnographer and also some of the access problems she encountered.

Chapter 4, by Alexander, has certain theoretical and methodological parallels with Hey, although this researcher conducts her study from a position of gender and racial difference. Alexander is interested in cultural identity, understood as fluid and heterogeneous, and how wider social relations of power are incorporated in the formation and expression of personal sexual/racial identities. She analyses the shared identity of a group of young black men ('the boys'), focusing on the group's internal dynamics and the ways it functions in the public sphere as a 'base for interaction and negotiation with wider society' (p. 94). It is not a fixed or bounded group but one which exists in and through its social interactions. Alexander is arguing against similar notions of underclass to those challenged by Bourgois and, particularly, against theories of black masculinity as pathological. She therefore aims to overturn or debunk certain existing assumptions.

Part III, 'Workplace practices', contains two contrasting observation studies. The first, by Leslie Salzinger, is a study of a Mexican export plant. Salzinger analyses the organization of the physical environment and work processes, showing how sexual subjectivities become incorporated in workplace relations and production. Her unit of analysis is therefore the workplace as a whole, including its physical layout and also the status of the plant within the larger transnational business organization and the electronics industry. She is interested in structural processes and practices rather than static structures. She is also interested in power, understood in a particular way. She analyses the workplace practices in terms of interpellation rather than coercion. In other words, she looks at how the workers respond to being 'hailed' (roughly, organized and generally regarded) in sexual terms, and how this response is simultaneously a participation in the production process. Salzinger therefore connects the macro scale of the workplace and organization with the micro level of individual subjectivity or sense of self.

This chapter demonstrates the range of data which the ethnographic researcher may use as evidence in a single study, although there is less explicit description of the data collection than in some other studies. The text includes accounts of the researcher's own observations, references to interviews, and direct quotations from talk directed to her (perhaps in interviews, perhaps in passing) and to other people (presumably overheard). She also reflects upon her own interactions and feelings. Other data, we can surmise, include official records, in-company records and perhaps news and academic articles on topics like the electronics industry and the Mexican economy. And of course there are the various sources listed in the references to the chapter.

Chapter 6 in this section, by Hutchins and Klausen, concerns a US study of pilots in a (simulated) airline cockpit. The researchers investigate work processes by employing a fine-grained analysis of talk between the pilots, analysing their talk and activities. Like Salzinger, they are interested in a unit which is larger than the individual person, but the focus here is on the effective operation of the workplace as 'the system that is composed of the pilots and the technology of the cockpit environment' (p. 139). This is analysed as 'a unit of cognitive analysis (p. 139)' and 'a system of *distributed cognition*' (p. 140). This focus derives from psychology but will be familiar to some students from other disciplines, such as education. Hutchins and Klausen want to demonstrate how flying a plane is not something which is 'done' by one person, acting as an individual expert. Rather, it is accomplished by a number of individuals coordinating their actions and using technology and a body of knowledge which has been developed by many people, over time. This may sound obvious: we are all familiar with the idea of a team, or a successful person who depends on her or his assistants. But Hutchins and Klausen are suggesting that the air crew interact so closely that they need to be understood as a single entity and not just as individuals working together. Human and non-human channels can be understood as alternative 'representational states' within the same system. One implication of this is that non-human entities can be ascribed human traits, like memory. Another implication is that administrators and designers who want to ensure that a task, like flying a plane, is accomplished more effectively, need to consider the system (e.g., how information is distributed within it), rather than the expertise of individuals.

Part IV contains two studies on the consumption of cultural products. The first, by a geographer, is an observation and interview-based study of the ways that tourists 'consume' the Taj Mahal. Edensor analyses the activities of different categories of tourist, Western and Indian, and in particular how they walk around the site and gaze at it, the activities which, he suggests, 'make' the space which they experience. Some tourists are limited or constrained in what they can do, for instance, because tour guides hurry them along. Others are freer to create a different experience through different behaviours. His evidence includes his observations of people, their accounts of what they do and feel, and his own behaviours and feelings. His quotations from their accounts can be seen as a means by which the researcher incorporates multiple voices in his text, although the interview extracts also serve as additional evidence, supporting his analysis of other data. The extracts presented here include a discussion of ethnocentricity, cultural imperialism and the position of an ethnographer conducting research in a different culture.

The second chapter in Part IV, by Kraidy, concerns people's consumption of the media, especially television. Kraidy conducted a study among Christian Maronite youth in Lebanon, investigating their responses to imported and local television programmes. Kraidy shares with Bourgois the broad aim of challenging theories which present people as the passive products of their life circumstances. He is disputing that identity is *imposed* on people, whether this is something done by predominantly Western media, which give everyone the same 'global' identity (an example of 'cultural imperialism'), or by former colonial rulers who destroyed local cultures and forced foreign identities on to the colonized peoples, or even by surviving local cultures which create a common identity for everyone living in a particular place. Kraidy suggests instead that the Maronite Christian young people he interviews enact 'hybrid cultural identities' in that they do not take up clear-cut positions which are 'either' Western 'or' Arab, either European/American or Lebanese, etc. Rather, in talking about and responding to television, novels and music, they 'articulate' (roughly, join together) different values and different discourses. Kraidy sees his interviewees (whom he calls 'interlocutors') as people who in these ways are actively making their own, hybrid cultural identities.

Kraidy suggests that Lebanon is a particularly appropriate case for the study of these issues because of its complex history as a 'crossroads civilization', its free media and the huge range of media and cultural products available. The people he interviews are in an especially complex position because they are Christian, not Muslim, and might therefore be expected to identify more with the West. The analysis sets up dualities including modern and traditional, Western and Arab, individual and communal. The argument is that the people interviewed do not occupy either side but move between and sometimes talk from a middle position. Furthermore, as someone who shares their identity, the researcher draws on his personal knowledge and experiences. He moves backwards and forwards between the two positions, as one of them and as ethnographer, which he variously describes as 'professional' and 'chronicler' (the one who writes and tells the story). This is what he describes as being a 'native ethnographer'.

The final section of the collection contains two studies of the provision of medical services. Chapter 9, by Griffiths, concerns care for mental health patients living in the community, in Wales. The main data are transcripts of talk from meetings in which teams of health workers negotiate the categorization and referral of patients. These transcripts record what was said, sequentially (including where speakers overlap or interrupt) and, to some extent, how it was said, recording laughter and other expressions of emotion ('Paah!'). This detail is similar to that in the transcript analysed by Hutchins and Klausen but Griffiths does not record body movements or direction of gaze, as they did. The form of analysis used here provides a bridge between ethnography and conversation analysis, incorporating the detail of context which is more characteristic of ethnographic studies with a close analysis of the interaction and 'moves' through which outcomes are jointly accomplished by speakers.[8] The focus is on how humour and laughter function to unite members of the team against or with expert proposals, specifically the referrals made by psychiatrists. By joking and laughing about proposals, team members can resist them and present alternative versions of the cases being discussed. In particular, they can move between two available discourses and 'sense-making frameworks' by which the same individuals can be constructed as either having mental illness or social problems.

The final chapter, by Dodier and Camus, is a study of the processes involved in the categorization of patients in the emergency department of a Paris teaching hospital. A key issue is the hospital's dual functions of openness and specialization. Dodier and Camus suggest that the staff are aware of a dual orientation of the hospital to provide, on the one hand, a public service which should be available to all, and on the other, highly specialized medical services, which of course implies selection. The analysis shows how the staff build up the 'mobilizing worth' of patients to decide on their priority and whether to provide free care for them. Although this is a qualitative study, it therefore uses a more formal analytic framework than in most ethnographies. The researchers define their basic concept, mobilizing worth, and the four dimensions which comprise it, then analyse their data using these. They indicate clearly what they count as evidence, namely, the *explicit* references which staff make, through their words and actions, to the factors which influence them. This, of course, does not, as Dodier and Camus put it, 'throw light on the silent influence of factors' (p. 238), which is a limitation of the study, as they acknowledge. More positively, it enables them to present succinctly the data on which their claims are based. This could be seen as a form of validation, because it enables the reader to 'check' the analysis, and as a return to claims of objectivity, because it seems to remove the researcher from the analytic process and to imply the possibility of replicating the study or at least carrying out a parallel one elsewhere. Alternatively, these could be seen as stylistic features whose effect is produced through the way the study is written up.

Taken together, the two chapters in Part V demonstrate very different approaches to the ethnographic analysis of collective decision-making. We can see parallels with other health service contexts, though these might differ in details, such as whether users pay for services. The approaches and findings of the two studies could also be relevant to other situations in which decisions must be negotiated, for example in different kinds of workplaces.

Although the collection is wide-ranging, these ten studies cannot, of course, provide a complete picture of the field. For instance, there are no studies of home life or education included (although Chapter 3, by Hey, is from a study conducted within schools), and the range of writing styles does not include the more innovative postmodern research texts. The headings under which the readings are organized show some of the major concerns across the field of contemporary ethnographic and qualitative work. It should be noted, however, that these are rich studies and other connections and divisions could have been drawn to produce rather different groupings. To mention just a few possibilities, many of the studies concern work practices, including those in Part V. Salzinger's analysis of 'gaze' within a production plant and Hutchins and Klausen's analysis of human technology interactions could also have been grouped with Edensor's study as examples of practices by which spaces are constructed. Alternatively, the section on gendered identities could have included

Salzinger's study on how sexual subjectivities are mobilized within the workplace, and Bourgois's, on the conflicts around identity experienced by his participants when they entered conventional workplaces, and also, of course, Kraidy's, on the hybrid identities constructed by young Maronite Christians in Lebanon. Readers are likely to find other connections and also to identify features of particular studies which are relevant to their own disciplinary and theoretical backgrounds and projected future research projects.

Acknowledgements

This Reader is part of the material for an Open University Masters course. I am extremely grateful for the advice of the External Assessor of the course, Professor Nigel Fielding, from the University of Surrey, and the assistance of the Course Manager, Eileen Potterton. My thanks also to Open University colleagues who acted as critical readers and contributed suggestions, including Martyn Hammersley, Elizabeth Silva, Pam Shakespeare, Jayne Artis, Karim Murji, Sharon Gewirtz, Gordon Hughes, Gail Lewis, Margie Wetherell, Karen Littleton, Steve Pile, Ann Phoenix, Jessica Evans and Helen Westcott. Thanks to Lynda Preston and Elaine Castle for secretarial help and technical support.

Notes

1. Two possibilities are Denzin and Lincoln, (1998a) and Hammersley and Atkinson (1995).
2. For a fascinating overview of this US social research, see Vidich and Lyman (1998). For a more extended account, which takes such research back to Thucydides, see Fielding (Chapter 9) in Gilbert (1993).
3. A rather different debate has centred on science's claims for itself: it has been challenged whether this is as detached, methodical and data-driven as has conventionally been claimed. See Hammersley and Atkinson (1995: Chapter 1).
4. See Billig (1999) for a discussion and criticism of these.
5. For a detailed discussion of the power relations within ethnographic research in anthropology, see Rosaldo (1989). The issue of power within the research relationship and process has been extensively discussed by feminist researchers: see, for example, Roberts (1981).
6. For a more extended discussion of these points, see Atkinson (1992) and Clifford (1986).
7. For a detailed discussion of assumptions about the relationship between research, policy and political reform, see Hammersley (1995: Chapter 7).
8. For a useful introduction to conversation analysis, see Wooffitt, in Wetherell et al., (2001: Chapter 2); also, Have (1999).

References

Atkinson, P. (1992) *Understanding Ethnographic Texts*. Qualitative Research Methods Series 25. London: Sage.

Baszanger, Isabelle and Nicolas Dodier (1997) 'Ethnography: relating the part to the whole', in D. Silverman (ed.), *Qualitative Research: Theory, Method and Practice*. London: Sage.

Billig, Michael (1999) 'Whose terms? Whose ordinariness? Rhetoric and ideology in conversation analysis', *Discourse & Society*, 10(4): 543–58.

Clifford, James (1986) 'Introduction: partial truths', in J. Clifford and G. Marcus (eds), *Writing Culture: The Poetics and Politics of Ethnography*. Berkeley and Los Angeles, CA: University of California Press.

Denzin, Norman K. (1997) *Interpretive Ethnography: Ethnographic Practices for the 21st Century*. Thousand Oaks, CA: Sage.

Denzin, N. and Y. Lincoln (eds) (1998a) *The Landscape of Qualitative Research: Theories and Issues*. Thousand Oaks, CA: Sage.

Denzin, N. and Y. Lincoln (1998b) 'Introduction: entering the field of qualitative research', in N. Denzin and Y. Lincoln (eds), *The Landscape of Qualitative Research: Theories and Issues*. Thousand Oaks, CA: Sage.

Gilbert, N. (ed.) (1993) *Researching Social Life*. London: Sage.

Hammersley, M. (1995) *The Politics of Social Research*. London: Sage.

Hammersley, M. (1998) *Reading Ethnographic Research* (2nd edition). London and New York: Longman.

Hammersley, M. and P. Atkinson (1995) *Ethnography: Principles in Practice*. London and New York: Routledge.

Have, P. ten (1999) *Doing Conversation Analysis: A Practical Guide*. London: Sage.

Roberts, H. (ed.) (1981) *Doing Feminist Research*. London: Routledge.

Rock, P. (1979) *The Making of Symbolic Interactionism*. London and Basingstoke: Macmillan.

Rosaldo, Renato (1989) *Culture and Truth: The Remaking of Social Analysis*. London: Routledge.

Seale, C. (1999) *The Quality of Qualitative Research*. London: Sage.

Silverman, D. (1985) *Qualitative Methodology and Sociology*. London: Sage.

Van Maanen, J. (ed) (1995) *Representation in Ethnography*. London: Sage.

Vidich, A. and S. Lyman (1998) 'Qualitative methods: their history in sociology and anthropology', in N. Denzin and Y. Lincoln (eds), *The Landscape of Qualitative Research: Theories and Issues*. Thousand Oaks, CA: Sage.

Wetherell, M., S. Taylor and S. Yates (2001) *Discourse as Data: A Guide for Analysis*. London: Sage.

Willis, Paul and Mats Trondman (2000) 'Manifesto for *Ethnography*', *Ethnography*, 1(1): 5–16.

Part I

At society's margins

1

Respect at work: 'Going legit'

Philippe Bourgois

Ethnographic methods and negative stereotyping

Any detailed examination of social marginalization encounters serious problems with the politics of representation, especially in the United States, where discussions of poverty tend to polarize immediately around race and individual self-worth. I worry, consequently, that the life stories and events presented will be misread as negative stereotypes of Puerto Ricans, or as a hostile portrait of the poor. I have struggled over these issues for several years because I agree with those social scientists who criticize the inferiorizing narratives that have predominated in much of the academic and popular literature on poverty in the United States.[1] At the same time, however, countering traditional moralistic biases and middle-class hostility toward the poor should not come at the cost of sanitizing the suffering and destruction that exists on inner-city streets. Out of a righteous, or a 'politically sensitive,' fear of giving the poor a bad image, I refuse to ignore or minimize the social misery I witnessed, because that would make me complicitous with oppression.[2]

This book consequently confronts the contradictions of the politics of representation of social marginalization in the United States by presenting brutal events, uncensored as I experienced them, or as they were narrated to me, by the perpetrators themselves. In the process, I have tried to build an alternative, critical understanding of the US inner city by organizing my central arguments, and by presenting the lives and conversations of the crack dealers, in a manner that emphasizes the interface between structural oppression and individual action. Building on the analytic framework of cultural production theory and drawing from feminism, I hope to restore the agency of culture, the autonomy of individuals, and the centrality of gender and the domestic sphere to a political economic understanding of the experience of persistent poverty and social marginalization in the urban United States.

This is an edited extract from Philippe Bourgois (1995) *In Search of Respect: Selling Crack in El Barrio* Cambridge: Cambridge University Press.

Traditional social science research techniques that rely on Census Bureau statistics or random sample neighborhood surveys cannot access with any degree of accuracy the people who survive in the underground economy – and much less those who sell or take illegal drugs. By definition, individuals who have been marginalized socially, economically, and culturally have had negative long-term relationships with mainstream society. Most drug users and dealers distrust representatives of mainstream society and will not reveal their intimate experiences of substance abuse or criminal enterprise to a stranger on a survey instrument, no matter how sensitive or friendly the interviewer may be. Consequently, most of the criminologists and sociologists who painstakingly undertake epidemiological surveys on crime and substance abuse collect fabrications. In fact, one does not have to be a drug dealer or a drug addict to hide the details of one's illicit activities. Even 'honest' citizens, for example, regularly engage in 'underground economy' practices when they finesse their deductions on income tax returns. In short, how can we expect someone who specializes in mugging elderly persons to provide us with accurate data on his or her income-generating strategies?

The participant–observation ethnographic techniques developed primarily by cultural anthropologists since the 1920s are better suited than exclusively quantitative methodologies for documenting the lives of people who live on the margins of a society that is hostile to them. Only by establishing long-term relationships based on trust can one begin to ask provocative personal questions, and expect thoughtful, serious answers. Ethnographers usually live in the communities they study, and they establish long-term, organic relationships with the people they write about. In other words, in order to collect 'accurate data,' ethnographers violate the canons of positivist research; we become intimately involved with the people we study.

With this goal in mind, I spent hundreds of nights on the street and in crackhouses observing dealers and addicts. I regularly tape-recorded their conversations and life histories. Perhaps more important, I also visited their families, attending parties and intimate reunions – from Thanksgiving dinners to New Year's Eve celebrations. I interviewed, and in many cases befriended, the spouses, lovers, siblings, mothers, grandmothers, and – when possible – the fathers and stepfathers of the crack dealers featured in these pages. I also spent time in the larger community interviewing local politicians and attending institutional meetings.

The explosion of postmodernist theory in anthropology in the 1980s and 1990s has critiqued the myth of ethnographic authority, and has denounced the hierarchical politics of representation that is inherent to anthropological endeavors. The self-conscious reflexivity called for by postmodernists was especially necessary and useful in my case: I was an outsider from the larger society's dominant class, ethnicity, and gender categories who was attempting to study the experience of inner-city poverty among Puerto Ricans. Once again, my concerns over these complicated issues are conveyed in my contextualization and editing of the tape-recorded crackhouse conversations. In fact, they are reflected in the very structure of the book.

While editing thousands of pages of transcriptions I came to appreciate the deconstructionist cliché of 'culture as text.' I also became acutely aware of the contradictory collaborative nature of my research strategy. Although the literary quality and emotional force of this book depends entirely on the articulate words of the main characters, I have always had the final say in how – and if – they would be conveyed in the final product.[3]

Critiquing the culture of poverty

El Barrio and the Puerto Rican experience in the United States has generated a disproportionally large literature. Puerto Ricans have been called the 'most researched but least understood people in the United States.'[4] The last major ethnographic work in El Barrio to receive national attention was Oscar Lewis's *La Vida* in the mid-1960s, and it illustrates perfectly the problems inherent in ethnographic method and in life history case studies more specifically. In fact, *La Vida* as well as Daniel Patrick Moynihan's 1965 report on the Negro family are frequently cited as the studies that scared a generation of social scientists away from studying the inner city.[5] Lewis collected thousands of pages of life-history accounts from one extended Puerto Rican family in which most of the women were involved in prostitution. The 'culture of poverty' theory that he developed out of this – and other – ethnographic data from Mexico, focused almost exclusively on the pathology of the intergenerational transmission of destructive values and behaviors among individuals within families. Lewis's approach is rooted in the Freudian culture and personality paradigm that dominated anthropology in the 1950s. He fails to note how history, culture, and political-economic structures constrain the lives of individuals. With the advantage of thirty years of hindsight, it is easy to criticize Lewis for his overly simplistic theoretical framework. Class exploitation, racial discrimination, and, of course, sexist oppression, as well as the subtleties of contextualized cultural meanings are not addressed in Lewis's psychologically reductionist descriptions of desperately poor Puerto Rican immigrants. Nevertheless, despite its lack of scholarly rigor, Lewis's compellingly written book on daily life in El Barrio and the shantytowns of Puerto Rico became a best seller in the United States, where it resonated with Protestant work ethic notions of rugged individualism and personal responsibility. Despite the author's progressive political intent and his personal sympathy for the socially marginal, critics interpret his volume as confirming the deep-seated contempt for the 'unworthy' poor that permeates US ideology.

It is no accident that it was an anthropologist who coined the concept of the culture of poverty and focused data collection on individual behavior. The simple practical fact of the discipline's methodology – participant –

observation – gives it access to documenting individual actions in minute detail. Structures of power and history cannot be touched or talked to. Specifically, in the New York City Puerto Rican context, the self-destructive daily life of those who are surviving on the street needs to be contextualized in the particular history of the hostile race relations and structural economic dislocation they have faced. Embroiled in what seemed like a whirlpool of suffering during my ethnographic research, it was often hard for me to see the larger relationships structuring the jumble of human interaction all around me. In the heat of daily life on the streets of El Barrio I often experienced a confusing anger with the victims, the victimizers, and the wealthy industrialized society that generates such an unnecessarily large toll of human suffering. For example, when confronted with a pregnant friend frantically smoking crack – and possibly condemning her future baby to a life of shattered emotions and dulled brain cells – it did no good for me to remember the history of her people's colonial oppression and humiliation, or to contextualize her position in New York's changing economy. Living in the inferno of what the United States calls its 'underclass,' I, like my neighbors around me and like the pregnant crack addicts themselves, often blamed the victim.

Political economy analysis is not a panacea to compensate for individualistic, racist, or otherwise judgmental interpretations of social marginalization. In fact, a focus on structures often obscures the fact that humans are active agents of their own history, rather than passive victims. Ethnographic method allows the 'pawns' of larger structural forces to emerge as real human beings who shape their own futures. Nevertheless, I often caught myself falling back on a rigidly structuralist perspective in order to avoid the painful details of how real people hurt themselves and their loved ones in their struggle for survival in daily life. Again, this analytical and political problem can be understood within the context of the theoretical debate over structure versus agency, that is, the relationship between individual responsibility and social structural constraints. The insights from cultural production theory – specifically, the notion that street culture's resistance to social marginalization is the contradictory key to its destructive impetus – is useful to avoid reductionist structuralist interpretations. Through cultural practices of opposition, individuals shape the oppression that larger forces impose upon them.[6]

The difficulty of relating individual action to political economy, combined with the personally and politically motivated timidity of ethnographers in the United States through the 1970s and 1980s have obfuscated our understanding of the mechanisms and the experiences of oppression. I cannot resolve the structure-versus-agency debate; nor can I confidently assuage my own righteous fear that hostile readers will misconstrue my ethnography as 'giving the poor a bad name.' Nevertheless, I feel it imperative from a personal and ethical perspective, as well as from an analytic and theoretical one, to expose the horrors I witnessed among the people I befriended, without censoring even the goriest details.[7] The depth and overwhelming pain and terror of the experience of poverty and racism in the United States needs to be talked about openly and confronted squarely, even if that makes us uncomfortable. I have documented a range of strategies that the urban poor devise to escape or circumvent the structures of segregation and marginalization that entrap them, including those strategies that result in self-inflicted suffering. I have written this in the hope that 'anthropological writing can be a site of resistance,' and with the conviction that social scientists should, and can, 'face power.'[8] At the same time, as already noted, I continue to worry about the political implications of exposing the minute details of the lives of the poor and powerless to the general public. Under an ethnographic microscope everyone has warts and anyone can be made to look like a monster. Furthermore, as the anthropologist Laura Nader stated succinctly in the early 1970s, 'Don't study the poor and powerless because everything you say about them will be used against them.'[9] I do not know if it is possible for me to present the story of my three and a half years of residence in El Barrio without falling prey to a pornography of violence, or a racist voyeurism – ultimately the problem and the responsibility is also in the eyes of the beholder.

[. . .]

'Goin' Legit': disrespect and resistance at work

I really wanna work legal. (Primo)

Everyone in Ray's network – including Ray himself – has had extensive experience working honestly. Most entered the legal labor market at exceptionally young ages. By the time they were twelve, they were bagging and delivering groceries at the supermarket for tips, stocking beer off the books in local bodegas, or running errands. Before reaching twenty-one years of age, however, virtually none had fulfilled their early childhood dreams of finding stable, well-paid legal work.

The problem is structural. From the 1950s through the 1980s second-generation inner-city Puerto Ricans were trapped in the most vulnerable niche of a factory-based economy that was rapidly being replaced by service industries. Between 1950 and 1990, the proportion of factory jobs in New York City decreased approximately threefold at the same time that service sector jobs doubled. The Department of City Planning calculates that over 800,000 industrial jobs were lost from the 1960s through the early 1990s, while the total number of jobs of all categories remained more or less constant at 3.5 million.[10]

Economists and sociologists have documented statistically that the restructuring of the US economy around service jobs has resulted in unemployment, income reduction, weaker unions, and dramatic erosions in worker's benefits at the entry level. Few scholars, however, have noted the cultural dislocations of the new service economy. These cultural clashes have been most pronounced in the office-work service jobs that have multiplied because of the dramatic expansion of the finance, real estate, and insurance (FIRE) sector in New York City. Service work in professional offices is the most dynamic place for ambitious inner-city youths to find entry-level jobs if they aspire to upward mobility. Employment as mail room clerks, photocopiers, and messengers in the high-rise office corridors of the financial district propels many inner-city youths into a wrenching cultural confrontation with the upper-middle-class white world. Obedience to the norms of high-rise, office-corridor culture is in direct contradiction to street culture's definitions of personal dignity – especially for males who are socialized not to accept public subordination.

[. . .]

First fired – last hired

None of those in Ray's network considered themselves to be victims. Their niche in the underground economy shielded them from having to face the fact that they were socially and economically superfluous to mainstream society. I watched Primo struggle with the glimmering realization of his profound economic vulnerability when one of his episodic attempts to reenter the legal economy coincided with the deepening of the recession that afflicted the US economy from late 1989 through 1991. At first Primo was totally confident. 'I've had like ten jobs before in my life. I dropped out of school at sixteen and I've been working ever since. Any asshole can find a job out there.' He almost enjoyed taking the subway downtown during daylight hours, marveling at the 'full cheeks' and 'cut hair' of the healthy-looking legally employed commuters.

When a half-dozen employers abruptly refused to hire him, Primo was able to blame his inability to find a job on his employment counselor, even though the newspapers were running euphemistically worded articles about the 'temporary interruption in America's growth' and 'the softening in the labor market.'[11] He defiantly 'fired' his counselor:

> *Primo:* I got a feeling this son of a bitch guy at the job center, my job counselor, was high. His eyes were always red. He lost my whole files. He was helping me without even knowing who the fuck I was. He sent me to so many fucking places, and nothing.
>
> That nigga' must have been on drugs. He was looking for my file all over his office. He's an idiot because that file was thick. It had all of the test'es I took.
>
> I told him, 'Maybe you're not supposed to be my supervisor. Why don't you look around to some other counselor?'
>
> He said, 'No, I had your file. I don't know where it's at.'
>
> He had a whole bunch of files, and I was hoping he would like look through the files and find mine, but mine wasn't there at all. It was like I never existed.

A month later, after another half-dozen employment rejections, Primo's self-confidence plummeted and his substance abuse escalated. He was living in flesh and blood the sense of personal powerlessness that impersonal market forces of supply and demand impose on vulnerable laborers during recessions:

> *Primo:* It's become hard to get a job now, I guess. It used to be easy to get a job, or maybe this TAP [Testing Assessment and Placement] Center I'm going to is sending me to the wrong places.
>
> I keep telling my job counselor, 'Why don't you send me to a place you haven't sent someone the day before, so that when they see me, it's definitely that they'll take me? Because when you send them a few people, then they're just not going to take me.'
>
> But I think my counselor agreed with the bosses to send them a few people, and 'whoever you like better you can keep.' Which is bad!
>
> I told him, 'Why don't you just tell them, just say, "We can only send you one person because we lack more people. We lack clients." '
>
> Instead this guy was sending me and everyone else. That makes your chances fucked up. Its like you got to battle it out to get a job.
>
> In the old days the TAP centers were better. Everytime they sent me to some company, boom! I'm hired, because they're not sending a whole bunch of people. Word!

The dramatic deterioration in 1990 of the number of jobs available in the entry-level legal labor market caught Primo by surprise. Not only did the recession make it hard to find a job, but Primo also had to confront his life-cycle developmental constraints: He was rapidly becoming too old to compete for the kinds of jobs that had been available to him when he had been an eager, teenage high school dropout just entering the legal labor force. Now that Primo was in his mid-twenties he had a several-year-long hiatus of unemployment that he was unable to justify to prospective employers. Primo internalized his structural marginalization. He panicked and spiraled into a psychological depression.

> *Primo:* I guess I was wrong, Felipe, about how easy it is to get a job.
>
> I was hearing on the news that there's a depression . . . an economic recession – or something like that. And I was thinking to myself, 'Damn! That's going to fuck up not only city, state, or federal workers, but it also fucks up someone like me . . . I guess – people that don't have skills, like me. This is fucked up.'
>
> It makes me feel fucked up, not being able to get a job. Because sometimes it seems like I like to be lazy.
>
> But you get tired of sitting around and not doing shit. I like to make myself useful, really – like I'm worth something. Not having a job makes me feel really fucked up, man.

Perhaps realizing that jobs are often found through personal connections, Primo began inviting his only legally employed ex-Game Room associate, Benzie, to hang out with him more often. Sure enough, Benzie began telling Primo about a possible opening in the kitchen of the downtown health club where he worked. The night before Christmas Eve he even motivated Primo to come to the office Christmas party to meet his supervisor. Primo arrived late, however, long after the upper-echelon administrators had left. He managed to meet only a few of the custodial workers, who were finishing off the leftover punch. Later that night, in his mother's housing project stairwell surrounded by beer, cocaine, and heroin, Benzie berated Primo for having ruined his chances of getting a job. During the conversation, however, Primo discovered the limitations of the job he had been so eagerly pursuing, and also whom he was competing with:

> *Benzie:* You remember El Gordo – that fat guy – at the party? Well, he's the one that I'm trying to get my supervisor to fire so that you can get the job.
> *Primo:* But all he be doing is washing dishes.
> *Benzie:* [a little flustered] I know . . . I'm in the back with him. I'm in charge of him. He's always fucking up. I keep trying to get him on point, but he doesn't take the job seriously.
> I keep telling my supervisor I know someone who really wants to work. But she's not hard on him. She feels sorry for him. And I feel sorry for him too, 'cause I know how he is.
> *Primo:* [suspiciously] What do you mean 'how he is'?
> *Benzie:* [ignoring the question] So Pops, your responsibility would be to wash dishes; but it's at six dollars an hour; and there's no place you could go to wash dishes that they'll start you off at six dollars an hours. They'll start you off at four or five.
> And after you work for a year you get a week vacation . . .
> *Primo:* [interrupting] Answer me. What's with El Gordo? Why everyone feel sorry for him?
> *Benzie:* [embarrassed] I mean he's slow, so he takes the job in a funny way.
> *Primo:* [worried] What do you mean he's slow?
> *Benzie:* I mean he's slow in the mind. He's got like a handicap. [defensively] Listen man, I'm only trying to help you out.

Benzie's mentally retarded colleague outcompeted Primo for the dish-washing job. Meanwhile, the logistics of Primo's personal life began falling apart. He had been squatting with his girlfriend, Maria, in her sister's project apartment opposite the Game Room. Maria's sister had fled to Connecticut with her husband and three children when her husband's drug-selling partner was found shot to death in their car. Primo and Maria were supposed to take charge of the continuing rent payments, but this was the same period when Ray had limited Primo to working two nights a week at the Game Room, and sales were slow. Maria found a job at a fast-food franchise, but this still did not provide them with enough money to meet their bare necessities. Primo was reduced to begging from his mother and sisters.

> *Primo:* Maria just started this week at Wendy's but she makes – net pay – about eighty something, ninety something bucks a week. Her welfare is a fucking piece of shit. She gets like not even forty dollars every other week. It's thirty-seven and some change because the cashiers keep something. Jesus that's bullshit money.

But me and Maria never starve, because if I don't have anything to eat at Maria's, I go to my mother's, or my other sister's, who just lives down the block.

Sometimes my mother looks me out. Twenty dollars, here and there. Sometimes she gives me food stamps, like once a month.

Within a few weeks of this conversation, failing to meet the Housing Authority rent payments, Primo and Maria were evicted. They were forced to separate, each returning to their own mother's high-rise Housing Authority apartment located in different projects in the neighborhood.

[. . .]

Shattered working-class fantasies in the service sector

It almost appears as if Caesar, Primo, and Willie were caught in a time warp during their teenage years. Their macho-proletarian dream of working an eight-hour shift plus overtime throughout their adult lives at a rugged slot in a unionized shop has been replaced by the nightmare of poorly paid, highly feminized, office-support service work. The stable factory-worker incomes that might have allowed Caesar and Primo to support families have largely disappeared from the inner city. Perhaps if their social network had not been confined to the weakest sector of manufacturing in a period of rapid job loss, their teenage working-class dreams might have stabilized them for long enough to enable them to adapt to the restructuring of the local economy. Instead, they find themselves propelled headlong into an explosive confrontation between their sense of cultural dignity versus the humiliating interpersonal subordination of service work.

Formerly, when most entry-level jobs were found in factories, the contradiction between an oppositional street culture and traditional working-class, shop-floor culture – especially when it was protected by a union – was less pronounced. I do not wish to romanticize factory work. It is usually tedious, tiring, and often dangerous. Furthermore, it is inevitably rife with confrontational hierarchies. On the shop floor, however, surrounded by older union workers, high school dropouts who are well versed in the latest and toughest street culture styles function effectively. In the factory, being tough and violently macho has high cultural value; a certain degree of opposition to the foreman and the 'bossman' is expected and is considered masculine.

In contrast, this same oppositional street-identity is dysfunctional in the service sector, especially among the office-support workers who serve the executives of the FIRE sector, where most of the new entry-level jobs with a potentially stable future are located. Street culture is in direct contradiction to the humble, obedient modes of subservient social interaction that are essential for upward mobility in high-rise office jobs. Workers in a mail

room or behind a photocopy machine cannot publicly maintain their
cultural autonomy. Most concretely, they have no union; more subtly, there
are few fellow workers surrounding them to insulate them and to provide
them with a culturally based sense of class solidarity. Instead they are
besieged by supervisors and bosses from an alien, hostile, and obviously
dominant culture. When these office managers are not intimidated by street
culture, they ridicule it. Workers like Caesar and Primo appear inarticulate
to their professional supervisors when they try to imitate the language of
power in the workplace, and instead stumble pathetically over the enunciation of unfamiliar words. They cannot decipher the hastily scribbled
instructions – rife with mysterious abbreviations – that are left for them by
harried office managers on diminutive Post-its. The 'common sense' of
white-collar work is foreign to them; they do not, for example, understand
the logic in filing triplicate copies of memos or for postdating invoices.
When they attempt to improvise or show initiative, they fail miserably and
instead appear inefficient – or even hostile – for failing to follow 'clearly
specified' instructions.

Their interpersonal social skills are even more inadequate than their
limited professional capacities. They do not know how to look at their
fellow service workers – let alone their supervisors – without intimidating
them. They cannot walk down the hallway to the water fountain without
unconsciously swaying their shoulders aggressively as if patrolling their
home turf. Gender barriers are an even more culturally charged realm.
They are repeatedly reprimanded for offending co-workers with sexually
aggressive behavior.

The cultural clash between white 'yuppie' power and inner-city 'scram-
bling jive' in the service sector is much more than superficial style. Service
workers who are incapable of obeying the rules of interpersonal interaction
dictated by professional office culture will never be upwardly mobile. In the
high-rise office buildings of midtown Manhattan or Wall Street, newly
employed inner-city high school dropouts suddenly realize they look like
idiotic buffoons to the men and women for whom they work. My argument
is that people like Primo and Caesar have not passively accepted their
structural victimization. On the contrary, by embroiling themselves in the
underground economy and proudly embracing street culture, they are
seeking an alternative to their social marginalization. In the process, on a
daily level, they become the actual agents administering their own destruction and their community's suffering.

Getting 'dissed' in the office

Both Primo and Caesar experienced deep humiliation and insecurity in
their attempts to penetrate the foreign, hostile world of high-rise office
corridors. Primo had bitter memories of being the mail room clerk and
errand boy at a now defunct professional trade magazine. Significantly, the

only time he explicitly admitted to having experienced racism was when he described how he was treated at that particular work setting. The level of racially charged cultural miscommunication at his work site is nicely illustrated by his inability to identify the name and ethnicity of his boss, just as she might have been unsure of what Latin American country he was from, and how to spell or pronounce his first name:

> *Primo:* I had a prejudiced boss. She was a fucking 'ho',' Gloria. She was white. Her name was Christian. No, not Christian, Kirschman. I don't know if she was Jewish or not.
>
> She would like to talk about me to whoever was over visiting in the office – you know, like her associates who would come over for a coffee break.
>
> When she was talking to people she would say, 'He's illiterate,' as if I was really that stupid that I couldn't understand what she was talking about.
>
> So what I did one day – you see they had this big dictionary right there on the desk, a big heavy motherfucker – so what I just did was open up the dictionary, and I just looked up the word, 'illiterate.' And that's when I saw what she was calling me.
>
> So she's saying that I'm stupid or something. I'm stupid! [pointing to himself with both thumbs and making a hulking face] 'He doesn't know shit.'

The most profound dimension of Primo's humiliation was not being called illiterate but, rather, having to look up in the dictionary the words used to insult him. In contrast, in the underground economy Primo never had to risk this kind of threat to his self-worth.

> *Primo:* Ray would never disrespect me that way, because he wouldn't tell me that because he's illiterate too, plus I've got more education than him. I almost got a GED.

Worse yet, Primo genuinely attempted to show initiative at Gloria Kirschman's magazine-publishing company, but the harder he tried, the stupider he felt when he inevitably failed. As he explains, 'It only gets worse when they get to know you.'

> *Primo:* So you, you know, you try to do good, but then people treat you like shit.
>
> Man, you be cool at first, and then all of a sudden, when they get to know you, they try to diss you.
>
> When I first got to my jobs, I was busting my ass and everything, but after a while, it's like, you get to hate your supervisor.
>
> I was disrespected a few times at that job when I didn't follow, like, the orders. When my supervisor told me to do a job one way, but I thought it was best to do it another way. She dissed the shit out of me a coupla' times. That lady was a bitch.

Quite simply, Primo was being exposed to the fact that he did not have the cultural or symbolic capital that would have allowed him to step out from behind the photocopy machine or the mail meter. He was claustrophobically surrounded by overseers from an alien but powerful culture:

> *Primo:* I had to be cool. Even when we used to get our lunch breaks, when we
> were supposed to be able to just hang, even then, the supervisors were right
> there.

Primo was both unwilling and unable to compromise his street identity and
imitate the professional modes of interaction that might have earned him
the approval and respect of his boss. It is precisely in moments like this that
one can see institutionalized racism at work in how the professional service
sector unconsciously imposes the requisites of Anglo, middle-class cultural
capital. His boss forbade him to answer the telephone, because objectively
a Puerto Rican street accent will discourage prospective clients and cause
her to lose money. Ironically, the confrontation over Primo using the
telephone occurred because he had been attempting to show initiative and
good faith by answering calls when he saw that his supervisors were busy
or out of the office.

> *Primo:* I wouldn't have mind that she said I was illiterate. What bothered me
> was that when she called on the telephone, she wouldn't want me to answer even
> if my supervisor – who was the receptionist – was not there and the phone be
> ringing for a long time.
>
> So when I answered it, my boss sounds like she's going to get a heart attack
> when she hears my voice. She'd go, 'Where's Renee?' – Renee Silverman – that's
> the receptionist, my supervisor.
>
> I'd say, 'She's out to lunch' – or whatever.
>
> And she would go, 'Is Fran there?'
>
> I'd say, 'Yes she is.'
>
> But, you see, it wasn't Fran's job to answer the phones. She was taking care of
> the bills and always busy doing some work. So I just said, 'She's probably out to
> lunch too.'
>
> That boss was just a bitch, because I answered the phone correct. There are so
> many different kinds of people out there in New York City that've got a crazy
> accent. They could be into real estate; they could be into anything. They just got
> their own accent. But that bitch didn't like my Puerto Rican accent.
>
> I don't know what was her problem; she's a fucking bitch.
>
> Okay, maybe I don't have the education to type; so I will not type. But don't
> diss me for answering the phones instead of letting it ring forever. Maybe it's
> important! Bitch!
>
> I used to answer it pretty well, man. But then after that – after she dished me
> – when I did pick up the phone, I used to just sound Porta'rrrrican on purpose.
> Fuck it.

[. . .]

'Fly clothes' and symbolic power

On a deeper level, the entire foundation of street culture and the unwillingness of people like Primo and Caesar to compromise their street identity is
a refusal to accept marginalization in the mainstream professional world.

The oppositional identities of street culture are both a triumphant rejection of social marginalization and a defensive – in some cases terrorized – denial of vulnerability. The ways office dress codes become polarized provide insight into this complex dynamic because clothing is a concretely visible arena encapsulating symbolic, or cultural, conflict. To my surprise, many of the crack dealers cited their inappropriate wardrobes and the imposition of demeaning dress codes as primary reasons for shunning legal employment. At first I dismissed the issue as trivial. It took me several months to realize how centrally this symbolic expression of identity articulates with power relations in the labor market.

The oppositional meaning of 'subcultural style' among youths and marginalized sectors of society has long fascinated sociologists.[12] Much of that material romanticizes and exoticizes the real pain of social marginalization. In contrast, of course, seen through the eyes of mainstream America, an inner-city youth's preoccupation with 'fly clothes' only confirms a stereotype of immaturity, petty irrationality, or even personal pathology.

When young inner-city men and women are forced to submit to powerful white women in the entry levels of the office-worker labor force, physical appearance becomes a fierce arena for enforcing or contesting power. Of course, on a more general level, this occurs whenever the crack dealers or anyone engrossed in street culture venture into the middle-class white world that dominates most public space beyond inner-city confines. Caesar, for example, highlights his experience of this tension in his angry reminiscences of office workplace confrontations. He had no idea when his clothes would elicit ridicule or anger. His vulnerability and powerlessness outside the street context is clearly expressed in his anger over the 'flexible' job description of his FIRE service-sector position. He mediates his objective powerlessness at work, through his preoccupation with the confusing office dress code.

> *Caesar:* When I worked at Sudler & Hennessey, the pharmaceutical advertising agency, they had a dress code and shit like that. I wore the tie for about three weeks, but, uhum . . . Bob – I mean Bill – he was my supervisor, an Irish son of a bitch, an old white guy – he told me I didn't really have to wear a tie if I didn't want to. So I didn't.
>
> Because for some reason, since I was new, like the new mail clerk there, and they was remodeling and shit, they wanted me to do like, all this wild work. I'd be taking down shelves, clearing dust, sweeping – dirty work.
>
> I mean I didn't wanna really do construction work in my good clothes. But I couldn't come in bummy, because my supervisor would tell me, 'Why you coming in like that?' Or 'Why you dressed like that for?' He meant, 'Like a hoodlum.' But I dressed good, like in nice baggies, and fancy shoes, and nice paisley shirts.
>
> But what I didn't like was that construction wasn't in my job description. I got hired to be a mail room clerk right. They never told me that they were going to be remodeling shit.

> But then they had that dress code right. I hated that shit. You see I didn't have
> no clothes back then because I was still goin' on mission [crack binges]. So really,
> like my first paycheck went for clothes, but then I had to replace the clothes I had
> fucked up at work.

In much the same way that Primo was humiliated by having to look up the word 'illiterate' in the dictionary, Caesar was hurt when his supervisor accused him of 'looking like a hoodlum' on the days when he thought he was actually dressing well. His problem was not merely that he did not have enough money to buy clothes but, rather, that he had no idea of which clothes to choose when he went to buy them. Losing this particular struggle over cultural capital has to be profoundly disorienting to the kind of person whose fly clothes on the street have always made him 'king of the crew,' as Caesar's teenage friend Willie had assured me.

In the same vein, several months earlier, I had watched Primo drop out of a 'motivational training' employment program in the basement of his mother's housing project, run by former heroin addicts who had just received a multimillion-dollar private sector grant for their innovative approach to training the 'unemployable.' Primo felt profoundly disrespected by the program, and he focused his discontent on the humiliation he faced because of his inappropriate wardrobe. The fundamental philosophy of such motivational job-training programs is that 'these people have an attitude problem.' They take a boot camp approach to their unemployed clients, ripping their self-esteem apart during the first week in order to build them back up with an epiphanic realization that they want to find jobs as security guards, messengers, and data-input clerks in just-above-minimum-wage service sector positions. The program's highest success rate has been with middle-aged African-American women who want to terminate their relationship to welfare once their children leave home.

I originally had a 'bad attitude' toward the premise of psychologically motivating and manipulating people to accept boring, poorly paid jobs. At the same time, however, the violence and self-destruction I was witnessing at the Game Room was convincing me that it is better to be exploited at work than to be outside the legal labor market. In any case, I persuaded Primo and a half-dozen of his Game Room associates – including Candy and Little Pete, who was then managing the Social Club crackhouse on La Farmacia's corner – to sign up for the program. Even Caesar was tempted to join.

None of the crack dealers lasted for more than three sessions of the job training program. Primo was the first to drop out after the first day's registration and pep talk. For several weeks he avoided talking about the experience. I repeatedly pressed him to explain why he 'just didn't show up' to the free job-training sessions. Only after repeated badgering on my part did he finally express the deep sense of shame and vulnerability he experienced whenever he attempted to venture into the legal labor market. In the particular case of the motivational employment program, clothes and appearance – style, once again – were the specific medium for resisting the humiliation of submission to a menial position in the service sector labor market.

Philippe: Yo Primo, listen to me. I worry that there's something taking place that you're not aware of, in terms of yourself. Like the coke that you be sniffing all the time; it's like every night.

Primo: What do you mean?

Philippe: Like not showing up at the job training. You say it's just procrastination, but I'm scared it's something deeper that you're not dealing with. Like wanting to be partying all night, and sniffing. Maybe that's why you never went back.

Primo: The truth though – listen Felipe – my biggest worry was the dress code, 'cause my gear is limited. I don't even got a dress shirt, I only got one pair of shoes, and you can't wear sneakers at that program. They wear ties too – don't they? Well, I ain't even got ties – I only got the one you lent me.

I would've been there three weeks in the same gear: T-shirt and jeans. *Estoy jodido como un bón!* [I'm all fucked up like a bum!]

Philippe: What the fuck kinda bullshit excuse are you talking about? Don't tell me you were thinking that shit. No one notices how people are dressed.

Primo: Yo, Felipe, this is for real! Listen to me! I was thinking about that shit hard. Hell yeah!

Hell yes they would notice, because I would notice if somebody's wearing a fucked-up tie and shirt.

I don't want to be in a program all *abochornado* [bumlike]. I probably won't even concentrate, getting dished, like . . . and being looked at like a sucker. Dirty jeans . . . or like old jeans, because I would have to wear jeans, 'cause I only got one slack. Word though! I only got two dress shirts and one of them is missing buttons.

I didn't want to tell you about that because it's like a poor excuse, but that was the only shit I was really thinking about. At the time I just said, 'Well, I just don't show up.'

And Felipe, I'm a stupid [very] skinny nigga'. So I have to be careful how I dress, otherwise people will think I be on the stem [a crack addict who smokes out of a glass-stem pipe].

Philippe: [nervously] Oh shit. I'm even skinnier than you. People must think I'm a total drug addict.

Primo: Don't worry. You're white.

Obviously, the problem is deeper than not having enough money to buy straight-world clothes. Racism and the other subtle badges of symbolic power are expressed through wardrobes and body language. Ultimately, Primo's biggest problem was that he had no idea of what clothes might be appropriate in the professional, service sector context. Like Caesar, he feared he might appear to be a buffoon on parade on the days when he was trying to dress up. He admitted that the precipitating factor in his decision not to go back to the job training program was when he overheard someone accusing Candy of 'looking tacky' after she proudly inaugurated her new fancy clothes at the first class. As a matter of fact, Primo had thought she had looked elegant in her skintight, yellow jumpsuit when she came over to his apartment to display her new outfit proudly to him and his mother before going to class.

[. . .]

The bicultural alternative: upward mobility or betrayal

Given the structural dynamic of ethnic succession by new immigrants at the lowest echelons of New York's labor force, the primary hope for upward mobility among New York-born Puerto Ricans lies in the expanding FIRE sector's need for office support workers – mail room clerks, photocopiers, and receptionists. Not only is this one of the fastest-growing subsectors of the city's economy, it also has the greatest potential for upward mobility as messengers get promoted to clerks, who get promoted to administrative assistants, and so on. Of course, these are also precisely the kinds of jobs that require subservient behavior anathema to street culture.

As noted earlier, success in the FIRE service sector requires an inner-city office worker to be bicultural: in other words, to play politely by 'the white woman's rules' downtown only to come home and revert to street culture within the safety of a tenement or housing project at night. Thousands of East Harlem residents manage to balance their identities on this precarious tightrope. Often, when they are successful, their more marginally employed or unemployed neighbors and childhood friends accuse them of ethnic betrayal and internalized racism.

I collected several righteous condemnations by Game Room habitués of their successfully employed neighbors who work downtown and adapt to high-rise office culture. Leroy, another cousin of Caesar's, who ran his own private crack operation, was especially adamant on the subject.

> *Leroy:* When you see someone go downtown and get a good job, if they be Puerto Rican, you see them fix up their hair and put some contact lens in their eyes. Then they fit in. And they do it! I seen it.
> They turnovers. They people who wanna be white. Man, if you call them in Spanish, it wind up a problem.
> I mean like, take the name Pedro – I'm just telling you this as an example – Pedro be saying, [imitating a white nasal accent] 'My name is Peter.'
> Where do you get Peter from Pedro?
> Just watch how Spanish people fix up their hair. When they get nice jobs like that, all of a sudden, you know, they start talking proper.

The bicultural alternative is not an option for Leroy, whose black skin and tough street demeanor disqualify him from credibility in a high-rise office corridor. I learned later that part of his articulate anger on the night I tape-recorded his denunciation of 'turnovers' was the result of his most recent foray into office work. He had just quit a 'nickel-and-dime messenger job downtown' (in order to return to crack dealing full time in his project stairway) shortly after a white woman fled from him shrieking down the hallway of a high-rise office building. Leroy and the terrified woman had ridden the elevator together and coincidentally Leroy had stepped off on the same floor as she did, to make a delivery. Worse yet, Leroy had been trying to act like a debonair male when the woman fled from him. He suspected the contradiction between his inadequate appearance and his chivalric intentions was responsible for the woman's terror:

> *Leroy:* You know how you let a woman go off the elevator first? Well that's what I did to her, but I may have looked a little shabby on the ends. Sometime my hair not combed, you know; so I could look a little sloppy to her, maybe, when I let her off first.

What Leroy did not quite admit until I probed further is that he too had been intimidated by the lone white woman. He had been so disoriented by her taboo, unsupervised proximity that he had forgotten to press the elevator button when he originally stepped into the elevator with her:

> *Leroy:* She went in the elevator first, but then she just waits there to see what floor I press.
> She's playing like she don't know what floor she wants to go to, because she wants to wait for me to press my floor. And I'm standing there, and I forgot to press the button.
> I'm thinking about something else – I don't know what was the matter with me. And she's thinking like, 'He's not pressing the button; I guess he's following me!'

Leroy struggles to understand the terror his mere presence inspires in whites:

> *Leroy:* It's happened before. I mean after a while you become immune to it.
> Well, when it first happens, it like bugs you, 'That's messed up. How they just judge you?' You know, they be thinking, 'Guys like that, they're a lot of dark guys running around.' It's like crazy.
> But I understand a lot of them. How should I say it? A lot of white people . . . [looking nervously at me] I mean Caucasian people – [flustered, putting his hand gently on my shoulder] If I say white, don't get offended because there are some white people who live in this neighborhood.
> But those other white people they never even experienced black people. They come from wealthy neighborhoods, and the schools they go to . . . no black kids there. The college they go to . . . no black kids there. And then they come to office buildings, and they just start seeing us.
> And you know, we don't have the best jobs. You know, how it is. I call them nickel-and-dime jobs. You know, we are not always as well adjusted or as well dressed.
> Sometime I come in a little sloppy. So automatically they think something wrong with you. Or you know, they think you out to rob them or something. So I like, . . . I don't pay it no mind. Sometime it irks me. Like, you know, it clicks my mind. Makes me want to write. I always write it down.

> Sometime I write down the incident, what happened. I try to make a rhyme [rap lyrics] out of it.

Of course, as a crack dealer Leroy no longer has to confront this kind of confusing class and racial humiliation.

I pursued this issue with another, older cousin of Caesar's – one who had actually 'made it' in the legal economy. He maintained a stable white-collar job in an insurance agency and had moved his family to the suburbs. His experience was particularly interesting as he had grown up in the neighborhood and had passed through a phase of heroin addiction. He still maintained acquaintanceships with some of his old street friends. At first he assured me that his escape from street culture had not necessitated any ethnic compromise. He saw it as part of a religious conversion. He and his family were devout Jehovah's Witnesses. At the same time, he did admit he had to hide the extent of his economic success when he returned to visit friends and family in El Barrio.

> *Caesar's cousin:* Half of my friends died: killings, overdose. But I stay in touch with the ones who are still alive. As a matter of fact, I just seen one tonight. He's still on methadone.
>
> My friends though, they don't see me as looking down on them, because I don't ever do that. They really don't know how I really live. They know I 'peddle insurance,' but I don't get heavy about it with them. It might make them feel uncomfortable. I never do that to them. So they don't see me as someone who's betrayed.

The tightrope of class and ethnicity is not quite as easy to balance in his new upwardly mobile world governed by a deeply institutionalized racism. The solution in his case has been to internalize the legitimacy of apartheid in the United States.

> *Caesar's cousin:* My kids' future is much brighter than mines' ever was. We live in a suburban situation. As a matter of fact, we may be one of the three Hispanic families in that general area.
>
> When I jog down the neighborhood, people get scared; people get nervous about me. It's not a problem for me, because I have self-confidence. I don't worry about it. It doesn't faze me at all.
>
> Every once in a while, I used to get a crank call in the house, saying, you know, 'Hey spic,' you know, 'spic' and other stuff, but I don't worry about that. [he giggles]
>
> In a sense, I've learned to be in their shoes. You see what I mean? Because I've seen what minorities as a group can do to a neighborhood. I've seen great neighborhoods go down. So I step into their shoes and I understand; I've learned how to be sympathetic. I understand their thinking.

Caesar and Primo are not capable of such sympathy and understanding; instead, they take refuge in the underground economy and celebrate street culture.

Notes

1. Benmayor, Torruellas, and Juarbe, 1992; Katz, 1986; Rainwater, 1994; Stansell, 1987; and Ward, 1989.
2. As the anthropologist Nancy Scheper-Hughes (1992: 172) notes in her ethnography of a Brazilian shantytown:

   For anthropologists to deny, because it implies a privileged position (i.e., the power of the outsider to name an ill or a wrong) and because it is not pretty, the extent to which dominated people come to play the role . . . of their own executioners is to collaborate with the relations of power and silence that allow the destruction to continue.

3. See Behar, 1993; Portelli, 1991; Rosaldo, 1980. Tape recordings are always difficult to edit, especially when they are in street idiom whose grammar and vocabulary differ from that of the academic mainstream. One of my biggest problems in editing, however, is the impossibility of rendering into print the performance dimension of street speech. Without the complex, stylized punctuation provided by body language, facial expression, and intonation, many of the transcribed narratives of crack dealers appear flat, and sometimes even inarticulate, on the written page. Consequently, I often deleted redundancies, dangling phrases, incomplete thoughts, and sometimes even entire passages in order to recover the articulate – often poetic – effect the same passage conveyed in its original oral performance. To clarify meanings, I sometimes added additional words, and even subjects and verbs, to sentence fragments. I also occasionally combined conversations of the same events, or on the same themes, to make them appear to have occurred during a single session within the text, even though they sometimes took place over a period of several months or several years. In a few rare instances of minor characters in the book, I conflated more than one person for brevity's sake.

   Having said all this, I tried as much as I could to maintain the grammatical form, the expressive vocabulary, and the transliterated Spanish forms that compose the rich language of New York-born Puerto Ricans who participate in El Barrio's street culture. Most important, I hope I have respected their message. Our conversations were usually in English with occasional Spanish words interspersed as a way of affirming Puerto Rican identity. Whenever a conversation, or a portion of a sentence was in Spanish, I have noted that fact in the text.
4. Rodríguez, 1995, citing G. Lewis, 1963.
5. Harvey, 1993; Katz, 1986; O. Lewis, 1966; Moynihan, 1965; Rainwater and Yancey, 1967; Wilson, 1987.
6. To name just a few examples of cultural production theorists and critical ethnographers of education, see Bourdieu, 1980; Devine, 1996; Foley, 1990; Fordham, 1988; Gibson and Ogbu, 1991; MacLeod, 1987; Willis, 1977.
7. In fact, I did exclude a number of conversations and observations I thought projected an overly negative portrayal of the crack dealers and their families out of context. Much of my 'censoring' occurred around descriptions of sexual activities. In several cases, I felt the passages might be considered straightforward pornography. I also wanted to avoid excessively invading the privacy of the major characters in the book, and I discussed these issues at length with all of them. Only one person actually asked me to delete some material from the epilogue, which, of course, I did. The problems of selection, editing, and

censorship have tremendous political, ethical, and personal ramifications that ethnographers must continually confront, without ever being confident of resolving them.
8. Scheper-Hughes, 1992: 25; Wolf, 1990.
9. Nader, 1972.
10. New York City Department of City Planning 1993 (January): 37, Table 6. In 1950, factory work provided 30 percent of New York City's jobs; by the early 1990s it provided only 10 percent. In contrast, in 1950 service jobs accounted for 15 percent of employment; by 1992 service work represented well over 30 percent of all city jobs. Just in the 1980s alone, manufacturing decreased 31 percent, whereas 'producer services' increased 61 percent and 'all services' rose by 16 percent (Romo and Schwartz, 1993: 358–9; New York City Department of City Planning Population Division, 1993).
11. *New York Times*, February 13, 1991: D1; *New York Times*, September 6, 1990: D 17.
12. Becker, 1963; Hebdige, 1979.

References

Becker, Howard S. (1963) *Outsiders: Studies in the Sociology of Deviance*. New York: Free Press.
Behar, Ruth (1993) *Translated Woman: Crossing the Border with Esperanza's Story*. Boston, MA: Beacon Press.
Benmayor, Rina, Rosa Torruellas and Anna Juarbe (1992) 'Responses to poverty among Puerto Rican women: identity, community, and cultural citizenship'. New York: Centro de Estudios Puertorriqueños, Hunter College. Report to the Joint Committee for Public Policy Research on Contemporary Hispanic Issues of the Inter-University Program for Latino Research and the Social Science Research Council.
Bourdieu, Pierre (1980) *The Logic of Practice*. Stanford, CA: Stanford University Press.
Devine, John (1996) *The New Panopticon: The Construction of Violence in Inner City High Schools*. Chicago: University of Chicago Press.
Foley, Douglas (1990) *Learning Capitalist Culture: Deep in the Heart of Tejas*. Philadelphia: University of Pennsylvania Press.
Fordham, Signithia (1988) 'Racelessness as a factor in Black students' school success: pragmatic strategy or pyrrhic victory?', *Harvard Educational Review*, 53(257): 293.
Gibson, Margaret and John Ogbu (eds) (1991) *Minority Status and Schooling: A Comparative Study of Immigrant and Involuntary Minorities*. New York and London: Garland Publishing.
Harvey, David L. (1993) *Potter Addition: Poverty, Family, and Kinship in a Heartland Community*. New York: Aldine de Gruyter.
Hebdige, Dick (1979) *Subculture: The Meaning of Style*. London: Methuen.
Katz, Michael (1986) *In the Shadow of the Poorhouse: A Social History of Welfare in America*. New York: Basic Books.
Lewis, Gordon K. (1963) *Puerto Rico: Freedom and Power in the Caribbean*. New York: Monthly Review Press.

Lewis, Oscar (1966) *La Vida: A Puerto Rican Family in the Culture of Poverty – San Juan and New York*. New York: Random House.

MacLeod, Jay (1987) *Ain't No Makin' It: Leveled Aspirations in a Low-Income Neighborhood*. Boulder, CO: Westview Press.

Moynihan, Daniel P. (1965) 'The negro family: the case for national action'. Washington DC: Office of Policy Planning and Research, US Department of Labor.

Nader, Laura (1972) 'Up the anthropologist – perspectives gained from studying up', in Dell Hymes (ed.), *Reinventing Anthropology*. New York: Pantheon. pp. 284–311.

New York City Department of City Planning (January 1993) 'Citywide industry study: labor force technical report'. New York: Department of City Planning.

New York Times (1990) 'Dollar off in heavy selling on talk of fed rate move', D17, 6 September.

New York Times (1991) 'Bush view upbeat on economy: recovery expected to begin in summer in economic report', D1, 13 February. David E. Rosenbaum.

Portelli, Alessandro (1991) 'Introduction', in *The Death of Luigi Trastulli and Other Stories*. New York: State University of New York Press. pp. vii–xvi.

Rainwater, Lee (1994) 'A primer on US poverty: 1945–1992'. New York: Russell Sage Foundation Working Paper No. 53.

Rainwater, Lee and William L. Yancey (eds) (1967) *The Moynihan Report and the Politics of Controversy*. Cambridge, MA: MIT Press.

Rodríguez, Clara E. (1995) 'Puerto Ricans in historical and social science research', in James A. Banks and Cherry A. McGee Banks (eds), *Handbook of Research on Multi-cultural Education*. New York: Simon & Schuster and Macmillan. pp. 223–44.

Romo Frank and Michael Schwartz (1993) 'The coming of post-industrial society revisited: manufacturing and the prospects for a service-based economy', in Richard Swedberg (ed.), *Explorations in Economic Sociology*. New York: Russell Sage Foundation. pp. 335–73.

Rosaldo, Renato. 1980. 'Doing Oral History.' *Social Analysis*, 4: 89–99.

Scheper-Hughes, Nancy (1992) *Death Without Weeping: The Violence of Everyday Life in Brazil*. Berkeley: University of California Press.

Stansell, Christine (1987 [1982]) *City of Women: Sex and Class in New York 1789–1860*. Urbana and Chicago: University of Illinois Press.

Ward, David (1989) *Poverty, Ethnicity, and the American City 1840–1925: Changing Conceptions of the Slum and the Ghetto*. New York: Cambridge University Press.

Willis, Paul (1977) *Learning to Labor: How Working Class Kids Get Working Class Jobs*. Aldershot: Gower.

Wilson, Julius (1987) *The Truly Disadvantaged: The Inner City, the Underclass, and Public Policy*. Chicago: University of Chicago Press.

Wolf, Eric (1990) 'Distinguished lecture: facing power – old insights, new questions', *American Anthropologist*, 92(3): 586–96.

2

Policing and public health: law enforcement and harm minimization in a street-level drug market

Lisa Maher and David Dixon

Introduction

Policing, place and people

This study is concerned with tensions in drug policing between commitments to law enforcement and to harm minimization, and with the harmful consequences to public health of the domination in policing practice of law enforcement. Reporting ethnographic research in Sydney's principal street-level drug market, and integrating perspectives from research in policing and in public health, we argue for a shift in policing priorities, rejecting suggestions that the law constrains the ability of police to subordinate law enforcement to other objectives.

The focus is on the policing of drug users and user/dealers in public space. Such work is primarily carried out by uniformed patrol officers, although plain clothes officers also contribute. These activities have to be placed in the context of other forms of drug policing. During the study period, the research site was subject to the attention of a considerable variety of other police sections and agencies, including local detectives and drug units, regional and district specialists, transit police, the NSW Drug Enforcement Agency, the Australian Federal Police, and the National Crime Authority. These activities interrelated, overlapped, and sometimes conflicted.[1]

Studies of drug policing often fail to discriminate except at a general level, for example between supply-side and demand-side strategies. This study indicates that more specificity is needed because of the under-acknowledged importance of street-level enforcement (Pearson, 1992). Despite the attention which specialist units attract, 'the current reality is that the bulk of drug law enforcement in Australia is conducted by non-

This article was previously published in *British Journal of Criminology* (1999) 39(4): 488–512.

specialized police' and 'the great majority of drug offenders taken before Australian justice systems are more likely to be "users" than "providers"' (Sutton and James, 1995: 113–19; cf. Green and Purnell, 1995).[2] As Sutton and James suggest, 'in the long term, comparatively neglected "street-level" issues are likely to yield the most important challenges and to yield the most significant returns for Australian drug law enforcement' (1995: x).

The study focuses not just on a particular kind of policing, but on such policing in a particular kind of place – Sydney's Cabramatta. Such specificity is necessary. Cabramatta is very different (socially, geographically and symbolically) from other drug-market locations such as, for example, an inner city 'red-light' area dominated by Euro-Australians. Cabramatta has the dubious distinction of being Australia's 'heroin capital'. But it is also Sydney's Asian city, and has been the subject of concerted attempts to promote it as a tourist attraction and an exemplar of Australian cultural diversity. Media attention has wavered between these negative and positive images, increasingly settling on the former. In the context of a public debate about race and immigration which became increasingly racist in the mid-1990s, Cabramatta is a 'symbolic location' (Keith, 1993), reference to which summons up fears of drug-related Asian criminality.

The social reality is rather different from either of these images. Cabramatta is a large, ethnically heterogeneous suburban centre in south-western Sydney. It is part of the Fairfield Local Government Area (LGA), which has the highest concentration of young people (aged 12–24) in New South Wales. Fairfield LGA also has the highest number of overseas migrants of any local government area in Australia, and the most diverse ethnic community. According to the 1991 Census, 61 per cent of young people in the area speak a language other than English and almost half (46 per cent) were born overseas (compared to the state average of 16.7 per cent). While unemployment in the area is generally higher than the state average, it is endemic among some groups – notably young people and the Vietnamese, Lebanese, Cambodian, Chinese, and Aboriginal and Torres Strait Islander communities.[3]

Contrary to media reports of domination by a ruthless Vietnamese gang (the '5T'), street-level heroin distribution in Cabramatta takes the form of a freelance market (cf. Curtis and Sviridoff, 1994: 157–8) dominated by Indo-Chinese user-dealers. While our research indicates that some dealers are 'taxed' by local gang members, the marketplace is not 'controlled' or monopolized by them, or anyone else.[4] Heroin is primarily distributed by individuals and multiple units of small entrepreneurs (mostly user-dealers) rather than mega-organizations or businesses. Entrepreneurial participation is relatively easy to accomplish, but is often short-lived and sporadic.

While the market is freelance, it is not open. Data from a related project which examined the characteristics of heroin purchases found that 92 per cent of respondents described the person from whom they last bought the heroin as 'Asian', with more than a third (39 per cent) estimating that the dealer was less than 20 years old (Maher et al., 1998). In a marketplace dominated by Indo-Chinese user-dealers, concepts of risk and respect clearly structure the participation of non-Asians. For some young Indo-Chinese people, territoriality is not merely a matter of economics, but an integral part of an oppositional street culture which provides them with a source of status and respect.

Heroin in Cabramatta has a reputation for being of higher quality than that sold elsewhere in Sydney.[5] It is typically sold in *caps*, small units weighing between 0.02 and 0.03 grams pre-packaged for individual sale. Caps are wrapped in a small piece of foil (often taken from the inside lining of a cigarette packet) and sealed in miniature balloons. The mean purchase price for a cap of heroin during the study period was $30.54 (range $12.50 to $45), with most purchases (84 per cent) costing between $25 and $35. The next most common retail unit was the *half-weight*: the mean purchase price of a half-weight during the study period was $180 (range $150 to $200; Maher et al., 1998).[6] During 1998, a new unit of retail sale known as the *quarter* emerged in Cabramatta: quarters typically sold for between $80 and $90 and, as the term suggests, ostensibly consist of a quarter of a gram of heroin (Maher et al., 1998).

Law enforcement strategies (in Cabramatta and elsewhere) are founded upon economic and social assumptions about the drug market. First, it is hypothesized that law enforcement drives up the street price of heroin which, in turn, reduces demand (Reuter and Kleiman, 1986). Secondly, it is expected that street-level law enforcement will disrupt the market and thereby 'accelerate the process by which users enter treatment programmes' (Gilman and Pearson, 1991: 112; see also Pearson, 1992: 16–17). A study by the NSW Bureau of Crime Statistics and Research challenges these assumptions, reporting that 'the rate of arrest for heroin use and/or possession exerts no effect on the street-level price of heroin or on the rate at which heroin users seek methadone treatment' (Weatherburn and Lind, 1995: iii).

This result is only superficially counter-intuitive. The impact of law enforcement (or lack thereof) should be understood as just one more example of how little criminal activity the police encounter in proportion to a 'dark figure' of crime, the dimensions of which can only be approximated. Our estimates suggest that between 18 and 78 million retail level heroin transactions take place in Australia each year. Using data from the Australian Bureau of Criminal Intelligence (1997) on the total number of heroin arrests in Australia in 1996–97, we calculate the overall risk of arrest per transaction as being between one in 2,600 and one in 10,900 transactions (Maher et al., 1998). Clearly, for those involved in high-frequency, low-volume transactions in areas such as Cabramatta, the risk per transaction may be greater. None the less, within the constraints of resources which can be realistically provided, police will never directly affect more than a relatively modest proportion of illegal drug activity.

If drug law enforcement does not achieve its objectives, then the social and economic costs in terms of crime and public health may be less acceptable. If, as the present study suggests, the concomitant public health risks are alarming, then current street-level drug policing strategies may be regarded as fundamentally flawed.

Drug policing: strategies and priorities

How does the street policing of drug users and user/dealers fit into broader policing strategies? It is widely accepted that policing efforts should be focused on the detection and prosecution of large-scale importers, suppliers, and traffickers, rather than users and user/dealers (Green and Purnell, 1995: 35). However, there is a significant disjuncture between enforcement agencies' commitment to targeting major drug offenders and the more prosaic reality in which enforcement impacts most on users and street-level dealers. This must be explained, first, in terms of the discursive presentation of the structure of the drug market, and, secondly, by placing drug policing in the broader context of public order policing.

Street-level participants in the drug market are redefined by police officers as potentially major players, or as the beginning of a trail to them. As one of Green and Purnell's interviewees responded: 'There's no such thing as a Vietnamese street dealer. They are all capable of importing a couple of ounces from relatives' (1995: 26). Other officers in the same study indicated that it was difficult to separate minor players from major because 'little jobs lead to bigger ones. We prosecute the little ones that we find along the way as well as the big ones they lead to' (Green and Purnell, 1995: 31). These 'fluid measures of seriousness which blur the distinction between major and minor drug offender targets' (Green and Purnell, 1995: 35) reinforce strategies based upon a pyramidal model of illegal drug organization which has been extensively criticized (Dorn and South, 1990; Ruggiero and South, 1995). Redefining police activity directed at the street user/dealer as part of a strategy aimed at the high-level dealer is a rhetorical, legitimating device.

Of course, drug policing has wider symbolic dimensions. In societies which regard illegal drug use as a challenge to moral and social order, drug policing delineates and defends 'the edges of our society' (Manning, 1980: 256). Doing so may be as significant as any instrumental effects of policing. In the case of drug policing in Cabramatta (as so often elsewhere), the 'edges of society' are racialized boundaries: a predominantly Caucasian police force seeks to control and discipline 'the slums of Cabramatta, its spiralling crime rate, (and) the almost pure Asian race that inhabits the streets and the drug scene there'.[7]

Drug policing must be understood, not just as a matter of specialist law enforcement, but also of a more general policing mandate which prioritizes order maintenance (Reiner, 1992: 212). In this context, street-level drug use and sale offend variously: as potential sources of disorder and violence, as improper 'disorderly' use of public space, as producing fears and anxieties among others in the community, and as expressions of immorality and social disutility. Drug policing, therefore, has to be located in a long history of public order policing which has focused on a variety of economic, cultural, and recreational practices in public space (Cohen, 1979; Dixon, 1991: Chapter 7). Street-level practices are determined by this mandate and its history as much as by policing strategies directed at the drug market.

Policy, discretion, and law in policing

We argue that public health considerations should be a prime determinant of drug policing activity. It is appropriate at this point to deal with a formulaic legalistic objection, which is to insist that policing is determined by the duty to enforce the law, and consequently that officers' activities cannot be restricted by directions intended to implement policy (cf. Jefferson and Grimshaw, 1984).

In a long tradition of research beginning with the American Bar Foundation project in the 1950s, it has been shown that law does not and could not dominate police activity (Dixon, 1997: Chapter 1; Ohlin and Remington, 1993). Policing is not just about law enforcement: crime fighting has never been, is not, and could not be the prime activity of the police . . . The core mandate of policing, historically and in terms of concrete demands placed upon the police, is the more diffuse one of order maintenance' (Reiner, 1992: 212). In carrying out such work, police officers are able to draw upon law as a resource of power, definitions and resolutions. As Chatterton suggests, we must suspend 'the conventional idea that laws are things to be enforced and (think) of them instead as resources to be used to achieve the ends of those who are entitled or able to use them' (1976: 114). Drug laws constitute such a resource, providing uniformed officers with authority to intervene to disrupt drug markets and harass participants, and with opportunities to make self-initiated arrests (see below).

In England and Australia, much is made of the supposed legally exceptional character of the police officer as constable (cf. Dixon, 1997: 75–6). It is claimed that officers cannot be directed how to perform their duty to enforce the law because the law requires them personally to be satisfied that legal criteria (e.g., reasonable suspicion) have been met (Jefferson and Grimshaw, 1984). Such arguments have a basic empirical flaw: police officers are part of organized departments, and are indeed directed in their duties every day. Their legal foundations are equally unreliable: as authoritative studies have shown (Lustgarten, 1986; Marshall, 1965), the legal implications of the 'office of constable' are largely mythical. There is nothing, either in empirical practice or in law, which makes an attempt to direct police activity in dealing with street-level drug users either unusual or legally problematic.

The longevity of the legalistic conception is primarily to be explained by its apparent attractions and ideological functions. It provides a mandate for policing – law enforcement as crime-fighting – which is much clearer and simpler than one which involves discretion and the interrelation of social policies and political considerations (Manning, 1997: Chapter 4). Disavowal of the power to choose has historically served police as a way of distancing themselves from misconduct and corruption (Remington, 1965: xvii). It is perhaps not surprising that some officers are wary of acknowledging their discretion in the aftermath of a major Royal Commission into corruption in the NSW Police Service (Dixon, 1999; Wood, 1997). However, as Scarman insists, 'the exercise of discretion lies at the heart of the policing function . . . Successful policing depends on the exercise of discretion in how the law is enforced' (1981: 63).

Critiques of legalism contributed significantly to the development of new conceptions of policing, such as community policing and problem-oriented policing (Goldstein, 1990; Moore, 1992). In these, law is displaced from its central position: policing is reconceived and redeployed as a flexible means of achieving a variety of public purposes. In such contexts, an insistence on the primary duty to enforce the law is merely anachronistic. To say that an officer must 'uphold the law, or is responsible to the law, is in practical terms meaningless' (Lustgarten, 1986: 11).

A central weakness of legalistic conceptions was always their lack of fit with the perceived reality of policing: as a series of studies demonstrated, police officers do not mechanically enforce the law (Dixon, 1997: Chapter 1). Our research, unsurprisingly, finds the same. Police officers in Cabramatta routinely deal with drug users not by arresting, but by removing or destroying drugs, equipment or money, and by warning, harassing and discouraging the drug user (Maher et al., 1997). Consequently, it is unconvincing to resist pressure for public health to be prioritized by citing legal duties of law enforcement. For police to present their work as the automatic application of law is, ironically, to understate the significance of their functions and the skill which policing requires (Bittner, 1990). In making decisions on how to police prohibited commodities and their markets, police officers must make choices. In this chapter, we suggest that another factor – public health – should be taken into account in making these choices.

Research methodology and demographic characteristics

In-depth ethnographic interviews and observational fieldwork designed to elicit information on the lifestyles and economic behaviours of street-level heroin users were undertaken in Cabramatta between February 1995 and February 1997. Initial ethnographic mapping identified geographic and social locations in which drug use and distribution occurred. It also identified dominant use patterns, acquisition and consumption sites, social networks, and demographic characteristics of the target population. Mapping data were collected through direct observation, informal conversations, systematic 'walk throughs' and the coding of locations.

This process provided the ethnographer with a map of the street-level drug using population which was subsequently used to develop a targeted sampling plan using the time-by-location method (Clatts et al., 1995). This involved the differentiation of potential participants by geography (street location) and time (of day and day of week) so as to achieve representation of all of the major segments of the street-level drug using population. Within this 'frame', efforts were made to secure appropriate age, gender and ethnic representation. In this respect, careful ethnographic research and the use of ethnographic mapping to inform targeted sampling can ensure more accurate representation than survey research which relies on self-selected or opportunity samples (e.g., recruitment through snowballing, advertising in newspapers, or notices in treatment centres).

As noted by Stimson, two of the principal strengths of ethnography for drug research are the ability to 'describe the social settings in which behaviour occurs' and the opportunities afforded by fieldwork to 'actually watch people doing things (rather than just talking about doing them)' (1995: 758). The fact that ethnography enables direct observation and analysis of behaviours and practices at both the individual and group level means that it is not dependent on drug users' self-reports. The combination of various data sources (observations recorded as fieldnotes, tape-recorded interviews, structured questionnaires and photographic images) permits information to be cross-validated (triangulated) and, where necessary, targeted for follow-up and clarification. As an additional measure, data collected for other projects by the authors in the same study site were triangulated against each other.

Once selected, potential participants were approached and the purpose of the study was explained to them. Participants were required to read and sign an informed consent outlining the possible risks and benefits of participating in the study. A total of 143 individuals participated in at least one in-depth tape-recorded interview (mean = three completed interviews, range 1–11). Data sources include 405 tape-recorded interview transcripts, more than 1,000 pages of typed fieldnotes, and 202 structured questionnaires on income and expenditure. Interviews were designed to elicit information in relation to a range of topics including demographics, childhood and family background, education and work history, social networks, drug use, crime, income generation and expenditure, impact of law enforcement, risk-taking, and experiences of treatment. Observational data in the form of fieldnotes were collected on each subject and on the nature, type and level of interactions between subjects in the study. Participants were paid $20 for each interview.

All participants in the research were current heroin users. Table 2.1 presents their demographic characteristics. Approximately half the sample were women. Anglo-Australians accounted for just over one-third (36 per cent) of the sample. The majority of participants (64 per cent) were from ethnic or cultural minority groups, with just under one-third (30 per cent) of Indo-Chinese background.

Table 2.1   *Sample characteristics (% unless specified)*

N	Experienced users* (n = 53)	New users** (n = 90)	Total (n = 143)
Gender			
Male	51	61	56
Female	49	39	46
Age (years)			
Mean	25.8	18.7	21.2
Median	25	18	20
Culture/Ethnicity			
Anglo-Australian	51	28	36
Indo-Chinese	19	36	30
Koori (Aboriginal)	15	2	8
Latin-American	6	9	8
Serbian-Australian	1	10	7
Pacific-Islander	0	6	3
Other NESB	8	9	8
Education (years)			
Mean	8.8	9.0	8.9
Unemployed	9.3	81	84
Current Residence			
Cabramatta	28	48	41
Other South West Sydney	42	31	35
Other	30	21	24

* Experienced users defined as those who had used heroin for more than two years at the time of first interview.
** New users defined as those who had used heroin two or less years at the time of first interview.

The mean age of participants was 21 years and a majority (77 per cent) were aged less than 25 years. Participants had an average of nine years of schooling and more than four-fifths (84 per cent) were unemployed at the time of the study. Most people who participated in the study resided in south-west Sydney: 41 per cent described themselves as residents of Cabramatta. One-third (34 per cent) had previously sought treatment for heroin use, but only 6 per cent (n = 8) were currently in treatment. Of these, seven were in methadone maintenance treatment.

Table 2.2 summarizes patterns of heroin use and routes of administration. The majority of participants (87 per cent) were predominantly or exclusively injectors. While those who currently smoked the drug only accounted for 13 per cent of the full sample, more than half (52 per cent) had initiated heroin use by smoking. Most participants were relatively recent recruits to heroin use, with a majority (63 per cent) having used heroin for two or less years. New injectors (70 per cent) were significantly more likely than experienced injectors (28 per cent) to report having made a transition from smoking to intravenous use. Preliminary analyses suggest that a combination of social, cultural, and environmental incentives are involved in the transition to intravenous use (Swift *et al.* 1997).

Table 2.2 *Patterns of heroin use (% unless specified)*

N	Experienced users* (n = 53)	New users** (n = 90)	Total (n = 143)
Heroin use (years)			
Mean	7.1	1.7	3.6
Median	6.0	1.5	2.0
Route of administration			
Inject	100	79	87
Smoke	0	21	13
Transition smoke-IDU			
Full sample (n = 143)	28	55	45
IDU (n = 124)	28	70	52
First drug injected***			
Heroin	77	89	84
Other drug	23	11	16

* Experienced users defined as those who had used heroin for more than two years at the time of first interview.
** New users defined as those who had used heroin two or less years at the time of first interview.
*** IDU (n = 124)

The effects of drug policing on public health

During the period of the study, Cabramatta was the focus of several high profile, intensive and sustained policing interventions. The findings presented here relate only to the activities of uniformed officers (beat police, mobile patrols, officers on horseback and dog teams), not to covert operations (undercover buy and busts).[8] While the latter target drug-dealers, the former also target users. However, in reality, there is no neat distinction between users and dealers at the street level: most dealers use, and indeed sell in order to finance their use. With this qualification, the findings presented here relate only to user-directed policing: i.e., interactions between uniformed officers and drug market participants at the street level. The impact of a highly visible uniformed police presence in Cabramatta has substantially increased the risk that those who participate in drug use and distribution will come to police attention. This has created a climate of fear and uncertainty which has resulted in a number of unforeseen negative consequences. We examine these in turn.

Oral and nasal storage and transfer of heroin

The intensity of policing in the area has encouraged both the oral and nasal storage and transfer of heroin. Most street-level dealers in Cabramatta store caps in their mouths. When a customer wishes to purchase, the dealer simply spits the cap(s) into his or her hand and passes it to the customer in exchange for the money. Such transfers often happen so quickly that they are invisible to the untrained eye. In some circumstances, the cap may be passed directly from mouth to mouth.

> Normally I take it in my hand and try and rub it on my clothes or something and clean it up a bit before I put it in my mouth. [You never put it straight into your mouth?] Sometimes if the police are really hot I do. Everyone does. I have even gone mouth to mouth, like kissing if things are really hot. (Rebecca, 17-year-old Anglo-Australian)

> When I get it I put it in my mouth. I wipe it sort of, rub it on my jeans a bit and then put it in my mouth because I don't want to get busted with it. If cops come, I just swallow it. (Gavin, 17-year-old Latin-American male)

Related research (Maher, 1996b), found that a majority of respondents (58 per cent) indicated that, on the last occasion on which they had purchased heroin, the dealer had retrieved the heroin from his or her mouth, with a further 10 per cent reporting that the dealer had retrieved heroin from his or her nose. More than two-thirds of the dealers were storing heroin in body cavities, risking exposure to blood and other bodily fluids. This may have implications for the transmission of tuberculosis, as well as blood-borne viruses, if the buyer then places the cap in his or her own mouth.

Until recently, dealers regarded oral storage of caps as an unproblematic tactic. If the police approached, dealers simply swallowed the caps and retrieved them later. While some might be irrecoverable, the cost was considerably less than being arrested.

> Before when I was dealing with (X), I think we had six caps each and a cop came up to me and I had to swallow all the caps and went around the corner and tried to vomit them up and I could only vomit three back up so I lost three caps you know. (Tien, 19-year-old Indo-Chinese male)

Police are now aware that dealers store heroin inside their mouths, and officers often attempt to prevent suspects from swallowing and to retrieve drugs from their mouths. These practices present significant risks both to suspects who are held in chokeholds and to police who put their fingers into people's mouths.

> Most of the cops are pretty cluey . . . They always ask to look in your mouth, like you know, 'Have you got anything in your mouth? Open your mouth' . . . I have even had a cop stick his finger in my mouth. (Harry, 34-year-old Koori male)

> Now when the cops grab you they try and put a hand around your throat so you can't swallow. They punch you in the back, try and make you cough it up . . . I have seen a lot of people get hit actually. (Chantelle, 23-year-old Anglo-Australian female)

In response to the police 'wising up' about the oral storage of caps, some dealers took to nasal storage of heroin.

He'll pull 'em out of his nose and say 'Put in your mouth quick'. Piss off . . . I wouldn't put them in my mouth. I have done, but only if the coppers are walking straight towards me and they're gonna question me and that. Then I'll put it in my mouth, but other than that, there's no fuckin' way in the world I'll put it in my mouth. Those cunts carry TB and everything, mate. (John, 27-year-old Anglo-Australian male)

I knew one bloke, fair dinkum, I've seen him pull ten caps, ten caps out of his nose. Mate, I don't know where the hell he puts 'em. He's gotta have a huge cavern at the back of his nose. Ten deals, no sweat mate, wrapped in foil and then in them little water bomb balloons tied up at the end. (Jack, 20-year-old Anglo-Australian male)

The increased risk of being busted has also resulted in a number of near-fatal overdoses as a result of people swallowing heroin in order to avoid detection by the police. In one instance observed during fieldwork, a young Vietnamese woman swallowed approximately two grams of heroin wrapped only in a tissue. Despite the potentially lethal consequences, she refused to go to hospital for fear of being arrested, choosing instead to force herself to regurgitate the contents of her stomach.

Reluctance to carry injecting equipment

Both observations and interviews suggest that users who inject in public settings in Cabramatta (streets, parks, alleyways, stairwells, toilets, car parks) are increasingly at risk of being interrupted by police either during preparation or actual administration. The most obvious consequence of this increased risk of being 'busted' is that some users are reluctant to carry injecting equipment. This means that, when they go to inject, they are less likely to have clean equipment. Some 'stash' their 'fits' (syringes) in nearby bushes, houses, or local flats, which may result in them being used by others.

We were in a house up the back and it's like in the kitchen section and there's like all fits and swabs and blood and stuff lyin' around everywhere, you know. And you open up one of the cupboards and up on the top shelf there's like fits up in there as well . . . He pulled one out that he said was his, you know, he puts it back each time he uses and . . . he changes it every day you know. He buys one in the morning and then, you know, he goes up there and has his shot and he leaves it up in that corner so he doesn't have to carry a fit around with him so if he gets shaken down by the cops he hasn't got it on him. (Jason, 24-year-old Anglo-Australian male)

Others engage in even more risky behaviours which are encouraged both by police practices and by the dearth of sterile injecting equipment outside business hours in Cabramatta.[9]

I was hangin' out like you wouldn't believe. I was sick, really severe cramps and I was like in major pain from the cramps and that and me insides were so like rotten that I was spewin' up bile y'know. And I was sweatin' and freezin' – just full on cold turkey. And I got on [bought heroin] and it was too early in the morning to get fits and there was no-one around that had any fits. I asked the dealer and he said no and I remembered that I saw a syringe like next to a drain. And I've seen it before and it's been there for ages. And I thought to myself 'HIV only lasts outside the body for three hours so I won't get that, and I've been immunized against Hepatitis B.' I've got Hep C already so I thought I'm hangin' out too much to wait so I just picked it up and used that. (Bon, 22-year-old Anglo-Australian male)

I know people that walk up the back of the flats and they're really bad, hangin' out. They can hardly walk. They're throwin' up everywhere and they spot a fit that someone has used and they just fuckin' fill it up with water a few times and squirt it out. (Kit, 23-year-old Anglo-Australian male)

Towards the end of the study period, there were a series of operations at Cabramatta Railway Station in which police ostensibly targeted people travelling without train tickets. Officers systematically searched those suspected of being drug users, inspecting arms for signs of injecting and examining clothing and bags for syringes and other evidence of drug use. Users reported that they were increasingly targeted by police and subject to street searches.

Every time they see me, they tell me 'What are you doing? Did you come to score?' You know, they nag and they search me, search my bag – in the middle of the street. I said 'Do you have ta to do it here?' Fuckin' embarrassing – why do this to me? What have I done? Fuck, I haven't done nuthin' and they'll just fuckin' empty my pockets, tell me 'Get on the train and go home. If you don't go and get on the train we're gonna arrest you' . . . and tell you to keep out of Cabramatta and all this stuff. (Taylor, 16-year-old Anglo-Australian female)

Some young people also reported that police had forced them to destroy their needles and syringes. This was particularly irresponsible late at night when the result was likely to be, not abstinence, but risky injecting practices.

[Why don't you carry fits?] Cops . . . You get hassled. They know [if] you've got a fit, you use. They pat you down, ask you have you got any fits on you . . . A couple of times I've pulled it out and they seen it and go 'Snap it, break it, put it in the rubbish bin' . . . just say that's the only fit you've got . . . and there's nothing open, you can't get nothing else and you haven't got none stashed or there's no-one around with any more fits. What are you gonna do then? (Alex, 23-year-old Serbian-Australian male)

While the possession of needles and syringes is not an offence in New South Wales, many new intravenous drug users (IDUs) and, in particular, Indo-Chinese users, were unaware of this. In any case, whatever 'law in the books' may provide, policing practice means that many IDUs fear that being found with a syringe will lead to harassment and further police attention, more intrusive searches, and warrant checks (see also Koester, 1994).

> They said to me they can charge me, they were going to charge me with self administer and all this. I just told them 'Fuck off, you can't, they're washed out, they're clean'.[10] They said 'Show us your arms . . . Don't lie to us. We can charge you. If you want to get smart, we'll start gettin' smart.' (Taylor, 16-year-old Anglo-Australian female)

> You haven't even done nothin' wrong. They grab you for doing nothin', find a fit on you and next minute they're doing a warrant check. (Bon, 22-year-old Anglo-Australian male)

For young women, gender issues in relation to police treatment may also condition their reluctance to carry syringes.

> Once a cop found a fit in my bag and he smashed it and broke my water. OK, that's bad enough, but it's the way they make you feel – made me feel like a real slut. They treat you like you are a prostitute or something just cause you've got a fit. (Suzie, 17-year-old Serbian-Australian female)

Users' perceptions of the risks involved in carrying syringes were clearly differentiated by age, gender, and ethnicity. Most experienced injectors did carry syringes, and many kept a supply of sterile injecting equipment at home. Older female IDUs claimed that it was easier for women and girls to carry syringes and less likely for them to be detected because they had handbags, whereas men had to carry bulky fitpacks in their back pockets. Many young injectors feared detection by their parents as well as by the police. Furthermore, for some young Indo-Chinese injectors, fear of identification as an intravenous drug user by their peers increased their reluctance to carry injecting equipment.

Increase in injection-related risk-taking

The overt police presence has also exacerbated the incidence of high-risk injecting episodes in the area. Users who inject in public or semi-public settings are anxious to 'get on' and 'get out'. This can mean using any syringe that is available if they do not have one: either borrowing one or picking one up off the ground.

> From the time when I'm just about to get it [buy heroin] 'til the time when I've just finished using, all that time is a major stress period. (Teddy, 20-year-old Pacific-Islander male)

Users are also less likely to have a 'taste' first or to measure their dose. Because they are fearful of interruption and anxious to get rid of the evidence, IDUs typically administer the drug in one dose, increasing the risk of overdose (especially if they have been using benzodiazepines or drinking alcohol).

It's like pigs in a trough. You gotta be quick. Hurry up, hurry up. Get me quick, put it away quick and then it's too late [to get busted]. Once you've taken it out of your arm, too late now, throw the fit in the box and say 'Well, the coppers can go and get lucky'. (Alex, 23-year-old Serbian-Australian male)

You just want to go quickly and have your shot in case the coppers come and that's how you get marks all over your arms and how come people overdose and stuff. (Kylie, 17-year-old Anglo-Australian female)

They [the police] hassle users and we are scared of being busted when we go and have a shot. People stress out and just want to have their shot and bolt. I'm more fearful now. There's no relaxing – scoring and using is stressful. (Arian, 36-year-old Anglo-Australian female)

Such fear and uncertainty are not conducive to safe injection practices. Our research suggests that street-based injectors are now less likely to use sterile injecting equipment and more likely to engage in unsafe drug preparation and division procedures, including needle sharing and the use of discarded needles, and to practise unsafe disposal (Maher, 1996a).[11]

You don't have time . . . to be there mixing everybody's gear [separately], you've gotta do it fast . . . Like I'm there mulling up and I've got my ear you know, listening for cars, you know, or for footsteps or the cops. (Susan, 19-year-old Latin American female)

The rush for the vein accumulates risk for many young people who are anxious and unskilled in injecting techniques. People are shaking, jabbing furiously, trying to get a vein, blood is flying around; in short, the worst possible injecting scenario.

I've been in a hurry and fucked my arm up because I'm scared of being busted. (Lazzares, 19-year-old Latin-American male)

I know I'm taking a risk. People are very scared 'caus we all know the cops go checking flats and everything. We hurry up and get out. (Kim, 16-year-old Indo-Chinese female)

Everyone's scared – paranoid. People are rushing. They lose things – drop their caps, drop their fits – panic. (Bob, 24-year-old Serbian-Australian male)

During these episodes, participants sometimes become paranoid or start arguing. Mistakes are made, such as drawing up too much solution from the communal spoon and having to squirt some back. This is a most effective way of spreading disease if the syringe has been used previously.

A couple of lines is a big deal. I sucked up too much [into a previously used fit] and they started spinning out, so I had to squirt some back. (Fatman, 20-year-old Anglo-Australian male)

It's money. I'm scared that I won't get the hit and I want to get more, as much as I can. And I was like, I must admit I am greedy but they always fight: 'Look, I only got ten lines' when she only had eight, so I had to put two more [lines] back so she had ten. I flick it and see how much and then I'll put it back in the spoon so she can get back it through the filter. We all do it. We flick and see how much and we say 'What did you get? What did you get?' I go, 'Look at you, you're greedy. See we've only got ten lines mate. Come on. Put some more back in.' And I'll have a stress attack. (Speedy, 16-year-old Anglo-Australian female)

The desire to 'get on, get it in, and get out' also means that users are less likely to dispose of their needles safely. Carrying used fits to a safe disposal bin risks being caught, so they leave them behind.

You rush and shit 'caus you're paranoid they're [the police] gonna come. I just get it done real quick and I don't care where I put the fits. Just have it, leave everything and go. (J.J., 15-year-old Anglo-Australian female)

Finally, many young people reported that they were too scared to carry identification in Cabramatta in case they were 'busted'. This can have problematic consequences in instances of accidents and overdoses.

The effective promotion of unsafe drug-injecting practices among a growing group of heroin users in an area with the state's highest concentration of young people should be a matter of considerable concern. Also of concern is the impact of policing practices on police–community relations.

It's like a crackdown on users – a persecution of users. It's over the top. They are physically more rough. They don't care who sees them doing stuff to people. They're breeding a whole new generation of people who will just resent and loathe law enforcement because of the way they see police treat people out here. They don't care who is watching. (Bananas, 41-year-old Anglo-Australian male)

Given that young Indo-Chinese heroin users are particularly over-policed, relations between them (and the communities from which they come) and the police should be a source of great concern.[12]

Displacement

Drug markets are rather like a squishy balloon: apply pressure to them in one place and there will be some diminution of the problem, yet it is likely that the market will balloon out in another place or on an adjacent site, involving new and possibly more cautious or sophisticated dealers and perhaps a different range of drugs. These outcomes are, respectively, examples of geographical, social and substance displacement. (Dorn and Murji, 1992: 170, n. 5)

Displacement of criminal activity has been recognized as a likely consequence of street-level law enforcement and of CCTV surveillance (Pease, 1997). Drug transactions, unlike, for example, certain types of theft, are labile polymorphous activities requiring only that the vendor and purchaser know how and where to make contact with each other. As such, they may be especially susceptible to displacement which, as Dorn and Murji note, can take a variety of forms. First, we examine the geographical dispersal of drug users and consumption sites.

Injecting drug users in Cabramatta utilize a wide range of locations to consume drugs. These locations represent hierarchies of risk (Friedman et al., 1992; Ouellet et al., 1991). Private settings include residential addresses and motel rooms. Semi-private settings include motor vehicles and abandoned houses. Public settings encompass the walkways, stairwells, and gardens of local flats, public toilets, hotel toilets and trains, as well as outdoor locations such as parks, underpasses, and car parks. Public settings are more likely to be used by young street-based injectors and some of these locations constitute significant health risks.

Vigorous policing may encourage the use of less desirable settings. In particular, locations used for collective injecting episodes are likely to be public, unhygienic, poorly lit and ill-ventilated. With the exception of public toilets, few provide access to running water and most are littered with injecting paraphernalia, including discarded syringes. Conditions in abandoned houses are notably poor.

> You go in there and you can't even see the floor, it's just full of [used] needles . . . there's needles everywhere. I reckon there'd be about a thousand needles. (Kylie, 17-year-old Anglo-Australian female)

> When you look at all these houses and that where people go to shoot up it's just unbelievable, unbelievable . . . I am just looking at a photo of myself shooting up now and I'm freaking out. I can't believe how filthy it was where we went yesterday and all the garbage and all the syringes and needles. Unbelievable. (Peter, 17-year-old Serbian-Australian male)

Many of these settings could be characterized as 'free' shooting galleries in the sense that they provide a 'space where IDUs regularly gather to inject drugs but where there is no admission fee' (Ouellet et al., 1991: 73). However, conditions in Cabramatta are conducive to the development of commercially oriented galleries where people provide places for others to inject for a fee (either drugs or money). Such developments are marked by the presence of individuals who support their use by injecting those who are unable or unwilling to inject themselves. While, in one sense, the establishment of commercial galleries may be desirable (i.e., presence of gatekeepers, potential for safe using norms and safe disposal), this is highly contingent on the type of galleries that emerge. For example, research in North America indicates that certain types of shooting galleries may serve as vectors for the transmission of HIV and other blood-borne viruses (Des Jarlais and Friedman, 1990; Marmour et al., 1987; Ouellet et al., 1991). There is also the danger that, in such settings, people, especially gatekeepers, are less likely to call an ambulance in overdose situations for fear of drawing attention to the premises.

One consequence of the vigorous policing of these locations has been a dispersal of the problems associated with having a large community of street-based injectors. Because the police have been successful in targeting known injecting locations in and around central Cabramatta, users have been forced to fan out in search of new, and as yet undiscovered locations.

> The police thing . . . [is] forcing us go further and further out. We had certain spots, you know, 2 minutes away from scoring, you had somewhere to go. Now it's you know, you're taking 15, 20 minute walks sometimes. (Steve, 38-year-old Anglo-Australian male)

> People get paranoid and they're always looking for new and more hidden places. All the close spots are very hot. There's a good chance of gettin' busted when you have a shot, so people are looking for new spots. (Bon, 22-year-old Anglo-Australian male)

Some residents, increasingly frustrated by the presence of drug users and drug-related paraphernalia, have installed locks and gates in order to prevent consumption in and around residential premises. Drug users who are part of the local community also resent what they see as the dirty habits of 'outsiders' who have no stake in the neighbourhood.

> They have no respect. Leave their fits everywhere and people piss in here [stairwell of flats] and be sick everywhere. They could go outside to do these sort of things. Plus like little kids live here – they shouldn't have to see this sort of stuff. (Tiffany, 17-year-old Vietnamese-Australian woman)

Dispersing drug users and using locations over a wider geographical area simply spreads 'the problem' further into the community. Over time, more flats, more parks and more families are affected and, in particular, the risks presented by discarded syringes increase. There are also risks to drug users associated with the dispersal of street-based injecting: seclusion may be fatal if a user overdoses. Cabramatta already accounts for a disproportionate share of overdose deaths in south-west Sydney, most of which occur in public places.[13]

Both the results of the present study and related research (Maher et al., 1997) suggest that current policing strategies may also threaten the tentative alliance between drug users and health professionals by displacing or driving drug users underground. Forcing heroin users to move around marginalizes and alienates them from communities and the rest of society, hampering outreach efforts directed at this population. New developments within at-risk communities may go unnoticed until it is too late. Police officers' insistence that intensive (or 'zero tolerance') policing is part of a multi-agency, problem-solving approach is, in this light, simply disingenuous.

While drug use has been dispersed, there has also been some displacement of the drug market. The unintended and undesirable consequence may be to make drugs available in neighbourhoods where they were previously scarce (Pearson, 1991: 74). Both field observations and interview data suggest that there has been significant growth in drug markets in adjacent suburbs. The emergence of a street-level heroin market in nearby Campbelltown has been a source of particular concern. Whether this is due to displacement from Cabramatta is unclear and controversial. However, there has certainly been geographical displacement within Cabramatta itself. Field observations suggest that many dealers who had previously operated on the street began to ply their trade in local shopping arcades. Others who had previously operated in the town centre shifted their business to the vicinity of a local primary school.

However, geographical displacement is not necessarily regarded as problematic. The police response has been to equate the problem to that of 'aircraft noise' which should be disaggregated in the interests of social equity. According to one senior police officer, 'we knew there was going to be a displacement effect . . . It is a bit like aircraft noise. We have to spread the problem about and not just have it centred on one suburb' (*Sydney Morning Herald*, 11 October 1997). From a public health perspective, this analogy is inappropriate not least because it assumes a finite population and discounts the possibility of reproduction. The adoption of a 'zero tolerance' policing policy which advocates the geographical displacement of drug problems clearly has the potential to produce more, rather than less, harm. Indeed, an epidemiological approach to the reproduction of heroin use and the transmission of blood-borne viruses suggests that the dispersal of heroin use and heroin markets may present more problems than it solves (Hughes and Crawford, 1972).

Intensive policing may also produce harmful forms of social displacement. As suggested above, there is some evidence to suggest that vigorous forms of street-level law enforcement may ultimately lead to more organized, professional and enduring forms of criminality and thereby exacerbate the social, economic and health costs of illicit drug use. First, observations and interviews suggest that the use of intermediaries became a more stable feature of the market as policing became more intensive. At minimal cost, the retention of a helper alleviates the need for the dealer to tout directly and provides some verification of authenticity of users if the helper knows, or is prepared to vouch for, the potential customer. If this is indeed the case, then street-level law enforcement activity may indirectly contribute to an increase in the complexity and sophistication of the market by encouraging functional specialization and hierarchical differentiation (Dorn et al., 1992).

Secondly, the availability of multiple means of making connection (whether personal, via touts and runners, or technological via mobile phones and beepers) increases displaceability. The police presence during the study period encouraged some dealers to move their business 'off the street' by relying on mobile phones, thereby minimizing the risk of detection and apprehension. Dealers who rely on mobile phones are well served by the market for stolen goods in Cabramatta where small, good quality mobile phones and reprogrammable cards are sought-after commodities. Thirdly, the introduction of a new unit of retail sale, the 'quarter' (see above) during the study period could also be seen as evidence of the market's capacity to adapt to external pressures. Indeed, insofar as the effect has been to minimize the number of transactions, the introduction of larger units of sale could be seen as a risk-reduction measure for both sellers and their customers. A fourth trend appears to be towards increased vehicular trade. Several streetcorners in Cabramatta are characterized by the presence of individuals who cater to these 'drive-by' customers.

> When they stop at the red lights you know a lot of the Asian guys just walk straight up to the car, 'Are you right mate?', you know, and a lot of the time you will see an Asian guy jump in the back of the car and they will just go for a drive somewhere and do the deal. (Rob, 17-year-old Anglo-Australian male)

> If anything is getting heavy they can just jump in the car and they can drive somewhere where the cops can't see them, away from everyone's eyes and then do the business. (Luis, 21-year-old Latin-American male)

In addition, structural changes in the wake of intensive policing have created a vacuum. As dealers leave the market (either because they are arrested or displaced), novices and those willing to work in a higher risk environment move in. Street-level dealing becomes more volatile and elusive, increasing the power of groups such as 5T. Intrusions may be met violently, as in a recent incident where a helper 'steered' a customer towards the 'wrong' dealer and had his throat cut on the street. On the other hand, 'bodgy' dealers (those who sell fake caps or half-weights) have become more common, especially during periods when there are few genuine dealers available as a result of fear and uncertainty induced by police operations.

> We'd see 'em coming. Suckers, you can just spot 'em. Just chop up some panadol [paracetemol]. (Stan, 23-year-old Serbian-Australian male)

The activities of 'bodgy' dealers have the potential to increase violence in the marketplace. Heroin users do not take kindly to being 'ripped off' and the illegal nature of the transaction necessitates resort to informal sanctions. During the study period, there were several reports of violence in Cabramatta associated with such transactions.

> Fake caps, that's bad enough but fake halves, you know they're just going to get killed. They think we're junkies but you might be sick and weak but you get so much anger getting ripped off – trying to get $200 whatever together and then you get ripped off. (Rebecca, 17-year-old Serbian-Australian female)

Intensive policing of this kind may have broader detrimental social consequences. There may be short- and long-term criminogenic effects:

> They [the police] make more crime by taking the gear off us – busting us so we have to do more rorts [income-generating property crimes]. Because every time

they bust someone having a shot, that person just has to go out and do another rort to get that shot back. (Frash, 18-year-old Anglo-Australian male)

A further unintended effect may be to encourage 'failed' user/dealers to resort to other types of crime in order to generate income. Deterring people from selling heroin and other related activities may not be the unproblematic social good which it is usually assumed to be (Grapendaal et al., 1995: 200). An increase in property crime, some of it involving violence, is a type of social displacement which receives insufficient attention. One of our participants, a 17-year-old Vietnamese-Australian female who had for several years supported her heroin use by street-level dealing, recently reported that, unable to sell heroin because of the police presence, she had held a knife to a shopkeeper's throat during a robbery. Clearly, some types of crime result in more direct harm than other types. The goal of public policy may need to be no more ambitious than minimizing the most harmful.

As regards substance displacement, there is some evidence that pressure on the heroin market has led to an increase in the illicit sale and use of diverted pharmaceuticals (primarily benzodiazepines[14] and methadone). An additional and significant form of displacement may involve route of administration, with some participants claiming that the police crackdown has encouraged users to make the transition from smoking to injecting heroin.

People are starting shooting up because of the police. Like a lot of the guys I know that used to smoke started shooting up in the last few months – I'm the only one left [smoking] . . . It's too hard to make any profit now with all the police and the cameras. They come and just stand there at the station and we have to move. When you smoke, you have to smoke a lot, so if they shoot up, they can use less. Like instead of smoking a halfweight, you can just have one or two shots. (Phuong, 20-year-old Indo-Chinese male)

It is too early to comment on the possibility of 'temporal displacement' (Dorn and Murji, 1992: 170). Cabramatta is currently the subject of even more intensive policing activity than during the period of the research reported here. Experience elsewhere suggests that whether the drug market regains its previous shape once this crackdown is relaxed is likely to depend upon social and economic change (Pearson, 1992; Sviridoff et al., 1992). If factors such as employment growth, gentrification or urban development are induced, the conditions for a street-level drug market may no longer exist. If they are not, saturation policing may be a short-term strategy which becomes a long-term liability.

In summary, the heroin market in Cabramatta has proved itself to be resilient with a considerable capacity to respond and adapt to police

interventions. Some of these adaptations are pathogenic and/or criminogenic, posing serious threats to public health and community safety.

From law enforcement to harm minimization

The conventional policy prescription at this point is drug law reform,
notably decriminalizing the possession of small amounts of some drugs.
There is increasingly significant support for such change. However, the
political reality[15] is that policing will be conducted in the context of
prohibition for the foreseeable future. Consequently, discussion should
focus on how drug prohibition could be best policed to minimize harm
(Pearson, 1992: 18).

Australia has a considerable reputation for its commitment to harm
minimization as the foundation of its national drug strategy. It is almost
conventional to contrast Australia favourably with the United States
(Nadelmann, 1992). While this contrast does have substance, its invocation
creates a danger of complacency. The research presented here suggests that
policy commitments to harm minimization are not matched by street-level
enforcement practices. Operational officers appear not to understand harm
minimization policies, feeling at best confused by directions (for example)
not to target clients of needle exchanges. They are little assisted by some
official guidance, for example on 'Drug harm minimization and practical
policing applications', which states the problem, but offers no solution:

> Some officers have a moral dilemma in reconciling policing needs with harm
> minimization. For example, a person caught injecting heroin is breaking the law
> and under strict law enforcement, should be arrested. Yet, with harm minimiza-
> tion, officers are asked to accept drug use and a programme that supplies users
> with clean needles and syringes. (*Police Service Weekly*, 1996: 3).

When 'policing needs' and 'harm minimization' are polarized in this way, it
is hardly surprising to find officers enforcing the law and regarding
proposed alternatives with cynicism.

More generally, this approach can encourage cynicism if harm minimization is perceived as a rhetorical rather than a substantive commitment. In
terms of policing strategies, it implies a partial (and consequently inadequate) adoption of problem-oriented policing: such a strategy, to be
successful, requires the active and knowledgeable involvement of operational officers in the programme (Goldstein, 1990). Problem-oriented
policing cannot be simply a tactic or 'law enforcement technology'. The
failure of police organizations to give substance to their commitments to
harm reduction cannot be explained at the level of poor communication or
even bad faith: responsibility lies much deeper, in the structures and
cultures of policing (Brown and Sutton, 1997: 21).

Harm minimization requires cooperation with non-police agencies committed to demand-reduction and public health. However, relations with such agencies are strained by police insistence on the priority of their definition of 'the problem' and by these agencies' lack of political influence and economic resources (Pearson et al., 1992). Throughout south-west Sydney, welfare and medical services are over-committed and under-resourced, and consequently limited in their ability to make an effective contribution. In Cabramatta, such services are scarce, under-funded, and under-staffed. Some local government leaders are publicly committed to a simplistic law-enforcement strategy, refusing to see the Cabramatta drug trade as anything other than an 'Asian crime problem'.

In a context such as this, arguments that street-level law enforcement should form part of harm minimization strategies are simply inappropriate. In the absence of adequate partners for inter-agency initiatives, police crackdowns are closer to 'heavy-handed scatter-gun approaches to law enforcement which fill the courts and prisons with people . . . [and] which result not only in harm to the individual . . . but also to the wider community' than to 'a more realistic and focused strategy by which the police direct their efforts against heavy end-users and user-dealers in order to push them into community-based programmes offering alternative life-styles' (Pearson, 1992: 26). It is symptomatic that, one year after the NSW Police launched its latest series of crackdowns in Cabramatta, the new health and welfare services which were supposed to accompany them were yet to materialize. A purportedly problem-solving, inter-agency initiative is experienced on the street as a crackdown which offers punishment as its only 'treatment option'.

In the context of under-resourced or ill-informed potential partners, the police have a particular responsibility to ensure that their own actions do not produce harm. As a well-resourced, politically powerful and strategically sophisticated organization, the NSW Police Service may have to take a more prominent role in reducing harm than would otherwise be appropriate. The discussion above makes clear that there is no legal impediment to the implementation of policies which go beyond law enforcement. This study strongly indicates that police officers should exercise their discretion in a way which takes full account of public health imperatives. This does not mean replacing law enforcement with unfettered discretion. The analysis above makes clear that police could not and do not fully enforce the law in this (or any other) area: police work is inherently discretionary. Some drug users are arrested, but the power to arrest and charge is a resource used to fulfil a fundamental mandate of public order maintenance. More frequently, other methods are adopted: police disrupt the activity, destroy the drugs, and/or move the user on. These are legitimate uses of discretion. However, under certain conditions, they are harmful to public health and inconsistent with policy commitments to harm minimization. Police make choices about how and when to enforce the law. Minimizing drug-related harm should be a factor that feeds into that choice.

Noting an example from a comparable area without the political and emotive resonances of drug control may be helpful. Many police departments in Australia, Britain and the United States issue instructions to police officers not to engage in (or to abandon) car chases in certain circumstances. Such instructions tell officers not to attempt to enforce the law, even though criminal offences (such as car theft) and violations of traffic regulations have occurred. Such instructions prioritize public safety: the safety of police officers, the persons in the stolen car and bystanders. This is one area in which a harm minimization policy is unproblematically adopted (Criminal Justice Commission, 1998; Homel, 1990). This example (including its lessons about the difficulties of implementing policy) could provide a starting point for developing a strategy for drug policing which takes harm minimization seriously.

Our study indicates that, as in the case of car chases, the *point* of intervention is crucial. Although there are a number of points along the continuum between purchase and use at which intervention is possible, current practice appears to be to intervene at the point of use. This is an obvious point of intervention: users are vulnerable, static and performing a complex procedure (preparing drugs, preparing the injection site, administering the drug). However, intervention (and the threat of intervention) at this point is, as our research makes clear, hazardous because it encourages unsafe injecting practices. The dangers for police officers should also be evident. Any intervention when needles are in use is dangerous, but some reported police practices (such as removing needles from people's arms during the injection process) suggest an alarming recklessness and a failure of police training to communicate information about health risks.

'Order maintenance' and some drug-related arrests are currently bought at the cost of serious public health risks to drug users, police officers and the broader community. Police officers should be directed, trained and encouraged to take public health into consideration when exercising their discretion in dealing with drug users. Using discretion in this way would not be improperly to abandon law enforcement. As has been made clear above, law enforcement is not currently the automatic police response, and structuring discretion by taking account of various policy imperatives is both legally impeccable and consistent with best practice in contemporary policing. The priority must be to shift police attention away from the period immediately surrounding self-administration. It is time that laudable policy commitments to harm minimization are given substance in policing practice by structuring police discretion around the priority of public health.

Conclusion

It is almost a cliché to point out that unsuccessful attempts to enforce prohibitions of widely desired goods and services have undesirable side-effects (Morris and Hawkins, 1970: 27). In the policing of prostitution, gambling, drink, and other drugs, a pattern has been established which was familiar in the eighteenth century: 'the inventions of the sharpers' are 'swifter than the punishment of the law, which only hunts them from one device to another' (Blackstone, 1769: 173).

Drug law enforcement has particular pathogenic and criminogenic costs. It is characterized by waves of activity: both the availability of resources and public or media pressure for action produce this pattern of crackdown and back-off. As we have seen, such a pattern appears to be particularly prone to unwelcome side-effects. Drug market participants adopt risky practices in storing, transferring and administering heroin. The illegal activity is not suppressed, but the threat of intermittent law enforcement encourages the development of a level of organization that protects participants and increases the potential for police corruption. Geographical, social, substance and temporal displacement may occur, and relations between police and ethnic minorities deteriorate.

As we have seen, specific types of illegal activity can be moulded in different ways by attempts to suppress or control them. Once it is accepted that suppression of an activity is impossible, the task of policing (assuming a continuing formal commitment to prohibition) is its regulation (Dixon, 1991). As Dorn and South suggest, the 'question is, given that we cannot totally prevent illegal drug markets . . . what kind of markets do we least dislike, and how can we adjust the control mix so as to push markets in the least *un*desired direction?' (1990: 186). Such questions need to be answered empirically. Our research goes some way towards providing some answers. The lesson from this study is that we know what *not* to do if we value public health and community safety.

If viewed solely from the short-term perspective of traditional law enforcement, the street policing of drug offences in Cabramatta may be judged a reasonable success: it generates respectable arrest and conviction rates. As quality of life or 'zero tolerance' policing attracts increasing interest, the criteria of success have shifted to disrupting the market and 'cleaning' up the town centre. The various ways in which the Cabramatta drug market has been displaced have been hailed as winning a drug war.[16] However, our research indicates that crackdowns, whether carried out in the name of law enforcement or quality of life, push markets in directions which are highly undesirable. Such 'successes' and 'victories' may be won at a cost which, in the long term, makes them not worthwhile.

Notes

1. In addition, an extensive CCTV system was established in the research site in 1997. For a discussion of this, see Maher et al. (1997).
2. While this chapter is primarily concerned with heroin, it should not be overlooked that almost half of all drug offences in NSW involve the possession of cannabis (Bureau of Crime Statistics and Research, 1997: 15, 48, 67).

3. These data are drawn from Australian Bureau of Statistics (1991), Fairfield City Council (1995) and Sullivan et al. (1995).

4. This corresponds with the findings of research on North American drug markets (Hagedorn, 1994). Our fieldwork in Cabramatta suggests that gang involvement in drug distribution and sales is oriented toward the economic survival of individual members and may be best understood as a response to high levels of unemployment and economic and social marginality. In particular, the 5T, as a 'cultural gang' (Skolnick, 1989), exists independently of the illegal activities in which it is involved and is perceived by many young Vietnamese people as a quasi-familial resource which places strong emphasis on loyalty, brotherhood, respect and physical protection (see also English, 1995; Long, 1996).

5. Based on 322 samples of heroin obtained as undercover purchases or recovered from persons arrested in Cabramatta. Weatherburn and Lind (1995) found a mean purity level of 58.7 per cent.

6. There appear to be several types of half-weights available for purchase in Cabramatta. 'Asian halves', which are reserved for Asian customers (usually street dealers), typically consist of a weighed half gram. Junkie or 'Aussie halves' (sometimes known as 'streeties') typically weigh between 0.3 and 0.4 grams. There is also a version of the half-weight in Cabramatta which is reserved for rank outsiders (i.e. non-Asian, non-regulars and non-locals). These 'tripper's halves' are the most expensive and may weigh less than 0.2 grams.

7. Letter, *Sydney Morning Herald*, 21 October 1996.

8. While these activities are clearly interrelated, in attempting to ascertain the impact of law enforcement strategies at the street level, it is necessary to differentiate the various policing strategies employed.

9. Sterile injecting equipment was only available from chemists and a secondary needle and syringe exchange outlet during business hours in the study period.

10. While possession of injecting equipment was decriminalized in 1987, self-administration of a prohibited drug remains an offence (Drug Misuse and Trafficking Act 1985 s. 12(1)) and a 'dirty' syringe could be used as evidence of this.

11. A survey (n = 202) conducted as part of this study found that more than a quarter (28 per cent) of participants reported using a needle after someone else and 42 per cent had lent their needle to someone else to use during the month prior to interview (Maher et al., 1998).

12. There is a prevalent insensitivity in the over-policing of young Indo-Chinese people (Maher et al., 1997) which is remarkably ill-advised given the documented costs of such policing activities in relation to members of minority ethnic and cultural groups in other jurisdictions (Keith, 1993; Scarman, 1981).

13. Between 1992 and 1996, 38 per cent of the 176 deaths attributed to heroin overdose in south-west Sydney occurred in Cabramatta. Deaths in Cabramatta were significantly more likely to occur in public settings (89 per cent v. 42 per cent) (Darke and Ross, 1998).

14. This development is of concern given the role of benzodiazepines in heroin-related deaths (Darke and Zador, 1996).

15. This is demonstrated by the remarkable controversy in 1997 over a proposal to prescribe pharmaceutical heroin to 40 people in the Australian Capital Territory. It became the subject of a heated, lengthy, national debate as if the

proposal was for national decriminalization rather than for a small-scale clinical trial.

16. See 'Police win war in drug capital', *Daily Telegraph* (Sydney), 20 April 1998; 'Outstanding success of Operation Puccini', *Police Service Weekly*, 1 June 1998: 4–5.

References

Australian Bureau of Criminal Intelligence (1997) *Australian Illicit Drug Report 1996–1997*. Canberra: Australian Bureau of Criminal Intelligence.

Australian Bureau of Statistics (1991) *ABS Census*. Canberra: Australian Bureau of Statistics.

Bittner, E. (1990) *Aspects of Police Work*. Boston, MA: Northeastern University Press.

Blackstone, W. (1769) *Commentaries on the Laws of England: Book 4: Of Public Wrongs*. Oxford: Clarendon Press.

Brown, M. and A. Sutton (1997) 'Problem oriented policing and organizational form', *Current Issues in Criminal Justice*, 9: 21–33.

Bureau of Crime Statistics and Research (1997) *Criminal Court Statistics*. Sydney: NSW Bureau of Crime Statistics and Research.

Caulkins, J.P., R.C. Larson and T.F. Rich (1993) 'Geography's impact on the success of focused local drug enforcement operations', *Socioeconomic Planning Science*, 27: 119–30.

Chatterton, M. (1976) 'Police in social control', in J.F.S. King (ed.), *Control without Custody?* Cambridge: Institute of Criminology. pp. 104–22.

Clatts, M.C., W. Rees Davis and A. Atillasoy (1995) 'Hitting a moving target: the use of ethnographic methods in the development of sampling strategies for the evaluation of AIDS outreach programs for homeless youth in New York City', in E.Y. Lambert, R.S. Ashery and R.H. Needle (eds), *Qualitative Methods in Drug Abuse and HIV Research*. National Institute on Drug Abuse Research Monograph 157, Washington, DC: US Government Printing Office. pp. 117–35.

Cohen, P. (1979) 'Policing the working-class city', in B. Fine, J. Lea, S. Picciotto and J. Young (eds), *Capitalism and the Rule of Law*. London: Hutchinson. pp. 118–36.

Collison, M. (1995) *Police, Drugs and Community*. London: Free Association Books.

Curtis, R. and M. Sviridoff (1994) 'The social organization of street-level drug markets and its impact on the displacement effect', in R.P. McNamara (ed.), *Crime Displacement*. New York: Cummings and Hathaway. pp. 155–71.

Criminal Justice Commission (1998) *Police Pursuits in Queensland Resulting in Death or Injury*. Brisbane: Criminal Justice Commission.

Darke, S. and J. Ross (1998) *Heroin-related Deaths in South Western Sydney*. NDARC Technical Report No. 52. Sydney: National Drug and Alcohol Research Centre.

Darke, S. and D. Zador (1996) 'Fatal heroin overdose: a review', *Addiction*, 91: 1757–64.

Des Jarlais, D. and S.R. Friedman (1990) 'Shooting galleries and AIDS', *American Journal of Public Health*, 80: 142–4.

Dixon, D. (1991) *From Prohibition to Regulation*. Oxford: Clarendon Press.

Dixon, D. (1996) 'Illegal betting in Britain and Australia: contrasts in control strategies and cultures', in J. McMillen (ed.), *Gambling Cultures*. London: Routledge. pp. 86–100.

Dixon, D. (1997) *Law in Policing: Legal Regulation and Police Practices*. Oxford: Clarendon Press.

Dixon, D. (1999) 'Reform, regression and the Royal Commission into the NSW Police Service', in D. Dixon (ed.), *A Culture of Corruption: Changing an Australian Police Service*. Sydney: Hawkins Press.

Dorn, N. and K. Murji (1992) 'Low level drug enforcement', *International Journal of the Sociology of Law*, 20: 159–71.

Dorn, N. and N. South (1990) 'Drug markets and law enforcement', *British Journal of Criminology*, 30(2): 171–88.

Dorn, N., K. Murji and N. South (1992) *Traffickers: Drug Markets and Law Enforcement*. London: Routledge.

English, T.J. (1995) *Born to Kill*. New York: Avon Books.

Fairfield City Council (1995) *Youth Needs and Issues of Concern: Fairfield Community Plan*. Fairfield: Fairfield City Council.

Friedman, S.R., M. Sufian, R. Curtis, A. Neaigus and D. Des Jarlais (1992) 'Organizing drug users against AIDS', in J. Huber and B.E. Schneider (eds), *The Social Context of AIDS*. Newbury Park, CA: Sage. pp. 115–30.

Gilman, M. and G. Pearson (1991) 'Lifestyles and law enforcement', in D.K. Whynes and P.T. Bean (eds), *Policing and Prescribing*. London: Macmillan. pp. 95–124.

Goldstein, H. (1990) *Problem-Oriented Policing*. Philadelphia: Temple University Press.

Grapendaal, M., E. Leuw and H. Nelen (1995) *A World of Opportunities: Lifestyle and Economic Behaviour of Heroin Addicts in Amsterdam*. Albany, NY: SUNY Press.

Green, P. and I. Purnell (1995) *Measuring the Success of Law Enforcement Agencies in Australia in Targeting Major Drug Offenders Relative to Minor Drug Offenders*. Payneham: National Police Research Unit.

Hagedorn, J.M. (1994) 'Neighborhoods, markets and gang drug organization', *Journal of Research in Crime and Delinquency*, 31: 264–94.

Homel, R. (1990) *High Speed Pursuits in Perth*, report to the Police Department of Western Australia.

Hughes, P.H. and G.A. Crawford (1972) 'A contagious disease model for researching and intervening in heroin epidemics', *Archives of General Psychiatry*, 27: 189–205.

James, S. and A. Sutton (1997) 'Joining the war against drugs?', in D. Chappell and P. Wilson (eds), *Australian Policing* (2nd edition). Sydney: Butterworths. pp. 147–64.

Jefferson, T. and R. Grimshaw (1984) *Controlling the Constable*. London: Frederick Muller/Cobden Trust.

Keith, M. (1993) *Race, Riots and Policing: Lore and Disorder in a Multi-racist Society*. London: UCL Press.

Koester, S.K. (1994) 'Copping, running and paraphernalia laws', *Human Organization*, 53: 287–95.

Long, P. Du Phuoc (1996) *The Dream Shattered: Vietnamese Gangs in America*. Boston, MA: Northeastern University Press.

Lustgarten, L. (1986) *The Governance of Police*. London: Sweet and Maxwell.

Maher, L. (1996a) 'Age, culture, environment and risk: contextualizing high-risk practices among new injectors in south west Sydney'. Paper presented at VII International Conference on the Reduction of Drug-related Harm. Tasmania, March.

Maher, L. (1996b) *The Illicit Drugs Reporting System (IDRS) Trial: Ethnographic Monitoring Component*. Sydney: National Drug and Alcohol Research Centre Technical Report.

Maher, L., D. Dixon, M. Lynskey and W. Hall (1998), *Running the Risks: Heroin, Health and Harm in South West Sydney*, NDARC Monograph No. 38. Sydney: National Drug and Alcohol Research Centre.

Maher, L., D. Dixon, W. Swift and T. Nguyen (1997) *Anh Hai: Young Asian People's Perceptions and Experiences of Policing*. Sydney: UNSW Law Faculty.

Manning, P. (1980) *The Narcs' Game: Organizational and Informational Limits on Drug Law Enforcement*. Cambridge, MA: MIT Press.

Manning, P. (1997) *Police Work* (2nd edition). Prospect Heights, IL: Waveland Press.

Marmour, M., D.C. Des Jarlais, H. Cohen, S.R. Friedman, S.T. Beatrice, N. Dubin, W. El-Sadr, D. Midvan, S. Yancovitz, U. Mathur and R. Holzman (1987) 'Risk factors for infection with human immunodeficiency virus among intravenous drug users in New York City', *AIDS*, 1: 39–44.

Marshall, G. (1965) *Police and Government*. London: Methuen.

Moore, M.H. (1992) 'Problem-solving and community policing', in M. Tonry and N. Morris (eds), *Modern Policing*. Chicago: University of Chicago Press. pp. 99–158.

Morris, N. and G. Hawkins (1970) *The Honest Politician's Guide to Crime Control*. Chicago: University of Chicago Press.

Nadelmann, E.A. (1992) 'Thinking seriously about alternatives to drug prohibition', *Daedalus*, 121: 85–132.

National Drug Strategy (1993) *National Drug Strategic Plan*. Canberra: AGPS.

Ohlin, L.E. and F.J. Remington (eds) (1993) *Discretion in Criminal Justice*. Albany, NY: State University of New York Press.

Ouellet, L.J., D. Jiminez, W.A. Johnson and W.W. Wiebel (1991) 'Shooting galleries and HIV disease: variations in places for injecting illicit drugs', *Crime and Delinquency*, 37: 64–85.

Parliamentary Joint Committee on the National Crime Authority (1989) *Drugs, Crime and Society*. Canberrra: Australian Government Publishing Service.

Pearson, G. (1991) 'The local nature of drug problems', in T. Bennett (ed.), *Drug Misuse in Local Communities*. London: Police Foundation. pp. 67–79.

Pearson, G. (1992) 'Drugs and criminal justice: a harm reduction perspective', in P.A. O'Hare, R. Newcombe, A. Matthews and E. Drucker (eds), *The Reduction of Drug-Related Harm*. London: Routledge. pp. 15–29.

Pearson, G., H. Blagg, D. Smith, A. Sampson and P. Stubbs (1992) 'Crime, community and conflict: the multi-agency approach', in D. Downes (ed.), *Unravelling Criminal Justice*. London: Macmillan. pp. 46–72.

Pease, K. (1997) 'Crime prevention', in M. Maguire, M. Morgan and R. Reiner (eds), *The Oxford Handbook of Criminology* (2nd edition). Oxford: Clarendon Press. pp. 963–95.

Police Service Weekly (1996) 'Drug harm minimization and practical policing applications', *Police Service Weekly*, 9 December 1996, p. 3.

Reiner, R. (1992) *The Politics of the Police*. Hemel Hempstead: Harvester Wheat-sheaf.

Remington, F.J. (1965) 'Foreword', in W.R. LaFave (ed), *Arrest*. Boston, MA: Little, Brown and Co.

Reuter, P. and M.A.R. Kleiman (1986) 'Risks and prices', in M. Tonry and N. Morris (eds), *Crime and Justice: An Annual Review of Research*, 7: 289–340. Chicago: University of Chicago Press.

Ruggiero, V. and N. South (1995) *Eurodrugs: Drug Use, Markets and Trafficking in Europe*. London: UCL Press.

Scarman, L. (1981) *The Brixton Disorders: 10–12 April 1981: Report of an Inquiry by the Rt Hon the Lord Scarman OBE*. Cmnd. 8427. London: HMSO.

Skolnick, J.H. (1989) *The Social Structure of Street Drug Dealing*. Sacramento: State of California Department of Justice, Bureau of Criminal Statistics.

Stimson, G.V. (1995) 'Never mind the quality, feel the width' (Comment on McKeganey's Editorial), *Addiction*, 9: 757–8.

Sullivan, E., M. Fahey, A. Bauman, G. Close, N. Nash and C. Kiernan (1995) *Health in South Western Sydney: An Epidemiological Profile*. Liverpool, NSW: South Western Sydney Area Health Service.

Sutton, A. and S. James (1995) *Evaluation of Australian Drug Anti-Trafficking Law Enforcement*. Payneham: National Police Research Unit.

Sviridoff, M., S. Sadd, R. Curtis and R. Grinc (1992) *The Neighborhood Effects of Street-level Drug Enforcement*. New York: Vera Institute of Justice.

Swift, W., L. Maher, S. Sunjic and V. Doan (1997) *Transitions between Routes of Administration among Caucasian and Indo-Chinese Heroin Users in South West Sydney*. NDARC Technical Report No. 36. Sydney: National Drug and Alcohol Research Centre.

Weatherburn, D. and B. Lind (1995) *Drug Law Enforcement Policy and Its Impact on the Heroin Market*. Sydney: NSW Bureau of Crime Statistics and Research.

Wood, J.R.T. (1997) *Final Report of the Royal Commission into the NSW Police Service*. Sydney: Government of NSW.

Part II

Gendered identities

3

'Not as nice as she was supposed to be': schoolgirls' friendships

Valerie Hey

'Grandiose revelations of the obvious': themes of girls' friendships

During the course of my fieldwork I collected the following 'exotic' note.

> Bernice if you must know I don't like you. And I know what you are going to do tomorrow tell your sis.
> No, I am not going to tell my sis of you. Marcia's started again (not really) Bernice.
> Oh yeh I bet you are. If you feel like being moody go ahead.
> I like you, you are being childish.

However, the pacification fails and the second writer joins the first in mutual insults as the text disintegrates into a slanging match:

> You are a little girl who follows shit stirrers.
> No that's not true. You must be a s.s.
> What's an s.s?
> Bloody hell s.s. = shit stirrer.
> Dopey Dur!
> I know you are.
> Well your language is. Well your language isn't very clear. SSABB. And if you don't know what that is well . . .
> So what I don't have to know what it means do I?
> Well I had to know what s.s. is didn't I? Well its silly slag and boffin breath.

Here represented in their most condensed and dramatic form are some of the themes of this book – issues of girls' intimacy, secrecy and struggle. Early on in her primary school, Jude (one of the subjects of this study) remembers sending a note to another girl: 'Will you be my friend? Tick in the box yes or no'.

This is an edited extract from Valerie Hey (1997) *The Company She Keeps: An Ethnography of Girls' Friendship* Buckingham: Open University Press.

Memories of girls' friendship exists as feminine subordinated 'tacit knowledges' (Corrigan, 1987; Johnson, 1986). This knowledge is often and surprisingly reactivated if we are the mothers of daughters. We are then made only too aware that girls are intensely preoccupied by the micro-politics of their girlfriends, as they insist on 'sleep overs' or worry alter-nately about invitations or exclusions.

Re/covering memories can provide (possible) confirming evidence of our own girlhoods. Reasons for the cultural suppression of school girl cultures are complex. There is for example, immense ideological pressure to restrict interpretations of these memories. Common sense claims these intricate relations as 'merely a phase' – as a demonstration of a 'natural' feminine capacity for 'caring'. Nostalgia combined with ideologies invested in denying the dangerous notion of complicitous feminine aggression may account for the ways in which we can slide over the violence and passion we might have felt as each others' girlfriends (Wolpe, 1988).

Charlotte Brunsdon (1978) has noted the persistence of the view that 'by nature women are inclined to be rather personal'. Certainly the social fact of girls' unique attachments to each other has often been naturalized. One significant consequence has been the minimum recognition of the 'social' within girls' personal forms. The ethnography which follows, in returning us to the terrain of loss and recollection – of girls' pleasure and pain in their friendship – asserts the claims of the social through identifying how it is variously written into the cultural forms of girls' relations with each other.

[. . .]

Learning your place: researching into girls' friendships

The data for this book is derived from a small-scale participant observation study conducted in two city schools in the mid-late 1980s (Hey, 1988). My first research site was Eastford School, a large mixed comprehensive set in a middle-class suburb. The second was Crossfield Girls' School, a smaller comprehensive situated in a predominantly working-class part of the same borough. Both schools taught the 11–18 age group.

Apart from my inexperience in conducting research, field relations at Eastford were also complicated by other factors: the circumstances of the school, the nature of the project (privileging girls) as well as by the choice of fieldwork methods (participant observation). Early field notes antici-pated such themes:

> Felt foolish 'cos I couldn't recollect the names of all the staff with whom I'd just been liaising. I kept calling Mrs Harris, Mrs Taylor, *felt just like a new girl*, overwhelmed by the bureaucratic nightmares that schools are (to newcomers). Not only do you have to remember the [layout of] buildings but also: staff

names; statuses; subjects; timetables; timings; routines; protocols and facilities.
(fieldnotes, Eastford)

Throughout my fieldwork I never quite managed to avoid this sense of being 'lost', literally as well as metaphorically suspended in a liminal space 'down among the women' – a location somewhere between childhood and adulthood (see Mandell, 1991; Walkerdine, 1985). In conditions of oppression, there are some tantalizing parallels therefore between 'becoming a girl' and 'becoming a feminist ethnographer' since both identities are necessarily wrested from the same contradiction, namely that in staking a claim to power we are threatened by loss of claims to femininity. As other female ethnographers have noted, being taken seriously as a field researcher is a condition that can just as easily be withdrawn as it can be granted (Warren, 1988).

Certainly the tensions of doing fieldwork (at Eastford) derived more from the gendered contradictions of working within a school unused to the discourse of equal opportunities, as they did from working across generational boundaries (Griffiths, 1995). It soon became evident that any woman outsider choosing to study girls was seen as problematizing the way the school treated its girls. If the context was dominated by unquestioned assumptions about masculine hegemony, then the simple tactic of deriding the research focus as 'feminist' cleverly insulated most of the senior male staff from its implications. I was confronted (like the girls) by the difficulties of 'learning a place' inside the school. In effect the 'discourse of derision' meant that I too, went underground.

[Here I discuss] aspects of my research experience in terms of its indivisibility from the material collected. The fact that I was studying girls in schools through the axis of their privatized friendships meant that the project was read in two conflicting ways – as simultaneously non-serious but also as a threat. Additionally the social spaces I wanted to investigate and the types of question I wished to explore were viewed not only by male 'gatekeepers' with a great deal of suspicion but also and perhaps not surprisingly by some of the girls (see Hey, 1988: Chapter 1; 1994 for a fuller account).

'Downwardly going' and 'upwardly mobile': two schools

Eastford was a school in crisis. One specific focus of this during the fieldwork was the disruption caused by union action in response to a national dispute. Staff morale was low, partly as a result of falling rolls and the resultant threatened redundancies and partly due to the headteacher's inability to manage divisions among the staff. The demise of the school's status as a boys' grammar school (prior to its amalgamation with the girls' grammar school under comprehensivization) was still the cause of nostalgic regret by the hard core of 'old masters' from the earlier regime. The backwash of the decision to amalgamate and become comprehensive *still* resonated in attitudes to the 'comprehensive' as opposed to the 'elite' children. In contrast, there was a strong pro-comprehensive 'left' position held by the union activists. The split was further elaborated around the call for union action. The senior management team and the 'old masters' declined while the majority of the staff complied.

These differences undermined the school's capacity to police the behaviour of its pupils, a situation which was intensified at a time of industrial sanctions. This in turn increased the difficulties of working in the school, because the pupils had understood only too well that it was possible to exploit the weakness of the system. Many of the most disaffected and demotivated pupils of both sexes simply voted with their feet.

The divisions and resulting tensions within the staff were reflected in the existence of three interconnecting but separate staffrooms. Senior male teachers – grammar school old masters – occupied the quieter, non-smoking end and created an ambience which aspired to that of an Oxbridge common room. The middle room was the domain of the union activists, while the remaining room was occupied by the non-aligned, a mix of staff room 'wags' (Cunnison, 1989) and crossword fanatics. The latter group were younger staff but it also included some older female part-time staff from the remedial department. I positioned myself with the relatively neutral group.[1]

Eastford School nevertheless enjoyed more advantages than Crossfield. It was located in a large expanse of playing fields near a prosperous residential area. Its intake still included many children from this affluent middle-class area. The other side of the school was fringed by some residual forms of corporate housing – postwar council estates. These estates provided most of the working-class pupils for the school.

Crossfield School was considerably more downmarket. It was situated near the site of a large gasworks built alongside the West Cross Canal, which had once been the basis of the area's industrial past. However, in the city, distinctions of class were highly volatile; some areas and indeed some roads were upwardly mobile and some distinctly downwardly going. Gentrification continued alongside dereliction in Crossfield, but the former had not yet erased the locality's proletarian character.

Crossfield School opened on its current site in the 1930s. The staff claimed it was closely identified with its neighbourhood and the predominantly female staff professed expertise in dealing with 'typical secondary modern' girls. The school ethos evinced a team feeling. However, like Eastford, there was also an eccentric subculture: 'school mistresses' who treated the 'gals' like 'young ladies'. This position, favoured by a particular generation of single women teachers, possibly reflected a class nostalgia for their own 'nice' girls' schools (Evans, 1991).

Crossfield's origins had a continuing effect, not only upon the school's reputation (almost as elusive a concept as a girl's!), but also in depressing the aspirations of the majority of its pupils. The identity of the school as a local white working-class secondary modern school was however changing because of the recruitment of Asian girls. This new intake was not only more affluent than the school's traditional pupils, but also more ambitious. Crossfield was also proving more attractive to Eastford's affluent white middle-class, disenchanted by the falling reputation of their neighbourhood school.

The fieldwork was undertaken prior to the intensification of the marketization of education (Ball, 1990; Bowe et al., 1992; Hargreaves and Reynolds, 1989), nevertheless, both schools were already under market pressure. The borough had a recognized over-capacity in secondary school places, for example Crossfield contracted from six entry classes (11-year-olds) to four over four years (though this trend had halted), and Eastford had decreased from nine entry classes to five over five years. In the climate of disappearing pupils, the local authority's commitment to a policy of community education was viewed with cynicism in both schools.

'Class issues': methods and methodological difficulties in researching into girls' friendships

> Very seldom does a start up sampling frame survive the lovely imperfection and intractability of the field. It must be bent and reframed. (Miles and Huberman, 1984: 38)

As the writers suggest, research in the real world is lived as a series of rapidly unfolding and occasionally unpredictable events about which one has to make practical decisions (Mandell, 1991; Skeggs, 1994). The fact that I had to recruit other girls to the study (from another school) reflected the power of male gatekeepers rather than the original intention (which was to make a one-site study).

In the process of implementing my research strategies I had also to make less dramatic compromises. These involved renegotiations about access to take account of the implacable routines of institutional life. Certainly my negotiations at Eastford were full of 'lovely imperfection' shaped as they were by my increasingly desperate attempt to find a suitable cohort of girls with whom I could spend a sustained period of time. There were two main dimensions to this. The first related to the formal mechanisms of schooling as an institution and the second concerned the girls' own informal responses to the school system and to me.

Any study of self-selecting groups like friends cuts right across the administrative divisions within formal settings like schooling (see Griffiths, 1995). The devices of the curriculum (subject specialization, academic differentiation, setting/streaming and the complex patterning of subject option choices) constitute public as opposed to private groupings.[2] My original intention to study older pupils proved impractical.

The only solution was to move down the age range. I thus solved the problem by choosing Ms Spencer's class (1S). My inexperienced trial and error approach (dipping in and out of classes while trying to establish access) was inadvertently beneficial. It was through visiting different groups and different classes that I had become visible throughout the school. [. . .]

At Eastford, my most systematic classroom observations featured the girls in Ms Spencer's class of 11-year-olds, where I focused upon three networks of girl friends. [. . .]

I undertook participant observation in Ms Spencer's class for approximately three terms, and followed the girls' transition into the second year, where they still had the same form tutor. I interviewed Ms Spencer, several senior members of staff and some of the year heads. I deliberately tried to keep my gaze upon the girls but could not avoid becoming familiar with some of the dynamics of the boys' relationships, as well as aspects of the gender dynamics between the boys and the girls. [. . .]

There were additional complications about tracking working-class girls higher up the school. Class at Eastford was literally strongly correlated with social visibility. In short, the older working-class girls were frequently absent. This affected my fieldwork decision-making in several ways.

Tracing an ethnography of girls' friendships both necessarily, as well as accidentally, tracks girls' multilevelled exploitation of school. My study records the degree to which girls variously experienced, as well as constructed, their own investments in its multiple possibilities. Was school seen as a social site for meeting friends as well as a source of academic prestige, status and display? Or alternatively was it predominantly the source of boredom, antagonism, disappointment and general social disempowerment, which only the solidarity of one's close friendships redeemed (Corrigan, 1987)? Correspondingly, research access to these various responses will map how, where and in what sense girls are invested in school, invested in schooling and friendship, invested in becoming particular sorts of girls (and indeed invested in cooperating with social researchers).

The more 'academic' or middle-class the girls, the more observable they were in classroom situations. 'Regular' girls meant for regular school observations. [. . .]

Opportunistic attendance called up a creative not to mention a pragmatic response. My relationship with Carol (a white working-class girl) at Eastford was characteristic of my countering tactic of opportunistic observation. I had to make myself available when she visited the school to sign on for morning or afternoon registration. Once we had rendezvoused she (and I) would disappear into the school surroundings. She only ever went to lessons when she liked the teacher. [. . .]

In short, the social conditions of data-gathering on girls' friendships in schooling reflected the relations of class and gender through which it was constituted.

[. . .]

Contracting research relationships at Eastford at a time which coincided with teachers' industrial action was just the wrong sort of luck common in fieldwork. Good will, essential to social organizations and their study, had almost evaporated. My negotiating position was not helped because my research question was understood as 'feminist research' and therefore construed as potentially subversive. One way the staff managed my actual presence was through parody. Shortly after my arrival the following 'advert' was circulated in the school bulletin: 'Item 411: "I have not found so great faith no, not in the whole of Israel". In pursuit of her research into Further Aspects of Femininity, Valerie Hey will be observing 3C . . . [etc.]'. On another occasion a physics master said about the same girls: 'You'd get more response from a brick wall. The best of luck!'

Allied to this were deeply embedded presumptions on the part of the boys (who outnumbered the girls by approximately two to one) that they were the most important people within schools (Clarricoates, 1987; Griffiths, 1995; Mahony, 1985). When one of the boys in a class challenged my right to study girls he was apparently told by the form tutor that 'social researchers study very bizarre subjects'. The teacher cited, as an example, someone she knew who was looking at 'fish symbolism in Shakespeare'. It is however also plausible that male resistance to being ignored expressed both boys' jealousy as well as power.[3]

During the course of the fieldwork I experienced some harassment – 'stare-outs' and mild verbal abuse from a few boys, who it seemed to me had taken upon themselves the role of conveying collective male disapproval. However this was manageable. What was less easy to manage was the dilution of access by their male elders.

Half-way through the fieldwork at Eastford, the headteacher summoned me to his room. He argued that my presence was proving too disruptive. He claimed that several male teachers found my presence in classrooms (I was sitting at the back with the girls) uncomfortable. He then conceded that if I wanted to continue talking with the girls I had to do so in their time but not in the school's. The head pointed to the disruption already caused through the teacher sanctions. He then secured this new access negotiation through offering me the opportunity to go into Crossfield School, where the head was a friend of his.

I remember being comforted in the midst of these alterations by the first maxim of Halcolm's Evaluation Laws: 'Always be suspicious of data collection that goes according to plan' (reported in Patton, 1990). In reality I managed to hold onto my research relationships (both inside and outside classrooms) at Eastford. This was achieved ironically through the practical assistance provided by numerous feminine friendship networks. Female members of staff and groups of girls persisted in talking with me, the staff letting me into their lessons and the girls continuing to tell me about themselves. Feminine marginalized cultures of social support became the means as well as the content of the research. However, establishing this base had not been without its own problems.

[. . .]

Field relations: trading in femininity – talking to the girls

Surviving marginalization at the same time as researching it emphasized the reliance one has upon those who are being studied. This research therefore was only made possible through the sponsorship of key individuals, most notably that offered by Saskia, Carol and Suzy (at Eastford) and Jude (at Crossfield).[4] These alliances were further embedded by my participation in the public spaces of the school as well as private (girls' locker room) cultures.

In the course of the fieldwork I played rounders; went on cross-country runs; attended registration/pastoral time; stood around on fields at play-time; ate in the cafeteria; sat in on swathes of lessons; occasionally visited the staffroom; went to school plays and end of term demob ceremonies and leavers' assemblies. Rushing around covering the official as well as the more illicit of girls' activities demanded, at 35, a certain stamina as well as a willing suspension of disbelief on the part of both the girls and myself. It was required not only by the demands of participant observation but also as a test of my commitment to the girls. I did draw the line occasionally (and so did the girls) but mostly I boldly went where the girls in my study boldly went, even if this meant bunking or going behind the bike sheds (so they could have a smoke). Interestingly and significantly the trial of my acceptability as a researcher (that is, that I would not tell the teachers) replicated the social tests of girls' friendships (see Griffiths, 1995; Hey, 1988; Horowitz, 1983; Llewellyn, 1980).

My fieldwork effectively involved a series of complex trade-offs (Skeggs, 1994). In the course of the study, the girls and I developed an implicit microeconomy of exchange and barter. The girls provided access to their social lives in return for certain tangible goods: my attention; advice; sweet money; access to a warm room; or absence from lessons (see Skeggs, 1994). These small trades are endemic in most field relations but because they smack of the marketplace there is very little reference to them and like a lot of the 'housework' of research, these details seldom surface in research reports or theses (though see Oakley, 1981).

In the course of my time in the schools I got to know about 50 girls reasonably well, 20 of these girls very well and three sufficiently well to have been invited to their homes and to have invited them to mine. One girl even sent me a note during a lesson. Others kept up communication after I left the schools, updating me on their present situations. Yet other girls sent me notes which they had stored away; others offered me diaries to read, I offered mine in return.

I only managed my study through the immense tolerance of the girls who accommodated me during lunch hours, free time at breaks, morning tutor times and who invited me home when they had been sent off the premises as a result of the no-cover action. There were girls (like Carol) who took me in hand and showed me the ropes, who let me tag along with them on their jaunts to the local prom and recreation ground. Neither I, nor my stomach, will ever forget our many visits to the Pond Cafe, safe refuge for so many of Eastford's working-class school refuseniks. However, willingness to indulge researchers is frequently constituted from the conditions of subjects' relative powerlessness (McRobbie, 1982).

A similar concern surfaces in this study. The girls' general toleration of a nosy intruder signified a potentially exploitative situation. Such conditions are an implacable fact of researching on those less powerful than oneself (see Measor, 1985). Looking back at my practice and accounting for my decisions, the issue as I see it of breaking the pretence that one can somehow (singlehandedly) dissolve the contradictions (of being a feminist working on girls' relative powerlessness) has meant my acceptance that research relations are necessarily made in, and constituted by, these conditions of difference.

Despite seeking to establish non-exploitative field relations, I was never able to evade the facts that as a white woman with a middle-class education not only was I generally more powerful than most of the girls but my agenda was in part to appropriate parts of their lives for my own use (see Measor, 1985). This is not to represent girls as powerless – in this I endorse Beverley Skeggs (1994) who also argues that girls' actions are about contesting power within terms which recognizes the force of social divisions.

Taking up this position is much more uncomfortable than assuming the orthodox cosier fantasy of imagining that our feminism secures for us the privilege of 'becoming one of the girls' through wishing away the differences between us and them. What is required is not only more reflexivity (about who 'we' are) but also a more finessed sense of how these power relations (including those of research) shift and are contested by their subjects/objects in the everyday (Davies, 1989; Hey, 1994; Patai, 1994).

In terms of my own practice I tried to be as clear about what I was up to as I felt was appropriate. But at all times during the research the girls knew that I was a researcher and that I was observing their interactions (even though rumours circulated that I was variously a social worker, headteacher, probation officer, police officer or someone's mum).

The debate about ethics is one of the most engaged and detailed within feminist methodology; there is a vast literature (Holland and Ramazanoglu, 1994; Oakley, 1981; Opie, 1992; Skeggs, 1994; Stacey, 1988). Inevitably issues of ethics become intensely focused when one is researching across the boundaries between the public and the private. As Johnson eloquently puts it, 'To render such accounts public is immediately to activate all the relations of power we traced . . . especially where the practice crosses the major cultural differences' (Johnson, 1986: 302).

I, too, am acutely aware of this dilemma, since insisting on moving the cultural backstage (of girls and schooling) to the front stage (particularly at this time when the mainstream research gaze is mesmerized by the government's agenda), opens up not only a proverbial can of worms for the dominant but also, as I have hinted, for feminism(s). My stance certainly (re)activated as well as captured/disrupted the dominant forms of power and their circulation since what was discovered was not, as other researchers imagine, 'collective images of a non-subordinated sense of self' (Ribbens and Edwards, 1995: 255) but precisely the conditions of contradiction and oppression (as well as their refusal) within which girls and ourselves live.

The point of my move to uncover the workings of power in the culture was not to search for a return to a buried originary feminine realm beyond the world of oppression (Brown and Gilligan, 1992; Ribbens and Edwards, 1995; Roland Martin, 1995) but to tease out the ways in which girls (and by analogy women) consent to, as well as resist, the multiple forms of subordinations, as well as to identify and analyse those occurrences when girls subordinate and oppress each other. Girl–girl social relations (as I have hinted) constituted a gendered (and hence collective) cultural code (see Frazer and Cameron, 1989). However this was not easily appropriable, since it was one of the conditions of girls' general cultural subordination that rendered girls' investment in privacy, secrecy and intimacy and each other. Therefore it was only through moving into the same covert realm where girls managed their relations that it became possible to understand how the borderlands worked as *private* feelings, *personal* affiliations and *personal* writings – where 'difference(s)' (if you like) could be traced in how girls (privately) lived their own antagonistic relations with and against each other. I take the view that furthering our understanding of girls means we have to occupy the interstitial spaces of schooling to reflect upon the cultural power activated there.[5] A defining moment in this research dilemma was when I discovered the significance of note-writing.

In/significances: a methodological and ethical note on schoolgirl notes

The significance of girls' notes only impressed itself on me after I had been involved in the research for several months. Insofar as teachers noticed girls' extracurricular activities they called girls' notes 'bits of poison' or 'garbage'. Girls referred to them as 'bits of silliness'. As far as I was concerned they were sociologically fascinating because they were important means of transmitting the cultural values of friendship.

It emerged that not only did these writings constitute visible evidence of the extensive emotional labour invested by girls in their friendships, they also comprised a 'pocket ethnography' of girlfriend work.[6] The correspondences materialized particular aspects of girls' interpersonal relationships to confirm that girls produced the private, encoded by feminine forms of power (Walkerdine, 1985).

A typical note would take the form of a piece of writing addressed to a specific girl. (Ninety per cent of what girls wrote about concerned their own relations with each other – only a few spoke about boyfriends.) The note was then passed more or less surreptitiously to the recipient who would then write back. The original author would respond and so on.

Other girls would act as postwomen, circulating the document between the correspondents.

In the course of my study I collected over 50 correspondence sequences from Erin and Saskia's group at Eastford School. From Crossfield School I collected about 20 others, predominantly from within Jude's group. I did not see boys engage in this activity. Evidence from other research indicates that boys do different things both in classrooms and within their friendships (Connell, 1987: 85; Mahony, 1985; Stanworth, 1981).

The struggle to take these notes seriously owed something to the difficulties of purloining these 'secret writings'. Girls were experts in these 'invisible' communication activities, and only a few teachers ever noticed them or wilfully intervened to eliminate them. Scrabbling around on the floor after double maths to retrieve the discarded letters was hard to explain to another adult. One of the teachers I spoke with scooped them up out her classroom dustbin to offer them to me, saying that they were 'little bits of garbage'. Becoming, as one colleague described it, 'an academic bag-lady' is at odds with the notion of research as a serious scientific endeavour.

Sometimes girls just left them on desks or floors. Towards the end of my year in the schools, I asked my key informants for any they might have retained, not expecting any response. To my surprise they provided me with more examples. Some of the girls had stored them for four years or more.

Equally, converting the 'garbage' into data presents other problems. The raw material persists in being the opposite of what data is supposed to be. Everything about this material conspired to render it unavailable as data. The word data carries sedimented meanings about self-importance and substantiality. And yet they retained for me sociological interest not least because some of these notes took the form of correspondence chains that lasted a week and included over 50 separate exchanges. The girls' notes were intentionally 'marginal'; for example, they were written on the margins of other more official writing. A number were written on the back of rough drafts of schoolwork. They were often difficult (if not impossible) to decipher. If I had not also been attending to the flux of the girls' friendships through observations and interviews I would have had little purchase upon their actual sequence, let alone their importance. That they are important, if fragmentary, moments in the making of schoolgirl selves is explored further.

[. . .]

'Being nice' and 'being bossy' – the management of dis/order among one group of girls

Make friends, make friends,
Never, never break friends

(children's chant from Opie and Opie, 1959: 324)

While Valerie Walkerdine noted the similarities between the prescriptive criteria of girlhood and those of feminine heterosexuality, she does not situate either girlhood or goodness in the contexts of class or race. Other writers argue that it is a *particular* classed and Anglo version of femininity which is constructed as the ideal type of pupil for all girls at school (Jones, 1993; Kenway and Blackmore, 1995).

The groups of white girls in my study related differently to the ideal type of girl pupil, and to the ideological imperative to be good. As we have noted, many of the girls (especially the middle-class girls) confirmed the criteria of goodness as central in their selection of a friend. Being disagreeable (bossy and openly assertive) was the exact antithesis of niceness. Pressures to *appear* compliant positively incited the subversive pleasures of committing disagreements to paper: note-writing materially assisted the task because it helped girls to avoid the damaging label 'horrid'. Erin's clique are discussing their preference for note-writing:

> *Erin:*   Well if we say things out loud people will hear that we are having arguments and start picking on us.
> *Sam:*   . . . or the teacher will tell us off 'cos we're talking in lessons . . .
> *Saskia:* . . . and it's safer to write notes sometimes. This morning we were writing notes . . . 'cos we want to go on a hack, a horse riding hack . . . 'em
> *VH:*   and they weren't spotted?
> *Saskia:* No.
> *Erin:*   [disagreeing] Yes . . . the teacher came round, she looked at it, Saskia, but she didn't say anything.
> *VH:*   Have you seen . . . do boys pass notes?
> *Erin:* ⎫
> *Saskia:* ⎬ [in unison] No.
> *Sam:* ⎭
> *VH:*   Why not?
> *Erin:*   They shout.
> *Saskia:* Yeh . . . but we enjoy doing it more this way.
>   (Interview of Erin's clique, Eastford School 2nd year)

In participating in these clandestine cultural productions Erin and her friends were learning not only to constitute their feminine subjectivities in (conditions of surveillance) as specifically classed forms of niceness, they were also defining themselves against the noisier and messier form of boys' overt behaviours (Mac an Ghaill, 1994; Walkerdine, 1985) and at another level also learning about their ability to resist such surveillance.[7]

Correspondences: inscribing the proper identity of a middle-class girlfriend

By the time I began my detailed fieldwork with the class of 1S, the girls had already patterned themselves into distinct subdivisions within the class on the basis of perceived class differences which had been expressed through notions about differences of 'ability' and 'cleverness' (Arnot, 1982). Erin's group consisted of Erin and Samantha (Sam) who formed the core relationship around which other relationships were predicated; Saskia, Anna and Tamara; Alexia, Olga and Clara. Saskia (according to her teacher) had always minded most about being positioned as outside the epicentre of the clique and compensated for this by having a brittle 'contingent' relationship with Anna (Davies, 1984: 258). To complicate matters further, Anna described Saskia as her best friend (this same distinction is played out later between Anna and Natalie). Ms Spencer told me that Anna had originally tried to set up a network with Natalie and Laura, but an early misdemeanour involving truancy had resulted in Anna (lower middle-class) being 'warned off' the other two (black and working-class) as a 'bad lot', by her teachers and her mother.[8]

Erin's clan thus consisted of the strong core of Erin and her best friend Samantha, surrounded by a looser set of alliances. This patterning had taken shape within the first weeks at school. By the time I began observing the clique, their social negotiations appeared to have stabilized, but the initial imbalances and instabilities – so common in the early stages of girls' struggles to establish relationships – reasserted themselves and continued to condition how this clique conducted their friendship over three terms.

At root was the dislocating effects of Saskia's affluence; more specifically it was the way she chose to manage her money that created endless problems within the clique's delicately poised system of friendship exchange. Her generosity, as the purveyor of endless sweets, treats and fad items, as well as her relentless social manipulations were acutely counterproductive – the former, because her largesse created resentment as her friends were unable to reciprocate, and the latter, because her mania for arranging things was construed as her being bossy and trying to buy friendship (see Griffiths, 1995: 85–8). The following account centres on exploring how Saskia's striving was read and resisted as bossiness.

If being good as a schoolgirl demanded the suppression of disagreements ('people will hear that we are having arguments and start picking on us'), then it was all the more important to invent a form of self-policing. I will focus upon three specific instances when Erin and her friends dealt with their disagreements through the ritual/regulation of a shared cultural code. The following detailed ethnographic account of what was in actuality endless hectic friendship transactions is traced (and to some extent fixed), through an analysis of their notes.

Saskia was the chief correspondent in her group because she was most interested in taking over its leadership. In the course of my time in Eastford I witnessed 50 or more note-writing episodes and Saskia was the originator of 30 of them. Within these texts it is possible to encapsulate aspects of the story of Saskia's struggle as her friends countermanded her quest of popularity *as* power.[9] Given that this process took place throughout the course of the time I was in the field, I cannot for obvious reasons represent, indeed I was not privy to, all of the manoeuvres among the clique. I am compelled to condense the serial nature of their struggles into three key dramatic episodes; they all concern the girls' different abilities to command and demand inclusion and exclusion.

Issuing and accepting or rejecting invitations was a key social practice of Erin's clique. It was Erin's speciality and Saskia's passion. As other commentators have noted, the powers to include and exclude constitutes the currency of how girls variously negotiate their relations with each other (Llewellyn, 1980; Nilan, 1991). Saskia therefore sought to position herself as the group's main social manager but this was always a miscalculation and she was never granted the status she so desperately wanted. In interpreting the girls' practices I was reminded of Gilbert Osmond in the novel *Portrait of a Lady*; he was said to hold parties purely for the pleasure of excluding people (James, 1987).

The use of the social resources of inclusion and exclusion within Erin's clique

Note episode 1[10]

It is important to bear in mind that the following note sequence covered only one day and included (insofar as it was possible to document) a 15-item exchange during a morning double history lesson and a subsequent 13-item exchange in the afternoon double general science lesson. All three main protagonists (Erin, Saskia, Samantha) took part in reading and writing the messages. These winged their way uninterrupted back and forth across the public space of the classroom. Girls' preoccupations did not interfere with their respective abilities to function formally, a finding which also says something about girls' skill in contriving their 'invisibility'. It is virtually impossible to conceive of boys being able, or indeed interested, in cooperating with each other in an equivalent cultural code.

Samantha was the main obstacle in Saskia's desire to become Erin's best friend. Saskia had to grasp any chances to outposition her. This opportunity optimally presented itself when Erin and Samantha fell out. In one such dispute Erin had then invited Saskia on a prestige trip to visit her father. Saskia, delighted by Erin's apparent interest in her, attempted to capitalize on the situation by issuing a counter-invitation to Erin (which specifically excluded Samantha) but this backfired since Erin had by then remade friends with Samantha. The following is the initial sequence establishing the details of the respective invitations.

> *Saskia:* I can invite one person to come to lunch because its only my brother in and he might not be in. Would you like to come for lunch? That way you can see the letter that my dad left, saying yes or no to [my] going with you.
> PS. I am looking forward to this weekend.
> Will I be staying the night at your dads?
>
> *Erin:* You will be staying the night if we go on the coach journey to Bayside. But if we go somewhere else on the train you might or might not.

Saskia: Oh! I see. I hope we can go on the coach to the fair and seaside. But if we don't will we go to Bayside or Albion Towers or what?

Erin: I don't know yet. Would you still like to stay the night if we don't go to the beach?

Saskia: Yes, please. I'd *love* to.

The notes then go into other details about the journeys and Saskia writes back again with enthusiasm:

Saskia: It sounds great fun. I can't wait. But would you like to stay for lunch with me today.

Erin's reply is an unequivocal YES! Saskia moves at this point to exclude other girls from this special invitation:

Saskia: Okay but Sam, Olga and Anna can't come do you mind?

Erin: Yes, but I want to come. Why couldn't Sam eat with us at your house?

Saskia: Because I can only invite one person at a time because only my brother's in. Sorry. When there was four of us my mum killed me because of the mess and because I didn't tell her and my brother can't handle three, otherwise you know I would. Don't say I'm making up excuses its not nice.

I have been unable to track Erin's response but from the next communication, it appears that Erin decided not to go for lunch, due to pressure applied by Samantha. Saskia's action is to withdraw the offer:

Saskia: I am sorry but I can't invite you to my house whilst I feel guilty I'd like to talk it over with you but thanks to Sam I can't. If Sam decides that I am not making it up then maybe I won't feel so bad. But she has said things that make me feel so bad.

The main struggle concerned Saskia's effort to make Erin into her property. This could only be accomplished at the expense of two other girls – Samantha (who was Erin's best friend) and Anna, her own contingent friend. Saskia's insistence tested Erin, which she tried to resolve through negotiating Samantha's inclusion.

At first Saskia's motives and behaviour remained obscure to me. I thought her initiating energies (she seemed to be *the* one to hold parties, organize outings and manage arrangements) showed her *centrality* to the group and so indicated popularity. However, it became increasingly clear through her notes that she was always trying (and failing) to secure a popular following. She identified popularity with becoming Erin's best friend, but in desiring and not achieving this outcome she conceded rather than accumulated social power.

Conversely, Erin retains her dominance within the elite group. She has considerable social power to command because she is desired rather than desiring. She can enjoy testing her power over Samantha by positioning herself with Saskia. She had after all punished Samantha through making her jealous.

Saskia wants what Samantha has, namely the friendship of Erin and with that the associated social prestige. In trying to control access to Erin, Saskia was prepared both to jeopardize the relationship with Anna (who was effectively ditched as a result of her accepting Erin's invitation) as well as suffer the anger of Samantha. The outcome seemed to be the worst of all worlds, guilt and feeling bad. She was after all, at this point exposed – unable to claim Erin and yet shown to be cavalier in her treatment of Anna.

By the end of the day an unsteady truce prevailed. The following day, however, tensions within the group erupted again. The immediate provocation was Erin withdrawing her invitation to Saskia (re the trip with her father) and reissuing it to Anna. It was impossible to capture reasons for this change of mind. However this is less serious than it might be, because it is not the absolute empirical details of these manoeuvres that are my analytic focus, but their prevalence as an indicative practice of the economy of feminine forms of power.

Erin's tactics are as revealing as Saskia's about how their particular economy worked. Her moves show again that she had a complex investment in provoking the powerful positioning of herself as the subject of all three girls' attention (namely Samantha, Saskia and Anna).[11] Having the ability to command and control these emotions displayed (as well as ensured) that Erin was the most popular and most powerful girl within the clique. Erin's capricious (?) change of mind/heart provoked another crisis within the clique. Now it is Saskia's turn to be full of indignation.

Note episode 2

> *Saskia to Erin:* That's right blame it all on me why don't you. And Erin just because I took the note away doesn't mean to say that you shouldn't [be] my friend. But I don't care you take Anna on holiday with you and forget about me that's the best thing to do.

Erin denies this, insisting on her preference for taking Saskia.

> *Saskia to Erin:* Well I don't want to go with someone who doesn't look like they like me. You just go off with Anna and have a nice two days away.

This is somewhat ingenuous given Saskia's previous practice, a point not lost on Anna who eventually joined in the correspondence, demanding from Saskia an affirmation of her precise status:

> *Anna to Saskia:* If you don't want to be my best friend any more just say yes or no and get it over and done with because I'm not going to wait any more and don't think I'm going to go crawling back because I wont.
> From Anna.

Saskia's reply was equivocal. She simply scribbled, 'I don't know'. Anna then wrote back, 'That's fin[al]'. However, this wasn't the end.

What appears to be at stake in these detailed (and apparently trivial) social dramas of intimacy are deeper meanings about belonging and striving for power and social prestige involving inevitable tensions over those girls deemed most popular. The girls in Erin's clique struggled with and against each other for the rest of the year. That they managed to keep the same personnel is intriguing. Anna and Saskia's relationship was in stasis as they both looked for other possible alliances but failed to secure them. They were therefore stuck with each other (Davies, 1984).

In the second year things changed. Setting practices disrupted the elite clique's social groupings. In the process certain girls were detached from their previous alliances. Natalie had previously been close friends with Laura. Laura's demotion to a lower set meant that in certain subjects Natalie was 'friendless'. This caprice of differentiation strengthened Anna's resources and the two girls reconnected and became allies. Interestingly, Anna characterized the relationship as casual, while Natalie claimed that they were best friends.

The immediate context to the following episode is Saskia (yet again) excluding Anna from an arrangement in which the larger group would all meet at lunchtime at Samantha's house.[12] Her new exclusion generated a new series of notes. Below is a complete transcript of this crucial exchange.

Note episode 3

Anna/Natalie to Saskia:	Saskia we are not your friend because you are a snide and you are not very nice.
Saskia to Anna/Natalie:	I did not [rest of this obliterated]
Natalie to Saskia:	because I am not OK GOT THE MESSAGE
Saskia to Natalie/Anna:	Why did Anna write the first one. Anyway I don't care what you say because words don't hurt. But I still like you both. Can't you answer.
Natalie/Anna to Saskia:	Don't you come cheeky to me girl.
Saskia to Natalie/Anna:	I'm allowed to say what I want to, it's a free world
Natalie to Saskia:	Don't bubble up your mouth on me girl. Get it slag.
Saskia to Natalie/Anna:	Why don't you try shutting up.
Saskia to Anna:	Is Natalie my friend?
Natalie to Saskia:	NO!
Saskia to Natalie/Anna:	If NO you don't like me. Then I don't have to do anything you say. If you were my friend then I would but you're not so I won't. [A naturalistic, relatively neutral drawing of Anna]
Anna to Saskia:	If you must draw my wonderful complexion draw it properly
Natalie to Saskia:	But shut your mouth cheeky
Saskia to Natalie/Anna:	I know but I have never been good at art. PS. Is Nattie still my friend

Natalie to Saskia:	NO
Anna to Saskia:	A drawing of Saskia with sticky up hair – teenage style – with arrows pointing to her chest with the phrase 'Saskia Stevens' and 'flat as a pancake'
Saskia to Anna/Natalie:	I don't care if that's what I look like. I like the hair cut though.

This note is one of the most elaborate that I collected. It has multiple discursive procedures. It contains both text and drawings which together orchestrate what has been called a 'discursive shift' (Rossiter, 1994: 4). Interestingly, Rossiter's analysis of girls' drawings shows girls representing their 'failure' in the 'bad party' as being underlined by girls, for instance Mandy draws several examples of the awfulness of exclusion and isolation and being ignored. 'In both sets of drawings the accusation of failure comes from *other* girls' (Rossiter, 1994: 17, my emphasis). Rossiter understands this as girls acting like 'the projected judges of each other'. On the contrary, girls appropriate this discursive repertoire and then transform it into a specifically feminine social practice. The effectivity of girls' particular power to wound each other is precisely because such judgements emanate from one's imagined allies (girlfriends) as opposed to the enemy 'other' (boys).

In the earlier episodes Saskia and her friends write within the terms of 'bantering' (Milroy, 1987) girl subjecthood, the social forms of which are referenced by the taken for granted common-sense pleasures of girls' friendship in issuing and receiving invitations ('I can invite one person'; 'I am looking forward to this weekend'; 'Yes but I want to come'; 'I am excited about going').

However by episode 3 Saskia is no longer able to call upon these resources because she is compelled to participate in an altogether more grown up (?) sexualized discourse. She is drawn as a 'sight' of 'the male gaze' (Rossiter, 1994: 4) and made to appear through 'other eyes' as 'a slag' and 'flat chested'. Rossiter identifies this transformation with the specific social practice of an early adolescent mixed-sex dance party (Rossiter, 1994). My material, however, suggests that the capacity of girls to reposition other girls within the regime of the male gaze is a *general* capacity of girls' friendships.

In terms of the particular sequence above, Anna, in alliance with Natalie, constructs Saskia within the powerfully subordinating gaze of hegemonic (hetero)sexuality. In this episode the move takes place precisely through an erasure of Saskia's identity as a subject of girlhood. This process is secured when she is 'objectified' after being made to dis/appear as a girl child and re/appear as a sexualized object lacking in heterosexual attractiveness.

The existence of the highly ritualized nature of the girls' exclusionary practices indicates cultural resources deeply embedded in normative gendered ideologies which cut across relations of social class. [. . .] Not only is Saskia now written off as a 'snide', she is literally (and metaphorically) drawn within another regime of meaning (of 'slag' and 'flat-chested') all the more effectively to exclude her from the pleasures of girlhood and feminine approval.

Understandably, these responses produced very painful feelings. Saskia gives explicit voice to her feelings in her earlier self-reflexive commentaries (see episodes 1 and 2). It is significant that she consistently tries to redistribute social blame onto other girls: Samantha (for being jealous and for not liking her, see earlier) and Erin (for excluding and for not liking her).

The last sequence shows her attempting to resist by *denying* her feelings. She tries to generate a third discourse of individual rights (of free speech for example). This is a bourgeois preoccupation but it is a weak position to make against the power of the stronger code of girls' friendship and the all-pervasive force of the male gaze. Through locating herself in the discourse of personal rights, she ultimately disqualifies herself from claims on the loyalties of other girls.

She also struggles simultaneously to pull back the girl position by attempting to neutralize the stronger discourse of heterosexuality (the not being attractive enough discourse; Hollway, 1984: 240) through a light touch of humour ('I don't care if that is what I look like. I like the haircut though') but to no avail. Saskia's insistence on trying to assume the social power of popularity/friendship without first meeting the criteria of its ethical structure and practical manifestation left her out of its very terms, 'If NO you don't like me. Then I don't have to do anything you say. If you were my friend then I would but you're not so I won't'.

Her persistent failure to honour co-dependencies was punished through the production of guilt and isolation. Not only was she positioned outside of the discourse of girls' friendship, she was also practically and effectively excluded from the group. She was ill for two weeks and in fact never returned to the school.

Negotiating feminine friendship and its associated powers is a delicate business, being always already constituted through the socially coercive presence of the male gaze, which endlessly seeks to position girls within its regulation. We have seen that a key sanction to disqualify a girl from friendship is to relegate her from claims to femininity by implying that she looks insufficiently attractive.

In examining the detailed workings of the early stages in the formation of relationships in one girls' group, we have seen something of what is at stake inside the culture of girls' friendship. Best friends are a specific feature of female relations (Griffiths, 1995; Llewellyn, 1980; McRobbie and Garber, 1980). Best friendship represents in dramatic form the features found more diffusely within the wider networks and understandably the struggles around the role are usually the most acrimonious because this relationship is the most invested.

The desire to become and the fear of being displaced as a girl's significant other appears to be what Erin, Samantha, Saskia and Anna all bring to the negotiations. However, girls' tangible desires for power through friendship have to be reconciled with its ethical rules. These social rules are premised on the exact opposite of undisciplined individualism. My understanding of the ethical basis and ethical rules of female friendship confirms what other researchers have discovered (Griffiths, 1995; McRobbie, 1978; McRobbie and Garber, 1980; Nilan, 1991). The central premises of girls' friendship are: reliability, reciprocity, commitment, confidentiality, trust and sharing. The repertoire of emotions that are provoked if these rules are broken are as powerfully felt and as dramatic as those that have characteristically been claimed as the sole prerogative of sexualized relations (Coward, 1986). Girls' 'divorces' are messy, as we can see in what happened to Saskia.[13]

One outcome of the pressure on girls to convert the wider loyalties of friendship into the exclusivities of best friendship is an implosion of individual power. It is not that girls in Erin's clique did not experience differential *feelings* of power through their ability to access other dimensions: being clever; being pretty; being good at games. They did. It is more that all of these other forms of cultural capital were incessantly evaluated within the domain of their friendships. Importantly therefore, in settling their alliances girls had to position themselves very carefully, lest their success in these other dimensions was perceived as disadvantaging one's peers (Davies, 1984).

Equally, being thought 'bossy' could be the way in which highly ambitious girls are socialized into disguising their competence. After all Saskia's worst fault, condensed in the phrase 'showing off', placed her not only outside of the rules of social reciprocity, it also undermined her claims to be suitably 'nice' – as we have seen, a routinely invoked middle-class feminine form. As one of her friends cryptically remarked, 'She wasn't as nice as she was supposed to be'.

Notes

1. Reinharz (1992) has a good overview of the wide-ranging literature about the respective arguments about appropriate distance and other matters relating to the ethics of research.
2. There is of course a relationship between the two – as most studies of girls' friendship note – that is, there is a marked tendency for girls to make friends with girls who they perceive as being like themselves. This is obviously related to the opportunity to make friends with girls who you are positioned with at school but it is also driven by the girls seeking out similarities.
3. See Reinharz's discussion of gendered fieldwork relations (1992: 58–64) See also Warren (1988) on the complexities of gender in fieldwork settings. It is fascinating to note that just as some boys were publicly annoyed because I *wasn't* studying them, some girls were annoyed because I *was*!
4. The discussion of trust and sponsorship in Griffiths (1995) is a recent and thoughtful example of the personal and intellectual demands of doing an ethnography, as well as exploring the reliance we, as fieldworkers, have upon the tolerance and help of girls.

5. For example, it became clear that girls' use of personal knowledge about each other constituted key cultural resources of power. This requires us to acknowledge just what it is some girls do to each other by appearing to be 'merely' making or breaking friends.

6. Weiner (1976: 11) cites an example of pursuing apparently insignificant leads.

7. Interestingly few social researchers have spotted these notes and their significance. There are literally passing references to them in (Davies, 1984: 258–60; Lever, 1976: 484; Pollard, 1984: 242). My field logbook is one long litany of the girls' respective fall-outs, show-downs and pranks – all done more or less surreptitiously through their sending of notes or whispers. [. . .]

8. Deliberate interventions into the choice of friends recurs throughout the ethnography, indicating the wider pressures being brought to bear upon how girls act even in their so-called private lives. [. . .]

9. Girls had a distinct vocabulary for allocating moral judgements in the economy of popularity/unpopularity. Another girl told me the meaning of the following terms: 'skank': a girl who is unreliable, who makes arrangements and then fails to honour them; 'snide': a girl who is said to have told a confidence to someone else and/or who leaves the prior friend; 'user': probably the most painful term. It is often used in situations where one person has been popular and for some reason is made unpopular. This person then makes friends outside the group.

10. I've retained the term girls give to describe this form of communication.

11. While becoming the object of three girls' desire is certainly a seductive position, it is also a predicament – a fact acknowledged by Erin in another note: 'I think if Saskia invites me and Olga to her house on Saturday then you can share me, but Saskia, it's up to you but you'd better invite someone else or two people will go off with each other and the other will be alone' (communication sequence 6, Item 10).

12. To prevent Anna from going, Saskia had taken it upon herself to tell Anna that Samantha's mother would be there. In the event this was untrue and Erin's clique minus Anna met at Samantha's house. According to my interview with Anna, this hit her very hard since she had lost her other source of social support (Natalie, who had made other arrangements). Social isolation and 'leaving a friend' is considered a serious breach of social etiquette.

13. In a closing interview with Saskia before she left the school, I asked her to comment on the changes within her relationships. She spoke of coming back from her holidays and, as she put it, 'some really good friends . . . didn't want to know me anymore'. She spoke specifically about being shouted at in the street and also recalled in elaborate detail another rejection process: the same girls made 'anonymous' phone calls to her home and left messages on the telephone answering machine (pretending to be the household's ex-au pair). As part of this attack Saskia was also accused by one of her 'enemies' of calling her mother a 'slag'. It was at this point, according to Saskia, that Saskia's mother interrupted the anonymous phone calls to reprimand the caller. The complex cultural relays between inside/outside schooling can only be hinted at in this example. There is an impreciseness about the girls' identities but there is no confusion about the continuity of practices centring upon secrecy, sexuality and exclusion. The premediated campaign suggests that collective punishment is being meted out in no uncertain measure. In the same interview Saskia stated that, 'You don't really need *best* friends when you can have *good* friends', and

optimistically anticipated her new (private) school through initial references to the 'warmth' and 'friendliness' of the girls, who she described as 'very nice'.

References

Arnot, M. (1982) 'Male hegemony, social class and women's education', *Journal of Education*, 164(1): 64–89.

Ball, S.J. (1990) *Politics and Policy Making in Education: Explorations in Policy Sociology*. London: Routledge.

Bowe, R., S.J. Ball with A. Gold (1992) *Reforming Education and Changing Schools: Case Studies in Policy Sociology*. London: Routledge.

Brown, L.M. and C. Gilligan (1992) *Meeting at the Crossroads: Women's Psychology and Girls' Development*. Cambridge, MA: Harvard University Press.

Brunsdon, C. (1978) 'It is well known that by nature women are inclined to be rather personal', in Women's Studies Group (ed.), *Women Take Issue: Aspects of Women's Subordination*. London: Hutchinson in association with the Centre for Contemporary Cultural Studies (CCCS), University of Birmingham.

Clarricoates, K. (1987) 'Dinosaurs in the classroom – the "hidden" curriculum in primary schools', in M. Arnot and G. Weiner (eds), *Gender and the Politics of Schooling*. London: Hutchinson for Open University Press.

Connell, R.W. (1987) *Gender and Power: Society, the Person and Sexual Politics*. Cambridge: Polity Press.

Corrigan, P. (1987) 'In/forming schooling', in D.W. Livingstone (ed.), *Critical Pedagogy and Cultural Power*. Boston, MA: Bergin and Garvey.

Coward, R. (1986) The company she chooses, *The Guardian*, 20 May.

Cunnison, S. (1989) 'Gender joking in the staffroom', in S. Acker (ed.), *Teachers, Gender and Careers*. London: Falmer Press.

Davies, B. (1984) 'Friends and fights', in M. Hammersley and P. Woods (eds), *Life In School: The Sociology of Pupil Culture*. Milton Keynes: Open University Press.

Davies, B. (1989) *Frogs and Snails and Feminist Tales: Preschool Children and Gender*. Boston, MA: Allen and Unwin.

Evans, M. (1991) *A Good School: Life at a Girls' Grammar School in the 1950s*. London: The Women's Press.

Frazer, E. and D. Cameron (1989) 'Knowing what to say: the construction of gender in linguistic practice', in R. Grillo (ed.), *Social Anthropology and the Politics of Language*. London: Routledge.

Griffiths, V. (1995) *Adolescent Girls and their Friends: A Feminist Ethnography*. Aldershot: Avebury.

Hargreaves, A. and D. Reynolds (1989) 'Decomprehensivization', in A. Hargreaves and D. Reynolds (eds), *Education Policies: Controversies and Critiques*. London: Falmer Press.

Hey, V. (1988) ' "The company she keeps" the social and interpersonal construction of girls' same sex friendships'. Unpublished PhD thesis, University of Kent, Canterbury.

Hey, V. (1994) 'The observation of infinite change: ethnographic evidence of girls' friendships'. Paper presented at BSA Sexualities in Social Context Conference, University of Central Lancashire, Preston, 28–31 March.

Holland, J. and C. Ramazanoglu (1994) 'Coming to conclusions: power and interpretation in researching young women's sexuality', in M. Maynard and J. Purvis (eds), *Researching Women's Lives from a Feminist Perspective*. London: Taylor and Francis.

Hollway, W. (1984) 'Gender difference and the production of subjectivity', in J. Henriques, W. Hollway, C. Urwin, C. Venn and V. Walkerdine (eds), *Changing the Subject: Psychology, Social Regulation and Subjectivity*. London: Methuen.

Horowitz, R. (1983) *Honor and the American Dream: Culture and Identity in a Chicago Community*. New Brunswick, NJ: Rutgers University Press.

James, H. (1987) *Portrait of a Lady*. Harmondsworth: Penguin Books.

Johnson, R. (1986) 'The story so far: and further transformations?', in D. Punter (ed.), *Introduction to Contemporary Cultural Studies*. London: Longman.

Jones, A. (1993) 'Becoming a "girl": post-structuralist suggestions for educational research', *Gender and Education*, 5(2): 157–66.

Kenway, J. and J. Blackmore (1995) 'Pleasure and pain: beyond feminist authoritarianism and therapy in the curriculum'. Paper presented at the Unesco Colloquium, 'Is there a Pedagogy for Girls?', Institute of Education, University of London, 10–12 January.

Lever, J. (1976) 'Sex differences in the games children play', *Social Problems*, 23: 478–87.

Llewellyn, M. (1980) 'Studying girls at school: the implications of confusion', in R. Deem (ed.), *Schooling for Women's Work*. London: Routledge and Kegan Paul.

Mac an Ghaill, M. (1994) *The Making of Men: Masculinities, Sexualities and Schooling*. Buckingham: Open University Press.

McRobbie, A. (1978) 'Working class girls and the culture of femininity', in Women's Studies Group (ed.), *Women Take Issue: Aspects of Women's Subordination*. London: Hutchinson.

McRobbie, A. (1982) 'The politics of feminist research: between talk, text and action', *Feminist Review*, 12: 46–57.

McRobbie, A. and J. Garber (1980) 'Girls and subcultures', in S. Hall and T. Jefferson (eds), *Resistance Through Rituals: Youth Subcultures in Post war Britain*. London: Hutchinson.

Mahony, P. (1985) *Schools for the Boys? Co-education Reassessed*. London: Hutchinson.

Mandell, N. (1991) 'The least-adult role in studying children', in F.C. Waksler (ed.), *Studying the Social Worlds of Children: Sociological Readings*. London: Falmer Press.

Measor, L. (1985) 'Interviewing: a strategy in qualitative research', in R.G. Burges (ed.), *Strategies of Educational Research: Qualitative Methods*. London: Falmer Press.

Miles, M.B. and A.M. Huberman, (1984) *Qualitative Data Analysis: A Sourcebook of New Methods*. Beverly Hills, CA: Sage.

Milroy, L. (1987) *Language and Social Networks*. London: Routledge.

Nilan, P. (1991) 'Exclusion, inclusion and moral ordering in two girls' friendship groups', *Gender and Education*, 3(1): 163–82.

Oakley, A. (1981) 'Interviewing women: a contradiction in terms', in H. Roberts (ed.), *Doing Feminist Research*. London: Routledge and Kegan Paul.

Opie, A. (1992) 'Qualitative research, appropriation of the "other" and empowerment', *Feminist Review*, 40(spring): 52–69.

Opie, P. and I. Opie (1959) *The Lore and Language of School Children*. Oxford: Oxford University Press.

Patai, D. (1994) 'When method becomes power', in A. Gitlin (ed.), *Power and Method*. New York: Routledge.

Patton, M.Q. (1990) *Qualitative Evaluation and Research Methods*. London: Sage.

Pollard, A. (1984) 'Goodies, jokers and gangs', in M. Hammersley and P. Woods (eds), *Life in the School: The Sociology of Pupil Culture*. Milton Keynes: Open University Press.

Reinharz, S. (1992) *Feminist Methods in Social Research*. New York: Oxford University Press.

Ribbens, J. and R. Edwards (1995) 'Introducing qualitative research on women in families and households', *Women's Studies International Forum*, 18(3): 247–58.

Roland Martin, J. (1995) 'A girls' pedagogy "in relationship"'. Paper presented at the Unesco Colloquium, 'Is there a Pedagogy for Girls?', Institute of Education, University of London, 10–12 January.

Rossiter, A.B. (1994) 'Chips, Coke and rock 'n' roll: mediation of an invitation to a first dance party', *Feminist Review*, 46(spring): 1–20.

Skeggs, B. (1994) 'Situating the production of feminist ethnography', in M. Maynard and J. Purvis (eds), *Researching Women's Lives from a Feminist Perspective*. London: Taylor and Francis.

Stacey, J. (1988) 'Can there be a feminist ethnography?', *Women's Studies International Forum*, 11(1): 21–7.

Stanworth, M. (1981) *Gender and Schooling: A Study of Sexual Divisions in the Classroom*. Pamphlet No. 7, London: WRRC.

Walkerdine, V. (1985) 'On the regulation of speaking and silence', in C. Steedman, C. Urwin and V. Walkerdine (eds), *Language, Gender and Childhood*. London: Routledge and Kegan Paul.

Warren, C.B. (1988) *Gender Issues in Field Research*. Newbury Park, CA: Sage.

Weiner, A.B. (1976) *Women of Value, Men of Reknown: New Perspectives in Trobriand Exchange*. Austin, TX: University of Texas Press.

Wolpe, A.M . (1988) '"Experience" as analytical framework: does it account for girls' education?', in M. Cole (ed. *Bowles and Gintis Revisited: Correspondence and Contradiction in Educational Theory*. London: Falmer Press.

4

'One of the boys': black masculinity and the peer group

Claire E. Alexander

Black macho: masculinity and the peer group

Very little has been written on issues of black masculinity in the British context. Although both Pryce (1967) and Cashmore (1979) remark on the significance of the male peer group in black youth culture, this remains very much an institution whose existence is assumed and significance unquestioned. Both place the peer group within the context of personal failure and frustration; a retreat to a collective identity – in each case, Rastafari – as a coping strategy in the face of racial rejection. For Pryce, the peer group is associated closely with the 'hustler' lifestyle, where older men act as role models for teenagers who are 'unemployed, homeless and in conflict with their parents' (1967: 35). Drawing upon the ascribed pathology of the black family, Cashmore similarly claims that the peer group constitutes the primary source of socialization for black youth; an alternative to their parents who 'provided only models of degradation and deprivation' (1979: 85). The black peer group thus constitutes a recoil from the forces of racism into a negative and hostile structure, which is oppositional in both form and intent. It also becomes inevitably associated with deviance and criminality (Lawrence, 1982).

The attitude of both Cashmore and Pryce towards black male peer groups can be seen to have its roots in traditional approaches to youth deviance. This places the peer group, black or white, within the context of social and psychological maladjustment (Cohen, 1955), in which the individual turns to a male subculture in order to compensate for social rejection. This forms an autonomous entity which is defined by 'negative polarity' (ibid: 28) to the norms of wider society, and creates an alternative value system through which marginalized youth can create the illusion of status and power. Although later studies recognize that such groups are

---

This is an edited extract from Claire E. Alexander (1996) *The Art of Being Black: The Creation of Black British Youth Identities* Oxford: Clarendon Press.

neither inevitably delinquent (Downes, 1966; Matza, 1964), nor necessarily opposed to social norms, it is this power inequality which remains the central feature of youth subcultural groups. Peter Wilmott notes in his study *Adolescent Boys of East London* that within the peer group, 'the adolescent boy can enjoy a freedom and equality he cannot find at school, at work or inside his family' (1966: 40). That the peer group constitutes a bid for power by marginalized groups lies at the centre of many studies of youth subculture; that this reach for control reinforces such marginality and re-creates the conditions for its existence has become something of a truism (Hebdige, 1979; Willis, 1977, 1978). Within this arena, black youth are seen as doubly disadvantaged – by race and by class position – and are perceived as inevitably 'contracultural' in their stance (Downes, 1966: 229). The black peer group is thus seen more as a cathartic expression of frustrated power and social maladjustment than of positive action and control.

Although youth culture is seen as an exclusively male arena, few studies focus directly on the construction of masculinity. Paul Willis's studies of working-class youth culture are the main exceptions in this area, although even these do not fully consider the position of women in subcultural discourse. The general dearth of material on gender relations can perhaps be explained partly by the absence of work on and by women in this area, but also by the highly structured perception of social realities which marks out subcultural theory. Subcultural groups are usually regarded as internally homogeneous and positioned in direct opposition to an overarching hegemonic order which constitutes 'Society'. Hall and Jefferson (1976) note that subcultures are not placed in simple opposition and have relation to both 'Society' and the parent culture; in practice, however, these subcultures are viewed as autonomous entities locked in conflict with an omnipresent and static social structure, by which they are ultimately subordinated. The focus has thus been placed on 'class' struggle at the expense of the multiple layers of social structure, which enable subordinated groups – both male and female – to enter into conflict with each other as part of an ongoing search for control. It is at these levels, lower than that of the ubiquitous and undefined 'Society', that black masculinity is lived out and achieves significance.

The 'living out' of black male experience has been considered more fully in relation to African-American men. In *Tally's Corner* (1967), Elliot Liebow studies an all-male, 'street corner' society, which considers the role of the man as father, lover, husband, and breadwinner, rather than as 'social problem'. His study reveals the complexity and variation within these roles in relation to the individual, and in their relation to both women and other men. However, Liebow's emphasis throughout is on problem-solving; on the expression of powerlessness rather than control. He writes, 'Here, where the measure of man is considerably smaller, and where weaknesses are somehow turned upside down and almost magically transformed into strengths, he can be, once again, a man among men' (Liebow, 1967: 136).

Exploitation, or power, becomes for Liebow a 'public fiction' within the street-corner context, an illusion distorted by the inevitability of personal failure. Liebow's study is of a world largely separated from wider society, denied its concerns, and set apart from its values and structures; a vision shared by Hannerz in his study of a black 'ghetto': 'The fact about the power of the ghetto . . . is that most ghetto dwellers neither have any nor are actively working to acquire any at present' (Hannerz 1969: 15). With a lifestyle characterized by sex, drinking, and women, the 'Street Corner Men' (ibid.: 57) are seen as symptomatic of personal limitation and lack of control, the product and enactment of absolute powerlessness. Ronald Taylor thus argues:

> A combination of contemporary social and economic factors conspire to limit the black male's access to status and economic resources. . . . The inability to function successfully in the male role . . . may be experienced as a loss in masculinity and social identity, which he may attempt to recoup by active involvement in the life of the streets. (1977: 2)[1]

This pathologized approach to black masculinity has recently been challenged by Mitchell Duneier in *Slim's Table* (1992). Focusing on a small, loose collectivity of older black men in a Chicago diner, Duneier writes of the group affirmation of respectability, self-esteem, and communal identity which lies at the heart of working-class black masculinity:

> They are consistently inner-directed and firm and they act with resolve; their images of self worth are not derived from material possessions or the approval of others; they are disciplined ascetics with respect for wisdom and experience; usually humble, they can be quiet, sincere and discreet, and they look for those qualities in their friends. (1992: 163)

Duneier contrasts this with the public expressions of 'ghetto-specific masculinity' (ibid.: 148) which characterize the younger black 'underclass'. He thus distinguishes between working-class 'maintainers' and the subcultural 'creators' of alternative status systems, such as drug dealers and gang leaders, who dominate the public arena (ibid.: 131). While affirming the heterogeneity of black masculinity at an individual, private level, therefore, Duneier simultaneously rehearses and reinscribes the homogeneity of 'black macho' at a public, 'street level'. Like Liebow, Hannerz, and Anderson (1978) before him, he finally adheres to a view of expressive young black male identity as a form of status-inversion; the catharsis of ultimate male powerlessness.

There is little doubt that the concept of power is central to any discussion of black masculinity. Most studies have, however, regarded black masculinity as an *alternative* to social status, rather than as an *extension* of it. 'Black macho' has been portrayed, therefore, as differing in kind rather than degree from the wider gendered power relations within Society at large. Machismo becomes a symbol of, and substitute for, the lack of power, rather than constituting an aspect of that power. It has thus been seen as inauthentic and illusory; something apart from, and opposed to, the wider structures of Society. As bell hooks argues:

> The portrait of black masculinity that emerges in this work perpetually constructs men as 'failures', who are psychologically 'fucked up', dangerous, violent sex maniacs whose insanity is informed by their inability to fulfill their phallocentric masculine destiny in a racist context. (1992: 89)

It is, however, only within the context of wider power relations – and as an extension of them – that black masculinity can be fully understood. In *Black Macho and the Myth of the Superwoman*, Michelle Wallace argues that it is in the search for 'manliness', as defined by dominant white society, that the origins of 'black macho' are to be found. It thus constitutes, for Wallace, a 'façade of power' (1990: 199), which is concerned with the negotiation of personal control through interaction. This control is, however, taken as a prerequisite for the attainment of social and economic power: the assertion of masculinity constituting an expression of individual worth. Lynn Segal notes, 'The issue of "manliness" was thus crucial to the confrontation between white men and black' (1990: 188). Black masculinity can be seen, therefore, to reify white Western notions of masculinity in the search for wider social control and to incorporate these within its creation. Kobena Mercer writes:

> There is a further contradiction, another turn of the screw of oppression, which occurs when Black men subjectively internalise and incorporate aspects of the dominant definitions of masculinity in order to contest the definitions of dependency and powerlessness which racism and racial oppression enforce. (1988: 112)

However, rather than a static, autonomous, and essentialized ideology, with a direct relationship to action, constructions of masculinity should be viewed as both historically and synchronically contingent, inescapably intertwined with the expression and contestation of power. Michel Foucault writes in *The History of Sexuality*:

> Sexuality . . . appears rather as an especially dense transfer point for relations of power. . . . Sexuality is not the most intractable element in power relations, but rather one of those endowed with the greatest instrumentality: useful for the greatest number of maneuvres and capable of serving as a point of support, as a lynchpin, for the most varied strategies. (cited in Jones, 1992: 95)

Black masculinity is then perhaps best understood as an articulated response to structural inequality, enacting and subverting dominant definitions of power and control, rather than substituting for them. Rather than a hostile and withdrawn entity, the black peer group can be seen as a base for interaction and negotiation with wider society. It forms a loose collectivity, which is internally neither homogeneous nor unified, and externally disparate in its intent and attitudes. The enactment of dominant norms and the restrictions of macro-structural constraints, however, render the lived expressions of black masculinity complex and often contradictory. Such tensions question the bounds of social constructions concerning 'race' and 'masculinity' and underline the fluidity of black male identity. As Segal notes: 'Black culture is also questioning the very notion of the "Black" subject. . . . In looking at the oppositional meanings inherent in Black masculinity today, the stress is on diversity' (1990: 203).

'One of the boys': control and the peer group

During my fieldwork, the constitution of my core group of informants proved remarkably diffuse. At times, it expanded to include men who were comparatively unknown to me; at others, it contracted to around four or five men that I knew well. My knowledge of the peer group was thus rather uneven, but reflected the dynamism and fluidity of the group as it was experienced by those it encompassed. Some general observations can be made, however.

First, the group was exclusively male; although women were sometimes present – as I myself was – at their meetings, they were never regarded as an integral part of the group. Far from being the 'honorary male', women tended to be 'carried with' the group more as an external adornment than an active participant. Secondly, the group was almost exclusively black; the notable exception being Satish, who is of Indian origin. Although he was generally accepted as part of the group, his ethnic origin was used frequently as a form of ridicule whenever tensions within the group arose. Thirdly, the peer group structure existed primarily in the public sphere. The boys were rarely together for any length of time within their home environments – although each knew the others' families – and usually gathered together only as a prelude to going out. Moreover, private knowledge between some members of the group was surprisingly slight; for example, when questioned, Ricky was unable to tell me Nathan's age or employment circumstances. Lack of knowledge of other spheres of life was relatively common, although this is not to deny the existence of close friendships between individual members of the group.

The core group, defined by Ricky and confirmed by others I asked, consisted of Ricky, Frank, Clive, Satish, Nathan, and Arif; it had formerly included Ricky's brother, Mike, and Shane, who was intermittently part of the group but had moved away the year before to pursue other interests. Its boundaries often expanded to include others such as Malcolm or Edgar, and more rarely to include occasional members, such as Ricky's cousin, Kevin, or Nathan's brother, Philip. The core group remained, however, relatively constant, although it did begin to fragment towards the end of my fieldwork for reasons which will be considered later.

The boys were, Ricky assured me, 'a unique group' (Interview, 9 Dec.
1990). In reality, however, this proved more a matter of self-perception
than fact. Each of the core members moved outside the boundaries to form
parts of other groups, perhaps with a degree of overlap in membership;
these interacted with the other groups only sporadically. Clive, for example, formed part of a sound system, of which Malcolm was a member:
although the other boys knew this group, they met only rarely at dances
and parties, and were never included en masse within the structures of the
boys' group. Clive also spent an increasing amount of time with some of
the men from work, whom he introduced rather selectively to his other
friends. Frank had a number of friends from the period of his return to
England, with whom he spent time; Satish had a circle of rather dubious
acquaintances from his days as car thief and amateur fence; while Shane, as
mentioned earlier, had moved away from the boys towards a group of
musicians, whom he considered more in keeping with his future plans.
Although these other groups were not considered threatening to the
structure of the original group, in the way that relationships with women
often were, they were often a site for role tensions. Each group was seen to
appeal to a different facet of the individual's identity, of which the other
groups had only limited knowledge. Ricky explained of his other friendships:

> They weren't part of the group really; basically they were my friends, but they
> just find it hard to like deal with C[live] and N[athan] and all that. Because them
> sort of guys, they feel rejected by guys like C[live] and N[athan]. They feel like
> someone's taking the piss out of them . . . there's a lot of frictions basically.
> (ibid.)

It is interesting to compare the boys' 'unique' group with Darnell's peer
group. He told me: 'Like, a lot of people from round my area, about six or
seven of them, we go round, and then you get like fractions; like this friend
knows that friend. Then it's a lot of people' (Interview, 24 Mar. 1991).
Darnell, it should be noted, is younger than the boys; his circle of
acquaintances stemmed mainly from school and the locale, whereas the
boys' friendships – with the exception of Clive and Ricky – were established after this period and tended to be more diffuse. Even so, Darnell's
friends had decreased in number since leaving school and had become more
tightly focused around shared ambitions and interests. He explained:

> When you are at school, you mix with all of them, but now they've gone their
> ways; some of them moved out of the area and like there's only a few of them left
> still. So you mix with less and less people . . . when you were at school, there was
> about forty people walking around same way. (ibid.)

His closest friends were those he 'raved' with, and, like Ricky, he admitted
to some tensions between this group and those with which it overlapped.
Darnell thus told me of one friend, Owen:

I see less and less of him everyday; he's strange. He raves, but he doesn't rave with *us*. He raves with his *other* friends. He might not like the people we go with: because if you like smoke weed 'Oh my God, you're bad', but with us, we don't mind what the people are really, as long as it's a good party. But if he doesn't like the look of the people, he doesn't want to go there. (ibid.)

The 'uniqueness' of the boys lay, therefore, not so much in the closed structure of the group, nor its particularity within black youth culture, as its self-perceived cohesion. That is, it was not the group itself which was unique or unusual, but the singularity of its defining ethos – at least in its own terms.

It is this ethos, an internal perception of what the group stood for to its members, which was the main source for membership. The group was not particularly distinguished by its history: although Clive and Ricky had known each other for about eight years, other relationships were more newly formed. Frank met Mike, Ricky's brother, about four years previously while they were both working in Pizza Hut; Arif and Nathan were introduced in a City winebar only about two years before. Other, older acquaintances, such as Edgar, had more recently moved away from the group and defined themselves against it. The boundaries of the group were thus perceived as relatively open to new members – male, of course, and generally excluding Asians and whites. These exclusions were articulated not on 'racial' grounds – indeed, most of the boys were keen to assert the existence of white friends – but on the grounds of 'cultural difference'. White men, I was told, do not share the same interests and expectations as black men. Malcolm told me:

I've got some [white friends], but not that many. I don't rave with them. . . . They're not so close; not close at all. I'm not racist, but the white ones, they've got their ways; they go to the pub a lot, and I'm not into it. I'm not someone [who] says 'let's go and have a pint', do you understand me? That's the reason why. (Interview, 12 May 1991)

On closer questioning, it transpired that the boys had very few non-black friends, and that these were regarded more as distant acquaintances. The boys were concerned, however, not to be seen as 'racist', and, more importantly, not to be seen as having an inability to deal with white people. Clive, who socialized occasionally with people from work, told me:

Basically, what I gather is that they don't have any black friends, so I'm a bit of a novelty. . . . It can be to your advantage, it can also be to your detriment as well. Sometimes you get all the old jokes 'you shouldn't be doing that, you should be cleaning', or 'you should be nicking videos or car stereos'. As I say, I'm thick-skinned, it's no problem. . . . I can go somewhere where I'm the only black guy in there and that's alright. (Interview, 16 Apr. 1991)

During my fieldwork, on only one occasion did the boys take a white man out with them – Danny, a friend of Satish's. The boys explained that because Danny had grown up with mainly black people he was able to relate to them and understand them in a way most white people could not. That power was a consideration in his inclusion was also obvious. Danny was accepted because in any confrontation he could be relied upon to take the part of the black group against any white men. He was thus dissociated from the power dynamic of most interactions with white men. Moreover, because Danny was short, round, and considered by most to be both quite stupid and slightly unstable, he was regarded as no threat to the image of the group or to its control.

Most of the boys defined the internal cohesion of the group in terms of shared expectations and ambitions. In theory at least, anyone who was male and black and shared these ambitions could become part of the group. Ricky explained:

> To keep up with the pack is exactly what it takes to go out with that lot. . . . It's almost like a pack of wolves running, and if you can't keep up, you're not part of the group. You know, keep up with the wildness, chasing girls, everything. (Interview, 9 Dec. 1990)

Ricky's metaphor is apt in a number of ways: first, it captures the overtly masculine nature of the group; secondly, it reveals the dynamic way in which the group functioned. The group itself only functioned *as* a group in relation to others; it thus incorporated movement and interaction within its very boundaries. When this external stimulation was not present, the group became much looser and more internally divided and competitive. The metaphor also encapsulates the notion of control, of power, which dominated the group in its external encounters; how this was inscribed by the group is hinted at in his last sentence, 'the wildness, chasing girls, everything'. This element was echoed by Frank, who defined the qualities of the group as:

> Personality. To do something that – to stick out among a crowd, not to blend in with the crowd; to be different. Just to show themselves as being themselves, not to be affected by what society says, or basically doesn't give a fuck. . . . Most of them are loud people; they're party people, they're the kind of people who make the atmosphere totally different; people walking up to their house would go 'wow, what have I been missing?' Those kind of people. (Interview, 5 Apr. 1991)

To a large extent, therefore, the internal cohesion of the group relied on the ability to elicit external responses; the relationships among the boys were primarily based upon external stimuli rather than internal, personal knowledge. When I asked Frank what had formed the core group from the much larger crowd in which they had previously moved, he told me:

> There were more then, but out of that more there was always that same group that would always be together. . . . I would say we were the liked. They all wanted to be with us, because they liked the way we moved; they copied what we

did. If we wanted to do this, do that, they always wanted to know what we were doing, how we were doing it. (ibid.)

For Frank, the ability to elicit these responses, this control, was a reflection of personal attributes, notably in relation to wider society: 'At the end of the day, I always knew what I was looking for; always knew what I wanted; always knew how to have a good time; always knew the kind of environment I liked to be in and didn't like to be in' (ibid.).

These personal ambitions were, in turn, translated into and reflected by the ability to 'perform' within a given social setting. To be able to control external responses in a social environment became a measure of one's ability to assert control in other spheres. In this, the values expressed by the peer group were a translation and transformation of wider societal values rather than the creation of an alternative; they were not 'contracultural' but rather an extension of wider social concerns and status judgements. For the boys, the ability to 'perform' was focused very much in the attraction of women: this was seen as asserting control as much over the other men present – black or white – as over the women themselves. Closely associated with this attraction was the presentation of external image, including the ability to dance, styles of dress, and the ability to communicate verbally. This latter ability, which Ricky termed 'the gift of the gab' (Interview, 9 Dec. 1990), was perhaps most central to this image, and the most closely connected to the wider issues of power, both within and outside the group. Also of crucial importance in the reach for control was the ability to assert physical control, should the need arise.

Membership of the peer group was thus grounded in an ability to conform to certain internal expectations and perform to an external audience. Such abilities were not, however, unproblematic in their execution. Ricky explained:

It depends; if you're no good with women, but you can fight, you're part of the group; if you're good with women, but you can't fight, you're still part of the group. It works that way, but it's better if you can do both. (Interview, 9 Dec. 1990)

In practice, the group proved rather uneven in its application of these standards. Arif, it was generally acknowledged by the others, was neither good with women, nor reliable in the event of any confrontation. He was included in the group primarily because of his association with Nathan. Nevertheless, Arif was accorded full status within the group, despite many personal animosities and misgivings by the others. Of primary importance in these decisions was the maintenance of at least the appearance of external unity. Clive told me: 'As long as they show the same values whilst in the company. . . . Whether they've got it or not – as long as they can show it' (Interview, 16 Apr. 1991).

The internal dynamic

Within this often impressive display of external unity, the reality of the boys' peer group was far from harmonious and uniform. Although there was no status hierarchy within the group, and no developed sense of personal competition – at least where the internal group norms were concerned – there existed a number of latent divisions and private hostilities which were manifest within the private arena. This 'backstage' could occur either within the domestic sphere or during an evening out, if no external audience was present. I never witnessed any conflict within the group when it was performing to an audience. The internal dynamic of the group was, however, revealing of the personal attitudes towards status and control, and towards the peer group itself.

On the whole, the enactment of personal hostilities remained very much at a verbal level; it was rarely translated into action. On only one occasion did a fight occur: this was between Frank and Satish over the use of the telephone in Ricky's flat, which I shared. Frank, who had long thought of Satish as ill-mannered and manipulative, accused Satish of exploiting our goodwill; while Satish, who thought of Frank as arrogant and bossy, accused him of interfering in his private business. In the row that ensued, the long history of this antagonism was replayed, with Frank finally threatening to hit Satish. The fight was prevented through Ricky's intervention, and Frank left. The others present, Ricky, Malcolm, and Clive, merely shrugged and told me that Satish was renowned for provoking Frank's infamous temper, and that it would all be forgotten within days – which it was. More generally, the boys were loath to admit openly to any private dislikes or conflict with their friends. They would, however, point out tensions between other members of the group. Moreover, as I lived with the boys for twelve months, it became possible to observe these tensions as they were enacted, both privately and within the group setting.

Personal tensions were both played out and assuaged through the constant verbal interplay which marked out any interaction within the group. This was focused primarily on the physical defects of the individual, which became the constant markers for ritualized insult. In her study of African-American teenagers, Folb has argued that 'These verbal games expose the points of genuine tension, anger, hostility and self-deprecation . . . experienced by young people in this society' (1980: 32).

Amongst the boys, however, these interactions were directed primarily at the individual rather than pointing to wider concerns and tended not to focus upon matters of personal social status. The main exception to this was the ridicule of the individual's girlfriend or partner, in which the man usually joined with some enthusiasm: the overall effect was thus more cathartic than injurious. Meetings of the group were characterized by references to Frank's receding hairline, Clive's mouth and weak chin, the gap in Nathan's front teeth, Arif's lack of height, Ricky's skinny legs, and so on. The focus moved from one individual to another, with the rest of the group uniting against the man under attack. Ricky commented:

> That's how they normally do it, they switch from one to the other; it's either they might start on C[live] and they go on to S[atish] and they go on to A[rif], you know, then they might take the piss out of F[rank]'s forehead. They look for something they can say, 'yes, that's a fault in that person' and then they won't leave it alone. (Interview, 9 Dec. 1990)

These insults also served to denote the core group at specific moments, although the content of this core remained quite fluid. More occasional members of the group, such as Malcolm and Satish, thus came under more intense, if not more hostile, fire. Malcolm was targeted mainly because the others considered him effeminate and Satish because of his ethnic origin and his lack of control over Dion [his girlfriend]. Ricky told me:

> It's like M[alcolm], even though he's part of the group, it's like one person takes the piss out of him, then everyone does. . . . He finds the guys a joke, but then again, as soon as he hears N[athan]'s name, he knows that he's in for a *hard* day. (ibid.)

Both Satish and Malcolm were especially valued within the group for their role as stooge. Resistance to this role by any of the boys was almost impossible to achieve; indeed, negative reactions tended merely to make the insults even more intense. Ricky told me that the ability to take the jokes was part of being in the group. Individual control could be asserted only by shifting the focus onto someone else.

The in-group joking thus functioned as a boundary marker, serving to include members and exclude outsiders, although these categories tended to shift according to context and the constitution of the core group at any given moment. Nathan, for example, was hostile to Malcolm and to Frank; Frank and Satish were often antagonistic; almost all the boys, except Ricky, despised Shane. These members were thus open to more intensive group ridicule at particular moments and personal antagonisms were more openly displayed when these parties were together. Such personal tensions did not preclude, however, the smooth functioning of the group. As Shane constantly made clear, although he disliked most of the boys intensely on a personal level, considering them 'hypocrites' (Interview, 5 Apr. 1991), this did not prevent him being part of the group. He told me, 'They amuse me when I want to be amused; they're there for me to have a laugh if I want to have a laugh: that's it' (ibid.). Shane's view of the group was thus primarily functional and expressed its externally-directed purpose: 'We like going out, dancing, talking to girls sometimes: but you know that's not really the thing I have in common with them, it's the thing I do when I'm with them. . . . I'm with the crowd' (ibid.).

The perceived functionality of the collective marked out most responses to the peer group. All the boys denied that they would go to their friends if they had personal problems; all articulated their relationship primarily in terms of external forces. Frank assured me that this was very much a gender difference:

> Men are not like women. Women come home and go to their friends – 'I missed my period': men don't talk like that. Obviously they don't have their period, but a man won't come and go 'F[rank], there's something wrong downstairs'. A man won't say that – we just talk about normal things. (Interview, 5 Apr. 1991)

As mentioned earlier, private, personal knowledge of other members of the group was often very slight. Liebow notes in *Tally's Corner* that 'Friendship thus appears as a relationship between two people who, in an important sense, stand unrevealed to one another' (1967: 206). Amongst the boys, however, this private knowledge was considered largely irrelevant; what was of significance was the social function of the group. This is not to deny that within the group some close friendships did exist at the personal level; however, these were not the foundation of the group's existence.

Darnell, for example, explained of his friends: 'We are all after the same things when we go out together. Check women and all that . . . we all like the same sort of music, we all like rare groove and a bit of reggae' (Interview, 24 Mar. 1991). Although Darnell was very close to one friend, Richard – 'My mum says, "if D[arnell] tells you a lie in Harlesden, and you go round towards Willesden and ask R[ichard] the same thing, he'll tell you the same lie"' (ibid.) – this friendship was expressed in terms of mutual interest rather than personal, private support. Darnell told me: 'You don't talk to the guys about your problems. Because they just go "forget them, man, come on, let's check a next one [girl]"' (ibid.).

Unlike Liebow's assumption that without private knowledge such relationships 'do not stand up well to the stress of crisis and conflict of interest' (ibid.: 180), the group's relationships were primarily turned outwards and oppositional in their formation. They functioned, therefore, largely autonomously from personal relationships and in response to external forces. This partly accounts for the fluidity of group boundaries, which worked to include and exclude as occasion demanded. Thus, when Ricky got into a fight at Hombres, the other boys present were immediately there to assist him: on this occasion the boundaries of the group expanded to include Danny. Depending on the nature of the oppositional force, the boundaries would also expand to incorporate other groups or be incorporated. On one occasion, the boys were called upon to help exact retribution on a group of white youths who had attacked a black acquaintance of theirs. Ricky immediately assembled as many of the boys as he could find, who left to seek out the offenders; this time as part of a much larger body of people. Of course, the oppositional nature of the group did not necessitate conflict; the boys would unite as strongly to assist the others in attracting women as in fighting. It should be noted that 'oppositional' in this context refers to a relational position rather than a hostile and absolute distinction.

The group functioned, therefore, mainly in the public arena, and internal interaction remained largely between generally perceived public persona. [. . .] Amongst the boys, each had an internally ascribed role, which was enacted whenever an audience was present. Clive, for example, was seen as the loud, extrovert member of the group, who could always be relied upon to break the ice in any encounter. As Ricky told me:

C[live] has no conscience; he will go with any group of girls, or anything like that, and if I wanted C[live] to go and chat with a group of girls, I'd say 'C[live] let's go over there' and C[live] would go over there and he breaks the ice and then I move in, and N[athan] and A[rif] – the rest of the vultures move in. (Interview, 9 Dec. 1990)

Nathan was seen as the aggressive member of the group; Frank as the intellectual and pacifier, the 'father figure'; Satish as being good with women. Ricky was generally accepted by the others as most personifying the desired qualities of the public role – attractive, a good dancer, a strong fighter, and, until he met Anne, something of a womanizer. It is significant that this role had little to do with what the other members of the group thought of Ricky's abilities in the private arena, where most considered him unemployable, lazy, and exploitative. Moreover, the public persona had little to do with what the boys were like in one-to-one private interaction, where most were quiet, serious, and reflective. The public roles were to some extent interchangeable: on the boys' nights out, each member of the group acted at different times both as a spur to, and a constraint upon, the group's excesses. Each reflected, however, a different aspect of the group's personality and enacted its norms.

The norms and internal mores of the group were inculcated and relived whenever the boys met. This mainly took the form of what may be described as an internal mythology, composed of stories surrounding the notable successes and failures of the group. After most evenings out, the events of the night were retold, discussed, and placed in an overall group context; notable happenings then became part of an 'imagined' history, which was often recounted at these sessions. Through stories of victorious fights, successful liaisons with women, triumphs over hostile police encounters, the boys celebrated and reasserted their control of their immediate environment. They also relived notorious failures, such as the time Nathan was turned down by women in a club five times in a row, or the time he split his jeans while busting splits in a dance-off; the time Shane was beaten up in a club for chatting up someone's girlfriend; the time Frank and Mike (Ricky's brother) picked up two especially unattractive Italian girls, and Mike leapt off the bus to avoid being seen with them. These latter stories served to remind the group of the situations which were to be avoided, and encapsulated by their denial the norms they sought to uphold.

The peer group is thus perhaps best understood as a collection of individuals joined internally by a set of assumed shared values and welded in opposition to external forces. Although within the group, divisions and personality clashes did occur, these were largely irrelevant in the enactment of a common aim; that is, control over the public sphere. This was achieved largely through the creation of a public image focused around dance, dress, and the attraction of women. Although this image has been traditionally understood as an alternative status system (Folb, 1980; Liebow, 1967), it can also be seen as the extension of mainstream concerns; a means of actively engaging in, rather than opposing, traditional criteria of power and success.

External interaction

'The boys' can thus be seen primarily as an interactive force, achieving significance only in opposition to other groups. The means of interaction was not, however, uniform. It should be noted that, since it functioned only in the leisure arena, the main groups it faced were of similar age; it rarely confronted either older people or figures of authority, except occasionally the police. Amongst its contemporaries, group action differed according to both gender and 'racial' origin; it also altered according to the environment and, indeed, the constitution of the group and its dominant mood at any given time. The interaction with women, at both a group and individual level, will be considered later; it should be noted, however, that attitudes to women were an integral part of control in a wider sphere and were therefore partially reflected in the attitudes towards other men.

Black social events were usually marked by a lack of overt competition and the assertion of communal solidarity. The boys' actions within these contexts were normally characterized by almost a lack of interaction. The boundaries of the group became much less clearly defined and more fluid, and its members functioned more as a set of individuals than a bounded collectivity. They were less likely to roam the venue, or seek to dominate, as they did in other environments, generally preferring to stand, drink, and occasionally dance a little.

Reactions to other black groups within a predominantly white environment proved more ambiguous. On the one hand, the boys were reluctant to 'run' other black groups, and there was rarely any sense of conflict. In many places the boys frequented, they recognized and acknowledged other black men, and often entered into friendly exchanges with groups they encountered on the street. On one occasion, we met a group of young black men who were on their first excursion in the City. The boys approached and surrounded the youths, who looked only about 19 years old and seemed intimidated, but the banter remained amicable and almost protective, rather than confrontational. They discussed places to go, commented on the clothes the youths were wearing and generally behaved as city-wise mentors. A similar approach was adopted with the many black men they encountered walking through the West End, notably around the Leicester Square area. Talk was of parties, new venues, and encounters the other groups had had with the police or white groups. This exchange of information was, of course, only between men – women were generally excluded. As one black woman I met in such an encounter commented, when we were both ignored, 'Girl, that's what you get for hanging around with niggers.' Among the black men frequenting the West End, then, there existed some feeling of solidarity. Ricky told me:

> You tend to see that you don't go and start trouble with your own blacks, basically because you're black yourself. . . . I mean, black people are in enough trouble as it is – so you don't start on your own black person. (Interview, 9 Dec. 1990)

On the other hand, black men were seen as the first targets of competition. The boys would always measure themselves against other black men in terms of dress sense, dancing ability, and general presence; they would then seek either to ally themselves with the competition, or – more often – to annihilate it, usually through dancing. This can perhaps be best understood as a struggle for control of the stereotypical symbols of 'black' style, which were the main source of status within these environments. The major concern, therefore, centred around issues of control; on the boys' continued ability to 'run' a place and make their presence felt. If they were ever defeated or felt a loss of control, the group would not return to the site for many weeks or perhaps ever. It is revealing that the boys tended to avoid venues that attracted a large black presence. Such a presence was articulated as a sign of decay, yet should perhaps be placed within the context of increased pressure to compete and a corresponding loss of assured control.

The main source of confrontation within these environments was, inevitably, white men. Although, on the occasions I was with the group, there was rarely any trouble, the boys did generally behave provocatively towards white men, and in the past there had been a number of fights. Interaction was not, however, necessarily confrontational. On many occasions, the boys would engage white men in friendly, if challenging, banter and draw upon their shared experience as London youth, City employees, East Londoners to assuage any conflict. Such encounters were, however, almost always competitive. One of the favourite themes for 'discussion' was, inevitably, penis size and sexual competence. In these, the boys retreated to a racial characterization and focused upon women as the basis for their control. The white men they challenged were then forced to compete for this control, yet from a shared overtly masculine stance. In the absence of other groups, this sexual competition was continued within the group, though in a less provocative manner.

That such provocation was intentional and instrumental is undoubted. Ricky told me, 'You go out to have fun and cause trouble, that's basically it. . . . it's a way of releasing tension' (Interview, 9 Dec. 1990). Rather than directly starting fights, the boys would act in such a way as to provoke a response and then act upon this response. They thus exerted dual control:

first, in provoking action on the part of the white men and, secondly, through physical strength. The initial manipulation of response was a crucial part of this activity and did not necessarily need the physical element to prove satisfactory. Ricky explained:

> You start trouble with the white guys. . . . C[live] would be over there like a shot, telling them that they're motherfuckers and everything else. It's that sort of thing. Or you can see a guy with a drink and say 'Oh, thanks mate' and you start drinking it. It depends how the white guys see it; we don't go and pick trouble with white guys because you say 'yes, pick some trouble with some white guys'; we have a laugh with them, and if they take it seriously, *then* you fight them; that's the way it works. (ibid.)

It is significant that 'having a laugh' always meant provocation by the boys directed towards someone else. On the occasions I was with them, I never saw them allow this initiative to be taken by others and directed towards them. The need for external stimuli meant, however, that the group was always open to outsiders and to constant interaction. Both within and between social venues, therefore, the boys were constantly drawing others within their boundaries. This often occurred within the context of the street. As the boys moved between winebars and clubs, they would often stop other groups, male or female or mixed, and engage them in conversation, which usually remained friendly. On other occasions, however, the boys would rely on their size and perceived racial stereotypes to challenge people they met directly; this challenge was exclusively directed at other men, but would often use women to achieve this. As Ricky explained to me:

> Say we're like walking down the street, there might be a girl and a guy walking; you touch the girl and you don't care that she's walking with her husband or boyfriend. You don't care, you just did it, just for a laugh. (Interview, 9 Dec. 1990)

In these encounters, which took place exclusively in the predominantly white environment of 'the City', the boys often articulated 'race' as a primary marker of the group's self-definition. This was used to exclude other groups which were then set up in opposition, so that the limits of control could be tested. However, 'race' was not the sole factor shaping the group's existence; indeed, the peer group was often posited upon general perceptions of common background or aspirations, gender roles, or socio-economic factors. The significance of 'race' was most obviously elided in confrontation with other black groups in the City, where 'race' was a unifying factor and difference was created and maintained using alternative symbols. Ironically, however, competition between these groups focused upon ownership of symbols in which 'race' and 'masculinity' have become indistinguishable (Gilroy, 1993: 7). 'Control' in these situations thus carried with it the implication of wider power relations in which 'race' was an integral factor.

It is interesting to compare the boys' behaviour in the West End with that of Darnell and his friends, who functioned almost exclusively in predominantly black environments. Like the boys, Darnell's group encompassed a fairly fluid membership, but, unlike the boys, it constituted at its largest a community-based grouping. The boys were, by contrast, a geographically dispersed entity which was formulated only within the public social arena, rather than related to any latent sense of 'community'. On the level of everyday interaction, Darnell's group tended to be inclusive rather than exclusive and was not inclined towards the confrontation and competition which marked out many of the boys' encounters. It thus became more like Liebow's 'personal community' (1967: 162), in which a network of acquaintances forms a locus for personal action rather than group interaction; an expression of community rather than control. This inclusive personal network, indeed, exempted the individual from the need to exert control within particular situations. Darnell told me of one night when, returning from a friend's house, he was confronted by a group of black youths. He continued:

> I saw all of them and like, you know, they was all reaching for their knife and whatever, and I walked up close to them and goes 'yeah, so what you load going to do?' And I knew about five of them anyway. And they goes 'oh, we didn't realize it was you, you know'. And I go 'if you didn't recognize me, what would happen?'; 'Don't worry, man, we would have stopped'. (Interview, 24 Mar. 1991)

Because Darnell knew members of the group, who formed part of his extended 'personal community', neither side felt the need to enact a display of power. The boundaries of the group dissolved and enabled Darnell to form part of it, if only temporarily.

Similarly, the extended peer group was crucial as a source of community identity and security; in this role, it functioned in opposition to other groups. Darnell told me of one occasion when his group, consisting of about forty youths from Harlesden, went to a park near Wormwood Scrubs, where one was attacked by some other youths for talking to a girl. He told me:

> So next Sunday, there's about 100 people. . . . Can you imagine it, two guys and about 100 people running after them . . . and they were hitting them and they was getting kick up and bruck [sic] up some ways. . . . It was bad, bad. (ibid.)

It seems likely that the extended base of Darnell's peer group was more a matter of context than essential difference. Were his friends to function outside a black environment, the group would almost certainly become more tightly bounded. This, indeed, was the case even in unfamiliar black environments, as Darnell explained:

> If you was out in the sticks, right – in some club in the country, like Birmingham – then you'd all go round like bad men. And then when people look at you and they want to say something to you; when they know you're from Harlesden, then they won't say nothing to you. (ibid.)

It is significant that Darnell should choose a geographically-based group identity among other black groups: this can be contrasted with the primary definition of the boys' group as 'black' within a white environment.

It would be misleading, however, to see Darnell's group as entirely free from the search for control. Although, unlike the boys, they did not compete overtly with other men, the group was formulated primarily as a force for social interaction. The focus for this interaction was not, however, other male groups – black or white – but women. The group's structures, in a predominantly black context at least, thus tended to include men and define themselves against women; 'Gender' not 'Race' became the primary basis for identification. Within a mainly white environment, the boundaries of definition and self-definition proved more complex, incorporating 'racial' as well as gender considerations.

Conclusion

The male peer group should thus be seen neither as a naturally formed and harmonious entity, nor as a defensive enclave in which the inadequacies of the group in wider society are turned inwards both to compensate for and consolidate these shortcomings. For the boys, the peer group formed a basis for interaction with wider society at street level and enacted issues of control and status within this arena. It was a loosely-based collectivity, whose boundaries were fluid, and internal relations complex. This enabled the boys to interact with different social groupings at street level in an attempt to empower themselves. Its operation was thus oppositional and relational, altering its definition according to context. Within a predominantly black environment, the peer group could expand to provide a 'community' stance, or contract to two or three men in interaction with women. Within a mainly white environment, these boundaries became more rigid in their opposition to other men, and more antagonistic.

Inter-group competition is then a primary force in the enactment and subversion of power relations; images of 'masculinity' in this arena constituting the yardstick by which success is measured. 'Race' in these encounters becomes a symbol denoting group boundaries. It is employed in relation to other groups, usually, but not exclusively, as a means of opposition. 'Race' is not, however, a sufficient or necessary basis for peer group formation: its meaning may alter according to the situation or be cross-cut by other considerations, such as those based on gender or class constructions.

[. . .]

'Writing culture': the limits of analysis

A study of identity constitutes something of a chimera: it reifies a momentary transaction, fixes what is constantly in flux; it creates, almost by default, the very essence it claims to deny. If, as Hall claims, 'Cultural identity . . . is as much a matter of "becoming" as well as of "being"' (1990: 225), such a study cannot but represent an artificial foreclosure of an ongoing and constantly transforming process (Harvey, 1990).

The present study is, then, subject to a number of constraints, in its scope and enunciation. First, it makes no claims to 'objectivity', or to what Shelby Steele has termed 'innocence' (Duneier, 1992: 138), 'a feeling of essential goodness in relation to others and, therefore, superiority to others' (ibid.). Rather, the work recognizes and accepts that the accounts presented here are, to some extent, the result of a negotiated and unequal encounter between a number of constructed Subjects and myself. The selections and interpretations offered here are my own, from a range of self-constructions presented to me by my informants: to this extent, they are 'fiction' (Clifford, 1986). Secondly, the study recognizes that, in the act of writing, these selections are further mediated and distorted; Harvey thus quotes Baudelaire, 'Writing tears practice and discourse out of the flow of time' (1990: 206). In denying claims to 'Truth', the research offers no alternative; it merely acknowledges its implication in the process of ethnographic creation.

Thirdly, it bears repetition here that the study makes no pretence of, or claims to, representativeness. By seeking to reveal some of the complexities of Black British youth identities, the study lays emphasis more on process than content. It does not, therefore, contend that the encounters, experiences, and reactions recounted should be taken as a general statement about all black youth: indeed, that would be replacing one definition of 'being black' merely with another. On the other hand, however, the process of negotiation and search for control that marked out all of my informants' interactions should not be regarded as unique or unusual. I would argue further that the processes of self-invention described here are not specific to Black British youth, but are applicable to other 'minority' groups, as well as, of course, to the dominant hegemonic group.

What this study has attempted to show is the creation of identities amongst a small group of black youth at a particular moment in time. It is a snapshot of the lives I witnessed and shared for twelve months between 1990 and 1991. The study is thus necessarily bound by time and circumstance: it does not aim to provide a historical overview and is wary of making sweeping generalizations. More than this, it acknowledges that since the fieldwork was completed, the lives of my informants have moved on and their identity construction has accordingly undergone transformations beyond the scope of this study.

Notes

1. Similarly, David Schulz writes of the 'problem' of black masculinity as a direct extension of the 'problem' of the black family: 'The problem of the Negro lower-class family is . . . the absence of an *adequate* masculine role model *enabling adaptation to the values* of the larger culture' (1977: 10–11; emphasis in original). This leads to the retreat into street life, where masculine roles are exaggerated and played out in what Schulz terms a 'ritualised exorcism' (ibid: 15).

References

Anderson, E. (1978) *A Place on the Corner.* Chicago: University of Chicago Press.

Cashmore, E.E. (1979) *Rastaman: The Rastafarian Movement in England.* London: Allen and Unwin.

Clifford, J. (1986) 'Partial truths', in J. Clifford and G. Marcus (eds), *Writing Culture: The Poetics and Politics of Ethnography.* Berkeley and Los Angeles: University of California.

Cohen, A.K. (1955) *Delinquent Boys.* Chicago: Free Press.

Downes, D.M. (1966) *The Delinquent Solution.* London: Routledge and Kegan Paul.

Duneier, M. (1992) *Slim's Table.* Chicago: University of Chicago Press.

Folb, E. (1980) *Runnin' Down Some Lines: The Language and Culture of Black Teenagers.* Cambridge, MA: Harvard University Press.

Gilroy, P. (1993) *Small Acts.* London: Serpent's Tail.

Hall, S. (1990 'Cultural identity and diaspora', in J. Rutherford (ed.), *Identity: Community, Culture, Difference.* London: Lawrence & Wishart.

Hall, S. and T. Jefferson (eds) (1976) *Resistance through Ritual* (London: Hutchinson).

Hannerz, U. (1969) *Soulside: Enquiries into Ghetto Culture and Community.* New York: Columbia University Press.

Harvey, D. (1990) *The Condition of Postmodernity.* Oxford: Basil Blackwell.

Hebdige, D. (1979) *Subculture: The Meaning of Style.* London: Methuen.

hooks, b. (1992) *Black Looks.* London: Turnaround Press.

Jones, J. (1992) 'The accusatory space', in G. Dent (ed.) *Black Popular Culture.* Seattle, WA: Bay Press.

Lawrence, E. (1982), ' "In the abundance of water the fool is thirsty": sociology and black "pathology" ', in Centre for Contemporary Cultural Studies, *The Empire Strikes Back.* London: Hutchinson.

Liebow, E. (1967) *Tally's Corner: A Study of Negro Street-Corner Men.* Boston, MA: Little, Brown & Co.

Matza, D. (1964) *Delinquency and Drift.* New York: John Wiley.

Mercer, K. (1988) 'Racism and the politics of masculinity', in R. Chapman and J. Rutherford (eds), *Male Order: Unwrapping Masculinity*. London: Lawrence & Wishart.

Pryce, K. (1967) *Endless Pressure*. Harmondsworth: Penguin.

Schulz, D. (1977) 'Growing up as a boy in the ghetto', in D.Y. Wilkinson and R. Taylor (eds), *The Black Male in America*. Chicago: Nelson Hall.

Segal, L. (1990) *Slow Motion: Changing Masculinities, Changing Men*, London: Virago.

Taylor, R.L. (1977) 'Socialization to the black male role', in D.Y. Wilkinson and R. Taylor (eds), *The Black Male in America*. Chicago: Nelson Hall.

Wallace, M. (1990) *Black Macho and the Myth of the Superwoman*. London: Verso.

Willis, P. (1977) *Learning to Labour*. Farnborough: Saxon House.

Willis, P. (1978) *Profane Culture*. London: Routledge and Kegan Paul.

Wilmott, P. (1966) *Adolescent Boys of East London*. London: Routledge and Kegan Paul.

Part III

Workplace practices

5

Manufacturing sexual subjects: 'harassment', desire and discipline on a Maquiladora shopfloor

Leslie Salzinger

On first entrance, the shopfloor is eerily familiar: the nubile women workers of managerial dreams and feminist ethnography, theory and nightmare are brought to life in its confines. Rows of them, darkened lashes lowered to computer boards, lids fluttering intermittently at hovering supervisors who monitor finger speed and manicure, concentration and hair style, in a single glance. Apparent embodiments of availability – cheap labor, willing flirtation – these young women have become the paradig-matic workers for a transnational political economy in which a highly sexualized form of femininity has become a standard 'factor of production' (Benería and Roldán, 1987; Elson and Pearson, 1986; Fernandez-Kelly, 1983; Fuentes and Ehreneich, 1983; Iglesias Prieto, 1987; Kamel, 1990; Sklair, 1993; Standing, 1989).

In this context, allegations of 'sexual harassment' surface repeatedly among critics and journalists, sitting uneasily amidst reports of job loss in the first world and exploitative wages and male unemployment in the third. However, few have stopped to investigate the relationship between the sexualization and the cheapening of production or its role in the transformation of working women into 'nimble fingers'. Within this ana-lytic vacuum, the language of sexual harassment serves to obscure more than it illuminates, as it focuses our attention on isolated, aberrant, generally dyadic interactions, rather than on social and organizational processes.

Although I spent 18 months doing participant observation in Mexico's border, export-processing ('maquila')[1] industry, it was during the months I spent in Panoptimex,[2] the plant described above, that I first began having difficulty responding to journalistic questions about sexual harassment. In Panoptimex, sexuality is an integral part of the fabric of production, an

This article was previously published in *Ethnography* (2000) 1(1): 67–92 essential aspect of the process through which labor is transformed into labor power and women into the 'docile and dextrous' workers of transnational repute. Within this context, there is nothing out of the ordinary about sexuality on the shopfloor. On the contrary, it is a fundamental element of the efficient operation of labor control and hence of production itself. Ironically therefore, it is only through removing the lens of 'sexual harassment,' with its focus on individual perpetrators and unwilling victims, that it becomes possible to see the role of sexuality on the shopfloor – that is to discern the systematic role of desire in constituting productive workers.

This is not to say that the journalists' repeated inquiries had no basis. Certainly, 'sexual harassment', as conventionally understood (cf. Fitzgerald's definition of the term as 'unwanted sex-related behavior at work that is appraised by the recipient as offensive, exceeding her resources, or threatening') (Fitzgerald et al., 1997: 15, quoted in Welsh, 1999: 172), is a problem in the maquila industry – as it is in a wide variety of industries and cultural contexts (Gruber et al., 1996). However, their questions envisioned psychologically or morally troubled individuals, impelled by obstreperous libidos, secretly targeting unwilling individual victims. In this framework, the organization is obscured by the image of the 'offender' and the ongoing constitution of consent is similarly hidden by the image of the 'victim'. Such a lens reveals important workplace problems, but in focusing attention on the isolated, closeted dyad, it impedes investigation of more social and systemic manifestations of shopfloor sexuality.

The academic literature on 'sexual harassment' is built upon many of the same underlying assumptions (Stockdale, 1996b; Welsh, 1999; Williams et al., 1999). The field is dominated by lawyers and psychologists, hence individuals – both 'targets' and 'perpetrators' – rather than organizations, become units of analysis. Frequently, this tendency is accentuated methodologically, as most analysts, whatever their disciplinary origin, recruit a cross-section of the population to survey or participate in experiments, rather than interviewing or observing people located within a single workplace.[3] This leads to a set of questions about the statistical likelihood of particular sorts of people harassing or being harassed, specific individuals' tendency to label these interactions as 'harassment' and predicted resiliency of 'targets' in the face of harassment. Even in studies where organizational structure is an explicit issue (Gruber, 1998; Hulin et al., 1996), workplaces themselves are treated as individual units within a set and sorted by particular characteristics, rather than investigated as productive wholes.

Just as the emphasis on individual perpetrators distracts researchers from analysing the role of sexuality in the workplace as a whole, so the emphasis on individual victims obscures the more subtle role of sexuality in the constitution of shopfloor consent.[4] Thus, investigators tend to focus on the impact of shopfloor sexualization on those explicitly targeted, at the expense of analysing its meaning for workers overall. Similarly, they highlight blatant coercion, and in so doing neglect situations in which women workers are successfully interpellated as sexual objects and so respond affirmatively, even enthusiastically, to being addressed as such (Althusser, 1971).[5,6,7]

In recent decades, the term sexual harassment has served an important intellectual and political function, drawing our attention to the common sexual coercion of women at work. However, precisely because of its capacity to name the problem, it has effectively come to stand in for all problematic workplace sexuality. As a result, its essentially psychological rather than social perspective increasingly constrains our capacity to analyse the role of sexuality in the workplace more fully. 'Sexual harassment' implies a process that is an intrusion in the workplace, rather than an integral part of production. That is, it highlights isolated, hidden, individual interactions at the expense of systemic, visible and structural processes. In addition, by focusing on dyadic interactions, it leads to questions about individual choices and the allocation of blame, rather than about the way in which a given workplace evokes particular sexual subjectivities in managers and workers alike. In so focusing our attention, it has come to impede our ability to investigate other manifestations of sexual exploitation at work.

Panoptimex

Panoptimex is a highly successful TV producer, a subsidiary of Electroworld, an enormous electronics transnational.[8] Since moving into its new building several years ago, the plant has been remarkably successful. Its production quantities and quality levels rival those produced by the same corporation at far higher cost in the United States. Recently, another TV assembler in the area, in the Mexican border city of Juárez, was so taken by its results (and look) that it bought the building blueprints for its second plant.

This success is directly, if unintentionally, related to the extreme sexual objectification of the plant's workforce. Visually oriented managers have created a structure of labor control in which everything is designed to produce the right look. In the process, they have designed a machine that evokes and focuses the male gaze in the service of production (Berger, 1972; Mulvey, 1975). The building is a panopticon, an architecture designed to control through visibility, a visibility that is ultimately as much about fostering self-consciousness as it is about the more mundane operations of super-vision. The logic which designed it is also at work in populating and managing it. Thus, a generation of managers accustomed to electronics factories full of young women have taken care to fill their own factory accordingly.

Labor control operates within this visually oriented context. The enactment of managerial practices based on men obsessively watching young women creates a sexually charged atmosphere, one in which flirtation and sexual competition become the currency through which shopfloor power relations are struggled over and fixed. In this framework, women are constituted as desirable objects and male managers as desiring subjects. Male workers become not-men, with no standing in the game. Far from impeding production, aggressive, often coveted, supervisorial sexual attention is the element through which labor control operates. Hence, in Panoptimex we find a workplace in which sexuality is integral to production, not an intrusion upon it. Rather than impairing efficiency through myriad isolated and closeted encounters, sexuality is made a highly visible and central element in the labor control process. Here, TVs are produced, not through the excision of distracting sexuality, but through the ongoing, systemic incitement of desire in production.

Over-seers

The structure of production on any given shopfloor is initially imagined and established by management. In the maquila industry, where capital faces a disorganized workforce and a captive state apparatus, this situation is particularly acute. These first decisions do not ensure managerial control, but they do set the context within which struggles over control will take place. Thus, in analysing the role of gender in production, we turn first to management: to the frameworks within which managerial 'common sense' is established and to the strategies that emerge from this cluster of understandings.

In Panoptimex, this common sense is remarkable for its consistent bias toward visual signs and symbols of success or failure. Management's visually skewed attention is the product of a cluster of forces – forces that are both institutional and discursive. Standard maquila accounting practices, the erosion of profit margins in the production of low-end TVs and the high internal mobility of top Electroworld managers combine to undermine a focus on costs and profits for their own sake and to encourage a focus on impressing headquarters instead. At the same time, these institutional predilections are solidified and underlined by the more general, visual rhetoric of TV production, in which 'the picture' is the frame within which everything is understood and evaluated.

This attitude has distinct consequences when it is turned from managers' bosses to their subordinates. Once focused 'down' – both literally and metaphorically – this visual attention is transformed into the gaze of sexual objectification. The focus on the 'look' of the factory, combined with a long tradition of women workers in electronics, leads to a rigid form of job-gendering, one in which filling the lines with young women becomes a goal in itself. Together, these institutional routines and attentional habits lead to a highly sexualized pattern of hiring and labor control – a pattern that, as we will see below, ultimately proves both pleasurable and titillating (if also disturbing) for the young women on the shopfloor, and in part because of this, proves remarkably effective in shopfloor control.

Projecting up

Production at Panoptimex occurs in a highly symbolic system, one in which appearances are as much the currency as dollars. To an extent, this is an issue throughout the industry. Most maquilas are far from any point of sale and their accounting systems are organized to 'make their budget'[9] rather than to make a profit. As a result, local managers find themselves more subject to the managers at corporate headquarters than to external competition. Their energy is directed accordingly. However, in Panoptimex, the tendency to make headquarter approval the primary goal of work on a daily as well as long-term basis is particularly accentuated. In just one example of this pattern, late in my sojourn in the factory, Electroworld was forced by international creditors to cut its workforce 10 percent across the board. The response in Panoptimex was a major effort – a bookkeeping effort however. No one was fired. No money was saved. But 10 percent of salaries were moved to the 'miscellaneous' category of the budget. Looking credible was enough, there was no countervailing price or profit pressure direct enough to undermine this entirely symbolic solution.

Two sets of institutional forces, intense price competition in the international TV industry and Electroworld career trajectories, frame Panoptimex's operations and evoke these responses. The first of these, the low profit margin in TV production, is a rarely discussed backdrop against which daily decisions are made on the shopfloor. 'TVs are not a business', the manager of Electrofeed, a local Electroworld parts-maker, tells me early on. 'If you had to face stockholders with only a TV business . . .', he shakes his head. The profit margin on the low-end TVs produced by Panoptimex are so slim, according to the plant manager Carlos Rodrigues, that making the budget frequently means literally selling below cost. So, why produce TVs at all? Because, he explains, it's worth it to Electroworld to keep its name in the marketplace in general. Once that's accomplished, profit can be made elsewhere – in VCRs, for instance. Here, it's not only Panoptimex managers who treat costs symbolically. The overall corporate decision to continue TV production is predicated on the calculation that it is worth it even under conditions in which it may not turn a profit on its own.

This sense among Panoptimex managers that appearances are paramount, and that the relevant audience is headquarters, is further encouraged by Electroworld's corporation-wide, managerial placement policies. Electroworld is an American subsidiary of an even larger European corporation. Panoptimex managers report to bosses in the United States, but their personal career trajectories move throughout the corporation as a whole. Top managers around the world are brought in for several-year periods and then moved on to keep them from being overly attached to – and hence losing their 'objectivity' about – the factory they're running. As one of them explained matter-of-factly, 'The truth is I'd get less emotional about fighting for this place than for my little radio plant in England'. This external staffing policy has obvious implications for the perspective of those, the current Panoptimex manager among them, brought in from the outside. Carlos is a Brazilian on a three-year contract. He began with Electroworld in Manaus, but most recently ran a plant in Singapore. He makes quite clear that his sights are set far above Panoptimex. He spends the better part of a first interview discussing details of the corporate structure and explaining where he'd like to be and when. These are no idle daydreams. His attention is firmly fixed on those who have the power to move him where he'd like to be.

These institutional patterns: a market in which profits cannot be the primary criteria for success; a structure of career opportunities in which top managers are not deeply tied to 'their' factories; and a set of accounting practices which formalize local managers' absolute reliance upon head-quarters, together encourage a highly symbolic attitude toward production. TVs still must be produced – if possible without huge cost overruns and of reasonable quality. However, top management attempts all this with an eye focused neither on 'the consumer' nor on 'the competition' but on the boss.

Seeing is believing

The institutional patterns described above *encourage* a focus on appear-ances, however they certainly do not ensure it. There is no question that these institutional structures are far more common among Juárez maquilas than is the plant's overwhelming focus on the look of things. What makes these structures so significant here is that they create an appearance directed context within which the visual rhetoric available in TV produc-tion can, and does, frame managerial perspectives on the shopfloor. In listening to Panoptimex managers, the sight-related criteria through which success and failure are assessed is striking and pervasive. Ultimately, this visual rhetoric is both symptomatic, and constitutive, of the habit of watching as a practice of control.

The general visual focus held throughout the factory emerges almost obsessively in Carlos's conversation – most clearly as the centerpiece of his triumphal autobiography. It erupts in a set of photos – pulled with practiced gesture from a top desk drawer – of a factory he ran in Singapore. 'It was all shit, just shit, girls working with garbage all around. Dark, ugly, I change all that. We paint, we make it nice.' He slams down the before-and-after pictures for emphasis, expostulating on the importance of color scheme and pointing out details of the shift. The color scheme is of particular importance, he points out, and his first act on arrival in Juárez was to paint Panoptimex in identical tones. His commentary on more daily management reveals the same emphasis. He discusses his capacity to see production from his office window at great length, describing calls down to supervisors on the floor to check on problems and remind them he is watching. This focus is even expressed when he discusses the importance of politic ignorance. Covering an eye with his hand he comments, 'I have to keep my eyes closed here all the time.'

This visual idiom of control is most clearly embodied in the physical structure of the shopfloor. Clean, light, spacious and orderly – the production area is the very image of a 'well-run' factory. Top managers are highly aware of, and invested in, this fact and they often boast about its attractiveness. The factory floor is not only easy on the eye however. It is *organized* for visibility – a fish bowl in which everything is marked. Yellow tape lines the walkways, red arrows point at test sites, green, yellow and red lights glow above the machines. On the walls hang large, shiny white graphs documenting quality levels in red, yellow, green and black. Just above each worker's head is a chart – one defect, three defects, perfect days. Workers' bodies too are marked: yellow tunics for new workers; light blue tunics for women workers; dark blue smocks for male workers and mechanics; orange tunics for (female) 'special' workers, red tunics for (female) group chiefs; ties for supervisors. Everything is signalled.

Ringing the top of the production floor is a wall of windows, a manager behind every one. They sit in the semi-privacy of the reflected glare, watching at will. From on high, they 'keep track of the flow of production', calling down to a supervisor to ask about a slow-down, easily visible from above in the accumulation of TVs in one part of the line, gaps further along, or in a mound of sets in the center of a line, technicians clustered nearby. It is from here that they show the factory to visitors, standing on the glassed-in balcony boasting about the plant's large capital investment and unique labor process. At one point, men with cameras watched for stealing from behind the glass walls, and it's common knowledge on the shopfloor that there are still cameras embedded in the ceilings for this purpose. They've set it up so that even the walls have eyes.

Hiring for looks

Panoptimex managers' focus on the look of things is expressed particularly clearly in the plant's gendered hiring practices. During the five years since Electroworld began producing entire TVs, including the two years since that process was moved into this showcase factory, years in which there was a dramatic 'shortage'[10] of young female labor in Juárez, they have virtually never had under 70 percent women on the line, rarely under 75 percent. The average age on the shopfloor continues to be under 20, and they have yet to place a man in the chassis-building section.

When asked about their absolute commitment to hiring women for most line jobs, Panoptimex managers tend to point out that electronics – certainly Electroworld – *always* hires women, whatever country they're in. Panoptimex's last manager comments matter-of-factly, 'electronics traditionally used female types', when I ask about the decision to hire women even when they're much harder to find than men. Other upper managers tell similar narratives.[11] Supervisors request not only the number of workers they need for their line, but the gender of each position as well. The personnel department puts a great deal of daily planning and energy into hiring the 'right' gender for the jobs available. The head of personnel in the plant details criteria for most line jobs, beginning with being female and young and continuing with slimness, thin hands and short nails. The criteria also include not being pregnant, using birth control and being childless or (if absolutely necessary) having credible childcare arrangements. The most basic of these requirements is being female, closely followed by a particular, sexualized body type and, as a result, on hiring days guards admit all the female applicants who come to the maquila gates, but only a previously specified number of men. The few men hired for what are known as the line 'heavy' jobs are not subject to the bodily strictures required of their female counterparts, but in their place are a substantially more demanding set of social requirements. Unlike their female co-workers, they need to be vouched for by the union or someone else already known in the plant, and they must present a certificate of high school graduation.

These criteria and practices are not unheard of among other Juárez maquilas. What sets Panoptimex apart is the lengths to which its managers went to ensure a female workforce even during the shortage of young women workers in the late 1980s, as their colleagues in other maquilas reluctantly began hiring men. Panoptimex managers decided to try to recruit workers from a village with an 'agrarian economy' an hour out of the city. In an extended 'PR' campaign involving all levels of the personnel department as well as top managers from other departments, they first courted the mayor, then treated the whole village to a picnic with mariachis, then knocked on all 150 doors in the village with pictures of the plant, and finally agreed to pay transportation for all young women willing to come to work in the factory. Four years later, these young women still work the lines, and Panoptimex is still paying for their transport.

Managers' framework in Panoptimex is relentlessly visual, and this perspective is expressed not only in their dealings with their superiors, but in their hiring and labor control practices as well. As a result, they hire assembly line workers who are overwhelmingly female and young – the age to be beautiful, and to be invested in that beauty – and then monitor them through obsessive observation. The essence of their hiring criteria is most succinctly expressed by a woman supervisor in another Electroworld plant, 'In Panoptimex they don't look for workers, they look for models – short skirts, heels, beauties . . .'. Not that Panoptimex workers are, at least not to my eye, more beautiful than young women in other maquilas. However, Panoptimex workers *are* hired as 'models' – hired to look the way managers expect workers to look. Sexual objectification is part and parcel of the hiring process.

In the fishbowl

Panoptimex managers' focus on control through vigilance is expressed throughout the factory in a hierarchy of sight. While top managers sit behind windows above the shopfloor, supervisors walk the lines below. And as supervisors walk the shopfloor, workers sit before them. In front of workers however, there is only their work and their individualized quality charts – co-workers glimpsed from the corners of their eyes. Shopfloor control is orchestrated through a set of embedded panopticons – managers watch supervisors and workers, supervisors watch (most) workers, workers watch themselves and, when they can, each other.

This picture is not the only one one might draw of this scene however. One might also describe men watching men watching women (and ignoring a few emasculated men). Or, one might more accurately include both these social realities: a panopticon in which male managers watch male supervisors watch women workers and ignore a few male workers. The hierarchy of sight is as defined by gender as it is by the relations of production, with predictable sexual effects.

Managers' attentional practices and the physical space they have spawned have constituted a highly visual system of labor control – a system that differentially affects women workers – the central objects of supervisorial attention – and male workers – the objects of their aggressive disregard. Although it can be described with no reference to sexuality, the tremendous interpellatory power of the plant's system of labor control comes from its organization of desire. Even the most cursory tour of the shopfloor reveals an intensely sexualized atmosphere, and conversations with workers only add to this impression. These subjectivities in turn have repercussions for the level of managerial control on the shopfloor, accounting both for the shopfloor's intense atmosphere of titillation and control and for its highly successful production record.

Super-vising

Unlike Electroworld's other maquilas in Juárez, Panoptimex produces a final product. From the beginning to the end of its long, looping lines, hundreds of tiny components are combined with monitors and cabinets to emerge as TVs, ready for sale. Production takes place in five long, looping lines – each one a perfect replica of the next. One hundred and twenty workers make up each line. Backs to their supervisors, eyes to their work, they repeat the same gestures a thousand times during the 9½ hour day.

The first part of the line assembles the TVs innards. This is chassis, the plant's most 'critical' operation. Here, several hundred miniature electronic parts are inserted into pre-punctured boards. The work is done by 40 seated young women, each of whom inserts 6–8 tiny, color-coded parts every 30-second 'cycle.' From there, the chassis is tested before moving on to the end of the line where ten young men, standing, attach it to monitors and cabinets. Turning the corner into 'final', the now recognizable TV re-enters the women's domain. Here the electrical system is assembled, wires soldered and twisted – the facsimile made real. On to the 'tunnel', where young women peer at the screen seeking straight lines, 90-degree angles and clear pinks and greens. Finally, the TV is ready for use. Once again, it moves into male territory at the line's end. Here it is packed, boxed and marked with one of a half-dozen brand names, finally rising to the ceiling in a glass tube and vanishing from sight. Soon it will re-emerge in warehouses on the other side of the border, last stop before the large chains that bring it to consumers throughout the United States.

As in almost all maquilas, the workers who produce these TVs are paid poorly even in local terms. Most workers took home roughly 40 dollars weekly during the period I studied the plant.[12] This is not a negligible amount of money, but it is well below what would be required to live independently in Juárez, and even this is contingent on perfect attendance. Missing a single day of work costs a third of the weekly paycheck. Seniority doesn't shift this, as promotion is extremely rare. As a result, three-quarters of the workforce is replaced over the course of the year. Not surprisingly, in this context, most workers are teenagers and live with family. Given this pay structure, labor control cannot depend too heavily on financial incentives or the hope of promotion. This is where the tremendous scrutiny under which workers operate in the plant, and the sexual self-consciousness that emerges from that scrutiny, becomes fundamental.

Lines are 'operator controlled'. The chassis comes to a halt in front of the worker, she inserts her components, and pushes a button to send it on. There is no piece rate, no moving assembly line, to hurry her along. But she hurries anyway. In this fishbowl, no one is willing to be seen with the clogged line behind her, an empty space ahead of her, managers peering from their offices above. And if she does slow momentarily, the supervisor materializes. 'Ah, here's the problem. What's wrong, my dear?' He circles behind seated workers, monitoring 'his girls' as he is monitored from above.

There are layers upon layers of supervision. Above the shopfloor hover those known below as 'the Americans' – top managers who, for all their varied origins, are marked by the US headquarters to which they report. Their presence is often noted by workers and supervisors seeking to explain the difference between Electroworld plants. A Mexican assistant personnel manager comments, '[at Panoptimex] there are visitors all the time, and the windows all around . . . all the time you know they're watching you.' And they do not only watch from afar. In the late afternoons Carlos and his chief of production descend to see more closely. Hands clasped behind backs they stroll the plant floor, stopping to berate a supervisor about a candy-wrapper lying on the floor or to chat with workers on the line.

Below the production manager are the supervisors. Two to each line, they are all Mexicans, all men,[13] most in their early 30s, all but one with some technical or managerial training. Both watching and watched, they are particularly sensitive to, and reflective of, the prevailing visual idiom in the plant. After several months in the plant, one supervisor told me of pervasive rumors among them that my car, a 15-year-old Ford with a smashed-up front, had an incredible motor camouflaged beneath its battered exterior. This visual expression of distrust, the assumption that something was hidden from the eye, expressed both their vulnerable position in the plant hierarchy and their immersion in a world of visual signs and symbols. True to this focus, they spend virtually all day standing just behind workers' shoulders – watching. They alternately compliment efficiency and deride mistakes, decide who can still work if they arrive late and who can't, initiate and bar conversations, commandeer and offer forbidden candies, lecture and cajole whenever quality or speed falter. Their attentions are not evenly distributed however. Although they are responsible for their entire half of the line, supervisors in chassis can generally be found in the section where components are inserted by hand, and supervisors in final can be found in the testing tunnel. That is, they hang out where the girls are.

The sense of being watched comes not only from being looked at in the moment, but through the managerial production of signs and symbols that are then available for surveillance. Above each worker's head is a chart, fully visible to her at all times, as well as to anyone walking by. Group leaders fill them out each day. Gold stars mark perfection. Green dots mark errors. Red dots mark trouble. This sense of exposure has consequences for workers' sense of self, and self-worth. A woman whose chart is full of green and red dots comments, 'I feel ashamed. It's all just competition. You look at the girl next to you and you want to do better than she does even though it shouldn't matter.' At the end of every day, announcements echo over the shopfloor as each line finishes its daily thousand TVs. In lines far from their quota, the group leader begins circulating anxiously at 3:00, an hour before shift's end, saying they should 'get a move on' or they'll be the only line who doesn't make it. The line always picks up speed at this point. When I ask a young woman generally notable for her jaundiced attitude what's going on, she shrugs: 'When they start congratulating the other lines for having finished and we haven't, you feel bad. Competition makes you work harder.'

Labor control in Panoptimex is achieved through practices – primarily but not exclusively visual – that speak directly to workers' sense of self. Whatever their center of attention in any single situation, managers' ultimate goal in the factory is to see that TVs get built to their bosses' satisfaction. They achieve this somewhat indirectly however, by focusing on who workers are, rather than on the work they do. In this process, worker subjectivities are directly addressed, and their success or failure as workers is easily conflated with their success or failure as human beings in general. This merging of workers' work and personal identities gives management tremendous leverage on the shopfloor.

This is not the whole story however. This leverage is achieved neither by addressing a concrete 'worker' identity nor a more abstract 'human' identity. The set of subjectivities addressed on the Panoptimex shopfloor are highly heterosexualized, and the narrative of shopfloor quiescence told above only begins to make sense as we investigate the substance of the subjectivities that are constituted and spoken to in the panopticon. Thus, in the pages that follow, I will retell the story above with the 'empty places' (Burawoy, 1979: 150) filled – investigating the impact, not of bosses watching workers, but of male bosses watching young female workers, of the male gaze in the service of managerial control. It is here that the depth of shopfloor control becomes comprehensible.

Ogling and dis-regarding

The visually-defined practices that typify labor control in this plant are imbued with sexual energies and gendered meanings when they are practiced in this girl-filled, guy-dotted space. Inside the panopticon, managers and supervisors are situated as voyeurs, while women workers are at the center of attention. Monitoring becomes the gaze of sexual objectification as soon as it locks upon them. Male workers, on the other hand, are at the periphery, beneath notice. Neither watching nor watched, they are as emasculated as their female co-workers are objectified. Thus, the visually-defined practices described above frame a highly sexualized set of meanings in and for production.

Supervisorial subjectivity reflects and embodies this symbolic framework. As the plant's official watchers in this gendered space, they, as much as their charges, are located in a sexual relationship. This is expressed in their initial self-presentation, as well as in their routinized daily behaviors. They are generally married with children, yet they openly flout their marriages on the shopfloor, and their children make appearances only in joking references to their manhood. They are required to wear ties, and from the booted, blue-jeaned 'cowboy' to the 'serious professional' they each stamp their line with an idiosyncratic version of this symbol of masculine predominance.

Beneath the gaze of these monitors, female and male workers are incorporated into production in distinctive ways. They are given different identification numbers, different uniforms, different jobs and are subject to different modes of supervision. Women do 'detail' work such as inserting components and checking quality; men do 'heavy' work such as assembling the cabinet and packing the finished product. On top of this base, other differences arise. Women sit, men stand. The center of the line is a female domain, its ends are male. 'Chassis', where there is a 1 to 15 ratio of group leaders to workers, is all women. 'Final', where there is a 1 to 27 ratio, is almost half men. Within final, the group leader does all communication with the men. This leaves the supervisor free to spend all his time with the women in his line. The cumulative, symbolic and practical effects of these differences are overwhelming. Women are central – watched, constrained, pinned down. Men are de-centered – ignored and relatively free to move.

The differences between men and women – and (also therefore) the meanings of femininity and masculinity in the plant – are marked as much by ongoing managerial behavior as by their initial setup in the structure of production. Every afternoon, Carlos walks the lines, all masculine and proprietary expansiveness, and 'jokes' with women workers – those who would be 'men' on the line he ignores. Among the women too, only some are recognized. As he walks, he stops and talks to an ever-changing favored few. These conversations are flirtatious and titillating, full of teasing on both sides, mild, blushing self-revelations on the part of workers, and pseudo-paternal supportiveness on his part. He does not stop at speaking either. It is well known in the plant that he has a mistress on the lines, as does the chief of production. Thus, every conversation is tinged by ambiguity and the flavor of forbidden sexuality.

The plant manager is not alone in this. His example is echoed down through the ranks, and in any case follows in a plant tradition that predates his tenure. Non-hourly workers, from low-level engineers on up, prowl the lines in search of entertainment of all sorts. In this context, supervisors take full advantage of their superior access. One of the workers favored by Carlos's attentions comments pitilessly on her co-workers. She reports that the supervisor on her line propositions everyone, and that some make the mistake of going out with him hoping that it will lead to promotions. Not she, however. It's obvious he's very 'hard' about all that. Another supervisor has a worker pregnant and is currently dating another, both on his line. As the due-date draws near, personnel staff tease him flirtatiously, threatening to tell his wife or throw him a baby-shower. He struts complacently. The norm is best encapsulated by workers' approving comments on one of his (also married) colleagues, who all agree is different from the others. 'Why, as far as I know', says one woman, 'He's only gone out steadily with one girl on his line, none of this using all the operators (i.e. workers).'

Supervisors not only use their position in production for sexual access, they also use a highly sexualized discourse around workers as a means of labor control. It is striking to watch them wandering their lines, monitoring efficiency and legs simultaneously – their gaze focused sometimes on fingers at work, sometimes on the nail polish that adorns them. Often supervisors will stop by a favorite operator – chatting, checking quality, flirting. Their approval marks 'good worker' and 'desirable woman' in a single gesture. Each supervisor has a few workers he hangs around with, laughing and gossiping throughout the day. It is not lost on their co-workers that these favorites eventually emerge elsewhere, in slightly higher paid positions on the line as well as among those with the self-confidence to enter the plant beauty contest. Through each day, managers and supervisors frame women workers as sexual beings, and sexual objects. In this process, women workers become vulnerable to personal, as well as work-based, evaluations.

Women workers are not the only ones controlled through heterosexual discourses. Sexuality is also the arena in which managers and supervisors struggle for predominance – both in individual cases and in the larger symbolic context. The shopfloor is rife with complaints by both supervisors and managers of ways in which the other group's sexuality undermines shopfloor discipline. One supervisor complains that Carlos's tendency to talk to some and not others undermines 'motivation' on the line. Another tells of being forced by the production manager to allow a worker in on a day she arrived late. 'OK', he reports agreeing resentfully, 'But then I'm not the supervisor any more.' There are stories of a line where the production manager's mistress throws her weight around, making the other girls cry and remaining exempt from sanction. And then there's the European O&E manager for Juárez commenting, 'In the Mexican environment . . . you can imagine what are the other things a young girl can offer to a supervisor . . . we've tried to crack down, but within the limits of the culture . . . macho is strong here.' In these incidents, supervisors and managers jostle for control of the shopfloor in order to legitimate and affirm their masculinity – which in this panopticon is about sexual mastery (or in the case of the European manager, about mastering their sexuality); and they jostle for control of women workers in order to legitimate and affirm their shopfloor power. In the process, a configuration of production and labor control processes are established that are as much about gender and sexuality as they are about efficiency and TVs.

These struggles over and through the mantle of masculinity also mark relations between management and male workers, although it's an unequal battle from the outset. Top managers casually belittle men who work on the line. Jones, the Juárez personnel manager, offhandedly exempts male line workers from the category of 'men' in explaining why they are not included in his general policy to pay men more than women: 'From a macho standpoint, a guy wouldn't take an operator's job.' Supervisors are less offhand, but equally scathing in their assertions. A supervisor finding a young man behind one afternoon is withering in his commentary, 'Just like I said, you have to keep an eye on these guys. He thinks he's some kind of Latin Lover . . .'. His target, a shy young man new to Juárez, looks at his shoes.

The managerial claims remain far more potent than that of male workers, in large part because they are reasserted in the structure of daily life in the factory. Just as women workers are disciplined within an essentially visual framework, so are their male co-workers. However, rather than being placed at the center of an immobilizing optic, male workers are relegated to its periphery – actively ignored. Men are physically segregated, standing at the line's ends. The plant manager does not even slow down as he passes them during his daily perambulations, and the supervisor is conspicuous in his absence.

Emasculation does undercut male workers' capacity to resist, but as a mode of control, disregard also has its dangers for management. Men on the line are subject to little direct supervision. They move relatively freely, trading positions among themselves and covering for each other during extra bathroom runs, joking and laughing, catcalling women as they pass by. Nonetheless, male workers' relatively autonomous physical location, while permitting some freedom of movement and the enactment of a few masculine rituals, also provides a powerful tool for managerial control. Supervisors can always move them out of male territory, and occasionally they do just that. When men on the line get too cocky, the supervisor materializes and brings it to a halt. Abruptly he moves the loudest of them, placing them in soldering where they sit in conspicuous discomfort among the 'girls' while the others make uneasy jokes about how boring it is 'over there'. Ultimately, the supervisor has the last word in masculinity. Male workers can challenge his behavior, but he can reclassify them as women. In such moments, he retains control precisely through this capacity to throw into question young male workers' localized gender and sexual identities.

Productivity at Panoptimex is born of the routinized sexual objectification of women workers by their male superiors. The plant's architecture and labor process incite and channel supervisorial and worker desire. In this context, supervisors become voyeurs and women workers, productive objects of the male gaze. Labor control is established within this relationship, as young women workers are under constant watch and evaluation – both as sexual and as productive subjects – and the few young men workers are ignored – also in both capacities. Thus, just as young women become subject through their admission to a category dependent on managerial approval, young men – neither watchers nor objects of desire – become subject through their inability to claim any category through which to act. Sexuality is neither hidden nor extraneous to production in this context. On the contrary, it is powerful precisely because of its very visibility. In this process, it emerges as central to worker compliance and managerial control and thus as an intrinsic aspect of the process of production itself.

Making 'models', making 'drifters'

In Panoptimex's labor control practices, workers are hailed as gendered and sexual beings, and as gendered and sexual beings of particular kinds. Workers' response to this address is not preordained. Insofar as they emerge from this process as productive subjects, it is due to their capacity and willingness to answer to this ascription, and to come to recognize themselves in these discourses. Thus, workers' factory-level experiences of themselves as (or as not) sexual subjects or objects, encapsulate the process through which sexualization operates through targets' desire, rather than 'against their will', even as it effectively objectifies and disempowers them.

Any glance at the Panoptimex shopfloor encounters a sea of stockinged legs and high heels, rows of meticulously curled bangs and brightly manicured hands, women painting their lips on every line. It is difficult to be a woman on the Panoptimex shopfloor without self-consciousness. The light, the windows, the eyes, the comments – each and all are persistently, glaringly evident. This gaze affects women at all levels in the plant. As the weeks go by, I find myself buying lipstick and agonizing over my outfit in the cold darkness of a predawn winter's morning. Despite my efforts, women in the plant are quick with more elaborate suggestions – why it's not that I'm not *feminine* they say diplomatically, but with a bit of makeup. . . . One young woman shows how much it matters, mentioning that she missed work the day before because she slept too late – too late, that is, to do her hair and makeup and still make the bus. To enter the plant as a woman is to be immersed in objectification – to be seen, to watch, and so to watch and see yourself.[14]

A young woman on the line tells her own story of transformation. When she started work she used no makeup, only wore dresses below the knee. Soon her co-workers began telling her she looked bad, that she should 'fix herself up'. So encouraged, she decided to be less shy. Today, mini-skirted and made-up, she reports she finally feels self-confident in the plant. As she speaks, her best friend surveys her physique with an affectionately proprietary air, 'They say one's appearance reveals a lot', she remarks. Later, they both appear at the Electroworld beauty contest, a poorly organized and attended affair except for the 50 contestants, many from Panoptimex, who infuse the occasion with a deep symbolic seriousness. The stories traded over cookies and shared lipsticks revolve around the lack of courage shown by those who 'chickened out' at the last minute and the value of participating, whether or not you win, as an act of bravery and an assertion of self-worth. There are also extensive discussions about those left behind, about the importance of representing those on one's line who lack the necessary bravery to be present themselves. To claim one's own desirability becomes an act of courage, independence, loyalty and solidarity all at once.

The ultimate arbiters of desirability, of course, are supervisors and managers. Workers gossip constantly about who is or is not chosen. On every line, they can point out those Carlos speaks to and those the supervisor favors – women only too happy to acknowledge their special status. For those so anointed, the experience is one of personal power. 'If you've got it, flaunt it!' Estela comments gleefully, her purple-lined eyes moving from her black, lace body-suit to the supervisor hovering nearby. This power is often used more instrumentally as well. On my first day in the plant, a young woman – known as one of the 'young and pretty ones' favored by managerial notice – is stopped by guards for lateness. She slips upstairs and convinces Carlos to intercede for her. She is allowed to work after all. The personnel office is incensed and the lines sizzle with gossip.

Gossip is the plant pastime and weapon of choice, as well as its most cited cruelty. 'Did you see him talking to her?' The lines bristle with eyes. Quick side-glances register a new style, make note of wrinkles that betray ironing undone. 'Oof, look how she's dressed!' With barely a second thought, women workers can produce five terms for 'give her the once over'

– words that shade in meaning from gossip about to cut down to censure. The issue of favoritism is a constant source of conflict, and everyone is always watching. Estela is a frequent target of sexual rumors, and she is torn about whether to be hurt or proud of her notoriety. The first time I meet her she boasts 'the other girls don't like me, I get on their nerves'. She turns to a co-worker, 'Isn't that true?' The other girl nods calmly. In this bounded space, femininity is defined and anointed by male supervisors and managers. Women workers have little to offer each other in comparison to the pleasures of that achievement and the perils of its loss.

If the young women in this plant have little to offer each other, the young men have even less for them. One unfortunate young man says he came here intentionally for all the women. 'I thought I'd find a girl friend. I thought it would be fun.' 'And was it?' I ask. There's a pause, 'No one paid any attention to me', he responds finally, a bit embarrassed, laughing and downcast. His experience brings scenes to mind: women on the line discussing the gendering of production, mocking men's 'thick fingers' and lack of attention to detail, giggling helplessly at the notion of a male group leader. I hear again a comment made by one of the women workers who returned to the factory after having quit. 'It's a good atmosphere here. In the street they (men) mess with us, but here, we mess with them a little. We make fun of them and they get embarrassed.'

In the face of such commentary, men on the line struggle to affirm a legitimate masculinity in production. Like their female counterparts, they also look to supervisors to affirm their gendered location. Unlike their female counterparts, however, both what they want and how they attempt to get it require confrontation rather than intimacies. Eschewing indirect appeals for legitimation, they make constant, carefully ritualized demands that the supervisor acknowledge their masculinity, both on the shopfloor and off. In *sotto voce* rebellions in the plant, they impugn their supervisors' manhood and imply his fear of theirs. 'If he has a problem, he should come tell us himself, not send Mari (the group leader) down. He's just afraid it could come to blows', complains Juan in a characteristic (and characteristically quiet) critique. A group in 'final' excitedly tells me what happened after I left their line's Christmas party. The supervisor showed up late and they asked him, 'So what's the story here, do we talk to you like the supervisor or like a man?' Needless to say, he said like a man. 'So we gave it to him, almost insulting his mother!' they reported with relish.

Despite such performances, the plant denies male workers' masculinity in its very architecture, and supervisors have no reason to undercut this. On the contrary, male workers' desperate desire for respect becomes a potent tool of control. When supervisors tire of the constant challenges and move male workers into female territory, the effect is dramatic. Once snatched from their domain and relegated to the 'womanly task' of soldering, even eye-stinging black smoke amidst broken ventilators evokes no complaints. In Panoptimex, to be male is to have the right to look, to be a super-visor. Gender and production relations are discursively linked. Standing facing the line, eyes trained on his work, the male line-worker does not count as a man. In the plant's central game, he is neither subject nor object. As a result, he has no location from which to act – either in his relation to the women in the plant, or in relation to factory managers. Just as his female co-worker becomes a productive subject through her response to managerial discourse, so does he. However, in her case the process has its pleasures. In his case, it is the lure of fixing things, the recurrent desire to remake an untenable, local gender identity, that ties him into factory life.

Within the panopticon, workers are incorporated into production through the pleasures and pains of sexual objectification, and it is only through their willing participation in these processes that they become effective. The framework embedded in the language of sexual harassment directs our attention to situations in which subordinates object to managerial overtures, at least internally. However, in Panoptimex, all workers are interpellated into production as sexual beings, and in responding to this address, they become participants in the process through which they are controlled. It is this participation which makes labor control in Panoptimex so effective and so troubling. 'Sexual harassment', recognizable and offensive, would not incorporate workers into their own subjugation, would not increase productivity, and would not affect those unattended to. However, the routinized operations of sexual objectification in Panoptimex accomplish all those goals, addressing workers as sexual and productive subjects simultaneously, and in so doing increasing supervisorial control and TV quality in a single move.

Making sexual subjects

Panoptimex is a highly monitored space, yet rather than weighing down production through cumbersome checks and antagonisms, supervisorial vigilance is woven into the very fabric of relationship between supervisors and workers, enhancing control and productivity simultaneously. Sexual objectification is central here, as it is within this process that the male super-visorial gaze evokes productive subjects, thus integrating sexual subjectivities directly into the structure of production. Rather than interfering with production, sexualized surveillance creates workers both willing and able to produce.[15]

This suggests a fundamentally different image of the role of sexuality in production than that which is generally highlighted by the term 'sexual harassment', yet it is, if anything, more consequential and problematic. Sexuality in the workplace is indeed sometimes extraneous, isolated and hidden. However, we see in the case of Panoptimex that it can also be intrinsic to production, social and highly visible – part of the basic infrastructure through which the factory operates. Much of the discussion of sexual harassment assumes that it is an impediment to production, and researchers tend to analyse its corrosive effects on productivity via increases in turnover, absenteeism and lowered morale (Hanisch, 1996; Knapp and Gustis, 1996). These studies conclusively demonstrate the destructive impact of individual, aberrant and stigmatized acts of 'sexual harassment' on individual productivity. However, when the labor process itself is sexualized, as is the case in Panoptimex, sexuality and desire can themselves become productive forces, more than compensating for the random inefficiencies they introduce into the production process by their outsize capacity to constitute productive subjects. For those disturbed by forced sexual contact, the managerial capacity to harness workers' most intimate sense of self in the service of production might give pause.

By the same token, in scores of workplaces, malicious or troubled perpetrators harass individual, unwilling victims. However, in Panoptimex, flirtation is a social relation that defines and frames the interactions of supervisors and workers overall. In this context, the sexualization of work becomes significant for everyone on the shopfloor, whether or not they are personally involved in sexual game playing. Recognizing this more generalized process in turn suggests that an exclusive focus on worker refusal and supervisorial culpability in identifying problematic sexual contact misses much that matters. The most effective forms of labor control are interpellatory structures in which productive subjectivities are evoked within daily shopfloor interaction. Panoptimex's mode of shopfloor control is of this kind, and its content is highly sexualized. Workers are addressed and incorporated into production only (although not exclusively) within this framework. Indeed, it is the very demography and architecture of the plant which incites desire in its occupants – supervisors and workers alike. Insofar as we look to the psyches of the particular individuals involved to explain this excess of shopfloor sexuality, we are missing its primary, structural catalyst. Factories produce widgets, but they also produce people. In Panoptimex, this production process is a sexual one. Neither the supervisorial voyeur nor the seductive factory girl are personality types, they are Panoptimex products.

This recognition returns us to where we began, to the production of the 'cheap, docile and dextrous' workers who are a staple of transnational production. Both managers and academic analysts tend to discuss this as a hiring issue. However, the central story of Panoptimex's success is not one of effective hiring, but of the effective interpellation of those hired. Both job choice and hiring in the industry is remarkably casual, and young women workers who end up elsewhere show little of the sexualized docility evident at Panoptimex.[16] In fact, Panoptimex workers are striking precisely for their uncanny resemblance to the sexual objects and productive subjects implicitly promised in advertising brochures by maquila promoters. The process through which they have been so constituted is a sexual one, and its power suggests how essential it is that we develop a language that makes it visible. 'Sexual harassment' is indeed important, but we should not let it obscure sexuality's other shopfloor incarnations. Insofar as sexual objectification is a significant mode of shopfloor control, it requires our attention and analysis.

Notes

1. 'Maquiladoras', or as they're popularly known, 'maquilas', are export-processing factories located in Mexico, generally along the country's northern border, which assemble parts produced in the USA for sale on the US market. The highest concentration of maquila workers is in Ciudad Juárez, where I did my research.
2. All factory, corporation and personal names used here are fictitious.
3. Williams (1997) and Hearn and Parkin (1995) make similar points. The over-representation of survey methods is evident in Stockdale's (1996a) collection, in which every essay based on empirical data uses either survey or experimental methods.
4. For defining analyses of the production of shopfloor consent in general, see Burawoy (1979, 1985).
5. The definition of sexual harassment as unwanted is so ingrained in the academic literature that the 1999 *Annual Review of Sociology* commissioned two separate reviews, one focused on coercive sexual contact and the other on 'positive and autonomous expressions of workers' sexual desire' (Williams et al., 1999: 73).
6. The troubling and intimate relationship between sexuality and power was first explored in depth by feminists in the 1980s (Snitow et al., 1983; Vance, 1984) and by Foucault (1980). Hollway and Jefferson (1996) raise these issues explicitly in the context of sexual harassment, however the discussion is focused on psychological rather than structural processes.
7. A few ethnographic researchers studying service industries (Guiffre and Williams, 1994; Loe, 1996; Rogers and Henson, 1997) have looked at the productive function and ambivalent worker experience of workplace sexuality. However, these studies don't explore the ways in which sexual interaction between superiors and subordinates can become an intrinsic element in labor control even in an industry in which femininity is unrelated to the product sold. Yelvington (1996) discusses sexuality at work in factory production, but he focuses on sexuality as a site of resistance rather than managerial control. Williams (1997) also calls for such studies.
8. The research on which this chapter is based is part of a larger study of four Juárez maquilas done over 18 months in the early 1990s (see Salzinger, forthcoming). I spent three of those months in Panoptimex. During that time, I spent every weekday wandering the shopfloor, sitting in personnel or meetings, or interviewing managers. Later, I interviewed 10 workers I knew well at my home.
9. Panoptimex managers propose a budget to their US superiors. Once accepted, their task is to spend no more than projected to assemble the promised quantity of goods. Spending more is a failure, but spending less is also penalized, as the following year's budget is cut accordingly.

10. This shortage of female labor is a reflection of how many young women are willing to work for below-subsistence maquila wages, not of how many young women workers are available in total.

11. The current plant manager is a notable and not terribly credible exception to this pattern. Having decided that as an American woman I am an advocate of 'gender-blindness', he eschews any consciousness of gender in conversation with me, repeating that nothing matters but the will to work. After one of our interviews, he is so concerned to prove this that he begins badgering the, extremely irritated, Juárez personnel manager to hire a blind man. The Panoptimex personnel manager makes her skepticism obvious when I mention his stance. Her response comes as no surprise, as Carlos's clear and not exactly disinterested preference for young women is an ongoing subject of office gossip.

12. Wages have since fallen further. Base pay is supplemented by a variety of coupons (e.g. for lunch and transportation) and yearly bonuses. Even with these additions, however, pay remains low. Some workers supplement their income by selling candy, jewelry, makeup and other items illicitly on the shopfloor. This is difficult in chassis because of the high level of supervision, but relatively easy elsewhere. Management doesn't interfere unless it becomes too blatant. As a wage subsidy, it has its advantages for them too.

13. There is one female supervisor, but she is on second shift. I have focused my analysis on first shift because, once managers leave their windowed offices in the evening, the panopticon is replaced by distinct modes of control.

14. Critiques of women's objectification have long been a staple of feminist theory (MacKinnon, 1982; Mulvey, 1975). Feminist analysis of its troubling pleasures have been less developed. Two authors who do discuss this are Chancer (1998) and Steele (1985).

15. Here sexuality functions as one of Foucault's (1979) 'disciplines'.

16. See Salzinger (1997) for a comparison of varied labor control strategies and their outcomes in distinctive shopfloor femininities and masculinities in the maquila industry.

References

Althusser, Louis (1971) 'Ideology and ideological state apparatuses (Notes towards an investigation)', in Louis Althusser, *Lenin and Philosophy and Other Essays*. New York: Monthly Review Press. pp. 127–86.

Benería, Lourdes and Martha Roldán (1987) *The Crossroads of Class and Gender*. Chicago: University of Chicago Press.

Berger, John (1972) *Ways of Seeing*. Middlesex: British Broadcasting Corporation.

Burawoy, Michael (1979) *Manufacturing Consent: Changes in the Labor Process under Monopoly Capitalism*. Chicago: University of Chicago Press.

Burawoy, Michael (1985) *The Politics of Production*. New York: Verso.

Chancer, Lynn (1998) 'The beauty context: looks, social theory and feminism', in *Reconcilable Differences: Confronting Beauty, Pornography and the Future of Feminism*. Berkeley, CA: University of California Press. pp. 82–172.

Elson, Diane and Ruth Pearson (1986) 'Third World manufacturing', in Feminist Review (eds), *Waged Work*. London: Virago. pp. 67–92.

Fernandez-Kelly, Maria Patricia (1983) *For We Are Sold, I and My People: Women and Industry in Mexico's Frontier*. Albany, NY: SUNY Press.

Fitzgerald, L.F., S. Swan and K. Fischer (1997) 'But was it really sexual harassment? Legal, behavioral and psychological definitions of the workplace victimization of women', in W. O'Donohue (ed.), *Sexual Harassment: Theory, Research and Treatment*. New York: Allyn and Bacon.

Foucault, Michel (1979) *Discipline and Punish: The Birth of the Prison*. New York: Vintage Books.

Foucault, Michel (1980) *The History of Sexuality*, Vol. 1. New York: Vintage Books.

Fuentes, Annette and Barbara Ehreneich (1983) *Women in the Global Factory*. Boston, MA: South End Press.

Gruber, James (1998) 'The impact of male work environments and organizational policies on women's experiences of sexual harassment', *Gender and Society*, 12(3): 301–20.

Gruber, James, Michael Smith and Kaisa Kauppinen-Toropainen (1996) 'Sexual harassment types and severity: linking research and policy', in Margaret Stockdale (ed.), *Sexual Harassment in the Workplace: Perspectives, Frontiers, and Response Strategies*. London: Sage. pp. 151–73.

Guiffre, Patti and Christine Williams (1994) 'Boundary lines: labeling sexual harassment in restaurants', *Gender and Society*, 8(3): 378–401.

Hanisch, Kathy (1996) 'An integrated framework for studying the outcomes of sexual harassment: consequences for individuals and organizations', in Margaret Stockdale (ed.), *Sexual Harassment in the Workplace: Perspectives, Frontiers, and Response Strategies*. London: Sage. pp. 174–98.

Hearn, Jeff and Wendy Parkin (1995) *'Sex at Work': The Power and Paradox of Organization Sexuality*. New York: St Martin's Press.

Hollway, Wendy and Tony Jefferson (1996) 'PC or not PC: sexual harassment and the question of ambivalence', *Human Relations*, 49(3): 373–93.

Hulin, Charles, Louise Fitzgerald and Fritz Drasgow (1996) 'Organizational influences on sexual harassment', in Margaret Stockdale (ed.), *Sexual Harassment in the Workplace: Perspectives, Frontiers, and Response Strategies*. London: Sage. pp. 127–50.

Iglesias Prieto, Norma (1987) *La Flor Más Bella de la Maquiladora*. Mexico City: Secretaría de Educación Pública.

Kamel, Rachel (1990) *The Global Factory: Analysis and Action for a New Economic Era*. Philadelphia, PA: American Friends Service Committee.

Knapp, Deborah and Gary Gustis (1996) 'The real "disclosure": sexual harassment and the bottom line', in Margaret Stockdale (ed.), *Sexual Harassment in the Workplace: Perspectives, Frontiers, and Response Strategies*. London: Sage. pp. 199–213.

Lauretis, Teresa de (1987) 'The technology of gender', in *Technologies of Gender: Essays on Theory, Film and Fiction*. Bloomington, IN: Indiana University Press. pp. 1–30.

Loe, Meika (1996) 'Working for men – at the intersection of power, gender, and sexuality', *Sociological Inquiry*, 66(4): 399–421.

MacKinnon, Catherine (1982) 'Feminism, Marxism, method and the state: an agenda for theory', *Signs*, 7(3): 515–44.

Mulvey, Laura (1975) 'Visual pleasure and narrative cinema', *Screen*, 16(3): 6–18.

Rogers, Jackie and Kevin Henson (1997) '"Hey, why don't you wear a shorter skirt?": structural vulnerability and the organization of sexual harassment in temporary clerical employment', *Gender and Society*, 11(2): 215–37.

Salzinger, Leslie (1997) 'From high heels to swathed bodies: gendered meanings under production in Mexico's export-processing industry', *Feminist Studies*, 23(3): 549–74.

Salzinger, Leslie (forthcoming) *Gender under Production: Making Subjects in Mexico's Global Factories*. Berkeley, CA: University of California Press.

Sklair, Leslie (1993) *Assembling for Development: The Maquila Industry in Mexico and the United States*. San Diego, CA: Center for US–Mexican Studies, UCSD.

Snitow, Ann, Christine Stansell and Sharon Thompson (eds) (1983) *Powers of Desire: The Politics of Sexuality*. New York: Monthly Review Press.

Standing, Guy (1989) 'Global feminization through flexible labor', *World Development*, 17: 1077–95.

Steele, Valerie (1985) *Fashion and Eroticism: Ideals of Feminine Beauty from the Victorian Era to the Jazz Age*. New York: Oxford University Press.

Stockdale, Margaret (ed.) (1996a) *Sexual Harassment in the Workplace: Perspectives, Frontiers, and Response Strategies*. London: Sage.

Stockdale, Margaret (1996b) 'What we know and what we need to learn about sexual harassment', in Margaret Stockdale (ed.), *Sexual Harassment in the Workplace: Perspectives, Frontiers, and Response Strategies*. London: Sage. pp. 3–25.

Vance, Carole (ed.) (1984) *Pleasure and Danger: Exploring Female Sexuality*. Boston, MA: Routledge & Kegan Paul.

Welsh, Sandy (1999) 'Gender and sexual harassment', *Annual Review of Sociology*, 25: 169–90.

Williams, Christine (1997) 'Sexual harassment in organizations: a critique of current research and policy', *Sexuality and Culture*, 1: 19–43.

Williams, Christine, Patti Guiffre and Kirsten Dellinger (1999) 'Sexuality in the workplace: organizational control, sexual harassment, and the pursuit of pleasure', *Annual Review of Sociology*, 25: 73–93.

Yelvington, Kevin (1996) 'Flirting in the factory', *The Journal of Royal Anthropology*, 2(2): 313–33.

6

Distributed cognition in an airline cockpit

Edwin Hutchins and Tove Klausen

Most people who travel frequently by air occasionally find themselves sitting in the passenger cabin wondering what is happening on the other side of the cockpit door. What are the pilots doing, and whatever it is they are doing, are they doing it well?

Although we cannot present data from an actual flight, we can provide the next best thing: data from an actual airline flight crew performing in a very high fidelity flight simulator.[1] Consider the transcript below, taken from a full-mission simulation of a flight from Sacramento to Los Angeles. It is the second flight of the day for this particular crew. They are about eight minutes out of Sacramento and are climbing through 19,000 feet toward their cruise altitude of 33,000 feet. The simulated aircraft is a Boeing 727–200, which requires a crew of three: Captain (Capt), First Officer (F/O) and Second Officer (S/O).

We open the cockpit door and peek inside. The Captain has just removed a departure chart[2] from the control yoke and is replacing it in his airway manual. The First Officer is flying the plane, monitoring the flight instruments and handling the controls. The Second Officer has completed his departure paperwork and begins a departure report by radio to the company offices on the ground.

Transcript

0216	S/O	xxx NASA nine hundred.
0224	S/O	Departure report.
	S/O	NASA nine hundred from Sacramento to Los Angeles International we have . . . fuel on board twenty seven point eight fuel boarded is not available out time is one six four five up time is one six five five.

This was previously published in Y.Engestrom and D.Middleton (1996) (eds) *Cognition and communication at work* Cambridge: Cambridge University Press.

0247	Capt	Oakland center NASA nine hundred request higher.
		{F/O reaches to vicinity of altitude alert setting knob when ATC begins transmission.}
0254	OAK24L	NASA nine hundred . . . roger contact Oakland center one thirty two point eight.
		{F/O pulls his hand back from the altitude alert knob when ATC says 'contact Oakland center.' 2.5 seconds after the end of ATC transmission, F/O looks at Capt}
		{Capt looks at F/O.}
0300	F/O	Thirty two eight.
	Capt	Thirty two eight?
	F/O	Yeah.
	Capt	OK
0303	S/O	That's correct, NASA nine hundred.
	Capt	One three two eight, NASA nine hundred.
		{Capt twists knob on radio console.}
		{F/O looks in direction of Capt}
0315	Capt	Center NASA nine hundred twenty one point seven for two three zero requesting higher.
0323		{S/O turns towards front of cockpit.}
0325		{F/O looks at Capt}
0325	OAK15H	NASA nine hundred . . . Oakland center climb and maintain flight level three three zero and expedite your climb please.
0327		{F/O reaches the altitude alert as ATC says 'climb and maintain.'}
0330		{When ATC says 'expedite your climb' S/O turns to the performance tables on the S/O work surface.}
0331	F/O	OK.
0333	Capt	Three three zero NASA nine hundred.
		{Capt leans toward and looks at F/O.}
		I didn't catch the last part.
0336	F/O	Expedite your climb.
	Capt	OK.
0339		{S/O reaches thrust levers and pushes them forward.}
0341	Capt	That's firewall thrust {Capt looks at F/O.}
	All	(Laugh).

Unless you know quite a lot about aviation, reading this transcript probably did not help you much in deciding what the pilots are doing and whether or not they are doing it well. Of course, in a very important sense, the question of interest to you as a passenger should not be whether a particular pilot is performing well, but whether or not the system that is composed of the pilots and the technology of the cockpit environment is performing well. It is the performance of that system, not the skills of any individual pilot, that determines whether you live or die. In order to understand the performance of the cockpit as a system we need, of course, to refer to the cognitive properties of the individual pilots, but we also need a new, larger, unit of cognitive analysis. This unit of analysis must permit us to describe and explain the cognitive properties of the cockpit system that is composed of the pilots and their informational environment. We call this unit of analysis a system of *distributed cognition.*

The excerpt of cockpit activity presented above is only approximately 1½ minutes in duration, yet it is very rich. It contains within it illustrations of many of the central concepts of a theory of distributed cognition. We will present and discuss these concepts by going through the elements of the example in chronological order and noting what the events in this example tell us about the nature of this particular system and about systems of distributed cognition in general.

This is a descriptive use of the theory. We will attempt to show that certain observed behaviors are instances of certain theoretical concepts. It is only by mapping from the data to a theory that we can generalize beyond the specifics of these observations. Establishing such a mapping from the data to the theory is itself a problematic cognitive activity. A short digression on method is in order.

The method of analysis

In some kinds of behavioral research, the mappings from observed events to the terms of a theory are taken to be obvious. In others these mappings are justified by 'operational' definitions. In our case, however, the theoretical interpretation of some events may depend on the meanings that the participants themselves attach to those events. Because the setting is not familiar to most readers, the mappings from events to theory are unlikely to seem obvious. Because of the complexity of the setting, it cannot readily be made familiar. And since the sort of thing an event is in the theory may depend on meanings that the participants attach to the event, there are no simple operational definitions of many of our terms. Instead, we must rely on an ethnography of the setting to provide the interpretive bridge from the structure of the recordings of activity to the terms of the theory of distributed cognition.

We have pursued a strategy of analysis in which we insist that the connections between the data and the theory must be established explicitly. Our analysis begins with video and audio recordings of the events in the cockpit environment. We take the video and audio records to be a first-generation representation of what happened in the cockpit. Some aspects of the setting are already lost in the video and audio. The camera angle leaves some parts of the environment obscured, for example. The camera mounted in the flight simulator records a black and white image from infrared sensors, so color is lost. Odors are not recorded by video. Although they are incomplete, the video and audio recordings are rich sources of data.[3]

From the video and audio recordings we create another representation of what happened in the cockpit, this time in the medium of print. We create a *transcript* of the verbal and other behavior, in the cockpit. This representation leaves out even more than the video and audio representations, but it is still rich, and for some analytic tasks, it is far superior to the raw recordings. Both the translation from real events to video and audio recordings and the translation from video and audio to written transcript is heavily theory laden (Ochs, 1979). The actual recorded acoustic signals are meaningless in themselves. It is only in interaction with the knowledge of a listener who understands the language that the acoustic signals become segmented into words. The role of transcriber knowledge becomes even more apparent where specialized vocabularies are employed. Most people in our culture do not speak 'aviationese' and just as it is impossible to transcribe recordings in a language one does not speak, it is impossible to transcribe discourse from technical domains without knowing something about the domain of discourse. As analysts, we know well that what people hear depends on what they expect to hear, and in a noisy technical environment very little can be heard at all without some expectations. This raises an important concern. If even the transcription process involves the tacit knowledge of the researcher, might the analysis be covertly shaped by the analyst's expectations?

One way to protect oneself from the possibility of unexamined assumptions driving the work is to attempt a form of 'objectivity' in which all assumptions are hopefully banished. Such approaches cling to a 'coding scheme,' a set of 'objective criteria' for the existence of instances of various classes of events. Every coding scheme, however, ultimately depends on the skills of coders to assign complex real events as instances of the coded categories. This in itself is a complex cognitive activity that is far from objective (Goodwin, 1994). We opt for another possibility, that is, making sure the assumptions do not remain unexamined (Duranti, 1985; Moerman, 1969). With this in mind, we ground the translation from video and audio record to transcription in an explicit set of propositions that are independently verifiable in the ethnography of the setting (Agar, 1986).

Consider a simple example from the excerpt above. The transcript indicates that at time 0327 the First Officer reached the altitude alerter. We know this is the correct description of this event because we have access to other resources. A diagram of instrument layout shows that the altitude alerter is located just where the First Officer reached. But there is more to it than that. Setting the altitude alerter is a meaningful action for the pilots at this point in time. Company procedures require that the altitude alerter be set whenever a new altitude is assigned to the aircraft.

From the transcripts we generate yet another representation of the events that were recorded. This is a description of the *actions* that took place. The stream of behavior in the transcript is segmented into culturally meaningful chunks and is related to an ethnographically grounded system of goals and expectations in which the actions achieve their meaning for the participants. Again, we attempt to be completely explicit about the grounds for the composition of every action. The development of ethnographic grounding leads us to many sources of cultural knowledge. These include operational manuals for the aircraft, the layout of the cockpit instrumentation and controls, crew training materials, published navigation procedures (commonly known 'rules of thumb' in aviation), interviews with pilots, and observations of pilots in actual flights, to mention only a few.[4]

A fourth representation of the events gives *interpretations* to the actions that were identified in the previous stage. Again, the translation from the action representation to that of interpretations is given an explicit grounding in an independently verifiable ethnography of the setting. Furthermore, even the richest ethnography may not uniquely constrain interpretations. Any particular identified action may have many meanings.

Finally, we draw on all of these representations to create the mapping from data to the theory. As the theory of distributed cognition unfolds in this chapter, the reader will recognize that this analytic device is modeled on the notion of the propagation of a representational state across a series of representational media. Each representation brings a different sort of information into the foreground. This is one of the central concepts of the theory. Unfortunately, we do not have the space here to give a complete explication of the process of analysis for even this brief excerpt. What we will do instead is weave together the data, the actions, the interpretations, and the ethnographic grounding as they are needed in a narrative that seeks to present a theoretical account of the observed events.

Analysis of the event

Let's begin with a brief summary of what we saw. This is the sort of description that a pilot would give.

As the crew approached the altitude to which they were cleared, the Captain called Air Traffic Control and asked for a clearance to a higher altitude. The controller handed them off to a high-altitude controller who gave them a clearance to their cruising altitude and instructed them to expedite the climb. The Second Officer increased the thrust and they continued their climb.

This is an entirely normal event. But now let us look much more closely and examine the cognitive properties of this system.

Cognitive labor is socially distributed

Flying a modern jet airliner is a job that cannot (at least not in current practice) be done by an individual acting alone. This is why your safety as a passenger depends on the properties of the crew/aircraft system rather than on the skills of any individual. The excerpt we have presented begins with the crew operating in a fairly autonomous mode. They are in a relatively light workload phase of flight; the stresses of the takeoff are behind them and they have now established a climb on a constant heading. The First Officer, who is actually flying the airplane, is the only crew member involved in time-critical performance at this point. The Captain is dividing his attention between housekeeping tasks (putting away a navigation chart) and monitoring aircraft and crew performance. In his role as 'pilot not flying,' he is also responsible for communications with the Air Traffic Control system (ATC), but there are no communication demands at the beginning of this example. Simultaneously, and quite independently, the Second Officer is involved in another kind of housekeeping task, making a report to the company of the condition of the flight. At this instant there is little explicit interaction among the members of the crew. Although no member of the crew is taxed by these circumstances, the system as a whole may still be doing more cognitive work than could be done by any individual alone. The fact that such systems proceed with several individuals working autonomously in parallel is well known and, from a theoretical point of view, easy to understand. Things become much more interesting when the members of the crew are required to coordinate their activities with each other.

Planning

At time 10:02:47, the Captain calls the Oakland, California Air Route Traffic Control Center (abbreviated to 'Oakland Center') low-altitude controller and requests a clearance to a higher altitude.[5] This is an important piece of evidence about planning in the cockpit. The aircraft is currently climbing through an altitude of about 19,000 feet. It is currently cleared to an altitude of 23,000 feet. This means that without a clearance to a higher altitude, it cannot legally climb above 23,000 feet. However, the flight plan[6] filed for this flight calls for a cruise altitude of Flight Level 330 (33,000 feet).

In this context, we can attribute to the Captain the goal of climbing to the filed cruise altitude of FL330 and, furthermore, we can attribute to him the goal of making the climb uninterrupted by leveling off at an intermediate altitude.[7] In order to realize these goals, the aircraft will need to have a clearance to climb to a higher altitude. The Captain's request is part of a plan to achieve the subgoal of getting the required clearance. In order to have this plan now, he must have been monitoring the progress of the flight. That is his job as Captain and as the pilot not flying.[8] He used the information available – present altitude, cleared altitude, cruise altitude, plus his knowledge of the legal status of cleared altitude and the role of ATC – to construct a plan. It's a tiny bit of action in the cockpit, but it is the tip of a large iceberg of information and knowledge.

Distribution of access to information

Up to now we have been primarily concerned with relatively autonomous activities of the crew. That changes when the Captain speaks. All members of the crew normally monitor the ATC frequency unless they need to be on another frequency for some reason.[9] The Captain's radio transmission can be heard by the First Officer. The distribution of access to information is an important property of systems of distributed cognition. The properties of the larger system emerge from the interactions among the interpretations formed by the members of the crew and the contents of those inter-pretations are determined in part by the access to information.

The trajectories of information

It is important to note that we cannot predict in advance where the information will actually go. For example, we do not know that the First Officer will actually attend to and hear the Captain's radio call. We do know from the structure of the setting and a knowledge of how the radios are operated that the First Officer could have attended to and heard any communication with ATC. This sort of knowledge permits us to establish a set of possible pathways or trajectories for information. Occasionally, the observation of particular pilot techniques may demonstrate possible path-ways that have not been anticipated on the basis of the normal operation in the setting. Once the possible pathways have been identified, it is possible to examine the data for evidence concerning where the information actually went. It is often possible, after the fact, to unambiguously determine that information has followed some particular trajectories in the system.

Formation of expectations

Given the content of the Captain's plan, we attribute to him an expectation concerning the reply from Oakland Center. His radio call is the opening turn in a conversation with a highly predictable structure. The expectation is that ATC will answer, saying something like, 'NASA nine hundred, climb and maintain flight level three three zero.' If the First Officer was attending to the Captain's request, he may also have formed this expectation. Note that at this point in the analysis we cannot confidently attribute this expectation to the First Officer. As was the case with the potential trajectories for information structure in the system, we cannot always know what cognitive consequences follow from the arrival of a particular piece of information. Thus, even if the information reached the First Officer, the development of an expectation about ATC's response is only a possibility. Additional evidence from the transcript would be required to support this interpretation.

In this case, more evidence is available in the form of the First Officer's reaching toward the altitude-alert setting knob as the ATC controller begins his reply to the request for a higher altitude clearance. The altitude-alert system is required by federal aviation regulations. The crew must set the cleared altitude into the window. The system sounds an alarm warning of approach within 750 feet of the assigned altitude. Altitude busts (flying through the assigned altitude) were a frequent and serious problem prior to the introduction of these systems. We believe the First Officer's reaching behavior is evidence of a plan to change the setting of the altitude-alert system in response to the expected clearance to a higher altitude. The currently cleared altitude (23,000 feet) is displayed. The First Officer intends to change the setting to whatever altitude ATC specifies. He expects the filed cruise altitude of 33,000 feet. The reaching behavior gives us an additional constraint on the ascription of an expectation to the First Officer.

This sequence shows how the distribution of access to information and a shared body of knowledge about the operation of the system permits the formation of shared expectations that are then the basis of coordinated actions by the crew. This is one of many events in this excerpt that highlight the cultural nature of this task performance and its reliance on shared knowledge. To the extent that coordinated actions of the crew are grounded in mental representations of possible but not yet realized states of affairs, we say that shared expectations are real.

Violations of expectations

As it turns out, the expectation is violated by the response of ATC. The expected clearance to a higher altitude is not forthcoming. Instead, the crew is instructed to contact another controller at Oakland Center – this time a high-altitude controller. This is a violation of the crew's expectations. Unable to carry out the planned change in the altitude-alert system, the First Officer withdraws his hand from the altitude-alert setting knob.

The frequency change instruction gives rise to a new expectation. All information from ATC is supposed to be acknowledged.[10] Both the Captain and the First Officer expect the Captain to acknowledge the instruction. But the Captain does not acknowledge the instruction immediately. Two and a half seconds after the end of the ATC transmission, the First Officer looks at the Captain. The First Officer's expectation of a timely acknowledgment has now been violated.

Intersubjectivity as a basis for communication

The next several actions are interesting because they establish one another's meanings. The Captain looks at the First Officer and says nothing. The First Officer says 'thirty two eight' to the Captain. Then the Captain asks, 'thirty two eight?' What is going on in this interaction?

It is useful to consider this interaction in terms of speech act theory (Austin, 1960; Searle, 1969). Speech act theory considers utterances as simultaneously being several kinds of acts at once. What a speaker actually says is called the locutionary act. The force of what is said is the illocutionary act, and the intended effect is the perlocutionary act. For example, saying 'Can you pass the salt?' at the dinner table has the locutionary force of a question: is the addressee capable of passing the salt? Of course, the speaker doesn't really want an answer to that question. The illocutionary force of the utterance is an indirect request for the salt to be passed. The perlocutionary act is an enticement to lead the addressee to pass the salt.

The First Officer's response to the Captain's glance is an elliptical version of the frequency that is to be acknowledged to ATC.[11] The locutionary aspect of this utterance is the specification of the frequency to be used.

That seems appropriate in context. But, what would have to be true of the world in order for that to be an appropriate thing to say? The illocutionary force is 'I am answering the question you posed by looking at me without saying anything.' That is, the First Officer's utterance assigns a meaning to the Captain's blank stare to which it is a response. It classifies the Captain's action of looking at the First Officer as a question about the frequency to be used. Once made, this assignment of meaning to the Captain's look is available for negotiation. The Captain could, for example, dispute the classification and claim that he knew the frequency. But he does not. The Captain's next utterance, repeating the frequency back with rising intonation, has an illocutionary force that concurs with the First Officer's classification of the looking behavior.

There is one more level of meaning in the First Officer's response to the Captain's look. The perlocutionary force or intended effect of the First Officer's utterance is to enable the Captain to continue with his job.

This interaction is evidence for the notion of interaction as the construction of a shared understanding of the situation in which the interactants find themselves. Certainly, the pilots entered this situation with a considerable amount of shared prior knowledge about how things are supposed to go or how they typically go. As they are members of a community of practice, we may expect that to be the case. In the course of their interaction, they use that shared knowledge as a resource to negotiate or construct a shared understanding of their particular situation. This constructed shared understanding of the situation is known as an inter-subjective understanding (Rommetveit and Blakar, 1979; Wertsch, 1985). As D'Andrade (1980) points out, what each participant in the situation knows is itself part of the situation being jointly understood. Following this notion of intersubjectivity, we would say that the First Officer's original looking at the Captain is evidence that he knows that the Captain is supposed to respond to the ATC call. The Captain's look at the First Officer is evidence that he knows that the First Officer knows that the Captain is supposed to respond to the ATC call. Finally, the First Officer's utterance is evidence that he knows that the Captain knows that the First Officer knows that the Captain is supposed to respond to the ATC call. It says, 'I know that you know that I know that you should respond.'

Intersubjectivity supports efficient kinds of communication. It is what permits human actors to intend and find meanings in many nonverbal behaviors and in the aspects of verbal behaviors that go beyond the literal locutionary force of the utterance. It was not just something in the Captain that made his glance at the First Officer so eloquent. Rather, it was the fact that this glance occurred in a context of intersubjectively shared under-standings about the nature of the current situation that permitted it to so smoothly and successfully communicate the Captain's need. Again, the shared expectations become real in the sense that they organize the behavior that determines the properties of the larger cognitive system.

It is important to note that this interaction depends on the intersubjective sharing of representations of aspects of the situation that were never made explicit by either of the interactants. There was no conversation about what each knew about what the other knew. The fact that these crew members can do this is all the more surprising when one considers that these pilots had never flown together before the day of the simulated flight. Prior to the reported excerpt they had flown one flight segment and had spent only about two hours together. Clearly, the grounds for the construc-tion of intersubjectively shared understandings depends on a very special distribution of knowledge in the pilot community.

Intersubjectivity is important for the functioning of the system of dis-tributed cognition because the trajectory of information in the system depended on the intersubjectivity of the crew. Norman (1990), in a paper on aviation automation, has pointed out that the communication between the current generation of automatic devices in the cockpit and the crew is primitive and leaves much room for improvement, especially with regard to providing the crew feedback about the condition of automated systems. Norman compares the case of a copilot flying an airplane with the case of an autopilot flying. He points out that if a copilot encounters a situation that requires unusual control inputs in order to maintain the desired flight path, the copilot is likely to say something about it to other crew members. An autopilot of the current generation, however, will simply make what-ever control inputs are required without notifying the crew. This has led to some near disasters. Some readers of Norman's paper have responded by saying that the state of the art in artificial intelligence would permit the automated system to represent the information that the pilot needs.[12] This may well be so, but the issue is not simply whether the automation could represent its own state. The issue is whether or not the system could interact with the pilots in the way that they interact with each other. With human interactants, we have seen that intersubjectively shared representa-tions permit a silent look in a particular context to have the meaning of a request for specific information. This sort of phenomenon is a reminder of the complexity and subtlety of human interaction. It is difficult to imagine what sort of machine could engage in this kind of interaction.

Distribution of information storage

The fact that the Captain succeeds in getting the required frequency from the First Officer illustrates another aspect of this system of socially dis-tributed cognition. The distribution of access to information is such that the First Officer also hears the communications with ATC, even though he is not responsible for radio communications. This permits the formation in the crew system of a redundant storage of information. Under ideal conditions, both the Captain and the First Officer (and the Second Officer if he is not otherwise engaged) will hear all ATC clearances. This means that if, for any reason, one of the members of the crew fails to attend to, store, or retrieve the information, it may be available from one of the other members of the crew. Such a redundant information-storage system is robust in the fact of local failures as long as there is a way to move information around inside the system. As we saw above, the communication of information inside the system can be quite efficient.

Redundant readbacks for error checking

Having gotten the frequency from the First Officer, the Captain reads the frequency back to the ATC controller. The expectations of the crew members are now met. Furthermore, the readback of the elements of any ATC clearance provides an opportunity for redundant error checking (Palmer et al., 1993). While there is no legal requirement to read back clearances, it is considered good practice in the aviation community and is the express policy of most airlines. It is normally thought that the error checking is to be provided by the ATC controller, but we can see that there is also a possibility of error checking of the readback by other members of the crew. Since both the original clearance and the readback are available not only to ATC, but to all members of the crew, including the Captain himself, every member of the crew has an opportunity to detect an error in the readback.

In the most general case, we can say that redundant error checking depends on a redundant distribution of access to information about the performance of the members of the crew. This is supported in other ways in the airplane cockpit. For example, civil transport aircraft provide duplicate flight instruments for the two pilots. There are several frequently cited functions served by these duplicate instruments. First, they permit either pilot to fly the airplane. Second, they provide a measure of redundancy in the event that the instruments on one side fail. Third, by cross-checking instruments, failures that might otherwise be difficult to detect can be discovered. Seen from the perspective of distributed cognition, these duplicate instruments serve yet another important function. They provide a redundant distribution of access to information that supports mutual monitoring between the crew members and is essential in the maintenance of intersubjectively shared understandings of, and expectations about, the situation of the aircraft. A similar argument can be made for the prominent position of the control 'yokes.' With the two yokes mechanically linked, it is easy for one pilot to monitor the flying style of the other without having to turn to watch.

There is a trend in current cockpit design to build two separate crew work stations for the two pilots. Mechanically linked control yokes are being replaced in some cockpits by side-stick controllers that are mounted outboard of the pilot's seats and are not mechanically linked to each other. From the perspective of individual pilot performance, side-stick controllers are functionally equivalent to (or perhaps superior to) control yokes. From the distributed cognition perspective, however, the side-stick equipped cockpit has a different distribution of access to information and this may affect the cognitive properties of the cockpit system. A similar situation is created by current implementations of the Flight Management Computer System (FMCS). Duplicate computer interfaces to the FMCS are provided to the two pilots. This appears on the surface to have the same desirable properties as duplicate flight instruments. This would be the case if they were in fact directly linked to each other. However, for perfectly good operational reasons, the actions taken on one interface are not necessarily reflected on the other. This results in a common complaint among pilots that unless extraordinary measures are taken to communicate intentions, one pilot may not know what the other is doing. And even if extra measures are taken, they often result in both pilots going 'head down,' one leaning across the center console to monitor a programming task as it is performed by the other.

The problems of restricted or nonoverlapping distribution of access to information have the potential to create difficulties in normal operations and may interfere more severely with training. Although, as one pilot remarked, 'the cockpit is a poor classroom,' a considerable amount of training takes place there.[13] Implicit learning through shared activity is an important component of learning a complex job like flying an airplane. It is possible to design computer systems with open interfaces (Hutchins, 1990) that support learning in joint action but this can only be done when the designer goes beyond the conception of the isolated individual user.

Propagation of representational state through the system

After reading back the frequency, the Captain tunes the number one communication radio to the specified frequency. This sets the radio to transmit and receive on the specified frequency. At this time, the First Officer glances at the Captain and at the frequency window of the radio. The First Officer has an expectation that the Captain will tune the radio to 132.80 MHz.

Notice the trajectory of the radio frequency information. It arrived in the cockpit as a string of spoken words. It went by way of the First Officer's memory to spoken words exchanged between the First Officer and the Captain, then by way of the Captain's memory to the readback and then on to the setting of the radio. Each appearance was slightly different from the one before it:

ATC:	'One thirty two point eight.'
F/O ↔ Capt:	'Thirty two eight.'
Read back:	'One three two eight.'
Radio:	132.80 MHz

We can see that the information moved through the system as a sequence of representational states in representational media. From speech channels to internal memories, back to speech channels, to the physical setting of a device. Its representation in each medium is a transformation of the representation in other media. Notice also that the various media in which the information is represented have different properties (Norman, 1993). Speech is ephemeral. It requires one to attend to information at the time it is delivered. Representations in the memories of individuals endure longer than those in speech. This is what permits the Captain to retrieve the information that was in the ATC instruction without having to ask the controller for it again. Although the ATC transmission had ended and was no longer available, the information in it was still represented in the memory of the First Officer. Finally, a portion of the information in the ATC instruction was imposed on the airplane itself, in the tuning of the radio. This is the same information that had been represented verbally, but now it is in a relatively durable representation, because the setting of the radio is continuously available and will not change until the next frequency is tuned.

This movement of information structure across various representational media and ultimately to the controls of the airplane itself is the essence of control of the aircraft and the way that coordination among aircraft is maintained. That is, if we step back and look at the entire aviation system and ask how it is that aircraft are kept separated from each other, we see that it is through the propagation of the representational state of descriptions of flight paths into the state of the aircraft controls themselves.

Distribution of labor again

With the radio now set to the appropriate frequency, the Captain contacts the Oakland Center high-altitude controller at 10:03:15. He is back to the point in his plan where he was with his original request for a higher altitude. That plan is still pending and is in fact somewhat more urgent now, as the plane is closing rapidly on its currently cleared altitude. In this case, he gives the current altitude of the plane and the altitude to which they have been cleared, then adds the request for a higher altitude.[14]

The Captain's radio call contains the current altitude and the altitude to which the aircraft has been cleared. We may ask where these values come from. The current altitude of the aircraft must come from the airplane's altimeter. Since the plane is climbing, this value is continually changing. Altitude is represented on the altimeter by the positions of two hands and a bar on the clock-like face of the gauge and also by a digital readout window. The Captain must transform this representation of altitude information into a spoken one. There are at least two possibilities for the source of the information about the altitude to which the plane is currently cleared. One is the Captain's memory. The airplane was cleared to flight level 230 about four minutes before the Captain's radio call and he may simply remember that altitude. The other is the altitude-alert system. Since the altitude to which the plane is cleared should always be shown in the window of the altitude-alert system, it is an alternate source of this information. In this case, it does not appear that the Captain consults the altitude-alert system, but we have seen many cases in which a crewman making initial contact with an ATC center will give the current altitude, pause, look at the altitude-alert system, and then give the altitude to which the aircraft has been cleared.

By this time, the Second Officer has completed his departure report and is again attending to the actions of the other crewmen. The captain's request is available to all members of the crew and leads them all to a shared expectation concerning the response from ATC.

Again, all members of the crew have the expectation that ATC will answer back with something like 'Climb and maintain flight level three three zero.' This expectation is partially met and partially violated. ATC responds to the request by saying 'NASA nine hundred . . . Oakland Center climb and maintain flight level three three zero and expedite your climb please.' As we shall see in a moment, the additional information 'expedite your climb' seems to be heard by the First Officer and the Second Officer, but not by the Captain. This bit of structure evokes in the First Officer and the Second Officer a model of the expedited climb while the Captain seems to still be thinking standard climb.

This ATC clearance spawns more work to be conducted more or less autonomously by the members of the crew.

Memory in the state of artifacts: the altitude-alert system

The First Officer now has the information he needs to set the altitude-alert system. As soon as ATC says, 'Climb and maintain' he knows an altitude is coming next and he reaches forward to the altitude-alert setting knob. The setting of the altitude in the window of the altitude alert system is similar to the setting of the radio frequency in that in both cases information that had verbal representation comes to be represented in the state of a device in the cockpit. In both cases, the representation in the medium of the device is much more durable than the representation in speech, and it is much less vulnerable to interruption or displacement by other information than the same information represented in individual internal memory.

The strategy of using physical state as a form of memory is widespread. Unfortunately, its very ubiquity may lead us to overlook its importance and miss its theoretical significance. Writing something down to remember it is a common example with which we are all familiar. This happens in the cockpit too. Each pilot has a small clipboard near at hand with slips of paper on which clearances and other information may be written. But in the cockpit there are also other sets of devices that both remember the information and act on it autonomously. The altitude-alert system is a simple example.

Computation by propagation and transformation of representational state: computing and using the maximum EPRs

The portion of the clearance that said 'expedite the climb' spawned some autonomous action on the part of the Second Officer as well. The expedited climb requires maximum thrust from the engines. The concept of the expedited climb leads, for the Second Officer, to the notion of setting the engines to maximum thrust. This is done by pushing the thrust levers forward until the engine pressure ratio (EPR) gauges read the maximum permissible values given the current air temperature and altitude. We attribute to the Second Officer the goal of setting maximum engine thrust. In order to achieve this goal, the Second Officer needs to know what the maximum EPR settings are.

When ATC says 'expedite your climb,' the Second Officer turns to the engine performance tables that are printed on the work surface below his instrument panel and finds the appropriate EPR values. With the EPR values in memory, the Second Officer turns to the thrust levers and pushes them forward while monitoring the readings on the EPR gauges for a match to the remembered values. Thus, having satisfied the subgoal of finding the EPR values, the Second Officer returns to the top-level goal of setting the engines for maximum thrust.

Here again, we see the propagation and transformation of representational state across a number of media. The Second Officer's model of the expedited climb included an implication of maximum thrust. He propagated that information (plus altitude and total air temperature) into the climb EPR table. That transformed the inputs into outputs of EPR settings for the engines, which he then propagated to the EPR gauges by manipulating the thrust levels. Some of the media across which this information was propagated are internal to the Second Officer, others, like the EPR table, thrust levers, and the gauges, are external.

The table that the Second Officer uses to compute the appropriate maximum climb engine pressure ratios is a mediating artifact of a special sort. Originally, the values in the table were determined by the engineers who built the engines. This involves both empirical testing and theoretical calculations. The knowledge that was gained through that process is now crystallized as a hard artifact: the EPR table. In the EPR table, the information is represented in such a way that the task of extracting the appropriate values is very simple.

Intersubjectivity and distribution of storage again

While the Second Officer was computing the maximum climb EPRs, and the First Officer was setting the altitude-alert system, the Captain also had a job to do. He was supposed to read the clearance back to ATC. At 10:03:33 he read back, 'three three zero NASA nine hundred.' This is just the part of the clearance that matched the Captain's expectations about what sort of clearance he was to receive. Since, as we noted above, the Captain's readback is also available to the First Officer, it is possible that the Captain's readback violated the First Officer's expectation that the readback would contain mention of the 'expedite your climb' portion of the clearance.

After his incomplete readback (which was not challenged by ATC) the Captain turned to the First Officer and said, 'I didn't catch the last part.' The locutionary force of this statement is simply that the Captain did not hear something. The illocutionary force is an indirect request for the First Officer to tell the Captain whatever the 'last part' was. An interesting question at this point is: how can the First Officer know what the Captain means by the phrase 'the last part'? The First Officer answers 'expedite your climb,' which is both a response to the illocutionary force of the Captain's statement and a claim about what the Captain meant by 'the last part.' The Captain immediately says, 'OK,' which indicates that the First Officer did know what the Captain meant.

One conjecture is that the First Officer could establish the meaning of 'the last part' on purely syntactic grounds. The instruction portion of the clearance consisted of two main clauses: 'climb and maintain flight level three three zero' and 'expedite your climb please.' Perhaps the 'last part' simply refers to the second main clause. We believe that such an interpretation is implausible because there are no pragmatic conventions for referring to grammatical structures in this way. More likely, the First Officer, on the basis of what he has heard from the Captain's readback, may already suspect that the Captain did not hear the instruction to expedite the climb. Or, even without forming this expectation, when the Captain says he didn't catch the last part, the First Officer may ask himself what the 'last part' could mean and may remember that just one second earlier the Captain left 'expedite the climb' out of his readback. In either case, the intersubjectively shared expectations about the Captain's responsibilities in this situation form the basis for effective communication.

Firewall thrust!

Having learned that the clearance was to expedite the climb, the Captain now shares the image of the expedited climb with the other two members of the crew. As the Second Officer reaches for the thrust levers and begins pushing them forward to the maximum-climb thrust position, the Captain turns to the First Officer and Second Officer and says, 'That's firewall thrust.' Notice that no command is given to the Second Officer to increase engine thrust. He performs his role here without explicit verbal interaction with the other members of the crew. This action is interesting in two ways. First, it is another example of a sort of seamless joint performance constructed by a team whose members met for the first time only a few hours before takeoff. It suggests a kind of interchangeability of human parts that is a striking cultural and social organizational accomplishment. Second, one has to wonder whether any crew member would do something as consequential as this without verbally interacting with other crew members if the action were not completely visible to the other members of the crew. Given the location of the thrust levers, any manipulation of them is quite accessible to both the Captain and First Officer. In other portions of the flight, especially when the crew is faced with an equipment failure, the Second Officer takes other actions that are not visible to the pilots and notifies them of what he has done. This is only to say that the Second Officer makes decisions about the distribution of access to information and organizes his verbal behavior to compensate for the fact that some of his actions are not available to the other members of the crew.

The Captain's comment 'That's firewall thrust!' and the reaction of other members of the crew establishes the distribution of awareness of the Second Officer's action. The phrase itself is a figure of speech. It is a form of trope known as a synecdoche. Its interpretation requires a bit of history. In the old days, when single-engine planes had an engine in the front and the pilot's cockpit directly behind the engine, there was a hopefully fireproof wall between the cockpit and the engine. In case the engine caught fire, this wall (the 'firewall') was supposed to protect the crew from the fire. Throttles (the piston engine equivalent of jet thrust levers) were pushed forward for increased thrust. Maximum thrust was achieved by pushing the throttle levers right up to the firewall, hence the expression 'firewall thrust.'[15] This colorful expression brings to mind an image of pushing the thrust levers all the way forward to the stops.

The locutionary aspect of this comment is inaccurate (it is not firewall thrust) and the illocutionary force of this statement is inappropriate (one would not push the thrust levers forward to the stops in this airplane except in an emergency because doing so would most likely damage the engines). The perlocutionary aspect of the statement, however, is an assertion by the Captain that he now knows what is going on. He understands that the aircraft is cleared to climb at its maximum rate and that such a climb will require increased thrust.

Discussion

In this chapter, we have considered only a tiny fraction of one simulated airline flight. Yet, a close examination of even this one excerpt illustrates a number of features of the cockpit as a cognitive system. Information processing in the distributed system can be characterized as a propagation of a representational state across representational media. In the cockpit, some of the relevant representational media are located within the individual plots. Others, such as speech, are located between the pilots, and still others are in the physical structure of the cockpit. Every representational medium has physical properties that determine the availability of representations through space and time and constrain the sorts of cognitive processes required to propagate the representational state into or out of that medium. Changes in the medium of representation of task-relevant information or in the structure of representations within a particular medium can therefore have important consequences for the cognitive conduct of the cockpit system.

The movement of information through the system has consequences for the formation of expectations and models of the situation of the aircraft. These expectations and models organize the behavior of the crew and, when shared, permit the crew members to coordinate their actions with each other. Furthermore, the movement of information among members of the crew sometimes depends on the crew members' assessments of their own states of knowledge and those of the others. The relationship between the cognitive properties of the cockpit system, as determined by the movement of representations, and the cognitive properties of the individual pilots is therefore very complex.

The analysis identifies a set of possible pathways for information through the cockpit system during ATC clearance-handling events. Some of the pathways observed are those that are anticipated by the design of the system. Others, which were perhaps not intended in the design of the system, nevertheless contribute to its performance characteristics. Although we can never know in advance which particular pathways for information will actually be used, the analysis of this event establishes a sort of existence proof for the observed pathways. As we have seen, there are many possible pathways for information in this system. In some cases the pathways are redundant so that if one is blocked, task-relevant information can still proceed via another. This redundancy appears to contribute to the robustness of the system in the face of local failures.

Certainly, the cognitive properties of the cockpit system are determined in part by the cognitive properties of the individual pilots. They are also determined by the physical properties of the representational media across which a task-relevant representational state is propagated, by the specific organization of the representations supported in those media, by the interactions of metarepresentations held by the members of the crew, and by the distributional characteristics of knowledge and access to task-relevant information across the members of the crew. Understanding the properties of individual cognition is therefore only a first step in an effort to understand how these more complex human cognitive systems operate.

Notes

1. The simulator is part of the NASA–AMES research facility at Moffett Field, California. It is a very high fidelity simulation. The cockpit simulator interior is

a real airline cockpit with all the appropriate instruments and controls. The 'box' is mounted on hydraulic rams that give it six degrees of freedom motion. High-resolution television monitors are mounted over the windows of the cockpit to provide complete computer-generated night and dusk visuals.

2. A Standard Instrument Department (SID) for Sacramento. This is a published procedure for departing the airport area. The aircraft has completed the departure segment and is in the *en route* climb segment of the leg, so this chart will not be needed again.

3. Our data stream is actually richer than this indicates. Because these are flights in a computer-controlled simulator, we also have data on the readings of all of the primary cockpit instruments and the settings of all of the controls for the duration of the flight. This data is very useful in reconstructing the description of the events as they occurred.

4. The highly rationalized nature of this domain makes this sort of documentation possible. It may be that this sort of analysis would be much more difficult to conduct in a domain that lacks the long history and explicit representations of procedures and concepts that is available for aviation.

5. This action-level description of the observed verbal behavior, 'Oakland Center United nine hundred request higher,' is based on ethnographic constructs involving the syntax (who is being called, who is calling, nature of request) and semantics of communications with ATC.

6. The flight plan is actually developed by company dispatchers rather than by the pilots themselves. The planning activity here does not concern the development of the flight plan itself, but what is required in order to fly the flight as planned.

7. The latter part of this claim depends on company policy with respect to procedures that maximize fuel economy.

8. On every flight segment one of the pilots is designated 'pilot flying' and the other 'pilot not flying.' This distinction marks a high-level division of labor. The pilot flying is responsible for the control of the aircraft, whereas the pilot not flying is responsible for communications. Flight crews usually alternate in these roles from one flight segment to another.

9. In this instance, the Second Officer is on another channel making his departure report. Among the crew up front, it is important to know who is listening to what and when. Normal procedures require a crew member to notify the other members of the crew when he is not monitoring the primary ATC frequency.

10. The Airman's Information Manual says, 'Acknowledgement of frequency changes: When advised by ATC to change frequencies, acknowledge the instruction. If you select the new frequency without acknowledgement, the controller's workload is increased because he has no way of knowing whether you received the instruction or have had a radio communications failure' (FAR-AIM, 1989, Chapter 4, Paragraph 193, Section d).

11. The format of the numbers and the knowledge of the frequencies allotted to VHF radio communications for ATC (from 118.0 to 135.95 MHz) make this an abbreviated but unambiguous statement of the frequency, 132.8 MHz.

12. D.A. Norman, personal communication.

13. This is in part because training is expensive and does not generate any revenue. Operators thus have a strong economic incentive to get pilots out of the training system and into revenue operations as soon as is legally possible.

Several months of actual flying experience seem to lie between legal qualification and real mastery of the cockpit.

14. The syntax of the initial contact with a controller is spelled out in the Airman's Information Manual, Chapter 4, Section 7, Paragraph 340: ARTCC communications.

15. Because the throttle levers are normally capped with balls, an alternate expression was 'balls to the wall.' In American automotive parlance, the equivalent expression is 'pedal to the metal.'

References

Agar, M.H. (1986) *Speaking of Ethnography*. London: Sage.

Austin, J.L. (1960) *How To Do Things with Words*. Oxford: Clarendon Press.

D'Andrade, R.G. (1980) 'The cultural part of cognition', *Cognitive Science*, 5: 179–95.

Duranti, A. (1985) 'Sociocultural dimensions of discourse', in T. van Dijk (ed.), *Handbook of Discourse Analysis* (Vol. 1). New York: Academic Press.

Goodwin, C. (1994) 'Professional vision', *American Anthropologist*, 96(3): 606–33.

Hutchins, E. (1990) 'The technology of team navigation', in J. Galegher, R. Kraut and C. Egido (eds), *Intellectual Teamwork: Social and Technical Bases of Collaborative Work*. Hillsdale, NJ: Lawrence Erlbaum Associates.

Moerman, M. (1969) 'A little knowledge', in S. Tyler (ed.), *Cognitive Anthropology*. New York: Holt, Rinehart & Winston.

Norman, D.A. (1990) 'The "problem" with automation: inappropriate feedback and interaction, not "over-automation"', *Philosophical Transactions of the Royal Society of London*, B. 327.

Norman, D.A. (1993) *Things That Make Us Smart*. Reading, MA: Addison-Wesley.

Ochs, E. (1979) 'Transcription as theory', in E. Ochs and B. Schieffelin (eds), *Developmental Pragmatics*. New York: Academic Press.

Palmer, E.A., E.L. Hutchins, R.A. Ritter and I. van Cleemput (1993, October) 'Altitude deviations: breakdowns of an error tolerant system', *NASA Technical Memorandum 108788*. National Aeronautics and Space Administration, Ames Research Center, Moffett Field, CA.

Rommetveit, R. and R.M. Blakar (eds) (1979) *Studies of Language, Thought and Verbal Communication*. London: Academic Press.

Searle, J.R. (1969) *Speech Acts*. London: Cambridge University Press.

Wertsch, J.V. (1985) *Vygotsky and the Social Formation of Mind*. Cambridge, MA: Harvard University Press.

Part IV

The consumption of cultural products

7

Tourists at the Taj Mahal: walking and gazing

Tim Edensor

[. . .]

This is a narrative based on ethnography; as a researcher based in a Western academic institution carrying out work in India, I was mindful of the notion that 'colonialism, ethnography and tourism are forms of intervention and expansion that inhabit the space cleared by the reach of Western power' (Little, 1991: 159). Like colonizers and tourists, ethnographers tend to objectify and spectacularize what they find through the mobilization of particular techniques. Moreover, all three are often relatively wealthy and powerful. Also like colonizers and tourists, I was arriving with a host of preconceptions, a predisposition to gaze in a particular way and a situated and institutionalized form of knowledge.

In recognizing that all forms of knowledge are situated, and in order to create a narrative without closure, I have incorporated a diverse range of stories, although of course, the final selection of narrative is my responsibility. Hopefully the voices in this book create a 'messy text' wherein multiple perspectives are conducive to the production of a 'communitarian moral ethic' (Denzin, 1997: xiv–xv) which informs the best ethnographies. This of course, is diametrically opposed to colonial knowledge, which erases the voice of the colonized and authoritatively enunciates objective facts about the space and culture it surveys.

Crick has recognized some of the parallels between tourists and ethnographers, especially insofar as they both reproduce conventional representations and discourses which codify how difference can be understood. Both also follow instrumental strategies whereby they may acquire experience and tangible rewards; tourists gain souvenirs and photographs whilst ethnographers, like myself, collect material for publication (Crick, 1991: 16). In recognition of some of the parallels between tourists and

This is an edited extract from Tim Edensor (1998) *Tourists at the Taj: Performance and meaning at a symbolic site* London: Routledge.

ethnographers, and in order to put myself in the picture as a performer in tourist space, I have, where appropriate, attempted to summarize the ways in which I narrated the Taj, walked around the site and gazed at objects of interest to me.

There has been a recent profusion of writing on the inevitable situatedness of research and theory within the social sciences which has acted to focus concern upon the extremely ethnocentric approaches of many Western ethnographers (Clifford and Marcus, 1986). These have been brought to book for failing to locate their ontological and epistemological framework within a particular culture. This emphasis has highlighted the necessity of locating the self in any ethnographic research. Despite the best intentions of the researcher, the elimination of ethnocentric bias cannot be completely expunged and it is as well to admit that any ethnography is bound to be affected by the culturally specific responses of the researcher. A careful reflexivity about the likelihood of making situated assumptions is advisable.

[. . .]

My approach in this study has been informed by Neumann's contention that:

> Tourist sites are an appropriate place for locating the broad debate over self and society. . . . Tourism is a metaphor for our struggle to make sense of our self and world within a highly differentiated culture . . . it directs us to sites where people are at work making meaning, situating themselves in relation to public spectacle and making a biography that provides some coherency between self and world. (1988: 22)

Renowned tourist sites such as the Taj Mahal are places where visitors are engaged in constructing and reproducing meaning and carrying out particular performances. As a global site, a destination for people who follow journeys of different scale, from the Western tourists to local visitors, these meanings vary greatly, are contested, and are articulated by different narratives and practices. As Urry says, sites are

> constructed through multiple texts which combine to produce a particular tourist text, albeit one whose meanings are shifting, unstable and contested. At the same time it is important to recognise that texts themselves are part of larger frameworks of signification, of narratives, concepts, ideologies, metaphors, practices. (1994: 238)

My aim is to identify the major ways in which different tourists make sense of the Taj Mahal, and also how they perform a diverse range of enactions at the site.

[. . .]

In order to specify the (changing) practices which tourists carry out, I have chosen to develop the metaphor of tourist performances. I consider performance to be useful conceptually since the constraints and opportunities that influence tourist's actions and experiences are important. I have noted that tourist spaces are differently regulated. If we consider these tourist spaces to be performative spaces, or 'stages', it is clear that certain types of performance are constrained by carefully managed stages, whereas less overtly controlled stages potentially permit wider scope for improvization. Similarly, tours are organized according to distinct spatio-temporal imperatives where restrictions on performance might be imposed by tour personnel, or conversely, individual travellers may be unsupervised. Thus, I will explore the relationship between different forms of tourist space and tour management, and tourist performance, specifically around narration, walking, gazing and photographing, and remembering, activities which continually reconstitute tourist space.

[. . .]

Walking

Tourism intimately concerns movement, that of a journey from an everyday situation to an extraordinary location. Tourism, as a set of embodied practices, is distinguishable from other social forms of practice. This passage through material space, as opposed to virtual movement, requires the activation of particular embodied techniques, dispositions and epistemologies which are enacted *in situ*. The aspect of tourist movement examined here is walking, a performance which 'entails movement through space in stylised ways' (Adler, 1989b: 1366).

Walking is an activity central to tourism. Landscapes are criss-crossed and imprinted with the bodily presence of the visitor, and symbolic sites are negotiated via various paths. Walking and moving through space partly constitutes places, as 'the habitual routines of "place ballets" are concretised in the built environment and sedimented in the landscape' (Shields, 1991: 53). However, the amount of time tourists spend walking, the paths they take, and the extent to which they veer from the established trails varies. Thus, both the modalities of walking and the diverse constitutions of place are shaped by the different spatial and temporal designs of tours.

I use the metaphor of choreography to convey the ways in which tourists' bodies are tutored in 'appropriate' ways and form patterns of collective and individual movement through tourist space. I have discussed the political significance of walking in the city described by de Certeau, the way in which pedestrians negotiate routes that conditionally free them from the regulated nature of the space they traverse. Game also reveals how through walking,

> things extra and other, heterogeneous details and elements insert themselves . . .
> practices . . . that cannot be put into representation, cannot be seen, fragmentary
> pasts that cannot be read by others. (1991: 153)

However, whether through the regulation exerted by the scrutiny of tour personnel, fellow travellers, or self-surveillance, bodies following strict choreographies are less likely to experience the sensuality excited by less rigid choreographies. Where there are opportunities for visitors to construct their own improvisational trails, a potential escape from dominant narratives and practices is enabled. Casual wandering, lounging, and 'hanging around' may specify a disposition that implies a different relationship between pedestrian and place. As Game points out, 'to wander is to err from the straight and narrow of linearity, of the order' (1991: 149), in this case, to deviate from organized passage through disciplined tourist space.

Places are also organized with modes of transit in mind. The kind of unilinear flows and obstacle-free streets of enclavic tourist space contrast with the numerous impediments and rough surfaces of heterogeneous tourist space. Tourist spaces, like certain cities, 'invite a writing of the stroll, others are closed, direct the walk, or make it impossible' (Game, 1991: 151). The variations of bodily contact and sensual encounter experienced by movement through these distinct stages structure the performances and choreographies of tourism. I will outline the diverse walking performances at the Taj, but within the context of the wider experience of tourist space.

For many tourists, especially those on package tours, their movements are shaped by a directedness that permits only a modicum of innovation. Since these tours are usually organized to fulfil the imperative to see 'as much as possible', to sample as many places as can be crammed in, the range of places to see and explore is paradoxically limited by a pre-determined, condensed itinerary. Moreover, the rigid dispensation of time necessitates the discouragement of lingering and so the opportunity to explore sites at a leisurely pace is often denied by tour personnel. Accordingly, most movement is encapsulated in buses, cars and planes and walking occurs only in brief bursts of collective sightseeing at attractions and by meandering through the regulated space of tourist enclaves; browsing in shops and restaurants, and wandering around gardens and golf-courses, stretching the legs over familiar territory.

In the structure of the holiday as a whole, for most package tourists the Taj is the most important sight/site on a visit to India. Of the several key attractions around which tours are organized, the Taj occupies centre stage. Tour organizers and guides whet expectations, emphatically predicting that the Taj will be the pinnacle of the trip. The site's centrality was conveyed to me by the tourists themselves who expressed how it was both anticipated and produced as the highlight:

> *Wanda (29, pharmacist, from London, on a two-week package tour)*: Most of our group have been completely and totally geared up to seeing it. This was the place we were all waiting to come to.

> *Phil (27, accountant, from London, on a two-week package tour with his partner)*: Everyone in our group kept saying it was going to be the highlight of the tour – and that's what all the tour guides were saying too.

After visiting the site, the assertion that the Taj was the highlight of the tour was retrospectively confirmed by 75 per cent of the package tourists I interviewed. It appeared to live up to the expectations of the majority of the package tourists and was favourably compared with other sights:

> *Anne (46, catering manager, from Leeds, on a two-week package tour with her friend)*: Well we liked the Red Fort, but the big thing has been the Taj. I mean, what a building. That was always going to be the highlight of the holiday.

Yet despite its central importance, most package tours only spend about one hour at the site. As I will discuss, this limited time is a matter of discontent for many tourists since visits to the Taj must be highly managed and organized so that what are considered to be the most important aspects can be crammed in.

At the Taj, obeying the instructions of guides and tour organizers, most package tourists follow prescribed paths, moving towards certain valorized spaces and features and not others. The performance of these disciplined collective choreographies constitutes a quite precise and predictable 'place-ballet' (see Figure 7.1). Bodies are tutored and disciplined, kept together and directed by assumptions about what is deemed 'appropriate', by group norms, and principally by the orders of the guide. Upon entering at its side, groups congregate upon the platform by the central gateway for a few minutes while the guide dispenses information and tour members take photographs. Following this, the central walkway is negotiated, the platform at the crossroads of the water-course provides another gazing and photography point for a few minutes, the marble base upon which the Taj rests is ascended and the tombs are explored, and occasionally the back of the mausoleum platform is traversed. Besides these areas, few other areas are explored and only a fraction of the possible spaces, views, and sensations in the grounds of the Taj can be experienced. These guided tours around the Taj are, with a few exceptions, highly regular. The tourist gaze is successively directed towards the following features as information about them is dispensed:

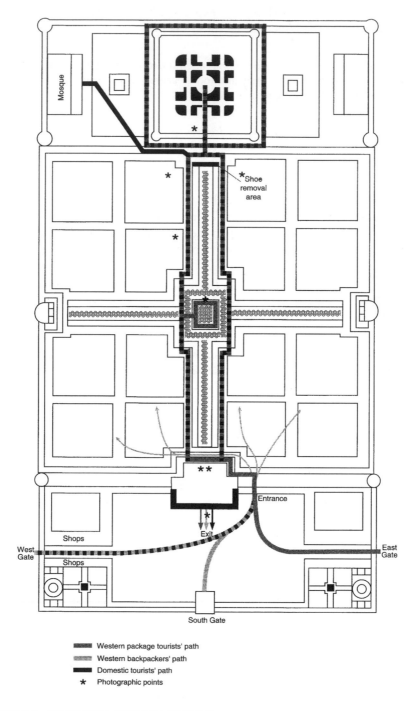

Figure 7.1   *Tourist paths around the Taj Mahal*

Stage 1 (by the central gateway): The Taj as a whole: the famous global image looking down the water-course to the Taj

1 a statement that the Taj is the most famous/greatest/largest building to love in the world; the romantic story of Shahjahan's love for his queen;
2 the extraordinary cost of the building; how long it took to complete; the numbers of workers; the myth that they had their hands cut off upon completion of the Taj to prevent any subsequent employment on other buildings;
3 architectural aspects: the special features synthesizing Hindu and Muslim traditions, notably the dome, the minarets and the symmetry of the building.

Stage 2 (at the central platform)
much photographing – this is conventionally the point from which individual portraits of tourists are composed. Also, most guides indicate the seat upon which the lovelorn Princess Diana sat when she visited the Taj.

Stage 3 (at the tombs or by the mausoleum)

1 description of the pietra dura inlaying with references to the types of stones used and always the application of a torch beam to the work to highlight its translucence;
2 the myth of the mooted construction of the 'Black Taj'; Shahjahan's imprisonment in the Red Fort by his son and his longing gaze towards his creation, the Taj.

These regular guide narratives, frequently mediated between the Orientalist themes of splendour, excess, cruelty and femininity, and the nationalist synthetic ideology restrict the interpretation of visitors by the transmission of packaged information. Between the guides, the tour operators and the tourists themselves, there is a constant bandying about of clichés, superlatives and ways of looking at the Taj. Emphatically this ingrained 'place-ballet' epitomizes the satisfaction of realizing anticipated consumption, and then quickly moving the party on to another site of consumption – following a visit to the Taj, as for any attraction on their tour, the next stop is invariably a craft emporium. In the case of the Taj, the retail outlet concerned usually sells marble-inlay products, echoing the recently gazed upon marble and inlay work at the building and further commodifying the Taj experience. Consequently, tour guides are anxious to get to the emporia as quickly as possible to maximize the amount of time, and therefore, money spent there, so that they can increase the opportunities for collecting commission on the purchases completed by the tour group. Since the whole Agra tourist industry is typified by schemes for gaining commission for guides, drivers and other tourist personnel, there is a powerful incentive for tourist workers and organizations to utilize strategies that boost their potential rake-off.

Walking around the Taj fits into a wider pattern of spatial control over tour members, echoing the extremely directed choreographies of other sites. Passage is very specifically timed so that a maximum time may be spent at each stop on the march around the building. The organizational imperative to keep the tour party together means that discipline is imposed upon those who stray too far. In fact, the need to keep groups in tight formation is emphasized shortly before the party enters the site. Guides issue warnings such as, 'Don't get lost or we will have to leave you behind', and, 'Beware of dishonest people who will try to take advantage of you'. The construction of the site as one where great care must be taken is certainly exaggerated since there are numerous tourist police present to prevent transgressions.

However, the tightly constricted movement of packaged tourists can result in considerable frustration. For many tourists, the view from the back of the Taj – the meandering Jamuna River, the herds of buffaloes, the washing of clothes and bathing people, and occasionally, the passage of smouldering funeral pyres from the burning ghats further upstream – represents a timeless vision of the 'real' India. Movement towards and through this less regulated space is strongly desired. Tourists express the urge to go down to the river, to mingle with the buffaloes and cow-herds and yet rarely do so because of the aforementioned time-constraints and their own fear of the apparent 'otherness' they are looking at.

Tourists also express frustration with the onslaught of information:

> Guy (48, lecturer, from Northampton, UK, on a ten-day package tour with his partner): The guide's been talking to us for about half an hour. He's taken us to various spots but he tends to bombard you with too much information. You try to have a look round but the guide says, 'Come on, we need to go' and he's only going to leave us on our own to do our own thing for a quarter of an hour.

But for many, given that a visit to the Taj is so eagerly anticipated and the main incentive for their trip to India, restrictions on time are the most keenly felt source of frustration, especially when they are whisked off to another craft emporium:

> Jeremy (63, lawyer, from Oxford, UK, on a two-week package tour with his partner): We've been here one hour, which isn't nearly enough time, but they say we've got limited time. We're going to see another marble shop now – thanks, but no thanks, we'd rather go for a beer.

> Phil (27, accountant, from London, on a two-week package tour with his partner): We went to the Taj and then straight after, to a marble inlay shop. They

showed us how they made the things and then did the hard sell. I mean, that's happened everywhere, in Delhi and Jaipur as well, and honestly, it does get a bit much.

Dawn (53, nurse, from New York, on a three-week tour with her partner which incorporates China, India and the UK): I've felt they've hustled us in some areas. I'd rather see the Taj than go shopping. You really get that everywhere you go on this tour. I mean, we've come all the way from New York to see the Taj, and then you've gotta go after a few minutes to some shop.

Yet despite this tension, many tourists seek distance from any external social interaction and a more physical engagement with the environment. Although the Taj is highly regulated and policed, unease at intrusions upon their progress around the site causes many package tourists to shrink from independent photographers and guides hustling for their custom. Upon reaching the platform on which the mausoleum stands, visitors are required to remove their footwear in recognition of its Islamic significance and as a mark of respect to the dead, and store them in an area by the stairs, leaving a small tip for the custodians. Domestic tourists go barefoot on to the platform but many package tourists prefer to pay an extra charge to keep their shoes on and tie a cloth bag around their feet. This provides an apt metaphor for the way in which package tourists insulate themselves from the physical sensations and imagined potential diseases in the Indian environment, forever retaining a certain distance from the crowds.

In heterogeneous tourist spaces where there is not the same form of surveillance, tourists traverse spaces where routes are not laid out, and activities are not tightly regulated. This is not to deny that there are particular touristic practices which adhere to a style of travelling, but there is the possibility of mobile exploration and escape from these norms. Where tourists have greater time at their disposal, they have the opportunity to explore a wider range of spaces on foot, to consider sights and attractions from different angles, to wander off the 'beaten track' and find a preferred spot. The average time spent in India by Western backpackers is 3.48 months. This time is generally unstructured and schedules tend to be improvised. Individual travellers, or those in small groups, therefore, tend to be more improvisational in their movement, contingent decisions to stay here or go there being made at short notice.

Many backpackers are aware of this distinction between themselves and package tourists, a demarcation they are keen to point out by way of emphasizing what they consider to be their superior, more individualistic mode of travel and their deeper level of perception. While many backpackers do visit the Taj Mahal, most assert that it is not central to their itinerary.

The following quote exemplifies the way in which this attitude influences their decision to visit the Taj:

David (26, writer, from Glasgow, UK, travelling on his own in India for six months): I feel very reluctant to pander to, to go to specific tourist type areas, particularly buildings and monuments. But there's normally a couple of times when I throw caution to the wind and go. I thought this would be a monument that I'd want to see, especially because of the energy of the place. I think that's what these kind of places are – high energy places – and that's what draws people to them. You can accumulate a lot of knowledge about a particular place but ultimately it's down to the actual vibrations and the emotional aspect.

It is notable that David stressed that he wanted to 'throw caution to the wind' in visiting the Taj. Presumably he felt that his status as an independent traveller might be compromised in some way and there is a clear notion that a traveller such as he should not 'pander' to these attractions. Also, he values emotional and spiritual responses in opposition to the collection and consumption of information about the Taj, and these are typical backpacker imperatives as we shall see. This indicates some of the motivations that impel such travel to India.

Although it is not a central focus of their travels, backpackers who do visit the Taj Mahal spend far more time there than any other tourists. Most stay longer than two days in Agra and thus make use of the opportunity to visit the nearby Taj (the area of backpackers' hotels is adjacent to the Taj) on more than one occasion. Many spend most of the day at the Taj and the average time spent there at any one visit is five hours. Since there is rarely any pressing need for them to keep to a schedule, many visit the Taj two or three times to 'hang out', socialize, watch people or read. Thus, time is not only spent gazing at the Taj but entails a diverse range of activities.

Having a greater control over their own use of time, backpackers cover a wider spatial range. The 'place-ballets' of backpackers tend to be less confined (see Figure 7.1). At the Taj, they wander over the whole area of the site, sit amongst the trees, sprawl out upon the lawn and stroll down lateral paths. This choreography incorporates a number of different movements as backpackers move from one spot to another, taking in the views or watching the passers-by. There are no regular locations at which backpackers position themselves and there are no external constraints over where they may roam. The Taj often serves as a site for social intercourse, backpackers often sit in groups and chat, or talk to domestic tourists or locals. Indeed, the space of the Taj represents something of a meeting place where they can sit and share experiences and recommendations about their travels.

These individual, improvisational movements indicate a desire to remain unrestricted. Indeed, backpackers do not usually employ guides to tour the Taj since this is believed to restrict their freedom in looking and moving. Likewise, most are not concerned with consuming a large quantity of information about the monument by reading about its history and architecture. It is generally considered better to gain more immediate impressions from the site than in consuming information, for it is through reflexivity and supposedly unmediated impressions that one can get a 'feeling' for the Taj:

Michael (39, strategic consultant, from Melbourne, Australia, travelling in India with his friend for one month): You can read about it but it doesn't help at all in experiencing it. It's the same with a guided tour. Having someone who explains the individual features is not of great interest. It's what stays in the mind; the essence.

Fiona (31, EFL teacher, London, travelling in India on her own for an unfixed period): I love the space here, it's beautiful, but I don't like to think about it in these ways: Why read about it? Why go on the guided tour? You have to meditate on it as a spiritual symbol.

The stress on this mode of consuming the Taj also connotes the afore-mentioned backpacker desire to be identified as different from the package tourist by virtue of their greater individualism:

Karl (59, semi-permanent traveller, from Enschede, Holland; has bought an Enfield motorcycle and is travelling around India for as long as he wants): I'm an individual. I don't like to follow a leader. And I don't like so many people round me. I like company, certainly, but not this way. When I have got my own impressions and worked them out, then I like to read about it.

Besides, the opportunities that they have for dialogue with both Indians and other diverse travellers at the site means that meaning can be nego-tiated and shared. In a sense, this also accords with the desire for self-realization and the notion that India forms a space in which such enlightenment can be achieved. This individualistic pursuit engenders a certain reflexivity amongst backpackers, which is manifest in the ways in which much of the time spent at the Taj involves meditation, sketching and journal-writing. The experiences confronted are reincorporated into located ways of containment and comprehension as part of a larger project of self-education, and the enaction of certain choreographies in tourist space is instrumental to this goal: the wandering through space absorbing stimuli and drifting off into fantasy and memory; the repose in yogic meditation; and the movement towards 'otherness'. This less-organized movement can lead to chance occurrences that destabilize culturally located epistemologies and common-sense impressions.

Another form of touristic choreographed movement, the most specific and formalized, is performed by those tourists who partake in ceremonial procedures to commemorate and signify their link with particularly sym-bolic sites. The rituals may be formalized calendrical occasions or individ-ual actions that inscribe the relationship between site and visitor.

Although there are certainly elements of such ritual performances in the disciplined tourist choreographies discussed above, I am referring here to the many Muslim visitors to the Taj, who stay for a much longer time than other domestic tourists, on average about three hours. They tend to approach the Taj with veneration and linger for a long time in the grounds. Collectively or singly, Muslims slowly walk around the mausoleum, read-ing the Quranic messages embedded in the structure, stand inside gazing upon the tombs, and sit on the marble terrace in silent contemplation.

A visit to the tombs of the emperor and his wife is a sacred activity in itself. Prayers are recited and visitors may stay in the chamber for several minutes as if paying homage to the departed. In fact, the Muslim guardians of the tombs, who keep a twenty-four-hour vigil inside the mausoleum in shifts, are known as *Khadims*, and are selected on a hereditary basis, some claiming descendance from the time of Shahjahan. Paid by the local government, these men also carry out specifically religious functions in regularly praying for the departed and defending the tombs. Muslim visitors also cross the square to visit the mosque to the East of the mausoleum, a space where few non-Muslim visitors go. Thus the movement of Muslim visitors follows a purposive and predictable spatial pattern. The very meaning of the space, saturated with notions of the sacred, informs a practice which is concerned with rapid movement to spiritually significant features.

Besides the constraining demands imposed by most package tours, most forms of group travel involve a certain amount of peer-group pressure. There are often demands to stay within the orbit of the group and engage in collective activities which limit individual trajectories. Group-oriented activity depends on the confining of individual desires. Thus, tourist groups that are not organized by a travel company nevertheless are disposed to 'stick together' and follow collective paths.

There are few solitary domestic tourists since a trip to the Taj is primarily an experience to be shared, usually with the family. This collective mode of travel highlights normative social life and identity, in which the family, caste group and community is integral to a sense of security. Social occasions such as religious rituals, pilgrimages, parties and holidays typically bring the members of extended Indian families together. About 75 per cent of domestic tourists are part of family groups, comprising from three to fifty persons, with the average group numbering approximately ten. As I have remarked, during pilgrimage season large coach parties of villagers visit the site *en route* to sacred centres. This communal approach to visiting places structures choreography.

These groups tend to stay extremely close to one another whilst walking around the Taj. Different points are stopped at collectively and tourists tend to move off *en masse*. This collective movement is not a matter of seeking safety in potentially dangerous space or a response to any perceived threat of epistemological chaos. Whereas package tours are regulated by agents such as guides, this place-ballet signifies a powerful sense of group identity and particular norms of collective spatial practice, such as a lack of self-consciousness about keeping one's distance. Most forms of leisure in India are similarly communally oriented.

The choreography of these groups is also shaped by the manner in which the Taj is consumed visually. The non-enaction of a romantic gaze means that domestic groups rarely linger at the entrance gazing upon the Taj. The usual procedure is for them to walk quickly down the central walkway, rapidly enter and exit the tombs, sometimes walk around the building, and then turn back, usually exiting without a backward glance. It is as if the building has been witnessed, admired, and is part of the day out but of no special affective importance, producing a series of movements which are not slowed down by reflexive contemplation.

The rapid coverage of space is reflected in the relatively short time that most domestic tourists spend at the Taj. Over half stay at the site for less than an hour and 25 per cent spend less than two hours there although occasionally groups will sit on the grass, chatting. However, this is rendered less appealing by the fact that in comparison to most other public spaces in India, regulation of the Taj prohibits eating in the grounds. Tourists complain that picnicking is very much part of the Indian day out and should not be forbidden. Due to this restriction, many visitors eat their lunches outside the site. One guide, Vinod, reported:

> Indians are great picnickers, they have a picnicking mentality. The average Indian has no great knowledge about the Taj. It is just a famous thing to see. Any outing is an excuse for a feast. If food was allowed in here, it would be a vast scene of families eating, litter everywhere.

Of course, if the rules restricting eating in the premises were relaxed, the choreographies of these visitors would take a very different form.

The social function of a visit to the Taj is reinforced by the belief that it is a good place at which to meet other Indian and Western tourists. Accordingly, groups frequently make contact with each other and step off the central paths to converse, and Western tourists are approached, chatted to and often photographed with the group. The national symbolic significance of the site and the co-presence of members of the 'imagined community' of India mean that national pride and solidarity – unity in diversity – can be celebrated:

> *Kusuma (22, housewife, from Bangalore, on a four-week honeymoon)*: The Taj makes us feel great about India, feel great love for our country. It reveals our culture to foreigners, and it's wonderful for all kinds of Indians to visit the Taj and meet people from all over the country.

Passage around the site then, is coordinated by the group. Like Western backpackers, domestic tourists have little interest in partaking in a guided tour, requiring neither information nor guidance:

> *Jaysing (31, sergeant in Indian Air Force, on pilgrimage to Mathura with a party of twenty-three)*: We have no interest in guides. What's the point? We can see it! A guide is not necessary for the enjoyment of the building. They only want money and to waste our time. We prefer to form our own impressions.

> *Ratilal (47, jeweller, from Ahmedebad, on pilgrimage to various sacred sites with a party of ten)*: We would have no freedom. A guide would restrict our movements and tell us where to go and what to look at, and so we would not use our own minds but concentrate on boring details.

Besides tourist use, the Taj is widely used by locals as a place to meet, stroll around, watch domestic and foreign tourists, worship, and hang out. As they are let in free at all times, local boys tease the tourists or plague them with requests for money when the tourist police are not around and, for them, the Taj serves as a large playground. Amongst the bushes and trees at the sides of the gardens, on the banks of the Jamuna, and all over the site, local boys play, weaving paths of childhood adventure.

Access for local adults is restricted to Fridays, when entry is free. On this, the busiest day, the influx of local Muslim worshippers visiting the mosque transforms the atmosphere of the site. For the local Muslims in Taj Ganj, the mosque is the most popular in the area. A second mosque also forms part of the Moghul complex, just outside the West gate. Because it is a religious building, local Muslims feel they should be granted access at any time and deeply resent what they regard as the unconstitutional entrance charge which effectively debars many of them from going as often as they would like:

> *Mehmood (30, shopkeeper)*: The Taj is a holy building therefore there should be no tickets for anybody. Why should there be obstacles put in the way of people to visit the Taj, a building they love, for religious reasons?

On Fridays, young local men approach foreigners and attempt to strike up conversations, practising their English and engaging in political, religious or other issues about which they are curious. This is a regular pastime for some of these youths. A fifteen-year-old schoolboy told me:

> *Sanjeev*: We like to look at the tourists, try and guess where they come from and then ask them. We come here every Friday after school and we like to talk to the tourists so that we can learn about different countries and also give information about our lives, and practise our English.

Meeting and conversing with strangers is a common leisure practice amongst Agran youth and the Taj is the pre-eminent site for this pursuit, and has been for many years. Besides being the site where local youths meet foreigners, several elderly men hang around on Fridays, reading, and frequently approach English visitors, with whom they feel they have an historical connection through colonialism and an affinity of interest in literature, in order to strike up discussions.

The temporal and spatial control which determines local use of the Taj, highlights how the site, like most major historical tourist attractions, is subject to surveillance. Tourist police prohibit 'undesirables' from entry, bags are searched, and certain types of behaviour are proscribed, such as touching artworks, eating and drinking, or failing to remove shoes in particular areas. Thus, spatial control has intensified, impacting particularly on locals. Local men told me that when they were younger and fewer visitors came to the Taj, they had much more freedom to do as they wished. There used to be no admission charge so they could go at any time, and the site was not policed to the extent that it is today. Consequently, the range of activities engaged in at the Taj was greater. One man summarized this change, highlighting how such activities were increasingly passive and visual:

> *Jawarhal (45, perfume seller)*: In the old days it used to be fun. We would come here any time we wanted to, and we would play cards and drink beer all afternoon. This has now been stopped and we are not allowed to do anything except just sit here and look.

This intensified control over the space of the Taj reflects the increased spatial regulation over tourist spaces in Agra. The control of access and movement in the Taj is apparently partly a response to the perceived threat of terrorist activity with the upsurge in communal tension in the past decade and lingering mistrust of Pakistan. The queues waiting to enter the Taj are subject to surveillance and kept moving by officious police. Bags and over-garments are checked and no electronic equipment other than cameras (though not video cameras) are allowed in. Once inside the grounds, tourist police stop visitors from picnicking and throwing litter and generally keep watch over the crowds. Control is maintained over touting and only officially sanctioned workers are permitted to ply their trade. Previously, the Taj was open for twenty-four hours and visitors were able to satisfy their desire to gaze at the Taj under moonlight, but this is now not possible since it closes at 7 p.m.

This surveillance and control extends to a rather different performance at the Taj which affects both tourists and locals, namely the commandeering of the Taj for the visit of foreign dignitaries. On these occasions, the site becomes even more policed than usual; tourists awaiting admission often have to wait until the VIPs have completed the visit and those who have already entered are ushered to the sidelines by baton- and rifle-wielding soldiers so that eminent visitors have an unimpeded passage down the central walkway. If an especially important foreign personage is arriving or one for whom stringent security is thought necessary then the Taj can be closed for a large part of the day, an enormous inconvenience for those tourists who have a limited stay in Agra. The space of the Taj then becomes totally subject to official control, all visitors or nearby strollers are subject to concentrated surveillance. Here then, the ultimate spatial control of the Taj is exercised by the Indian government who at this official level, further inscribe the Taj as the pre-eminent attraction for visitors to India.

My own spatial performances at the Taj were varied. In order to identify the regularities of performance and the diverse spatio-temporal patterns by which tourists organized their tours of the Taj, it was necessary to spend as much time as possible at the site. Unlike tourists then, and more akin to the many workers at the site, I spent long periods of most days over a six-month spell carrying out work *in situ*. Much of the time I spent sitting at the most obvious vantage points – upon the three platforms – so that I could identify the routes taken by tourists. At other times I would follow guided tours, listening to guide's commentaries and the remarks of tourists, and also cover all marginal areas of the site so that I could identify ways in which particular tourists might be drawn to them. Interviews with domestic tourists were usually recorded on the platform of the mausoleum, so that the tourist police were less likely to see my small secreted cassette recorder, and interviews with backpackers were generally carried out on the lawns. It proved difficult to interview package tourists at the Taj given their limited time and the extent to which they were required to adhere to their party. This meant that I had to carry out research in the evening at the hotels in which they stayed, when there was more time and no pressure from tour personnel. To maximize opportunities for ethnographic research and to ensure I interviewed a wide range of tourists, I had to follow the choreographies of a large diversity of visitors. My walking performances of necessity followed many and various routes. Whilst this sort of research meant that I had to be disciplined and instrumental in my strategies for information retrieval and hence in my movements, this was frequently foiled. Because I became something of a familiar fixture at the Taj, I was apt to be engaged in conversation at any point with local visitors and guides, often important key informants, who might interrupt any ethnographic strategy I was pursuing. Thus, out of politeness and a desire to converse, research had to be combined with pleasure. In this sense, then, besides being a site of work, the Taj was for me, as it is for other workers at the site, a stage upon which sociable encounters were played out.

The distinctive walking performances that I have described impinge upon the ways in which the tourists gaze upon the Taj Mahal. For instance, the coverage of particular routes dictates the angles and views that can be consumed, the length of time spent at the site determines the degree of scrutiny the monument can be subject to, and the norms of collective behaviour condition the importance of gazing to experience the Taj, as I will now discuss.

Gazing

The visual dominates the sensory consumption of tourist attractions much as it prevails in the image-saturated societies of contemporary capitalism. In the ocularcentric West it has been considered 'the noblest of the senses' (Crawshaw and Urry, 1997: 177) and yet according to Howes, this sensual preoccupation means that other senses such as smell and hearing are underdeveloped (1991: 170). In tourism, gazes are socially organized around a set of techniques which lay the basis for visual performances. The ascendancy of the ocular has arisen out of historical tendencies to construct tourist sites in particular ways, and construct a normative set of gazing practices. As Urry contends, 'to gaze as a tourist is to insert oneself within a historical process and to consume signs or markers of particular histories'

(1992: 182). Thus the organization of tours emerges from situated aesthetics and ways of seeing which reflect particular ideologies and norms.

For Western tourists, Adler avers that 'sight itself has been differently conceived in the course of tourism history'. For instance, she describes how sixteenth-century travellers were more concerned with discursive performance and learning than ocular absorption. Thus the word was considered more important than the image, and the ear and tongue predominated over the eye (Adler, 1989a: 8). Gradually, however, experiences gained through sight came to be perceived as mirroring reality. At first, the duty of the traveller was to classify and quantify things seen through an 'emotionally detached, objectively accurate vision' (ibid: 14). However, by the end of the eighteenth century this was replaced by a more romantic gaze as

the well trained 'eye' . . . made authoritative judgements of aesthetic merit, as travel itself became an occasion for the cultivation and display of taste. . . . Experiences of beauty and sublimity, sought through the sense of sight, were valued for their spiritual significance to the individual who cultivated them. (Adler, 1989a: 22)

These romantic performances were encouraged by, and stimulated, the development of the picturesque tour which normalized the contemporary notion that visual contemplation of the extraordinary is appropriate, and that such a practice develops the sensibilities of the onlooker. The obligation to gaze in this affective way continues to inform much contemporary tourism and yet there is now a proliferation of things, people and sites to gaze upon, transforming them into touristic spectacles. There are various techniques to regulate and direct the tourist gaze. The products of the media and the images disseminated by magazines, adverts, tour brochures, films and TV drama and travel programmes confirm and introduce objects worthy of gazing upon. These common-sense notions as to what sorts of features ought to be gazed at are frequently ordained by guides, guidebooks, information boards and signposts which direct tourists to 'outstanding' features. MacCannell (1976) terms this secondary inscription of significant attractions 'sight sacralisation'. The kind of landscape constructed here is a curious one where the unquantified and ill-defined terrain of non-tourist space is punctuated by tourist spectacles against which it is the backdrop. Following this selection of objects to be gazed upon, particular techniques of visual representation frame tourist performances and experiences. The collection of souvenirs, postcards and photographs help to order the 'range of often disparate and relatively unconnected sights' (Urry, 1992: 181) and structure the tourist gaze.

But whilst there are predominant tour technologies that are reinforced by normative tourist performances, tourist gazes are performed in different ways and are directed to a range of objects, as Urry has described, distinguishing between types of tourist gaze (1992: 184). I will show how different visual performances may be enacted at the same place.

Tourism involves both the collection of archetypal quotidian cultural signs of otherness (Culler, 1981), and the journey to gaze upon extraordinary places. There are 'common-sense' hierarchies of those attractions most deserving of such attention, as the popularity of various seven wonders of the world in the nineteenth century indicates. Whether remarkable or quotidian, sights have come to capture metaphorically the essence of a place. However, rather than gaze upon places and objects in any pure or natural form, tourists confront a series of cultural discourses that distinguish places in terms of particular values. We see a 'canyon-as-a-geological-wonder', 'a field-as-historical-battleground' or 'a painting-as-a-work-of-genius' (Neumann, 1988: 22), and the theming processes discussed increasingly frame and mark out these distinctions.

For most Western tourists, the Taj continues to be the principal site for gazing at, and consuming India. As an example of the sights and signs collected by contemporary tourist-semioticians, the Taj, as a constructed symbol of the 'Other', is a synecdoche for India. Although globally the most famous and reproduced sight of India, and therefore, in a sense, 'already seen', it nevertheless remains the focus of the tourist gaze, notwithstanding the existence of landscapes in India that offer manifold juxtapositions of images, visual diversity and unpredictable sights.

In the colonial era, a British travel writer asserted that, 'Once one has seen the Taj, one has no further interest in the town of Agra. The descent from the topmost pinnacles of sublimity to the ordinary fatuousness of everyday is ridiculous' (Steevens, 1909: 40). Likewise, some Western package tourists declare that seeing the Taj was their only motivation in choosing India for their holiday destination:

> Bess (62, retired head teacher, from Staffordshire, UK, on a two-week package tour with her friend): I had no great desire to come to India at all, except to see the Taj and see another Wonder of the World.

> Grace (over 70, retired ward sister from Nottingham, UK, on a two-week package tour with her friend): I was not particularly interested in coming to India – it held no great attraction for me – but I did want to see the Taj Mahal. I have always wanted to see the Taj Mahal before I die.

To travel to India solely for the pleasure of gazing upon one building testifies to the production of the Taj as an important global site and a symbol of India. The intensity of tourist expectations and the significance of the site further generates the compulsion to gaze romantically at the Taj.

Tourist personnel work to produce normative gazes, 'coaching tourists into the right sort of gazing through both tuition and exemplification' (Crang, 1997: 150). On highly structured tours, tour personnel screen out sights that are considered unimportant or unpleasant and direct the tourist gaze to key sites. At such sites, the gaze is further directed towards only specific features as I have indicated above in my description of tours around the Taj and the specific bites of information and objects highlighted by guides. *En route*, other scenes can only be witnessed at speed, and as a series of fragmented images, it may be difficult for tourists to incorporate these sights into an epistemological framework, and consequently they are discounted, not fitting into the visual highlights which the tour promises and is designed to accommodate. Such tours and condensed schedules require the inculcation of a 'spectatorial' gaze to facilitate the rapid collection of images as groups serially move from site to site, seemingly epitomizing a 'postmodern' consumption of 'depthless signs'. Yet the opportunities for enacting a sustained 'romantic' gaze are apparently limited by these condensed schedules.

For although the desire of package tourists is to gaze romantically at this 'picturesque' or 'sublime' object in solitary immersion, this is thwarted by the numbers of tourists at the Taj. Echoing the colonial convention that scenes were best depicted without 'natives' cluttering up the picture, many package tourists expressed surprise and disappointment, bemoaning the hordes that spoil the serenity of the scene and clutter the romantic vista:

> *Maureen (45, housewife, from Manchester, UK, on a two-week package tour with her friend)*: The Taj has beauty, balance, equilibrium – it's just beautiful, serene actually. I mean, you could just sit and look at it all day – apart from the milling crowds. But if you could just block them out, you could just sit and look at it.

> *Irene (42, receptionist from Sheffield, UK, on a ten-day package tour with her partner and another couple)*: What's surprised me, and it affects the atmosphere, is all the people – because it ought to be a peaceful place to rest and look but all those people – it's just too crowded, which is a shame.

The longing to experience this Western visual convention, which stresses the value of looking at scenes in blissful solitude, epitomizes a tourism which conceives the world as a place to be looked at; a visual consumption of cultures on display which edits out perceived unsavoury aspects.

However, since the structure of the tour and the commission requirements of tourist workers usually keep visits short, some tourists return, chaperoned by tour guides and drivers. This compulsion to view the Taj at sunrise or sunset partly satisfies their desire to gaze in solitude and spend more time at the site:

> *Dorothy (66, retired head teacher, Staffordshire, UK, on a two-week package tour with her friend)*: Well, we didn't get that much time there this morning so I went back this evening as well, to see it in the sunset, so I've spent virtually the whole afternoon there, and it was still perfection.

Again, a major complaint made by package tourists at the Taj is that the tight structure of the tour does not allow sufficient time for solitary detachment and contemplation of the building:

> *Michael (47, soft-furnishing retailer, from Buxton, Derbyshire, UK, on a two-week package tour with his partner and co-manager)*: I think that's the thing,

with this schedule it really is tight for time and the guide's got to get everything in. At the Taj today, we just had no time to look at the thing, and we want to look – I mean that's what we came for.

Many tours are organized so that they visit the Taj at sunset and/or sunrise. This timing of the gaze continues the influence of a particular nineteenth-century discourse which is rooted in colonial methodology of how to consume 'romantic' sights. Nearly all accounts from this time discuss the time of day which provides the most favourable conditions in which to gaze upon the Taj. As the debate on the most fruitful time to gaze intensified, the proponents of particular times were labelled 'morningites', 'eveningites', 'moonlighters' and 'mid-dayers'. For instance, in Hamilton's guide, *The Taj Mahal Of Agra*, there is a chapter titled, 'When should the Taj be visited?' (1937: 23–9).

This is now echoed in all contemporary guidebooks, which elucidate the benefits of timing one's gaze during particular periods of the day. This discourse exerts a powerful influence on contemporary tourist itineraries and practice. A majority of package tourists are concerned with gazing at the Taj at particular times of day, notably at sunrise and sunset (security measures restricting entry after dark have curtailed tourists gazing during the most celebrated time for gazing, at full moon).

The Agra Development Corporation has capitalized on this desire to be captivated by the Taj at special times by introducing a new pricing policy whereby admission to the Taj between 7 a.m. and 10 a.m., and 4 p.m. and 7 p.m. is one hundred rupees. At all other times it remains 20 rupees. This has generated much opposition amongst Indians since it effectively prevents most of them from visiting during the periods when admission is more expensive. Recently, there were even proposals to install powerful lights to simulate the effect of moonlight upon the Taj, in order to satisfy tourist desire.

Whilst Western package tourists are often frustrated in their desire to gaze romantically at the Taj, the backpackers who visit the site have plenty of time in which to indulge such a visual performance. Although back-packers can view the Taj from a wider range of angles than package tourists, and despite their claims to individuality, many backpackers do enact a romantic gaze towards the Taj, and are more located in a Western tradition of tourism than they think. Indeed, such apparently footloose travellers often rely upon the selective criteria of the *Lonely Planet Travel Survival Kit* to inform them about what should be gazed upon. The greater time at their disposal means that any desire to engage in solitary visual immersion may be realized.

Colonial India frequently served as a realm of the 'other' where, it was believed, 'authenticity' and the 'mystical' could be discovered. The contemporary mutation of this trope is in the search for alternative psychic and spiritual experiences, the quest for enlightenment or self-discovery that continues to impel young Westerners to visit India, and influences backpackers' practices and interpretations at the Taj. Practices associated with the transcendental and mystic properties of Eastern religions, such as yoga and meditation, are performed on the lawns of the Taj. And this tendency to imagine India as the dominion of the metaphysical, the opposite of Western rationalism, is reflected in certain dispositions towards gazing upon the Taj. A romantic gaze is enacted but one informed by a valorized mystical 'otherness':

> *Mattheus (24, student, from Frankfurt, Germany, travelling on his own in India for four months)*: It's a very proud building. And it has an aura, you know – you can feel it. And when I saw it the first time I heard a sound like 'Om'.

Accordingly, this way of looking at the Taj highlights how the space of the 'other' becomes enchanted, especially at selective symbolic sites which have become the focus of Western 'New Age' spiritual sentiments.

Likewise, the persistent pursuit of cheap drugs by many Western travellers means that the space of the Taj can be explored by pharmacologically inspired imaginations resulting from *bang lassi*, a yoghurt drink containing hashish, widely sold to backpackers in the local cafés in Taj Ganj. At 15 rupees, this is a very cheap way to get 'high' and many travellers spend a day at the Taj stoned, watching the surroundings for hours. Other drugs such as 'grass' or LSD are also popular ways of enhancing the experience:

> *Robert (23, traveller, has been travelling around India and South Asia for two years and has no plans to stop)*: It's fucking brilliant! I came here this morning. It was great; really lovely. Well, man, I took a tab of acid before coming down here. Fucking brilliant, man – a trip at the Taj! That's why I came down here. It's like, so intricate, and things were moving all over the place, I can tell you!

Nevertheless, although backpacker visions of the Taj are informed by romantic conventions which may mutate in drug-induced hallucinations, the availability of time, the space for reflexivity, and the improvisational nature of much backpacker movement means that unorthodox, sometimes critical views of the Taj emerge from intense gazing:

> *Clive (30, 'jack of all trades', from Wellington, New Zealand, has been travelling for four months and does not know how long he will stay in India)*: The Taj is the thing you're supposed to see, isn't it? I was impressed when I first set eyes upon it. But you know, to be honest, it seems rather overrated. Is it really so beautiful? And when you think of what it represents – the ego of a ruler – it makes you squirm to think of what else could have been done with the money.

In addition, surprising sights and changing conditions are witnessed by the sheer amount of time spent at the Taj by many backpackers:

> *Gordon (47, Buddhist monk, originally from Sydney, Australia, he stays in various monasteries throughout Asia, intends to stay in India for three months)*:

This is my eighth time here. The first time, I slept in the gardens here. In the space of twelve hours, I saw this place with sunset, full moon, rain and sunrise. I played a flute in the gardens and then watched a corpse float down the river with a vulture perched on it.

Although backpackers generally enact a romantic, intense gaze at the Taj, as I will subsequently examine, in the heterogeneous tourist spaces which they inhabit, the performance of such a gaze is not possible. Unlike at the Taj, there are no markers or attractions delineated by the tourist industry, few normative codes of behaviour and frames of reference. Indeed, there is little possibility of sustained gazing because of hazards, the movement of people and vehicles and continual distractions. Rather, incomprehensible and untranslatable sights present a visual cavalcade that mobilizes the enaction of a distracted gaze. However, it is clear that although certain spaces present a highly managed appearance and are designed to channel gazes, this can break down under critical scrutiny, where the enaction of unorthodox performances and oblique ways of looking reveals unexpected aspects, cracks in the carefully regulated edifice of disciplinary and commodified spaces.

Urry considers that what he terms the 'collective' gaze involves a less reflective mode of looking (1990). Contrasting with the intense self-absorption of the solitary romantic gaze, this gaze is conditioned by affiliation to the group. In this case, the solidarity of the group is para-mount and a trip to a symbolic site might, for instance, be a relaxing day out for a family to a local tourist attraction, or a group visit where collective witness may be deemed appropriate.

The notion that the Taj is a symbol of India is also articulated by many domestic tourists, yet the gaze that they perform is of a different kind to Western visitors. Of the domestic tourists I interviewed 35 per cent cited their desire to visit a 'wonder of the world', and 80 per cent stated that they want to see the Taj because of its fame. Questions as to why they wanted to visit the Taj were often reproached as being too obvious; the reasons were straightforward and commonplace, the responses below being typical of those given by a majority of domestic interviewees:

Rakesh (31, civil servant, from Delhi, on a day trip with a family party of seven): As a tourist I want to visit especially beautiful and famous places. We came here as a sightseeing excursion so that our children can see this national monument.

Jadhav (51, civil servant, from Delhi, on a day trip with a family party of nine): We came quite simply to see a famous historical place, of course.

Naaz (20, history teacher, from Mumbai, on pilgrimage to Ajmer with a family party of five): Because its a wonder of the world. We have heard about the fame of this monument from early childhood and we have wanted to see it for a long time.

Thus it is the fame of the Taj that attracts people, its renowned beauty and history. Although first identified as a world wonder in the colonial era, the notion has been appropriated by Indians to enchant their sense of national identity and prestige. However, the desire to see the symbolic site is not accompanied by a desire to gaze at or experience the Taj intensely. Instead, a visit to the Taj is typified by a communal *witnessing* of a national monument with family, friends or fellow-villagers, as well as millions of other Indians. More than anything else, this shared gaze celebrates the collective identity of the group, and reinforces national identity. In this case, although there is no directing of the gaze, peer-group norms constrain the visual range of what can be gazed upon by their insistence on collective witness.

This collective gaze is not intense. The Taj is looked at briefly, along with the tacit recognition that it is a remarkable building of national significance. However, an aesthetic appreciation is not the result of being awe-struck, but reflects a common-sense understanding that the Taj is an achievement of excellence. Most domestic visitors use single adjectives to describe the building, such as 'unique', 'beautiful', 'marvellous', 'magnificent', 'world-class', 'artistically excellent'. There is little sign of the defeated struggle for adjectives to capture the object of the intense gaze, the conjuring up of exotic, mystical and ethereal imagery to describe the Taj common amongst Western visitors. The unreflexive, non-analytical gaze is criticized by some Western tourists on the grounds that a hurried, unserious and distracted passage around the Taj whilst conversing and laughing fails to mobilize the appropriate form of looking. In the opinion of these critics, this reflects an incompetent tourist performance:

> Linda (33, financial consultant, London, on a three-week package tour with her friend): I think Indians are really crap tourists. They just don't know how to be tourists, rushing around, talking all the time and never stopping to look at anything – even here at the Taj Mahal!

This response highlights the extent to which tourist performance is typified by an entrenched set of codes which circumscribe which enactments and dispositions are appropriate. Where two forms of tourist performance coincide on the same stage, the potential for one group to participate or appreciate as an audience the performance of the other group may be curtailed by these conventions.

The failure to enact an intense, contemplative gaze does not mean that such practices are absent in Indian social life, but that a tourist visit to a famous building is not an occasion to perform them. However, any response that emerges out of a more reflective engagement with the Taj tends to be diverted towards other than aesthetic aspects, again producing critical interpretations. These more phlegmatic impressions include:

> Chaturvhaj (60, trader, from Saurashtra, Gujarat, on pilgrimage to Mathura with a party of fifty villagers): At first, I was impressed, but upon closer

inspection it gives me little pleasure. The white marble is beautiful but not the red sandstone which is not a pleasant material and spoils the artistic effect. The Taj is not a particularly important place although the place has been immortalized.

> *Ilias (53, foreman in construction, from Bangalore, on holiday with a family party of ten for three weeks)*: A wealthy king has shown his pride by squandering an enormous amount of wealth which he could have used for the welfare of the poor. But it is no better as a building than many modern architectural structures, and what use does it have?

Other ways of looking at the Taj could be called mediatized, since as the pre-eminent romantic site in India, it is often used as a stage in a more conventional sense, as a setting for a 'masala' movie. The influence of these films is considerable and people, especially children, re-enact scenes and dances from movies and perform songs, testifying to their power to colonize the popular imagination. Many visitors recall movie scenes when they visit the Taj (particularly the 1961 epic *Leader*, starring Dilip Kumar and Vijayantimala), in a sense superimposing a filmic image on the scene before them. Recently, a Tamil film called *Nagma* was filmed at the Taj. For many, these films are the most familiar source of information about the site:

> *Pandit Maharaj (40, religious singer, from Vrindaban, on a day trip with a party of fifteen friends)*: I haven't read much but there is a movie about the Taj Mahal which we've watched many times. And coming here, we remember the song where Mumtaz sings *What you've promised you must carry out*, about Shahjahan's promise to build the Taj for her.

However, not all domestic tourists perform a collective or mediatized gaze at the Taj. Whilst the romantic gaze described above primarily involves the contemplation of an aesthetic(ized) object, what I term the 'reverential' gaze focuses on the divine, the sacred or the commemorative. Indeed, a reverential gaze may not even have the object itself at the forefront of its focus but rather view it as a symbol, a metaphor or metonym for a religion or community. This visual performance may be collectively enacted as when a sacred or highly symbolic site is visited during a ritual or pilgrimage, or it may be performed by solitary devotees. Muslim visitors to the Taj enact a reverential look as they consume the sacred site, particularly intensifying their gaze towards the mosque, the tombs and the Quranic script inscribed on the buildings. This gaze is not particularly concerned with consuming romantic scenes or even collecting mental images but is a means to an end; a route towards significant spiritual feelings which are not exhausted by the visual. It is formed through adherence to religious duty and ritual rather than being motivated by a desire to consume beauty or the sublime.

The gaze is as central to ethnography as it is to tourism. Urry has described the 'anthropological' gaze which is solitary but less concerned with romantic gazing and more with scanning sights and actively interpreting their meaning (1992: 184). This approximates my own gazing performances, and indeed that of any ethnographer. Rather than the Taj itself, the objects of my gaze were tourists and their guides, the routes they took and performances they enacted. When I first arrived at the Taj, although I had been there before, I was inevitably drawn to the spectacle of the mausoleum, but gradually this no longer provided the central focal point as my gaze became more diffuse, and extended to the rest of the site – to the trees swaying in the breeze, to the brilliant green flashes of parrots on the wing, to the bullock carts used by gardeners, and the host of workers maintaining and restoring the site. My initial romantic gaze also became dislocated as I listened to the critical accounts of some tourists and began to doubt whether the Taj was as magnificent as was claimed, and finally, this romantic aura vanished with the site's familiarity to me. Moreover, as I became conscious of the other sensual elements of the site – the different sounds of footfalls on marble and grass, the shrieking interruptions of parrots, the stench of the river and the sweet aroma of *bidis* (cigarettes), the sound and touch of the humid breeze – the visual stimuli were complemented by other sensual nourishments.

[. . .]

References

Adler, J. (1989a) 'Origins of sightseeing', *Annals of Tourism Research*, 16: 7–29.
Adler, J. (1989b) 'Travel as performed art', *American Journal of Sociology*, 94: 1366–91.
Clifford, J. and G. Marcus (1986) *Writing Culture: The Politics and Poetics of Ethnography*. Berkeley, CA: University of California Press.
Crang, P. (1997) 'Performing the tourist product', in C. Rojek and J. Urry (eds), *Touring Cultures: Transformations of Travel and Theory*. London: Routledge.
Crawshaw, C. and J. Urry (1997) 'Tourism and the photographic eye', in C. Rojek and J. Urry (eds), *Touring Cultures: Transformations of Travel and Theory*. London: Routledge.
Crick, M. (1991) 'Tourists, locals and anthropologists: quizzical reflections on "otherness" in tourist encounters and in tourism research', *Australian Cultural History*, 10: 6–19.
Culler, J. (1981) 'The semiotics of tourism', *American Journal of Semiotics*, 1: 127–40.
De Certeau, M. (1984) *The Practice of Everyday Life*. Berkeley, CA: University of California.
Denzin, N. (1997) *Interpretative Ethnography: Ethnographic Practices for the 21st Century*. London: Sage.
Game, A. (1991) *Undoing the Social*. Milton Keynes: Open University Press.
Hamilton, J. (1937) *The Taj Mahal of Agra*. Simla: Liddell's Press.
Howes, D. (ed.) (1991) 'Sensorial anthropology', in D. Howes (ed.), *The Varieties of Sensory Experience: A Sourcebook in the Anthropology of the Senses*. Toronto: University of Toronto Press.

Little, K. (1991) 'On safari: the visual politics of a tourist representation', in D. Howes (ed.), *The Varieties of Sensory Experience: A Sourcebook in the Anthropology of the Senses*. Toronto: University of Toronto Press.

MacCannell, D. (1976) *The Tourist*. London: Macmillan.

Neumann, M. (1988) 'Wandering through the museum: experience and identity in a spectator culture', *Border/Lines*, Summer: 19–27.

Shields, R. (1991) *Places on the Margin*. London: Routledge.

Steevens, G. (1909) *In India*. London: Blackwood.

Urry, J. (1990) *The Tourist Gaze*. London: Sage.

Urry, J. (1992) 'The tourist gaze "revisited"', *American Behavioural Scientist*, 36: 172–86.

Urry, J. (1994) 'Cultural change and contemporary tourism', *Leisure Studies*, 13: 233–8.

8

The global, the local, and the hybrid: a native ethnography of glocalization

Marwan M. Kraidy

Several scholars have recently criticized the concept of globalization as an overriding process referring to 'both the compression of the world and the intensification of consciousness of the world as a whole' (Robertson, 1992: 8). From a variety of traditions associated with anthropology, cultural studies, and postcolonial theory, these critics have argued that global cultural discourses are mitigated by symbolic local practices. Their formulations have coalesced on the locus of cultural hybridity, theorized in terms of *mestizaje* (Martín-Barbero, 1993), creolization (Hannerz, 1987), hybridization (Pieterse, 1994), and hybridity (Bhabba, 1990, 1994; García-Canclini, 1989, 1990; Hall, 1991a, 1991b). These conceptualizations, focusing on hybrid intersections of the local with the global, were a welcome turn at a time when the field of international communication was ensnared in a sterile opposition between the 'cultural imperialism' and 'active audience' formations. Theorizing the implications of cultural studies' entrance into (international) 'new worlds,' Grossberg exhorted us to move cultural studies beyond 'models of oppression' (1993: 8), including the colonial model of oppression aligned with cultural imperialism, and the transgressive model of oppression and resistance identified with the active audience approach.

This chapter is a response to Grossberg's exhortation. In it I focus on the 'transformative practices' (Grossberg, 1993: 8) that define the intersection of globality and locality, and narrow down on the unavoidable issue of identity. I explore the ways in which cultural identities are reconstructed by Maronite youth in Lebanon at the intersection of global and local discourses. Rather than looking at how global media impact locality, I pose locality in its cultural complexity. I then ask how locality is best analysed and what importance communication practices may have in its constitution. I advocate 'native ethnography' as an adequate methodology to

This article was previously published in *Critical Studies in Mass Communication* (1999) 16: 456–476.

understand the articulation of local practices with global discourses. Arguing that locality is inevitably a hybrid space, I will provide empirical data about the conditions of the formation of hybridity, addressing a gap in the emerging field of international media studies which has remained largely oblivious to the phenomenon of hybridity.

Lebanon and the Maronites

Enduring metaphors have described Lebanon as a crossroads civilization, a buffer zone between Christianity and Islam, a point of contact between East and West. In fact, Lebanon's identity itself is highly contested by the different ethno-religious communities that make up its population. One of the world's smallest states, Lebanon is also one of the world's few countries that are entirely composed of ethnic minorities. At the heart of Lebanon's existence lies a fundamental identity dilemma: is Lebanon a unique country with a diverse ascendance and Western affinities, distinct from its Arab environment? Or is Lebanon inseparable from the Arab world, sharing its values and identity? This question has ensnared Lebanon in a permanent identity crisis leading to occasional sectarian flare-ups culminating with the 1974–1990 war.

The Maronites of Lebanon are one of the most prominent Christian communities in the Middle East. Among the conflicting views about Maronite origins (Chabry and Chabry, 1987; Mélia, 1986; Tabar, 1994; Valognes, 1994), the Phoenician roots theory has historically been an identity discourse demarcating Maronites from their Arab/Muslim environment. More than other communities in Lebanon, the Maronites are caught in a position betwixt and between West and East, Christianity and Islam. Their historically close relationship with France allowed the Maronites to play a dominant role in post-World War II Lebanese politics, but Maronite political clout declined during the 1975–1990 war. After years of political and cultural prominence, the Maronites have experienced a new identity crisis (*Réfléxions*, 1993), lived by Maronite youth in a context of chaotic media proliferation.

Lebanon's unique experience with the media was noted by several scholars (Boulos, 1996; Boyd, 1991; Harik, 1994; Kraidy, 1998; Rugh, 1987). With the freest media system and the highest literacy rate in the Arab world, Lebanon's population has access to dozens of mass media with conflicting ideological allegiances and diverse programming in Arabic, French, English, and Armenian. In 1995, more than 50 television stations and more than 150 radio stations catered to Lebanon's estimated 3 million inhabitants living in a country of 4,105 square miles (twice the size of the state of Delaware). Even in 1998, with only a handful of stations licensed by the 1994 Broadcasting Law (Kraidy, 1998), choices on Lebanese television range from MTV videos, the *Simpsons* and *Beverly Hills 90210*, passing through British comedy, French drama, German documentaries,

Mexican *telenovelas*, local dramas, public affairs programs, game shows, Egyptian soap operas, and Christian and Muslim religious programs. The radio menu is also varied, and includes classical Arabic songs, Lebanese folk songs, Armenian pop, French oldies, American and British rock, Latin pop, classical and modern music, jazz, blues, and heavy metal. Movie theaters feature the latest American, French, and Arab productions, and a lively press, published in Arabic, French, English, and Armenian, reflects Lebanon's diverse constituencies.

International communication, cultural studies and cultural hybridity

Until recently, the debate raging in international communication about the relation between global media and local cultures was strongly polarized. On one hand, critics of media and cultural imperialism relentlessly under-lined global cultural inequities (Guback and Varis, 1982; Mattelart, 1983; Schiller, 1991, 1992; Varis, 1984). These researchers shared the beliefs that international flows of media and cultural products were unbalanced in favor of Western industrialized countries and were dominated by a few media multinationals from those countries. On the other hand, some critics of popular culture and media reception noted active audiences grouped in interpretive communities (Ang, 1985; Fiske, 1987; Morley, 1980, 1983; Radway, 1984). These scholars were united in their view that active audiences resisted and re-appropriated media messages, reinvesting them to their advantage in their daily lives. The chasm between these two positions appeared irreconcilable as imperialists condemned the 'cheerful surveyors' of active audiences (Schiller, 1991: 16), whereas proponents of active audiences spoke of the other position as 'ultimately debilitating in its pessimism' (Fiske, 1991: 105).

That polarization ensnared cultural studies in an opposition between the global and the local (Grossberg, 1993); the former fetishizing cultural studies as a 'traveling theory' (1993: 3), and the latter focusing on local politics at the expense of theory. An intermediary approach was needed that recognized power inequities *and* audience activity. Meanwhile, a number of studies focused on less polarized international media relations, complex receptions patterns by audiences, and mitigated perspectives on issues of dependency and imperialism. It includes academics from both the 'imperialism' and 'active audience' groups, in addition to researchers not closely associated with either position (Ang, 1990; Boyd, 1984; Fiske, 1994; Hall, 1991a, 1991b; Liebes, 1988; Liebes and Katz, 1990; Mattelart and Mattelart, 1992; Morley, 1995; Straubhaar, 1991). Morley (1995), whose The 'Nationwide' Audience (1980) launched the active audience ethnography movement, warned of the 'pendulums and pitfalls' of the active audience theory, while recent writings by Mattelart (1994, 1996) and Mattelart and Mattelart (1992), who are strongly identified with the imperialism paradigm, acknowledged the sites of subjectivity and hybridity as important arenas of inquiry in international communication. Even Ang, a pioneering voice in the active audience formation, cautioned that 'audiences may be active in myriad ways in using and interpreting media, but it would be utterly out of perspective to cheerfully equate "active" with "powerful," in the sense of "taking control" at an enduring, structural or institutional level' (1990: 247). This *rapprochement* between the 'active audience' and 'cultural imperialism' traditions is discernible in two landmark essays where Stuart Hall (1991a, 1991b) proposed to disarticulate local/global questions from their 'somewhat closed, somewhat over-integrated, and somewhat oversystematized formulations' (1991b: 41). Hall acknowledged that global mass culture had a homogenizing impact on local values but recognized the role of local reception in shaping the communication process, seeing global culture as a peculiar form of capital which can only 'rule through other local capitals' (1991a: 28). Hall's formulation (1991a, 1991b) acknowledges both power relations and audience activity in international communication processes.

While hybridity has been a salient framework in anthropology, literary theory, and postcolonial studies, international communication research and media reception studies explicitly focusing on cultural hybridity remain rare (see Naficy, 1993; Tufte, 1995). The concept of hybridity is particularly useful in our attempts to consolidate bridges between disparate communication research traditions. The polarization between the global and the local is based on the assumption that they are separate realms connected by the mass media. This alleged distinction glosses over years of osmosis between different national and cultural entities. For centuries immigration, trade relations, colonial expansion, political alliances, wars, and invasions have contributed to blending heterogenous elements of different cultures. As a result, in Kwame Appiah's words, 'we are all already contaminated by each other' (cited in Pieterse, 1994: 178). The considerable leaking between 'local' and 'global' undermines any approach that considers them discrete categories. Perspectives focused on cultural hybridity, unencumbered by assumptions of separatedness between local and global spheres, are a sound framework for grasping complex local/global interactions.

By focusing on hybridity, emerging theoretical formations indirectly question the axioms of the imperialism/global versus active audience/local debates. Postcolonial theorists pioneered the discussion of hybridity (Bhabba, 1990, 1994; Tiffin, 1995). Whereas Bhabba (1994) displaced hybridity from its biological context of miscegenation into the semiotic realm of culture and the political field of power, Tiffin recognized the hybrid fabric of postcolonial cultures caught in a 'dialectical relationship between European ontology and epistemology and the impulse to create or recreate independent local identity' (1995: 95). However, hybridity is not restricted to postcolonial cultures, for it is clear that hybridization is an inevitable course for all cultures. This recognition led Hannerz (1987) to see the world undergoing a process of creolization, whereas Pieterse (1994) advocated an understanding of globalization itself in terms of hybridization.

A growing body of Latin American scholarship has focused on hybridity as both a process and a product of symbolic practices acted out by communities consuming national and transnational media and popular culture. The works of Colombian media critic Jesus Martín-Barbero (1993) and Argentinian-Mexican anthropologist Nestor García-Canclini (1989, 1990) stand out in both their theoretical innovation and their specific focus on the interlace of the local and the global. Martín-Barbero (1993) opposed the separation of production, message, and reception in the communication process. Placing the burden of meaning construction on all three communicative contexts, he adopted the term *mediations* to refer to symbolic meaning-creating practices. Rejecting the notion of pure identity, Martín-Barbero used the concept of *mestizaje*, loosely translated as creolization, which he defined as 'continuities of discontinuity and reconciliations between rhythms of life that are mutually exclusive' (1993: 188). García-Canclini (1990) coined the term *cultural reconversion* to suggest that local cultures adapted to global influences without being destroyed because tradition is re-articulated in modern processes. In *Culturas Híbridas* [*Hybrid Cultures*] (1989), García-Canclini described Latin American countries as hybrid cultures where previously separate cultural systems mingle, symbolic interactions are deterritorialized, and impure genres rule. Thus, García-Canclini (1989) argued cultural hybridity is constructed by circuitous power dynamics where globality is negotiated by locality via semiotic detours. The usefulness of Martín-Barbero and García-Canclini's approaches lies in that they consider local/global interactions both as process, 'cultural reconversion' or 'mediations,' and as product, '*mestizaje*' or 'hybridity,' rejecting the polarity between global (production and dissemination) and local (reception) of mass mediated culture. Their dual examination of both local everyday life and transnational media, with a focus on the hybridity of their intersection, provides a heuristic theoretical blueprint.

A recognition that all contemporary cultures are to some extent hybrid is required to understand the micropolitics of local/global interactions. I am not adding a new argument to the 'betwixt-and-between culture' theme, for we have to recognize that both global and local cultural formations are inherently hybridized. I am rather exploring the terms of hybridity. The question therefore is not about whether identities are hybrid, but rather about the types of formation that recreate and flesh out these hybrid identities. Hybridity is thus construed not as an in-between zone where global/local power relations are neutralized in the fuzziness of the mélange but as a zone of symbolic ferment where power relations are surreptitiously re-inscribed.

Native ethnography and hybrid cultures

As a slippery and constantly shifting entity, hybridity is not easily grasped, rendered, and understood. Inhabiting an interstitial space between local traditions and global modernity, hybridity requires a pliant methodology grounded in a flexible epistemology. As an embodied method of cultural inquiry focusing on everyday life, ethnography has for a long time been the method *par excellence* for cultural studies scholars. The internationalization of media and cultural studies mandates new ethnographic methods if we are to understand the articulation of local matrices with global processes. This re-direction of the ethnographic lens was advocated by Appadurai (1991), who invited ethnographers to investigate the micropolitics of locality: '[T]he task of ethnography,' Appadurai wrote, 'now becomes the unraveling of a conundrum: what is the nature of locality, as a lived experience, in a globalized, deterritorialized world?' (1991: 200). To understand the mutual articulation of local and global processes, ethnographers must be able to negotiate their intersection. In this respect, Abu-Lughod (1991) coined the term *halfies* to refer to 'people whose national or cultural identity is mixed by virtue of migration, overseas education, or parentage' (1991: 137), claiming that the anthropological practices of halfies unsettles the anthropological boundary between self and other. By belonging simultaneously to both local and global realms, halfies are capable of understanding the hybridity inherent at their intersection. In the following pages, I will theorize and advocate *native ethnography* as a method for understanding hybridity.

As a native of the Maronite community in Lebanon with the lived experience of the local scene under study and the familiarity with global media and cultural discourses acquired during graduate training in the United States, I was a halfie who qualified as a 'native' ethnographer. Amidst the uneasy movement between fieldwork and theorizing, I was perplexed by what I first saw as a theoretical oxymoron: How can I be a *native* ethnographer of a *hybrid* culture? I saw native ethnography as a sub-genre of critical ethnography with an imperative to excavate power vectors from cultural matrices. I was therefore committed to include voices other than mine in my manuscript, rejecting the Other-As-Theme of traditional anthropology in favor of the Other-As-Interlocutor (Theunissen, 1984). In a critical context, the word 'native' bears ambiguous connotations. The recognition that power permeates knowledge construction begs an ontological question about what constitutes a 'native.' The postulated purity that 'native' denotes in opposition to a putative contaminated 'hybrid' is a mere superficial clad, since national, cultural or ethnic identity is itself a fragmented and maculated construction. Rather than resorting to dubious claims of authenticity, the 'native' ethnographic project must then be an appropriation of voice by a subject whose speaking position is located on the borderline between two worldviews: that of the 'native' culture, the culture of intimate, taken for granted, quotidian knowledge, and the worldview of the ethnographic, academic, systematic, and, therefore, instrumental knowledge.

The native ethnographer is a translator positioned between different and sometimes antagonistic, worldviews. As a native, the researcher *knows* the culture under study which according to Geertz implies 'grasping a proverb, catching an illusion, or seeing a joke' (1974: 45). Native ethnographers articulate this intimate native knowledge with global discourses by enacting a hybrid posture. The hybridity of the native ethnographic discourse resides in its ability to bring identity and otherness in contact only to undo their fixity. Clifford contended that from an ethnographic perspective, identity 'must always be mixed, relational and inventive' (1988: 10). As an enunciative modality, native ethnography is able to show that hybridity is not a contradiction of identity, but its quotidian, inevitable, systematic condition.

Between 1993 and 1998, I returned to Lebanon for periods ranging between four and ten weeks, for a total of twelve months, residing mainly in the Mount-Lebanon region, northeast of Beirut. I had corresponded about my research with some interlocutors I already knew who had recruited others for the study. From that point of view, my *entrée* to the field was a homecoming, and rapport in some ways offered itself. Nevertheless, my *entrée* was a rite of passage whose challenge was mainly on the conceptual level rather than the physical. Physically, I was not entering but re-entering a somewhat familiar setting. In this sense I did not face the challenges many ethnographers have to overcome in order to gain *entrée* into and establish rapport with the community under study. Conceptually, however, I had to come to terms that I was looking at social acquaintances as a *field* of inquiry.

In the summer of 1993, I took extensive field notes and collected 50 open-ended questionnaires containing ten self-reflexive statements about media consumption and cultural identity using a snowball 'sampling' approach. Based on the data from the essays and field notes, I designed an interview protocol to conduct 15 in-depth interviews in 1994. I focused on ten interlocutors, five female and five male, here referred to by pseudonyms. Fuad, 27, has a bachelor in philosophy and manages a fast food restaurant. Antoun, 26, runs his own optician's shop. His neighbor, Adib, is a 23-year-old male dentistry student at a private Lebanese university. Adib's friend Elham, 25, is a video artist working for one of Lebanon's numerous advertising agencies, whereas her friend Karine, 23, works for a television production house. Twenty-five-year-old Maha works for a cultural center. Peter, 24, is a fifth-year medical student at the public Lebanese University. Attending different faculties at the same university are Serge, 22, a fourth-year male engineering student, and Rima, a 22-year-old woman studying law. Rima's friend, Marianne, is a 21-year-old advertising major at a private university. Serge and Rima are from rural areas while all the others lived in or around Beirut. I expanded my data with more extensive field notes and additional rounds of interviews with my interlocutors in several visits to Lebanon in 1995, 1996, and 1997. Native fieldwork thus fleshed out and sobered native ethnographic theorizing.

Native ethnography's betwixt-and-between speaking position, blending lived experience and systematic inquiry, has a heavy bearing on the techniques of critical ethnography itself, for ethnography is primarily about constructing meaningful episodes of life-histories when the self inquires about and with others *in situ*. Initially elicited by the researcher, the dialogue ideally fuses ethnographer and interlocutor in an intersubjective conversation where each is altered by the interaction with the other. This conversation between ethnographer and interlocutor sets two dialectics in motion: a dialectic of identity and a dialectic of otherness, both triggered by the question 'Who am I?' The dialectic of identity feeds on the recuperation of shared past experiences between the researcher and the narrator, whereas the dialectic of otherness is maintained by the differences emerging in the dialogue between the two. Ethnographic intersubjectivity is thus established.

The question 'Who am I?' carries bilateral implications for the native ethnographer: It is simultaneously a 'who am I?' reflexively posed to a Self and a 'who am I?' intersubjectively posed to an Other. By virtue of the dialectic of identity and the ensuing recall of shared experiences, the Other becomes inextricably fused with the Self. The dialectic of otherness first became manifest when I realized that my new status as an ethnographer eclipsed my previous social allegiances. I was investigating persons, probing their lives, and scrutinizing their motivations and actions from a scholarly vantage point. They too became aware of my professional motivation. This 'will to knowledge' created perplexity towards my changing roles as my interlocutors perceived me to have become 'less spontaneous' and 'more goal-oriented.' The dialectic of difference thus permeated my fieldwork.

The dialectic of identity was manifest in the tension between my native position as 'chanticleer of sentiment' and my ethnographic position as 'chronicler of data' (Bennett, 1990: 568). This constant hat switching brought home to me the instrumentality of my ethnographic endeavor. Karine, for instance, complained that our conversations were 'annoying' because they were 'making things emerge that [she] wished remained buried deep in [her].' At the same time, she felt 'good to talk about those things.' Karine's ambivalent revelation about the therapeutic dimensions of intersubjectivity was echoed in the gratitude expressed by interlocutors as my research looked into 'what [they] always live and think about without being able to formulate in words.' My interlocutors repeatedly brought back shared memories, such as social events or episodes of the war we both had witnessed. Perhaps more important, interlocutors intentionally glossed over issues they assumed I was familiar with, such as the description of young Maronites' social life. I often had to insist to elicit first-hand descriptions. They would question my persistence, such as Maha saying to me 'you know exactly what I am talking about! Why do you want me to repeat it?' In a stunning reversal of the critical imperative to give voice to the native, the native, assuming my speaking position to be the same as theirs, gave voice back to me. My only resource to mitigate that self-silencing position was a heightened awareness of it as I recalled Foucault's (1976) critical interpretation of confession as an instrument of power and control.

Other epistemological implications of the native ethnographic experience emerged when I had to negotiate bifurcations that inevitably occur when dealing with multiple languages since interlocutors used a typically Lebanese middle-class linguistic mixture of Arabic, French, and English. I had to convert this polyglot, embodied speech into a monolingual ethnographic account in English. Gellner (1970) underscored the options for a cultural translator facing a description or statement in a local language. Although there is an infinite set of sentences in the ethnographer's own language, 'there is no third language which could mediate between the native language and [the ethnographer's own]' (1970: 24–5). Native ethnography reverses this order in that the native language is the ethnographer's own whereas the language of the final record is not. Several print references and personal verifications helped me negotiate this linguistic labyrinth by translating stories into data while keeping alive the meaningful nuances imbricated in them. Two recurring themes, 'The West' and 'The Arabs,' emerged in interlocutors' narratives as two competing spheres between which young Maronites articulated media discourses with quotidian practices.

Between tradition and modernity: 'The West' and 'Arabs' as dialogical counterpoints

Ethnographic data strongly suggest that young Maronites articulated their identities between two competing discourses, *modernity* and *tradition*, that they saw constructed by the mass media. Sweepingly identified as 'the West' and 'the Arabs,' these two discourses functioned as dialogical counterpoints whereby meaning was created at their intersection. An overriding concern among my interlocutors was their inability and unwillingness to exclusively belong to one or the other of what they saw as two irreconcilable worldviews. This double-voiced posture embodies Bakhtin's definition of linguistic hybridization, which is applicable to the wider cultural realm:

> What is hybridization? It is a mixture of two social languages within the limit of a single utterance, an encounter, within the arena of an utterance, between two different . . . consciousnesses, separated from one another by an epoch, by social differentiation or by some other factor. (1981: 358)

Simultaneously identifying with Western and Arab cultures and rejecting both of them, young Maronites embodied hybridity in that they inhabited what Bhabba (1992) called a 'third space,' living on both sides of the symbolic faultline without allegiance to any. This intermediary location was underscored by Peter who said:

> In some ways, we resemble Arabs. In other things, we resemble Europeans. Nothing makes you distinct as a Maronite Lebanese . . . you have falafel and you have hamburger. Where is Lebanon? . . . a creative mixture of the hamburger and the falafel . . . they put humus inside a hamburger or some blend of that sort. . . .

Struggling to position themselves somewhere between two worldviews, interlocutors used 'Maronite' and 'Lebanese' interchangeably, underscoring their vision of Lebanon as a hybrid space between tradition and modernity. Most Maronites acknowledged being Arabs or 'similar to Arabs' by virtue of language and geographical location, and of values such as hospitality and social compassion that they perceived as typically Arab but rejected to identify with strong social and religious conservatism, authoritarianism, and anti-Western attitudes that they associated with Arabs. On the other hand, young Maronites identified with the West's commitment to personal freedom and civil liberties but criticized perceived Western individualism and sexual promiscuity. Identifying the Arab world with tradition and the West with modernity, as what Martín-Barbero called 'tempos of develop-ment' (1993: 187), young Maronites articulated both discourses with the cultural matrices permeating their consumption of media and popular culture.

The Arabs and tradition

Arab societies are traditional in the sense that they place emphasis on community and on the nuclear family as the prime social unit rather than the individual. Maronites interlocutors strongly identified with nuclear family values, social compassion, and hospitality associated with Arab society but rejected other Arab values. In the Arab world, autocratic regimes are the rule and Islam permeates the social, cultural, and political fabric of most societies. In that sense, Arab cultures are socially and politically conservative, and were perceived as such by young Maronites.

Because of the prominence of Egyptian soap operas in the Arab world, this television genre epitomized Arab programs for young Maronites. Interlocutors referred to the portrayal, in their eyes, realistic of Arab society riddled with parental and political authoritarianism, social con-servatism, and religious restrictions. Peter said he liked *some* Egyptian movies because they 'go in depth into Egyptian society' and treated some of the serious problems in it such as 'corruption, injustice, and inefficiency.' Providing examples of 'inefficiency,' Peter said that these movies 'explained why the bus never arrives on time and why accidents happen, because drivers are not qualified . . . and mechanics . . . not competent.' This statement, manifesting a clearly exclusionary, even neocolonial, reading, cast backwardness as a characteristic of the traditional Arab world in opposition to the perceived technical efficiency and competence of Western modernity.

Other interlocutors echoed this understanding and associated Arab productions with Mexican *telenovelas*. These programs, dubbed in Arabic by Lebanese actors, have been a popular genre in Lebanon since the late eighties and have become part of an informal cultural 'industry' including clothing, music, gossip, and popular jokes. For programmers, they are a viable alternative to expensive local productions. In addition, dubbing *telenovelas* in Arabic opens lucrative possibilities for exporting them to the rest of the Arab world. The popularity of Mexican *telenovelas* has meant good audience ratings and, in turn, big advertising revenues. However, the fact that Mexican *telenovelas* were put in the same category with Egyptian soap operas was surprising. Interlocutors found both genres to be highly melodramatic, even histrionic. This would have been acceptable to them if the acting had been good, but according to all interlocutors, both Egyptian soaps and Mexican *telenovelas* displayed poor acting. Watching a *telenovela* while conversing in Karine's house, Elham derided the characters because they kept 'howling, crying, and whining.' Whereas Maha criticized the convoluted plots and the lack of verisimilitude in *telenovelas*, the ethnographic account suggests that Mexican and Egyptian programs lacked appeal because interlocutors could not identify with the 'very remote' (Serge) and 'irrelevant' (Karine, Antoun) stories, characters, and experiences.

Fieldwork suggested that American norms of production, writing, and acting were the standards by which interlocutors judged media programs. In her inquiry into consumption in post-communist Hungary, James (1995) found that slick production values symbolically marked Westernness to her Hungarian respondents. This may explain why young Maronites relegated *telenovelas* to the non-Western, Arab symbolic category. Besides the prominence of American, epitomizing Western, productions as a referent by which to judge other programs, the fact that Mexican *telenovelas* were dubbed in classical – that is, literary – Arabic might have played a major role in making my interlocutors position Mexican *telenovelas* within the 'Arab' worldview. Young Maronites identified more with elements of American series while criticizing and rejecting some other facets of American programs.

The West and modernity

Associated with modernity, the West was described by young Maronites as a place of individual freedom and 'love for knowledge,' two aspects that they strongly identified with what they saw as a typically Maronite 'openness to other cultures.' By 'other cultures,' interlocutors referred to 'the West.' In one of the conversations I had with Fuad, he articulated the cultural space of Francophony, a strong cultural presence within the Maronite community, as a marker of openness to the West which according to him was 'better than wearing a veil and not see beyond a couple of meters.' This statement reveals an opposition between the West, here represented by Francophony, and the 'Arab/Muslim' alluded to by the reference to the veil. Fuad declined to adopt Francophony as his identity but preferred it to the field signified by the veil which in his opinion was a metaphor for short sightedness and stagnancy. Antoun, Serge, and Karine expressed similar, one could say neocolonial, views about the veil. Whereas to Fuad, Francophony connoted openness, 'Arab/Muslim,' symbolized by the veil, conjured to interlocutors narrowness of view and social strictures. Young Maronites' reading position thus marked their own rules of inclusion and exclusion, of Selfhood and Otherness.

Young Maronites articulated the discourse of individual freedom primarily with American television programs, with *The Cosby Show* and *Beverly Hills 90210* mentioned the most. Young Maronites liked *90210* because they connected their personal lives with the characters'. Maha and Karine emphasized that the television series showed a higher degree of freedom and openness in intimate relationships than they had personally experienced, and Peter and Antoun told me that they used the program in their daily lives, drawing on its events to articulate their social identity. *The Cosby Show*, broadcast in Lebanon in the eighties and early nineties, also emerged as a major text. Interlocutors indicated that they watched it with their families. Marianne told me how she 'exploited' *The Cosby Show* to gain more freedom from her parents: she would discuss the relationship between the parents on *The Cosby Show* and their daughters, arguing that although the parents were socially conservative, they allowed their daughters to go out on dates because they trusted them. Marianne strongly believed that the show helped her reduce parental restrictions.

In contrast to that favorable reading of *The Cosby Show*, most interlocutors criticized 'many' American movies and television programs for containing 'cheap, purely commercial, sexual scenes' (Elham, Maha), or to portray 'excessive promiscuity between teenagers' (Serge, Rima). Whereas Adib argued that such scenes were 'OK because, to an extent, they [reflected] real life,' Antoun and Peter recognized that some movies, such as *Basic Instinct*, effectively used sexuality for dramatic and aesthetic values. When I probed them about their own social and sexual freedom, interlocutors pointed out that they enjoyed less freedom than American youth, but believed that they endured less restrictions than Arab/Muslim youth, thus positioning themselves, again, between the contrapuntal 'Western' and 'Arab' discourses.

Television emerged as my interlocutors' medium of choice. They adopted and rejected elements from both Arab and Western programs, underscoring symbolic leakage between the two worldviews, and speaking at their point of contact. As a general strategy, this hybrid enunciative posture harnessed three everyday life tactics: a propinquity towards consuming ostensibly hybrid texts, quotidian acts of mimicry, and nomadic reading strategies.

Consumption, mimicry, and nomadism thus enacted hybridity as the daily condition of Maronite youth identity.

Enacting hybrid identities: consumption, mimicry, and nomadism

Hybridity as consumption

After Baudrillard defined consumption as 'an active mode of relationships . . ., a mode of systematic activity and global response upon which the entirety of our cultural system is founded' (1968: 275), thinkers like Bourdieu (1979), de Certeau (1980/1990), and the active audience formation gave consumption its *lettres de noblesse* as the prime meaning-making everyday life activity. Oddly, interlocutors began with literary examples to explain how they gravitated towards hybrid television and musical genres. They revealed a predilection for consuming ostensibly hybrid publications. Citing Milan Kundera and Tahar Ben Jalloun, Fuad said that he 'love[d] and identified with border-crossing writers,' living 'between two or more worlds' and 'perpetually looking for an identity of their own.' Antoun, Maha, Adib and Peter also mentioned Lebanese-French author Amin Maalouf and the anti-colonial *négritude* formation in Africa as favorite writers.

Some claimed admiring Rushdie as a typical 'in-between' (Fuad) writer. Because of the controversy caused by Rushdie's *Satanic Verses* and the outrage of Muslim clerics throughout the Arab and Muslim worlds, a symbolic alliance with the West via Rushdie's books ostensibly serves to differentiate the Maronites from their Muslim neighbors. However, some interlocutors criticized the *Satanic Verses* for its offending content to Muslims while at the same time praising Rushdie's other books, thus assuming an 'in between' position, once again symptomatic of hybridity. On yet another level, the fact that interlocutors claimed that they had access to Rushdie's books, banned in Lebanon since the publication of *Satanic Verses*, reflects another tactic of cultural poaching through the acquisition and consumption of prohibited material.

The Lebanese television industry has historically shunned local dramatic productions and favored less costly Egyptian, French, and American imports. The few locally produced television dramas focused on village life or historical events. *The Storm Blows Twice*, a 1996–97 Lebanese dramatic series, marked a break with that tradition in its daring treatment of contemporary social issues. The series depicted a society caught between tradition and modernity, with characters, including women, struggling to keep a balance between family and career, conservative social norms, and individual freedoms. Religious restrictions are questioned, social taboos broken, and controversial issues tackled in the program. Characters explicitly discussed premarital sex and divorced women were positively depicted pursuing successful careers. This is unusual in conservative Arab societies.

Young Maronites especially appreciated that *The Storm Blows Twice* broke social taboos in a daring but not offensive manner. In doing so, interlocutors said, characters in *The Storm Blows Twice* picked the best from tradition and modernity but did not completely embrace either of the two. Young Maronites closely identified with the daily negotiation of the two worldviews.

The enactment of hybridity is strongly manifest in my interlocutors' infatuation with the music of Fairuz and the Rahbanis, who are one of Lebanon's most famous cultural exports, enjoying a nearly mythical status in Lebanon and the Arab world, and an appreciation in Europe and North America. Fairuz and the Rahbanis' monumental *œuvre* blended Lebanese folk melodies with modern music. Ziad, the son of Fairuz and Assi Rahbani, introduced jazz to Lebanese music. Revealing hybridity's dual assimilationist and subversive thrusts, Peter describes Ziad's music as 'very homogenous' and yet 'pluralistic' but 'not fragmented,' stressing that the 'harmonious mélange' of Rahbani's 'Oriental jazz' was 'the greatest music ever.' Whereas Elham described the music as a 'unique mixture of . . . conflicting cultural legacies,' like Hebdige's cut 'n' mix Caribbean musics (1987), Fuad and Antoun agreed with Peter that Ziad's music was 'influenced by so many musical forms and currents, but . . . [was] different from all of them.' In Fuad's words:

> You cannot discern different structural musical elements in his music. You cannot say this part is jazz, this other Arabic. It is a unique and innovative blending. Just like his father was influenced by classical music but never let it dominate his music, Ziad is very subtle in mixing differences. Others have been trying to blend Western and Eastern music, but the result is artificial. It has no genius and no creativity.

Thus the resonance of Stuart Hall's rhetorical question: 'Are there any musics left that have not heard some other music?' (1991a: 38).

The assertion predominant in interlocutors' narratives that Fairuz and Ziad Rahbani were 'typically Lebanese,' and Elham's description of their music as 'more Lebanese than the cedar,' underscores how important hybrid texts were to young Maronites. Since the cedar is the quintessential symbol of Lebanon, such a hierarchical reversal posits Fairuz and the Rahbanis as the paramount cultural text, indeed the only cultural matrice that all young Maronites I spoke with identified with unconditionally. It also posited Lebanon itself as a hybrid national space. This preference for hybrid cultural products reveals the importance of 'cultural proximity' (Straubhaar, 1991) in audience tastes and choices.

Hybridity as mimicry

Early in my fieldwork, I noticed that many young Maronites mimicked snapshots of Western lifestyles. My interlocutors validated my observations and made several unsolicited remarks about mass media's perceived role in the phenomenon of imitation. Antoun claimed that young Maronites liked to live 'the European way, or the American way,' in his own words, 'maybe because of all [those] programs on television. . . .' As an example, Antoun invoked the 'torn jeans fashion' which he imputed to the influence of *Music Television (MTV)*. Using the same example of torn jeans, Peter spoke of a 'tremendous phenomenon of imitation of everything Western, particularly from the United States.' Claiming that fads took 'phenomenal proportions' among young Maronites, he argued that 'things [were] swallowed rapidly, snatched up, as if [young people were] waiting for something new to swallow in order *to fill an unbearable void*' (emphasis mine). Invoking 'this urge to imitate,' Serge told me how sentences from *Beverly Hills 90210* became 'leitmotifs, repeated over and over again: the word "man," for instance. Also "hi guys," "I've had it" and others.' Serge concluded that *90210* had become a cult series in Lebanon because 'young people really [identified] with that bright picture of happy shiny boys and girls.'

Interlocutors, in a somewhat self-criticizing tone, stated that the phenomenon of imitation of Western fashion and lifestyles among young Maronites was mostly on the superficial level of appearances rather than mentalities and actions. In other words, it is a phenomenon of simulation. Baudrillard (1983) established an interesting connection between dissimulation and simulation. '[T]o dissimulate,' he wrote, 'is to feign not to have what one has,' while 'to simulate is to feign to have what one has not' (1983: 5). According to Baudrillard (1983), simulation means concealment of the non-existence of something; in other words, it is the display of a simulacrum, a copy with no original. Interlocutors' adoption of simulative strategies reflected a perceived lack of cultural identity wherein simulated action masks the absence of such an identity. Hence, mimicking Western popular culture served to symbolically fill a void. Elham explained, first in Arabic: '*We have a fragmented identity lost between two or three languages, between different worldviews. This leads to a crisis. An identity crisis*' (emphasis mine). She proceeded in French: '*Nous sommes . . . cheval entre deux cultures* [we are straddling two cultures]. We do not really have any identity; *the stronger your feeling of not having an identity, the more you want to pretend to have one*' (emphasis mine).

Young Maronites thus constructed their identity by using hybridizing acts of mimicry and simulation. Simulation, because 'it is simulacrum and because it undergoes a metamorphosis into signs and is invented on the basis of signs' (Baudrillard, 1987b: 59), serves to hide that a void exists and to project the impression that the void does not exist. As such, simulation helps young Maronites to navigate a cultural realm whose matrices irrevocably slip into hybridity. Baudrillard claimed that resorting to simulation is a manifestation of deterritorialization which is 'no longer an exile at all . . . [but rather] a deprivation of meaning and territory . . .' (1987a: 50). Nomadic tactics in my interlocutors' everyday life underscored that deprivation of meaning and territory.

Hybridity as nomadism

Media audiences have been theorized as nomadic communities of 'impossible subjects' (Erni, 1989), inhabiting no physical space, only discursive positions (Allor, 1988). In Grossberg's words, audiences are 'located within varying multiple discourses which are never entirely outside of the media discourses themselves' (1988: 251). In order to understand how young Maronites weave their hybrid identities, we need to articulate their media consumption with a variety of social, political, and cultural factors – local and global. More precisely, we need to look at the quotidian tactics young Maronites mobilize to make sense of these manifold factors. Mouffe embraces Derrida's notion of the 'constitutive outside' which sees every identity as 'irremediably destabilized by its exterior' (Mouffe, 1994: 109) and argues that identity is relational. From this perspective, the relationality of Maronite identity with its 'Western' and 'Arab' dialogical counterpoints is manifest in nomadic identity postures. In this context, Peter expressed his reluctance to identify himself as an Arab when he is among Westerners because of his weariness of being associated with Western stereotypes of Arabs. Antoun strongly expressed this context-bound nomadism when he said:

> Sometimes yes, I am an Arab, but only sometimes. It depends. If a Christian asks me 'are you Arab?' I will say 'yes.' If a Muslim asks me the same question, my answer will be 'no.' Why? Because if you are a Christian in an Arab country, you lose your rights and freedom.

This sweeping statement underscores the insecurity felt by a member of a minority whose apprehensions are expressed differently depending on the context. The multitude of competing identities and worldviews living cheek-by-jowl in Lebanon imposes on young Maronites nomadic tactics of identity construction and display. Thus young Maronites are *cultural chameleons*, nomads who blend with the different settings they cross.

Etymologically, the term 'nomad' stems from the Greek 'nomos,' meaning 'an occupied space without limits,' and the Greek 'nemo,' which means 'to pasture' (Laroche, 1949, cited in Deleuze, 1994: 309). Thus, a 'nomad' is someone who lives in an open space without restrictions. Furthermore, 'pasture' connotes a temporary sojourn in a particular location which the nomad leaves after having used what it had to offer. The term nomad does not necessarily imply physical movement from one place to the other. In *Nomadology: The War Machine* (1986), Deleuze and Guattari explicate differences between nomads and migrants:

> The nomad is not at all the same as the migrant; for the migrant goes principally from one point to another, even if the second point is uncertain, unforeseen and not very well localized. But the nomad only goes from point to point as a consequence and as a factual necessity: in principle, points for him are relays along a trajectory. (1986: 50)

Conflating Maronite and Lebanese identities, Fuad suggested that following nomadic identity construction strategies reflected the fact that Maronite Lebanese '. . . *roam . . . in search of several identities*' (emphasis mine). Fuad lamented how slippery and blurred Lebanese, and especially Maronite, identity was. Of it he said:

> It is impossible to paint a portrait and point to it and say 'this is the Lebanese.' It is the Lebbedeh [traditional head dress] and the Sherwel [traditional pants] now, jeans and T-shirt some other time, and (smiling) maybe the [Indian] sari at some other occasion . . .

Fuad appeared to suggest that nomadic itineraries of self-definition were triggered by an absence of identity, resulting in a perpetual, circuitous, and never satisfied, search for an identity to adopt. This constant change of territory following peripatetic trajectories reflects the continuous evacuation of meaning inherent in the construction of hybrid cultural identities.

Conclusion: glocalization, hybridity, hegemony

Departing from theoretical formulations of international interactions converging on hybridity, this paper explored the intersection of global and local media and cultural spheres in terms of the hybrid cultural identities enacted by young Maronites in Lebanon. I focused on the quotidian practices by which young middle-class Maronites develop and maintain a cultural identity located on the faultline between Western and Arab worldviews. In consuming media and popular culture, young Maronites use tactics of consumption, mimicry, and nomadism to weave the hybrid fabric of their cultural identities. In doing so, they identify with key elements from the cultural capital made available by a plethora of media. These constitutive elements were mainly US and Lebanese television programs, with the exception of the music and songs of Fairuz and Ziad Rahbani who emerged as favorite cultural texts. On the other hand, other programs such as Egyptian soap operas and Latin American *telenovelas* were harshly dismissed for their perceived poor dramatic and production qualities. By setting their own rules of inclusion and exclusion, young Maronite audience members used favorite and unpopular programs as dialogical counterpoints between which symbolic codes and cultural discourses were harnessed to construct, preserve, and defend hybrid identities. These identities were articulated as being part of both Western and Arab discourses but simultaneously different from both.

Responding to Appadurai's call for 'ethnographic cosmopolitanism' (1991: 192), I designed and used the method of native ethnography. A branch of critical ethnography, native ethnography occupies an intermediary position on the border between different worldviews. Because of their hybrid ability to negotiate a variety of traditions and contexts, native ethnographers are uniquely positioned to understand and conciliate these different cultural systems. As such, this study is an 'ethnography of the particular' (Abu-Lughod, 1991: 149), concerned with the explication of ways in which extralocal events and processes are articulated locally by people making do in their everyday life. As an enunciative modality, native ethnography demonstrates that hybridity is not a negation of identity, but its quotidian, vicarious, and inevitable condition. Native ethnography can thus be a significant contributor to the true internationalization of media and cultural studies.

The empirical data generated in this study in the form of personal narratives suggests entangled articulations of global and local discourses. However, we need to retain an important lesson from the literature on cultural imperialism, for despite its perceived unsubtlety, this perspective has unraveled inequities and power imbalances in international communication. The fact that 'the West' was one of two overriding cultural worldviews revealed by young Maronites is witness to the ubiquity of Western popular culture. Besides, the hegemonic overtones that colored some young Maronites' perspective on 'the Arabs' merit further empirical investigation and theoretical contemplation in addition to class and gender issues. Nevertheless, instead of looking at power in unifying terms of two distinct poles (the global and the local) locked in an unequal relationship in which the former dominates the latter, we need to trace, map, and study what Grossberg (1997) referred to as the 'messy reality' of power in society. Rather than perceiving global/local interaction in terms of oppression and resistance, we should focus on power differences as they are manifested in everyday life 'modalities of action' and 'formalities of practices' (de Certeau, 1980/1990: 51). If we are to understand local/global encounters, the discussion should focus on axiological *and* ontological grounds, adding 'how' questions to '*why*' and '*in whose interest*' questions. We need to recognize with Murdock that 'although [global] arenas circumscribe options for [local] action, they do not dictate them. There is always a repertoire of choices' (1995: 92). More empirical cross-cultural research is needed to tackle these local options and to ground the underlying threads of and to better grasp the experiential manifestations of cultural hybridity.

Furthermore, we should perhaps adopt terms that better reflect global/local encounters than the now cliché 'globalization.' The term '*glocalization*' obtained by telescoping 'globalization' and 'localization' is a more heuristic concept that takes into account the local, national, regional, and global contexts of intercultural communicative processes. The term has already been used in marketing, sociology, and geography (Galland, 1996; Robertson, 1995). The communication discipline, more specifically international and intercultural communication research, could benefit from conceptual inroads made in other fields especially when these inroads carry a reinvigorating interdisciplinary potential. It is with this potential in mind that I propose a conceptualization of hybridity as *glocalization*, at the intersection of globalization and localization.

A deeper understanding of global/local interfaces can be achieved if empirical investigation departs from the following theoretical stances. First, we need to commit to the recognition that cultural hybridity is the rule rather than the exception in that what we commonly refer to as 'local' and 'global' have been long hybridized. Although historians have for years offered competing theories about the origins of the Maronites, young Maronites are more concerned with understanding and preserving their hybrid identities than eager to seek untraceable and mythical origins. This offers additional evidence to Stuart Hall and others' argument that inter-cultural contacts and their manifestations testify that 'it is hybridity all the way down' (Rosaldo, 1993: xv). Therefore, hybridity needs to be under-stood as a tautology rather than as a causation, hence the reading of globalization itself as hybridization (Pieterse, 1994).

Second, we need to acknowledge that hybridity is not a mere summation of differences whereby eclectic symbolic elements cohabitate. Rather, hybridity is the dialogical re-inscription of various codes and discourses in a spatio-temporal zone of signification. As such, conceptualizing hybridity entails re-formulating intercultural and international communication beyond buoyant models of resistance and inauspicious patterns of domina-tion. The articulation of hybridity with hegemony is a step towards exiting the material/symbolic, political economy/cultural studies impasse. Such a leap would entail moving beyond an understanding of local/global inter-actions in strictly dialectical terms where the mingling of a variety of foreign cultural elements allegedly neutralizes differences. We need to theoretically establish and empirically investigate the quotidian tactics of hybridity as a knotty articulation of the dialectical and the dialogical. Articulating the poetics of meaning construction and the politics of consent formation, such a perspective looks at hybridity as an assertion of differ-ences coupled with an enactment of identity, as a process which is simultaneously assimilationist and subversive, restrictive and liberating. In this endeavor, it may be helpful to remember Trinh Minh Ha's remark that 'no matter how desperate our attempts to mend, categories will always leak' (1989: 94).

References

Abu-Lughod, L. (1991) 'Writing against culture', in R. Fox (ed.), *Recapturing anthropology: working in the present*. Santa Fe, NM: School of American Research Press. pp. 137–62.

Allor, M. (1988) 'Relocating the site of the audience', *Critical Studies in Mass Communication*, 5: 217–33.

Ang, I. (1985) *Watching Dallas*. London: Methuen.

Ang, I. (1990), 'Culture and communication: towards an ethnographic critique of media consumption in the transnational media system', *European Journal of Communication*, 5: 239–60.

Appadurai, A. (1991) 'Global ethnoscapes: notes and queries for a transnational anthropology', in M. Fox (ed.), *Recapturing anthropology: working in the present*. Santa Fe, NM: School of American Research Press. pp. 191–210.

Bakhtin, M. (1981) *The Dialogical Imagination: Four Essays*. (M. Holquist, ed.; C. Emerson and M. Holquist, trans). Austin: University of Texas Press.

Baudrillard, J. (1968) *Le système des objects* [*The System of Objects*]. Paris: Éditions Gallimard.

Baudrillard, J. (1983) *Simulations*. New York: Semiotext(e).

Baudrillard, J. (1987a) *The Ecstasy of Communication*. New York: Semiotext(e).

Baudrillard, J. (1987b) *Forget Foucault*. New York: Semiotext(e).

Bennett, J. (1990) 'On being a native: Thoreau's hermeneutics of self', *Polity*, 22(4): 559–80.

Bhabba, H. (ed.) (1990) *Nation and Narration*. Routledge: London.

Bhabba, H. (1992) 'Postcolonial authority and postmodern guilt', in L. Grossberg, C. Nelson and P. Treichler (eds), *Cultural Studies*. New York and London: Routledge. pp. 56–66.

Bhabba, H. (1994) *The Location of Culture*. Routledge: London.

Boulos, J.C. (1996) *La Télé: Quelle histoire!* [*Television: What a History!*]. Beirut: Fiches du Monde Arabe.

Bourdieu, P. (1979) *Distinction: Critique sociale du jugement* [Translated as *Distinction: A Social Critique of the Judgement of Taste*. London: Routledge and Kegan Paul]. Paris: Minuit.

Boyd, D.A. (1984) 'The Janus effect? Imported television programming in developing countries', *Critical Studies in Mass Communication*, 1(4): 379–91.

Boyd, D.A. (1991), 'Lebanese broadcasting: unofficial electronic media during a prolonged civil war', *Journal of Broadcasting and Electronic Media*, 35(3): 269–87.

Chabry, L. and A. Chabry (1987). *Politique et minorités au Moyen-Orient: Les raisons d'une explosion* [*Politics and Minorities in the Middle-East: The Reasons for an Explosion*]. Paris: Maisonneuve & Larose.

Clifford, J. (1988) *Predicament of Culture*. Cambridge, MA: Harvard University Press.

de Certeau, M. (1980/1990) *L'Invention du quotidien: 1. arts de faire, nouvelle édition* [Translated as part of *The Practice of Everyday Life* (1984). Berkeley: University of California Press]. Paris: Gallimard.

Deleuze, G. (1994) *Difference and Repetition* (P. Patton, trans). New York: Columbia University Press.

Deleuze, G. and F. Guattari (1986) *Nomadology: The War Machine*. (B. Massumi, trans). New York: Semiotext(e).

Erni, J. (1989) 'Where is the audience? Discerning the (impossible) subject', *Journal of Communication Inquiry*, 13(2): 30–42.

Featherstone, M., S. Lash and R. Robertson (eds) (1995) *Global Modernities*. London: Sage.

Fiske, J. (1987) *Television Culture*. London and New York: Routledge.

Fiske, J. (1991) *Understanding Popular Culture*. London and New York: Routledge.

Fiske, J. (1994) *Media Matters: Everyday Culture and Political Change*. Minneapolis, MN: University of Minnesota Press.

Foucault, M. (1976) *Histoire de la sexualité I: La volonté de savoir* [Translated as *The History of Sexuality, vol. I: An Introduction* (1978) (R. Hurley, trans). New York: Pantheon]. Paris: Gallimard.

Galland, B. (1996, autumn) 'De l'urbanisation à la glocalisation' ['From urbanization to glocalization'], *Terminal*, 71/72.

García-Canclini, N. (1989) *Culturas híbridas: Estrategias para entrar y salir de la modernidad* [Translated as *Hybrid Cultures: Strategies for Entering and Leaving Modernity* (1995) (C. Chiappari and S. López, trans). Minneapolis, MN: University of Minnesota Press]. Mexico City, Mexico: Grijalbo.

García-Canclini, N. (1990) 'Cultural reconversion' (H. Staver, trans), in G. Yúdice, J. Franco and J. Flores (eds), *On Edge: The Crisis of Latin American Culture*. Minneapolis, MN: University of Minnesota Press.

Geertz, C. (1974) 'From the native's point of view', *Bulletin of the American Academy of Arts and Sciences*, 28: 27–45.

Gellner, E. (1970) 'Concepts and society', in B.R. Wilson (ed.), *Rationality*. Oxford: Basil Blackwell. pp. 18–49.

Grossberg, L. (1988) 'Wandering audiences, nomadic critics', *Cultural Studies*, 2(3): 377–90.

Grossberg, L. (1993) 'Cultural studies and/in new world', *Critical Studies in Mass Communication*, 10(10): 1–22.

Grossberg, L. (1997, November) *Everything You Wanted To Know about Cultural Studies But Were Afraid To Ask*. Presentation at the National Communication Association annual convention, Chicago.

Guback, T. and T. Varis (1982) 'Transnational communication and cultural industries', *Reports and Papers on Mass Communication*, 92. Paris: UNESCO.

Hall, S. (1991a) 'The local and the global: globalization and ethnicity', in A.D. King (ed.), *Culture, Globalization and the World-system: Contemporary Conditions for the Representation of Identity*. London: Macmillan. pp. 19–40.

Hall, S. (1991b) 'Old and new identities, old and new ethnicities', in A.D. King (ed.), *Culture, Globalization and the World-system: Contemporary Conditions for the Representation of Identity*. London: Macmillan. pp. 41–68.

Hannerz, U. (1987) 'The world in Creolization', *Africa*, 57(4): 546–59.

Harik, I. (1994) 'Pluralism in the Arab world', *Journal of Democracy*, 5(3): 43–56.

Hebdige, D. (1987) *Cut 'n' Mix: Culture, Identity and Caribbean Music*. London: Routledge.

James, B. (1995) 'Learning to consume: an ethnographic study of cultural change in Hungary', *Critical Studies in Mass Communication*, 12(3): 287–304.

Kraidy, M.M. (1998) 'Broadcasting regulation and civil society in postwar Lebanon', *Journal of Broadcasting and Electronic Media*, 42(3): 387–400.

Laroche, E. (1949) *Histoire de la racine nem-en grec ancien* [*A History of the Root Nem-in Ancient Greek*]. Paris: Klincksieck.

Liebes, T. (1988) 'Cultural differences in the retelling of television fiction', *Critical Studies in Mass Communication*, 5(4): 277–92.

Liebes, T. and E. Katz (1990) *The Export of Meaning: cross-cultural Readings of 'Dallas'*. New York: Oxford University Press.

Martín-Barbero, J. (1993) *Communication, Culture and Hegemony: From the Media to Mediations*. London and Newbury Park, CA: Sage.

Mattelart, A. (1983) *Transnationals and the Third World: The Struggle for Culture*. Westport, CT: Bergin and Garvey.

Mattelart, A. (1994) *Mapping World Communication: War, Progress, Culture*. Minneapolis, MN: University of Minnesota Press.

Mattelart, A. (1996) 'Généalogie des nouveaux scénarios de la communication' ['Genealogy of the new communication scenarios'], in J.L. Berdot, F. Calvez and I. Ramonet (eds), *L'Après-Télévision-Multimédia, Virtuel, Internet: Actes du colloque '25 images/seconde'* [*After Television: Multimedia, Virtual, Internet: Proceedings of the Colloquium '25 Images/Second'*]. Valence, France: CRAC.

Mattelart, A. and M. Mattelart (1992) *Rethinking Media Theory*. Minneapolis, MN: University of Minnesota Press.

Mélia, J. (1986) *Chez les chrétiens d'Orient* [*At the Christians of the Orient*]. Beirut: Dar al-Majani.

Morley, D. (1980) *The 'Nationwide' Audience: Structure and Decoding*. London: BFI.

Morley, D. (1980) 'Texts, readers, subjects', in S. Hall et al., (eds), *Culture, Media, Language*. London: Hutchinson. pp. 163–73.

Morley, D. (1983) 'Cultural transformations: the politics of resistance', in H. Davis and P. Walton (eds), *Language, Image, Media*. London: Blackwell. pp. 104–19.

Morley, D. (1995) 'Active audience theory: Pendulums and pitfalls', *Journal of Communication*, 43(4): 255–61.

Mouffe, C. (1994) 'For a politics of nomadic identity', in G. Robertson, M. Mash, L. Tisckner, J. Bird, B. Curtis and T. Putnam (eds), *Travelers' Tales: Narratives of Home and Displacement*. London and New York: Routledge. pp. 105–13.

Murdock, G. (1995) 'Across the great divide: cultural analysis and the condition of democracy', *Critical Studies in Mass Communication*, 12(1): 89–94.

Naficy, H. (1993) *The Making of Exile Cultures: Iranian Television in Los Angeles*. Minneapolis, MN: University of Minnesota Press.

Pieterse, J.N. (1994) 'Globalisation as hybridisation', *International Sociology*, 9(2): 161–84.

Radway, J. (1984) *Reading the Romance: Feminism and the Representation of Women in Popular Culture*. Chapel Hill, NC: University of North Carolina Press.

Réfléxions sur la crise de la communauté maronite [*Reflections on the Crisis of the Maronite Community*] [Document] (1993, 3rd quarter, 1994, 1st quarter) *Les Cahiers de L'Orient* (pp. 221–51).

Robertson, R. (1992) *Globalization: Social Theory and Global Culture*. London: Sage.

Robertson, R. (1995) 'Glocalization: time-space and homogeneity-heterogeneity', in M. Featherstone, S. Lash and R. Robertson (eds), *Global Modernities*. London: Sage. pp. 25–44.

Rosaldo, Renato (1993/1989) *Culture and Truth: The Remaking of Social Analysis*. London: Routledge.

Rugh, W. (1987) *The Arab Press: News and Political Process in the Arab World*. Syracuse, NY: Syracuse University Press.

Schiller, H.I. (1991) 'Not yet the post-imperialist era', *Critical Studies in Mass Communication*, 8(1): 13–28.

Schiller, H. (ed.) (1992) *The Ideology of International Communication*. New York: Institute for Media Analysis.

Straubhaar, J.D. (1991) 'Beyond media imperialism: assymetrical interdependence and cultural proximity', *Critical Studies in Mass Communication*, 8(1): 39–59.

Tabar, P. (1994, spring) 'Power in Maronite political and historical discourse', *The Beirut Review*, 7: 91–114.

Theunissen, M. (1984) *The Other: Studies in the Social Thought of Husserl, Heidegger, Sartre and Buber.* Cambridge, MA: MIT Press.

Tiffin, H. (1995) 'Postcolonial literature and counter-discourse', in B. Ashcroft, G. Griffiths and H. Tiffin (eds), *The Postcolonial Studies Reader.* London and New York: Routledge. pp. 95–8.

Trinh, T., Minh Ha (1989) *Woman, Native, Other: Writing Postcoloniality and Feminism.* Bloomington, IN: Indiana University Press.

Tufte, T. (1995) 'How do *telenovelas* serve to articulate hybrid cultures in contemporary Brazil?', *The Nordicom Review*, 2: 29–35.

Valognes, J.P. (1994) *Vie et mort des chrétiens d'Orient: Des origines à nos jours* [*The Life and Death of the Christians of the Orient: From the Origins to the Present Day*]. Paris: Fayard.

Varis, T. (1984, winter) 'The international flow of television programs', *Journal of Communication*, 34: 143–52.

Part V

Working to provide medical services

9

Humour as resistance to professional dominance in community mental health teams

Lesley Griffiths

This chapter contributes to the sociological study of humour in health care settings by analysing its use by social workers and nurses in community mental health teams (CMHTs) dealing with referrals made by consultant psychiatrists. It is about humour and hierarchy, and specifically about humour as a strategy used by rank-and-file team members to resist or attenuate instructions coming from powerful professionals.

There is, of course, already an extensive literature on humour and health care but much of this centres on the affiliative and emotional functions of humour, rather than its use as a modality of resistance.[1] Social scientists have long recognized the significance of humour as a mechanism for managing tension in social relationships (Coser, 1958, 1959, 1960; Goffman, 1961; Radcliffe-Brown, 1940). In the health care sphere humour has, *inter alia*, been portrayed as something that helps staff to deal with difficult communications, comfort and reduce anxiety in patients, express frustration and anger, relieve tensions, bond together and enhance work satisfaction (Astedt and Liukkonen, 1994; Bottorff et al., 1995; Lieber, 1991; Mallet and Ahern, 1996; Wender, 1996; Yuels and Clair, 1995). Emerson (1973) makes the important point that humour allows staff and patients to raise forbidden topics that would be difficult to discuss in 'serious' discourse:

> Joking provides a useful channel for covert communication on taboo subjects. Normally a person is not held responsible for what he does in jest to the same degree as he would be for a serious gesture. Humour, as an aside from the main discourse, need not be taken into account in subsequent interaction. It need not become part of the history of the encounter, or be used for the continuous reassessment of the nature and worth of each participant, or be built into the meaning of subsequent acts. For the very reason that humour officially does not 'count', persons are induced to risk messages that might be unacceptable if stated seriously. (1973: 269)

This article was previously published in *Sociology of Health and Illness* (1998) 20(6): 874–895.

Although Emerson's research focuses on staff/patient interaction, and the management of sensitive topics such as staff competence or death, this insight can also be applied to interaction among health care staff.

Rose Laub Coser (1960), in her research in a state mental institution, found that senior staff utilized humour to mock junior staff and thereby support the existing status structure. Less frequently, those at the bottom employed wit to express rebellion against instructions from seniors, though never when the latter were present. However, these findings may not do full justice to the complexity of humour as a resistance strategy across health care settings. I will show that there are situations where organizational subordinates use humour in the presence of superordinates, and that this serves clear interactional purposes, both in negotiating respective roles in a division of labour and in seeking to influence emergent decisions about cases. The significance of humour in hierarchical work organizations is that it allows subordinates to signal dissent, short of a serious statement of opposition or withdrawal of cooperation. Humour signals that social tensions exist, without exposing the dissenters to the consequences that would follow from a direct challenge to authority. In Emerson's (1973) terms it allows interactants to suspend implicit rules about forbidden topics, and – within particular situated interactions – make unacceptable messages acceptable.

Studies like the present one illuminate two aspects of institutional work-life. The trans-situational aspect incorporates those limits and possibilities which are available to members as members of a particular organization. CMHT members are subject to constraints arising from the institutional locus of their work, such as the expectation that the main business of team meetings is the processing of patients, or understandings of the legal framework of care and the available treatment and disposal options. These constraints are trans-situational in the sense that they provide a backdrop to all events taking place within the organization, and exercise members in local, particular situations. At the same time members deal with particular issues or items in interactions which are unique, despite sharing the contextualizing background of the organization. In concrete, situated interactions they negotiate how any one patient will be dealt with on this occasion. This study employs analysis of talk to illuminate both the situated negotiations of members and the trans-situational structures of power and knowledge to which they orientate in these negotiations. I approach this by examining the 'referencing work' (Griffiths and Hughes, 1994) that occurs as organization members use symbolic resources to draw attention to certain discourse frames or social structures that shape their work, while ignoring others. My concern is with the selective framing of macroscopic constraints that impinge on a situation, so that aspects compatible with a favoured course of action are accentuated, while contradictory aspects are disattended or rendered irrelevant. Among these symbolic resources is humour, which I argue provides an effective means of challenging a framing proposed by organizational superiors and suggesting an alternative interpretation of events.

Humour emerged as a pervasive feature of CMHT work, featuring in almost all the tape-recorded meetings. It was central to CMHT members' skilful negotiation of potential points of conflict between immediate work pressures and wider organizational requirements, such as the tension between individual workloads and the duty to deal with the large numbers of patients requiring care in the community. In the empirical sections of the paper I describe how humorous challenges to the psychiatrist's medicalized version of a case often provided a way for CMHT members to resist excessive workloads. By implicitly constructing patients in non-medical terms – as the sufferers of normal problems of living or as 'malingerers' – team members harnessed trans-situational understandings about the boundaries of the target population to control the entry of patients to their caseloads.

The study and the setting

The two CMHTs studied were set up in 1991 in response to the *All Wales Strategy for Mental Health*. Each CMHT comprised community psychiatric nurses (CPNs) and social workers specializing in mental health and a team psychiatrist. Both operated in urban areas, serving predominantly working-class populations. One team had accommodation both at the psychiatric hospital and in the social services area offices; the second team was split between a local health centre and the area offices. The two CMHTs studied were selected on pragmatic grounds and there is no suggestion that they represent opposite poles on a theoretical continuum. They were simply the first teams operating in an area where several other CMHTs were planned.

Ethnographic fieldwork was carried out over a twelve-month period. Access was negotiated in the first instance with senior NHS and Social Services staff, and then with individual team members. All participants were informed of the aims of the research and gave permission for audio-taping of meetings and interviews. Names and places have been changed to ensure anonymity. This paper draws on transcribed data from weekly team meetings. Initially twelve successive weekly meetings were observed and recorded for each team. As part of the larger study, unstructured interviews were carried out with all team members and relevant senior NHS and Social Services staff, but these are not fully reported here. Additional background data were collected by attending local mental health strategy discussions and meetings of voluntary sector agencies, some of which were also tape-recorded.

Transcripts of meetings were analysed using an inductive approach. Tapes and transcripts were studied in conjunction, examined for general patterns and coded. Some qualitative research is guilty of a form of reductionism arising from the use of short data extracts abstracted from context (Burnard, 1995). As a deliberate policy, this paper uses extended data extracts to convey a better sense of the form and sequencing of interactions. However, this is intended as an ethnographic study rather than an example of mainstream conversational analysis (CA), and I consider it unnecessary and impracticable (given the length constraints of a standard journal article) to use the full range of transcription conventions utilized in CA research. My approach has been to use a more eclectic form of discourse analysis to address the broader concerns relevant to a case study of professional practice (cf. Atkinson, 1995). An analysis at this level illuminates features of social organization that shape the work of the CMHTs, but admittedly passes over specific aspects of speech exchange systems that could be addressed in more focused CA studies.

Contrasting versions of teamwork

The psychiatrists had been the most powerful actors in shaping local arrangements, and each had opted for a different role and a different way of constituting weekly team meetings. The *Team A* psychiatrist favoured a division of labour in which a semi-independent team drew upon his clinical expertise, but exercised its autonomy in managing work activity rather than through involvement in diagnosis or clinical review. He did not generally attend meetings, and the function of meetings was characterized as 'allocation'. The *Team B* psychiatrist similarly emphasized his expert clinician role, but was prepared to involve the team more directly in some areas of clinical decision-making. The weekly gatherings were presented as 'clinical review meetings', which the psychiatrist or his senior house officer always attended. Although referrals and the basis of referral decisions were not usually discussed in *Team B*, nurses and social workers would frequently feed back their assessments of patient progress to the psychiatrist, so that cases were subject to an ongoing review in which all team members played a part. In this team the allocation function was also present, but was carried out as a brief preliminary to the weekly meeting or – with the occasional urgent case – outside the meeting. Referrals to *Team A* came from GPs directly or from the psychiatrist; in *Team B* all referrals came through the psychiatrist.

CMHT work may be seen as people-processing work, not dissimilar to the work of other 'street-level bureaucrats' (Lipsky, 1980) who exercise discretion in categorizing a clientele and providing a service. CMHT members develop routine ways of managing the work of allocating cases, classifying patients, and monitoring progress through the talk of the meeting – what we might call 'talking the work'. However, there are striking differences in the way definitions of patients and CMHT work are constructed in the two teams, which seem to be directly attributable to the participation or non-participation of the psychiatrist and the framing of the meeting as 'allocation' or 'review'.

On the surface one psychiatrist has embraced the team concept and participated fully, while the other has taken a more qualified position, with a more distant relationship with the rest of the team. However, in practice, both approaches had the consequence of keeping substantial decision-making authority with the psychiatrist, albeit with different costs and risks. The *Team A* psychiatrist gains the time and professional detachment from the team which non-attendance at team meetings allows, but through his absence creates the space for other team members to resist his definitions and instructions. The *Team B* psychiatrist structures meetings to encourage full staff participation in discussions and an appearance of joint decision-making but – because of his control over referrals, hospital admissions, prescribing, and wider professional contacts – continues to be the most powerful team actor.

Humour as resistance

Humour is an important feature of meetings in both teams. In part this reflects a shared concern with the volume of work coming through from the psychiatrists, and a perception that many referrals involve patients who are not seriously mentally ill. From time to time, team members challenge the patient history put forward by the referring psychiatrist, and seek to re-formulate the information to suggest an alternative explanation for the patient's behaviour. Often these challenges are packaged as humorous comment.

In *Team A* these comments are addressed, not to the absent psychiatrist, but to the team leader who makes the referral request on the psychiatrist's behalf and must report back to him. Typically the team leader introduces the referral in the format of the case report, cast in the standard language of case presentation, and making heavy use of direct quotations from the referral letter and attached papers. Team members respond by questioning the team leader about the case, and sometimes suggesting re-formulations of the history. Without an author to provide clarification, the referral letter must stand on its own: it is scrutinized for sense and consistency, and for evidence that the referral is appropriate. *Extract 1* illustrates the delicate interplay between team leader (TL) and team, as the team's scepticism about the referral becomes clear. 'Rory' is the psychiatrist.

Extract 1

```
1 TL:   Right. Ray Daniels, 8, W_____ Rd, C_____,
2       referred by Rory, seen at South health centre on the
3       30th of April, he's going through a divorce from his
4       wife, and he believes she has been unfair to him, she
5       has stolen his car and sold it=
6 N1:   =Paah! Good for her           Stolen his car=
7 N2:                  ⌊Heh heh⌋ heh heh ⌊heh heh⌋
```

```
 8  N1:    =That's my girl=
 9  N2:    =Hmmmmmm Eeeeh//heh
10  SW1:   I think that's unspeakably low, that's possibly
11         the worst thing a woman could do
12  N1:                    ⌊I think that's absolutely⌋ brilliant
13  N2:    Heh heh   heh heh heh
14  SW1:             ⌊heh he   heh heeh
15  TL:                       ⌊It's not very nice and not only his
16         car but his jacket as well
17  SW1:   Ooo/aoh
18  N1:    ⌜Nooooh, not his jacket haah ha haaah
19  N2:    ⌊⌊Noooooh
20  SW2:   Oooahhhh=
21  TL:    =And has taken his furniture and has gone to live with
22         her mother
23  N1:    Ooh//no
24  N3:    What ahh   How about the microwave?
25  TL:    She has apparently also taken the microwave
26  N1:                    ⌈ha ha ha   huuh heh⌋
27  TL:    =and television
28  N1:           ⌈Hah ha ha   heeh heeh heeh
29  N2:                       ⌊uh huh huh huh huh huh=
30  TL:    =I feel sorry for this//chap
31  SW2:   Heh    heh heehh
32  N2:           ⌈Heeh hah ha=
33  N1:    What diagnostic category is that then?
34  N3:         Desmond's got empathy here=
35  TL:    ⌊⌊Well, he                 =He tends to cry a lot
36  N1:    =Why?=
37  TL:    =He has three children, two by his wife's first
38         marriage and one by theirs. His appetite//
39         is poor
40  N1:    ((inaudible overlap))
41  TL:    He has attempted suicide New Year's Eve when he had
42         been drinking. Is he known to anybody?
43  N2:    No=
44  N1:    =A lot of people do that New Year's Eve though,
45         don't th//ey?
46  N2:    eh heh eh heeeh=
47  SW2:   =Can't face the new//year
48  N2:    Heh eh heeeh
49  TL:    He is reluctant to go back to his home situation and
50         is and is due in court on the 12th of May and=
51  N2:    ⌈There's nothing there⌋
52  TL:    =also the 4th of May for assault
53  SW1:   Ooo//oh
54  SW2:        Oooh
55  N1:    ⌊⌊((inaudible overlap))
56  TL:    He is being prosecuted for assault
57  N1:    Oh=
```

```
 58 TL:    =Oh, she is prosecuting=
 59 SW2:   =He gave her a pasting
 60 TL:    He admits to drinking five pints a//night
 61 SW2:   Sue was there. Sue would know
 62 N1:    Heh heh he doesn't heeh heh
 63 SW2:                    [[heeh, heh heeh
 64 TL:    Past medical history nil, except the patient had been
 65        in before. He also tried to ahh kill himself on New
 66        Year's Eve. Well there we are
 67 N1:    Oh all right
 68 N2:    What's he referred him for?
 69 TL:    Hey?
 70 N2:    What's he referred//him
 71 N1:    Poverty
 72 TL:    I've got (all the details) on his marital problems.
 73        Summary: a 37-year-old married man who is
 74        undergoing divorce for the second time. He drinks
 75        approximately five pints a night=
 76 N1:    =And the re//st
 77 TL:    And is depressed due to the impending divorce
 78        from his second wife. He's put him on Prozac, he
 79        says refer to social services for urgent
 80        attent//ion
 81 N1:    Nooo not=
 82 TL:    =due to his chronic housing problem
 83 SW3:   What is he looking at? What is his housing
 84        problem? He's got a house
 85 N2:    With nothing in it=          heh hehh heh
 86 N:                      =Nothing [in it heh ha heh]
 87 SW3:   =The best thing to do now . . . (inaudible). Well he should
 88        see a solicitor shouldn't he?
 89 N1:    Yes, if he . . . What about STEPS, Desmond, for him?
 90 TL:    Well you see, the tone of this suggests to me that his
 91        alcohol abuse isn't the thing that's concerning him at
 92        this point=
 93 N1:    =No but that's what they all think at STEPS as well=
 94 TL:    =Yeah that's right and he's presumably depressed
 95        about his wife leaving him and seeking a divorce.
 96 N1:    So what will we do, send Jane up for therapy
 97        three times a week?
 98 N3:    Yeah, Jane, get him another house
 99 N1:    Get him a woman
100 N2:    Huh heeh/heh
101 N3:    By next week
102 N2:    Huummh heh
103 SW1:   Give him one
104 SW2:   Hehh heh heh heh          Oh Jane=
105 N1:         [Huuh huuuh hu] uuh          =No, you want to cure
106        him not kill him
107 TL:    You see, I mean, social services, for urgent
```

```
108          attention due to his chronic housing problem. Well have
109          we got any houses//then?
110 SW2:     Is it a chronic//prob
111 SW3:     Well, he's . . . He's got a house, a council house.
112          They won't give him another house=
113 N1:          No
114 TL:      [[There's . . . There's insufficient information here²
```

Mulkay (1988) has suggested that humour depends on a juxtaposition of disparate elements in such a way that familiar patterns are challenged by other less obvious ones, so that an interpretive shift occurs. There is 'a sudden movement between, or unexpected combination of, distinct interpretive frames' (1988: 26). Sacks (1992) has described the way in which second speakers in arguments hold the stronger position as they are able to draw attention to weaknesses in the case being made by the first speaker. He pays special attention to the role of clarificatory questions, which, while hearable as a simple request for information, can also allow for the introduction of a new interpretation. Taken together these two ideas offer us a way of developing an explanation for the way humour is used in this team.

The inter-disciplinary nature of CMHTs means that members have available to them two discourses and thus two sense-making frameworks within which they can categorize patients. Social workers draw on a set of ideas which tend to 'normalize' or 'socialize' symptoms which might be presented within a medical model as evidence of mental illness. The nurses in the team move between this social discourse on symptoms and the medical discourse of the psychiatrists. The kind of interpretive shift between frames that Mulkay refers to often occurs as team members challenge the medical framing of the case by offering an alternative social framing packaged as humorous content. Typically, such interventions will suggest an interpretation of supporting case-report information which casts doubt on the appropriateness of the referral by poking fun at it. While the referral report de-personalizes the 'case', the team's challenge reverses that process and reconstructs the case as a person with human motivations.

Coming from the second speaker's position, such challenges have the strength that they can be constructed elliptically as comments or questions requiring further clarification, rather than as a direct contradiction of the preceding formulation, and the risk to the speaker is further reduced by their overtly humorous nature. Unlike a serious evaluation which must be heard seriously and responded to, humorous challenges leave open the possibility that the next speaker will ignore the attempted frame shift and reassert the serious agenda of the meeting. Yet if sufficient support for the challenge can be mustered, a change of agenda may be forced. In *Extract 1* the shift of frame comes as a nurse (N1) offers an evaluative comment, 'Good for her. Stolen his car. That's my girl!' (lines 6–8), after the first segment of the case presentation. Although this is ostensibly an evaluation of the action of the client's wife who has stolen his car, it also serves as a channel to mount a challenge to the referral as a serious matter.

Glenn (1995) draws a useful distinction between 'laughing at' and 'laughing with', which helps to shed light on the affiliative and disaffiliative functions of laughter in CMHTs. Glenn notes that conversational laughter contributes to displays of both alignment and distancing, but that 'which (if either) laughter helps accomplish at any particular moment may be displayed and redefined over several turns' at talk (1995: 43). In negotiating laughter's affiliative status, participants attend to: the nature of the utterance to which laughter refers ('the laughable'); the first laugh; any (possible) second laugh by another participant; and subsequent activities. In a typical 'laughing at' situation: the 'laughable' identifies some co-present member as the butt of a joke; the first laugh will be from the perpetrator or another participant (as opposed to the putative butt); there is shared laughter from others present (but not the butt); and subsequent talk continues on the topic taken up in the 'laughable', with possible attempts at repair.

The sequence that includes the 'good for her' comment displays many of these features. Although the butt at first appears to be the referred patient (whose status as the kind of patient presented in the referral is cast in doubt), it becomes apparent that the absent psychiatrist ('What's he referred him for?'), and his proxy, the team leader ('Desmond's got empathy'), are also implicated. The first laugh (at line 7) comes not from the staff member who produces the humorous challenge (N1) but from a second community psychiatric nurse (N2). One may hypothesize that, in the hierarchical CMHT context, there are advantages for the perpetrator of a 'laughable', in terms of minimizing the risk of offending superiors, if the first laugh comes from another team member. When a social worker (SW1) uses irony to extend the joke at lines 10–11 ('that's possibly the worst thing a woman could do') and joins in with the second laugh at line 14, it is clear that at least three participants support the challenge. The team leader takes up the joking tone with his comment at lines 15–16 that it is not only the car but 'his jacket as well'. In the subsequent talk the joking tone is amplified and another nurse (N3) becomes involved (line 24). A shared team alignment begins to emerge, which is at odds with the account of the case contained in the referral letter. Team members construct an alternative version which highlights the tragi-comic elements of the wife's appropriation of domestic property, the assault of the wife by the husband, and the current situation of a man living in an empty house and affected by heavy drinking and depression.

A significant shift in the direction of the interaction comes at line 30. In continuing the joke ('I feel sorry for this chap'), and laughing with the team, which serves affiliative functions for him as he selects the role of team member, the team leader opens the way for other members to raise the issue of the point of the referral. N1's sarcastic question about the nature of the diagnosis (line 33), and N2's mocking answer that the team leader has 'got empathy there' (line 34), threatens to turn the joke on him. The team leader risks being 'laughed at' and distanced from the rest of the team, while at the same time having lost the authority he might have retained by resisting the earlier frame shift to the humorous mode. He tries to steer talk back to the serious business of the referral by quoting from the psychiatrist's letter, but other team members respond by asserting the basic normality of the case (and by implication the absence of underlying mental illness) culminating in the suggestion that the problem is 'poverty' (lines 44–5, 47, 61, 71). This takes place in a stretch of talk where the team leader's paraphrasings of the psychiatrists' points are challenged, and in which team members eventually move to offer alternative suggestions for action (seeing a solicitor and referral to a voluntary agency – STEPS). These suggestions support the construction that the case is not suitable for treatment by the team. At lines 107–9 the team leader changes tack by acknowledging the inappropriateness of the CMHT referral for what is presented as a 'housing problem'. He finally suggests that there is 'insufficient information' to proceed (line 114). Later the discussion moves on to the type or advice or help that this client could get, and the need for a policy to cover referrals of this kind. The social work team leader is obliged to take the case back to the psychiatrist, but has managed to re-formulate the problem as one of lack of information – something that can be communicated to the psychiatrist with less risk of offence than straightforward refusal to accept the case.

The dynamic of meetings in *Team A* is substantially shaped by the communication of information between absent psychiatrist, mediating team leader and team. Rank-and-file team members use humorous comments to signal their unease about certain referrals to the team leader, who must then choose whether to respond to this by delaying acceptance of the referral. The team leader's position as the link between team and psychiatrist gives rise to a difficult dilemma: an over-close identification with the psychiatrist risks negative reaction from the team, but open opposition is even more damaging because it challenges the operative system of referral and allocation. To maintain credibility with team members the team leader needs to be seen to have a degree of detachment from the psychiatrist, but – at the same time – must chair meetings in a way that ensures that the process of referral and allocation continues to be taken seriously. In *Extract 1*, the team leader is able to distance himself from the referral by locating the psychiatrist as its author, and even commenting negatively on the reasonableness of its content: 'well have we got any houses then?' (line 109). This technique is used on several occasions by this team leader, who has a social work institutional affiliation which is problematized at times by his 'managerial' role in this team.

Negotiating laughter's affiliative status

In *Team B*, humour is again a resource that less powerful team members can put to work to question the psychiatrist's definitions and preferred course of action. *Extract 2* involves a male client who is significantly underweight and complains of a variety of illness conditions, for which no physical basis has been established. The case is little different from cases referred back in *Team A* as inappropriate or requiring more information, and team members use similar strategies to communicate scepticism. However, in *Team B* the psychiatrist (P) is present to respond to team members' humorous jibes and resist their attempts to reframe the situation.

Extract 2

```
 1  P:     I Mean I think a lot of it is driven by him
 2         consciously, and it's malingering and it's manipulating
 3         things. But I'm sure there's an unconscious element
 4         here, gaining a lot. I mean I was asking him how it's
 5         affected his life, this not being able to hold solids
 6         down and the story was like that he spends his time on the
 7         sofa, watching TV and sipping this high calorie stuff
 8  N1:    Yeah, I asked him if he went out and he said, no, he
 9         said, I can't, I'm not strong enough to walk
10  P:     Good, good, so I mean I thought that was it, if there
11         was anything we could do it's to look at that, at the
12         secondary gain that he's getting, that you know, he
13         has . . . he's ill and therefore he doesn't have to do
14         anything in the house or anywhere else, he just sits
15         there ((multi-turn segment omitted))
16         OKay. I mean I wonder just, er if we've any input it's
17         to look at the secondary gain for him and . . . and try and
18         push him out of the house. I mean I'm aware that it's
19         probably . . . I mean it's attention he wants. I think it's
20         some form of attention . . . some form of intervention
21  SW1:   Where does he live, John?
22  N1:    Hmmmmp?
23  SW1:   Where does he live?
24  N1:    Redbridge
25  SW1:   Redbridge. Oooh get him to the club man. Cos he could
26         come to the club if we get him off the sofa
27  N1:    Yeah get him on the bus, it's right on the main//road
28         ((inaudible overlap)) Yeah=
29  N1:    =nearly opposite Val
30  SW1:   Is it? Right. We ought to get her to go there,
31  N1:    He heh heh heh
32  P:                 heh heh heh
33  SW1:   She'd sort him out. heh heh heh heh
34  P:                    ⌈heh heh heh
35  N1:                   ⌈heh hheh
36  N2:                   ⌈heh heh//hehh
37  SW1:   And have some cash heh heeh
38  N1:                       ⌈Yeh ha heh heh heh=
```

39 P: =But I think it there's one thing we could to, it's
40   that: look at the secondary gain and try and shift
41   that. Like get him involved with things
42 SW1:   Yes=
43 P: =Because I can imagine he just drifts from place to
44   place with his symptoms and he sits in a certain area
45   for a certain space of time and goes into the hospital
46   and he gets attention and then whenever he gets known=
47 SW1:   =Hmmm=
48 P: =and he gets a bit of negative feedback he moves on
49   somewhere. But I mean that's like a typical
50   Munchausen's. All that energy and drive to get
51   attention, if you could divert it somewhere else, he'd
52   be Prime Minister.
53 SW1:   hm//hhhmmmm
54 N2:   heh heh
55 P: But I wonder if that's . . . if that's probably all. I mean
56   I said to the GP that that's all we're going to be able
57   to do. And I said to him like you know anything else
58   is going to be counter-productive. If it gets to the
59   point where he does collapse and it's a real collapse,
60   then he's need to go to a medical ward to be re-fed ahm
61   but not here.
62 SW1:   Would he come to the club Phil?
63 N1:   Well I didn't ask him really, I asked him about his
64   social life and he said he didn't have much social life
65 SW1:   Well tell him then, tell him that we . . . we've got the
66   ambulance calling up the valley to pick him up. heh
67   heh heh heh
68 N1:   ⌈Heh heh heh
69 N2:   ⌈yeah heh heh
70 P: That's . . . that's in a sense, I mean . . . The thing about
71   this chap, that that's a more socially acceptable=
72 N2:   =Yes=
73 P: =place and it's more acceptable for him. It's
74   intervention, it's help and it's him being special,
75   which is all these sort of issues that go round chaps
76   like this. I mean maybe=
77 N2:   =Tell him they'll drip feed him down there. heh heh
78   heh
79 N1:   ⌈Heh
80 SW1:   ⌈Heh heh heh
81 P: Tell him it's a special club for you know whatever
82 N2:   ⌈shove him on the bus⌋
83 N1:   For malingerers
84 N2:   Heh heh heh heh heh heh heh
85 SW1:   ⌈heh hehh heh heh heh
86 P: ⌈heh heh
87 N1:   ⌈heh heh hehh heh heh
88 P: I think that=

```
 89  SW1:  =Would be great for the patient heh//heh
 90  N1:   heh heh heh.
 91  N2:        [huuh heh heh
 92  P:    I mean he's malingering, but there's always an
 93        unconscious element to these people
 94  SW1:                        [Yes]
 95  N2:        Hmmm
 96  N1:   [[Yes
 97  P:    I mean you can get like ((pause)) I'm sure there is a
 98        hysterical conversion bit to this chap
 99  N1:   Hmmm
100  P:    You know he shifts all over the place . . . the way he
101        shifts his symptoms is so typical of that
102  N1:   That's right
103  P:    I think if he was a straightforward malingerer, I mean
104        maybe I'll get to the point of saying that, I don't
105        know. But I have a feeling he's typical Munchausen's
106  N2:   Hmmmmm=
107  P:    =That what you need to do is just say, yeah, you've got
108        a problem, we'll help you with it, and if the help is
109        just getting him to the club or whatever, getting him
110        involved somewhere, just getting him out of the house,
111        I think maybe is all we can do, yeah?
112  N1:   Mmmmm
113  P:    But I'll send you the . . . I've got a file here
114        which I haven't written up, I'll do it
```

Here the interplay between the medical and social definitions of psychiatrist and team members, overlaps with attempts by the psychiatrist to preserve the medical frame as serious, and by social worker and nurse to juxtapose elements of a humorous frame that pokes fun at the patient and challenges the medical interpretation of the case. As in *Extract 1*, some team members appear doubtful about the presence of psychiatric pathology. Scepticism is introduced by the social worker's query at lines 25–6 about the difficulty of getting the patient 'off the sofa', and the joking observation that a second patient (Val) living nearby would 'sort him out' (with its obvious sexual innuendo). The remarks elicit laughter from several team members. The psychiatrist attempts to re-assert the primacy of the medical framework by talking of the need to 'look at the secondary gain' (line 40) and formulating the patient's behaviour as 'his symptoms' (44). 'Secondary gain' here is used as a technical term which is represented as a symptom of mental illness rather than being used as a moral evaluation. He suggests that the patient is 'typical Munchausen's' (lines 49–50), and talks of the possibility of a 'real collapse' (line 59). However, the psychiatrist's attempted return to the medical frame is resisted as the social worker produces another joke (lines 65–7). Once again he gets others to join in the laughter, and once again the psychiatrist tries to re-assert the serious medical agenda (line 70).

But a CPN (N2) again brings talk back within the humorous frame in line 77 ('they'll drip feed him down there').

Glenn emphasizes that 'laughing at' and 'laughing with' alignments are 'not fixed but changeable, sometimes equivocal, and subject to moment by moment negotiation' (1995: 48). There is the possibility that the butt of an intended joke may succeed in transforming the interaction to convert disaffiliative laughter to affiliative laughter. This may be done by demonstrating a shared appreciation of the joke, or perhaps by adding a new slant which turns it to the butt's advantage. This is what the psychiatrist appears to be working towards as a way of managing the implied challenge. His contribution in line 81 ('Tell him it's a special club for you know whatever') appears to link back to his serious reference in line 74 to the mental states of 'chaps' of this kind ('it's him being special'), and thus modify the joke so that it supports his previous formulation. The problem is that in sharing the joke he lays himself open to a sarcastic rejoinder from the CPN: 'For malingerers' (line 83). This subverts the attempted shift to the 'laughing with' format by casting doubt on the basis of the referral.

In line 92 the psychiatrist moves forcefully to regain the floor. He acknowledges that the team's version has some validity ('I mean he's malingering'), but sets this within the context of 'hysterical conversion' and the typical symptomatology of an established disease syndrome (Munchausen's). In this he receives support from N2 and N1, who produce appreciations to signal agreement with his account (lines 95, 96, 99, 102, 106, 112). While it is not clear that the dissenting members are wholly convinced, the psychiatric definition is publicly sustained, and the psychiatrist's suggestions for action are enforced.

Although the exchange patently reflects the psychiatrist's power to push through decisions, even in the face of team resistance, there are indications that this is exercised with some ambivalence and restraint. Having formulated a course of action in lines 107–10, the psychiatrist uses a pronoun shift to signal shared responsibility for treatment 'just getting him out of the house I think maybe is all we can do, yeah?' (lines 110–11). By this use of the final 'we' and the construction of the closing remark as a question, the psychiatrist offers the team the possibility of defining his preferred outcome as one they all support. However, though the nurse's response ('mmmmm') at line 117 can be heard as ambiguous, the psychiatrist uses the next turn to state that the case file will be sent to the team and effectively cuts off further discussion.

The above exchange highlights the continuing reality of professional dominance in the apparently democratic context of the *Team B* setting. While the psychiatrist stops short of any bald assertion of decision-making authority in the face of the humorous challenge, he carries the argument by emphasizing his specialist expertise in psychiatric diagnosis (notably through his references to the typicality of symptoms). This is an effective tactic, though one that may have negative consequences for team unity if repeated too often. Challenges to definitions which are framed humorously are permissible since they allow for the withdrawal of the challenge without loss of face on the part of the challenger. However, a challenge made outside this frame and based on claims to superior expertise, for example, would pose a serious threat, both to the psychiatrist's expert status and to the cooperative ethos of teamwork. The psychiatrist's problem is that excessive emphasis on specialist medical knowledge will also have negative consequences by devaluing the contribution of the other disciplines to the team enterprise.

Humour and team building

One well-documented way of building in-group identity is to contrast group values and behaviour with those of a disvalued other who remains outside the group (Burke, 1969). In *Team A*, shared dissatisfaction about inappropriate referrals from the absent psychiatrist appears to promote a sense of common membership of a team defined to exclude him. Humour plays a part in this process and, as we saw earlier, creates a dilemma for the team leader, who must display membership of the team but also maintain a good working relationship with the psychiatrist. The team leader steers a middle course, joining in team banter while trying to attenuate the challenge it poses to the referral process and the current organizational framework.

The psychiatrist in *Team B* must deal with a similar tension. On the one hand, humour may help to build a team identity in which he too wishes to have a part, but the current of resistance expressed in joking remarks needs to be managed and perhaps responded to. As illustrated in *Extract 2*, the psychiatrist may use an approach similar to that adopted by the *Team A* leader, and attempt to keep the subversive possibilities of humour in check. However, the presence of the psychiatrist, as originator of the referrals, in the meetings also allows him to play a more proactive role and harness humour to support the version of 'team' that he favours. *Extract 3* contains a segment of interaction where the psychiatrist makes a joke at his own expense.

Extract 3

```
 1   SW:   You'll be pleased to know that Rebecca P_____ is much
 2         better this week
 3   P:    Oh, she owes me a tenner
 4   SW:   Heh Heh
 5   P:    Did I tell you the story?
 6   N1:      No
 7   SW1:  [[No ((inaudible phrase))
 8   P:           ((inaudible overlap)). (I'll have a bitch). Came
 9         out of the estate agents in Grovetown one day last week
10   N1:   heh heh heh heh
```

11	SW1:	[Heh heh heh
12	P:	About half five came out pouring . . . it was pouring with
13		rain, you know. And there's Rebecca standing with her
14		tee shirt and her jeans all soaked. So//she
15	N1:	((inaudible)) then?
16	P:	So she's been up to see Paul//you know
17	N1:	Yeah yeah=
18	P:	=this boyfriend, who's one of George Brown'
19	N1:	[I thought it was all over
20	P:	Well I thought it was over after the last episode
21	SW1:	I thought she broke off the engagement between one bus
22		stop to the other=
23	N1:	=heh heh heh
24	P:	heh heh. Yeah. Well apparently it was all on again
25		that week and she'd gone up. I think she hadn't told
26		Lisa she was going to see him
27	N1:	hmmm hmmm=
28	P:	=So she's kind of going behind the family if you like
29	SW:	hmmm
30	P:	But he had dumped her again
31	N1:	Oooahh=
32	P:	=And he kicked her out of the house, and so she'd just
33		been wandering around Grovetown soaked. So of course
34		I had to=
35	SW:	Haah hu//ha
36	P:	She . . . She said, I've no money with me
37	SW2:	Ha//hah hah
38	P:	(Understand why I got into it)
39	SW2:	Huh huh huh Good Samaritan
40	P:	I//know I
41	SW2:	ha ha ha huu
42	P:	Of course all I had was a bloody tenner in my pocket=
43	SW:	=Hah hah hah//ha
44	P:	So I give her a tenner
45	SW:	=Oh brilliant=
46	P:	So if you see her she owes me money
47	N1:	[heh heh heh=
48	P:	=She owes me//a tenner
49	SW:	(Oh don't you worry about that) heh heh ha ha ha[3]

This story fulfils a number of affiliative functions for the psychiatrist and the team. It situates the psychiatrist as a person who operates within the same mundane reality and who is subject to the same everyday contingencies as other team members. His account has him 'just coming out of the estate agents' (line 9). This is a reference to the fact that he intends to buy a house in the area (an everyday activity that any one of them might be engaged in), and also draws attention to the chance nature of the encounter. The construction stresses the story-teller's lack of control over the events that followed, and in this context serves to de-emphasize the psychiatrist's authority and superior status within the team. The story concludes with Rebecca borrowing ten pounds because, 'of course, all I had was a bloody tenner in my pocket' (line 42). This locates the psychiatrist as the butt of a self-made joke: he felt obliged to lend Rebecca some money, but would have preferred a smaller amount, except that the only money he had in his pocket was ten pounds. Again the psychiatrist is minimizing his superiority: this is the sort of situation which anyone might fall into, especially team members who deal with awkward customers. He is also emphasizing his familiarity with the clients: he knows Rebecca well enough for her to ask him to lend her money, and to comment in intimate terms on her relationships with men. The story appears to serve its purposes well: segments of the account are interspersed with appreciative laughter (lines 4, 10, 11, 23, 35, 37, 39, 41, 43, 47, 49) and other verbal markers of appreciation (lines 17, 29, 31, 39, 45).

Later at the close of the case discussion, the psychiatrist acknowledges the social worker's original comment that Rebecca is much better and reinforces the message of the job well done. 'She's good, she's good you know [. . .] Great stuff'. Although these verbal reaffirmations of the reality of cooperative working may be largely symbolic, the careful display of a self which emphasizes the common ground between the psychiatrist and team members, when set against the unequal power of the different participants, allows team members to construct their relations as collegial rather than hierarchical ones.

In *Team B*, where the psychiatrist makes himself available for routinized face-to-face interaction with his team members, his contribution to the joint production of what the team is and what the team does is different from the contribution provided by the non-attending *Team A* psychiatrist. One significant advantage available in face-to-face interaction is the ability to respond to frame shifts initiated by other team members, by moving between frame and countering challenges as they occur. By contrast the medical case report used by the absent *Team A* psychiatrist is readily challenged and often defeasible simply by switching frame.

These contrasting strategies affect the psychiatrists' ability to determine the patient population accepted onto team caseloads (see Griffiths, 1997). With the psychiatrist present, both psychiatrist and team have a voice in accepting patients, so that the boundary between 'appropriate' and 'inappropriate' referrals is a boundary which is jointly constructed and jointly owned. The *Team B* psychiatrist interactionally accomplishes the task of establishing that boundary against alternative suggestions from the team as to its limits. This contrasts with the situation in *Team A* meetings, with an absent psychiatrist, where the boundary between 'appropriate' patients and others is strongly contested, and where team members locate the boundary so as to exclude many of the patients whom the psychiatrist wishes the team to take.

Conclusion

My data contain many more examples similar to the extracts presented above, where lower status staff use humour to challenge team leaders or psychiatrists. This suggests that Coser's (1960) finding that the use of humour by subordinates in face-to-face interactions with superiors is rare, cannot be generalized to all health care settings. One explanation for the frequency of humorous challenges in my study may lie in the situation of the multi-disciplinary CMHTs as an innovative organizational reform imposed on staff who must make it work. Hatch and Ehrlich (1993) suggest that humour, being often constructed on a foundation of contradiction and incongruity, provides a revealing window on members' experiences of paradox and ambiguity in organizations. Studying humour provides a way of exploring how organization members cope with difficult or changing situations. There is a similarity with Radcliffe-Brown's (1940) argument that humour becomes functional when people are brought into situations which contain an element of disjunction as well as conjunction: situations where there is a divergence of interest that might lead to conflict but also a practical need for close contact without strife. He applies this analysis to changes in social status in tribal societies, as, for example, may occur with members of two families when a marriage changes their relationship.

CMHTs are clearly organizations which manifest a high degree of paradox and strain. They are intended to exemplify team working, but must also accommodate existing occupational hierarchies and the professional power of the psychiatrists. The need to work closely together is contradicted, not just by status differences, but also by different disciplinary perspectives that favour different explanations of mental illness. Team members are bound together by the need to conform with the current orthodoxy in mental health policy, but – because the teams are so new – have not fully worked out their respective roles and decision-making powers. Humour reflects these paradoxes and strains. It helps rank-and-file team members to support each other in dissent, and communicates their dissatisfaction to organizational superiors. Superordinates too, join in the banter to avoid being marginalized and to try to deal with implicit challenges packaged as jokes.

It would be possible to construct my argument in functionalist terms so that subordinates' humour is seen as a way of 'letting off steam', which does not fundamentally challenge the status quo. Probably the messages that staff convey in jokes would not be pursued in serious discourse, and may be more a ritual statement of complaint than an indication of real opposition. Yet the balance between humorous and serious dissent is a fine one, and humour clearly carries risks. If kept within permissible boundaries, humour may be seen as an integrative mechanism that allows unavoidable tensions to be expressed and managed. But, as noted by Douglas (1968, 1975), jokes often involve a confrontation with the dominant social pattern, and can disrupt that pattern by giving voice to its inconsistencies and irrationalities. Both CMHTs studied were relatively new and still adapting to changing circumstances, and there was certainly a possibility that uncontrolled humour might undermine the legitimacy of powerful professionals and the work routines they had developed. *Team A*, in particular, went through a difficult period as opposition to referrals took an increasingly open form. The team only moved towards something like a position of equilibrium as it became clear that the non-attendance of the psychiatrist at meetings created space for members to exercise more decision-making authority (by delaying acceptance of patients onto case-loads or to reformulate cases as 'non-urgent') than the official 'allocation' function provided for. Resistance within the team put pressure on the team leader, with the consequence that meetings developed as events where the suitability of referrals became a legitimate topic for discussion, and when team members were able to block acceptance of some clients. At the same time, the team leader continued to feed through the majority of referrals in accordance with the psychiatrist's wishes. This uneasy compromise was less about functional adaptation than about the calculation by those involved that a breakdown of relationships between team and psychiatrist would damage both sides. One important policy implication of the type of conflict described in this chapter is the difficulty, perhaps impossibility of providing a 'needs-led' service. The extracts presented here and many like them show the ways in which patient 'needs' are always shaped by organizational imperatives to which staff are orientated.

Notes

1. Issues concerning humour, power and resistance have received more attention outside the health care sphere. See Dwyer (1991), Powell and Paton (1988) and Zijderveld (1983).
2. In line with the views expressed in the introduction, I use a simplified transcription system which includes the standard symbols for overlaps, simultaneous utterances and continuous utterances, but does not record such things as timed pauses, intonation, sound and pitch (for an account of the standard conversation analysis transcript notation see, Button and Lee, 1987: 9–18). The symbols used in the chapter are as follows: '[and]' indicates the beginning and end of overlapping utterances; '//' indicates the place where an overlapping utterance printed in the next line of the transcript begins; '=' '=' indicates that one utterance continues immediately on from another. The transcripts contain as much as I can decipher of the spoken exchanges, but may omit some overlaps and truncated utterances. Given the importance of the positioning of laughter for the analysis, I have made every effort to identify placement and the identity of participants, but acknowledge that some overlapping laughter and laughter fragments may have been omitted. The mention of STEPS in the extract refers to a voluntary agency dealing with drug and alcohol abuse.
3. Brown is a consultant psychiatrist. Lisa is Rebecca's sister.

References

Astedt, P. and A. Liukkonen (1994) 'Humour in nursing care', *Journal of Advanced Nursing*, 20: 183–8.

Atkinson, P.A. (1995) *Medical Talk and Medical Work*. London: Sage.

Bottorff, J.L., M. Gogag and M. Engelberglotzkar (1995) 'Comforting: exploring the work of cancer nurses', *Journal of Advanced Nursing*, 22: 1077–84.

Burke, K. (1969) *A Rhetoric of Motives*. Berkeley, CA: University of California Press.

Burnard, P. (1995) 'Interpreting text: an alternative to some current forms of textual analysis in qualitative research', *Social Sciences in Health*, 1: 236–45.

Button, G. and J. Lee (1987) *Talk and Social Organisation*. Clevedon: Multilingual Matters.

Coser, R.L. (1958) 'Authority and decision making in a hospital: a comparative analysis', *American Sociological Review*, 23: 57–63.

Coser, R.L. (1959) 'Some social functions of laughter: a study of humour in a hospital setting', in J.K. Skipper and R.C. Leonard (eds), *Social Interaction and Patient Care*. Philadelphia, PA: J.B. Lippincott Company (also in *Human Relations*, 12: 171–82).

Coser, R.L. (1960) 'Laughter among colleagues', *Psychiatry*, 23: 81–95.

Douglas, M. (1968) 'The social control of cognition: some factors in joke perception', *Man*, 3: 361–76.

Douglas, M. (1975) *Implicit Meanings*. London: Routledge and Kegan Paul.

Dwyer, T. (1991) 'Humor, power and change in organisations', *Human Relations*, 44: 1–19.

Emerson, J.P. (1973) 'Negotiating the serious import of humour', in A. Birenbaum and E. Sagarin (eds), *People in Places: The Sociology of the Familiar*. London: Nelson.

Glenn, P. (1995) 'Laughing at and laughing with: negotiations of participant alignments through conversational laughter', in P. ten Have and G. Psathas (eds), *Situated Order: Studies in the Social Organisation of Talk and Embodied Activities, Studies in Ethnomethodology and Conversational Analysis No. 3*. Lanham, MD: International Institute for Ethnomethodology and Conversation Analysis and University Press of America.

Goffman, E. (1961) *Asylums*. New York: Doubleday Anchor.

Griffiths, L. (1997) 'Accomplishing team: teamwork and categorisation in two community mental health teams', *The Sociological Review*, 45: 59–78.

Griffiths, L. and D. Hughes (1994) ' "Innocent parties" and "disheartening" experiences: natural rhetorics in neuro-rehabilitation admissions conferences', *Qualitative Health Research*, 4: 385–410.

Hatch, M.J. and S.B. Ehrlich (1993) 'Spontaneous humor as an indicator of paradox and ambiguity in organisations', *Organisation Studies*, 14: 505–27.

Lieber, D. (1991) 'Laughter and humour in critical care', *Dimensions of Critical Care Nursing*, 5: 162–70.

Lipsky, M. (1980) *Street-level Bureaucracy. Dilemmas of the Individual in Public Services*. New York: Russell Sage Foundation.

Mallett, J. and R. Ahern (1996) 'Comparative distribution and use of humor within nurse–patient communication', *International Journal of Nursing Studies*, 33: 530–50.

Mulkay, M.J. (1988) *On Humour: Its Nature and Its Place in Modern Society*. Cambridge: Polity Press.

Powell, C. and G.E.C. Paton (eds) (1988) *Humour in Society: Resistance and Control*. London: Macmillan.

Radcliffe-Brown, A.R. (1940) *Structure and Function in Primitive Society*. London: Cohen and West.

Sacks, H. (1992) *Lectures on Conversation* (2 vols) (edited by G. Jefferson). Oxford: Blackwell.

Wender, R.C. (1996) 'Humor in medicine', *Primary Care*, 23: 141.

Yuels, W.C. and J.M. Clair (1995) 'Laughter in the clinic: humour as social organisation', *Symbolic Interaction*, 18: 39–59.

Zijderveld, A.C. (1983) 'The sociology of humor and laughter', *Current Sociology*, 33: 1–103.

10

Openness and specialisation: dealing with patients in a hospital emergency service

Nicolas Dodier and Agnès Camus

The functioning of hospital emergency services is at the heart of a recurring question in hospitals, a question that is becoming increasingly acute: how to reconcile the principle of openness to the very heterogeneous demands for medical care that are spontaneously directed to the hospital, with the concern to select patients in terms of their match with the medical specialties? The hospital's openness to spontaneous demands has taken many forms: the association with charity under the *Ancien Régime*; the creation of a 'public assistance' scheme for the care of the indigent in the nineteenth century; the emergence, after the Second World War, of the concept of the hospital as 'a public service open to all' and adapted to users' demands.[1] This openness co-exists, particularly in teaching hospitals, with the need to specialize to a high degree in fields at the cutting edge of medicine and biomedical research (Jamous, 1969; Lejonc et al., 1993; Vassy and Renard, 1992). The hospital's dual role generates an increasingly tense situation. On the one hand, because of its openness to all types of demands, the hospital tends more and more to be solicited by people affected by the growing importance of the social question in contemporary societies (Castel, 1995). On the other hand, hospital services are tending to select their patients on ever more stringent criteria, either to ensure a patient profile adapted to harsh budget restrictions, or to recruit patients that correspond to the trend towards biomedical innovation (Dodier and Camus, 1997).

This dual function of the hospital can be seen at several levels, first of all, in a polarization of settings. On the one hand are places that we might describe as 'open': services dealing with internal or general medicine (Herzlich, 1973; Lejonc et al., 1993), and the emergency room, which in large hospitals is organised as a genuinely independent service. These services receive all sorts of demands, many of them associated with their

This article was previously published in *Sociology of Health and Illness* (1998) 20(4): 413–444.

role as a 'neighbourhood' service for the district in which the hospital is located. Conversely, there are also 'selective' areas, such as services associated with specialties dealing with a limited range of pathological conditions. They are anchored in medical-scientific networks, of the same type as the sociotechnical networks studied by Michel Callon (1989) and Bruno Latour (1989). The notion of 'neighbourhood' is no longer meaningful, in that their relationship to space is not with an actual territory, but with a network (Mol and Law, 1994). However, the dual role of the hospital also affects the internal organization of certain services. It can be seen again at the very core of the ambiguity surrounding the role of the emergency hospital service. On the one hand, these services are characterized by their *accessibility*, as implied by the very concept of emergency. A person who applies to a service 'in an emergency' must be able to do so rapidly and take priority over other demands. An emergency service must be able to bypass the usual formalities for gaining access to medical attention: the need to make an appointment, deadlines for treatment, the relevant administrative formalities, opening hours. However, at the same time, the emergency service, as a specialized service, must also answer to another concept of emergency: *a restricted range of conditions* or symptoms generating a more or less serious life-threatening situation. In this sense, emergency services belong to a set of specialized networks using specific skills and equipment (Peneff, 1992): the SAMU (mobile medical emergency unit); the fire brigade; the '999' or emergency police unit; general practitioners (GPs) specializing in emergency medicine; intensive care units. This applies even if emergency medicine itself does not exist as a specialty in the same sense as the other specialties taught in the course of medical training.

The flow of demands attracted by the accessibility of emergency services is documented in many works. Some of these confirm the heterogeneous nature of these demands (Béland et al., 1991; Mannon et al., 1987); others highlight the function of this accessibility for deprived persons (Béland et al., 1990), people in danger of becoming disconnected from society (Genell and Rosenqvist, 1987a), in contact with psychiatric services or in a situation of solitude (Genell and Rosenqvist, 1987b). The effect of this duality on the actual work undertaken by emergency services has also been examined in several studies carried out from an ethnographic standpoint (Dingwall and Murray, 1983; Hughes, 1988, 1989; Jeffery, 1979; Mannon, 1976; Roth, 1972a, 1972b; Roth and Douglas, 1983, all in the English-speaking countries; Peneff, 1992 in France). This research shows that the way in which patients are dealt with depends on the way in which they are *categorized, in situ*, by staff, much more than on exclusively clinical criteria. The analytical frameworks adopted to understand the way in which patients are dealt with in emergency services raises questions on several different levels. The first is related to the intention behind this categorization. Some research emphasizes the distinction made by staff between 'good patients' and 'bad patients'. For example Roth and Douglas

(1983) suggest, on the one hand, that patients are 'deserving' or 'undeserving' depending on the social worth attributed to them and, on the other, that they are 'legitimate' or 'non-legitimate' depending on whether or not their demand matches the concept which personnel have of their own work. Jeffery (1979) distinguishes between 'good patients' and 'rubbish patients'. The merits of this approach is that it shows that the reception given to patients in the emergency service reflects sharply contrasting reactions: on the one hand, there are patients for whom mobilization is immediate and unequivocal; on the other, there are patients for whom everything in the reaction of staff tends to cast doubt on the very legitimacy of their presence. The drawback of this approach is that it tends to 'congeal' the work of categorization by creating a dichotomy. It reflects only one aspect of staff's reactions, since through these categories of good and bad patients, it refers to the two extremes of a much more complicated range of mobilization. Categorization of patients by staff does not only concern questions of eligibility, but also the constant establishing of orders of precedence between patients, via a series of small operations, in the framework of management of a flow of demands distributed between the different actors in the department (physicians, nurses, nursing auxiliaries, etc.). Barring obvious exceptions, nothing in our own observations, at least, suggests, for example, that the very long wait that must sometimes be endured by certain patients results necessarily from an intentional decision made by staff at the outset, categorizing them straight away as bad patients. In many cases, their having to wait is more a result of being pushed down the order of precedence by new priorities established between cases in the course of time and as new patients arrive. In order to understand these gradients of mobilization, we shall start with the notion of *mobilizing worth*, by which we mean what, in each patient, triggers the particular degree of mobilization of staff with respect to him/her, in gradually establishing his/her place in the order of precedence.

The second question concerns the different dimensions involved in categorizing patients. These dimensions are heterogeneous, given the openness of emergency services to all types of demand, which makes analysis rather difficult. If we seek, as Jeffery did (1979), separately to reconstruct criteria for the origin of the categories of good patients and bad patients, we run into problems of consistency, as Dingwall and Murray (1983) have pointed out. When the comparison adopted is too simple, such as between a judgement made on social grounds and a judgement made on clinical grounds (Dingwall and Murray, 1983; Roth and Douglas, 1983), we may end up lumping very different cases together in a single category. For example, Roth and Douglas (1983) lump together in the category of patients who are negatively perceived in terms of their social worth, attempted suicides, hysterical and bizarre behaviour, vague complaints, dirty, smelly patients, hippies, women with scanty clothing, young unmarried pregnant women who have attempted an abortion, drunks, pelvic inflammatory disease. In Jeffery's (1979) work, we find a hotchpotch of the same type between rubbish patients – trivia, drunks, overdoses, tramps – but also nutcases, smelly, dirty, obese patients. Mannon (1976) distinguishes three categories among 'problem patients': helpless, drunk and drugged, regulars. In terms of clinical judgement, the authors obviously have difficulty in identifying a single dimension in the judgement made about patients: hence, although they believe that outpatient cases, that is, cases that are not real emergencies, are not legitimate for staff, they also note that some of them have high mobilizing worth, since they arouse interesting clinical problems (Roth and Douglas, 1983: 85). This discordance can only pose a problem for the framework of an analysis that treats the clinical aspect of judgement as an indivisible whole.

In this article, we attempt to define distinctions between the different dimensions that go to make up the patient's mobilizing worth, and to undertake a systematic analysis of each of them. To avoid casting our net too wide, we evaluate the respective weight of these dimensions in the actual work, finally retaining only the most important. For this article we have chosen four of them. The first two can be lumped together under clinical judgement, but arouse reactions of different types: the degree to which the case can be seen as a life-and-death situation, and the intellectual interest of the case. The third is related to the social aspects of the demand and the fourth to the responsibilities of physicians who send patients to the emergency service. The patient's worth is made up of several dimensions. Various authors have mentioned this point during their observations (e.g., Roth and Douglas, 1983: 94). Here, it should be used as a theoretical central point of the analytical framework: several markers may potentially contribute to this mobilizing worth; each may arouse different reactions, some of which tend to accelerate and others to delay mobilization.

The complexity of staff reactions is not only a question of the combination of different dimensions whose effects may be quite contradictory, but an internal characteristic of the judgement made within the framework of each dimension. We suggest that for certain dimensions – and notably, as we shall see, for the intellectual interest of the case and the social aspects of the demands – staff reactions are not unequivocal. Rather, they should be seen as a complex of reactions which are not without internal contradictions, even for each person who is called on to deal with a given patient. This situation is not specific to the emergency services. On the contrary, much is to be gained by looking at it in the light of theoretical developments contributed in the last ten years in terms of the sociological approach to action. As recent works tend to suggest,[2] we shall here look at the general assumption whereby people wishing to make judgements in a given situation can refer to a large number of possible justifications. Far from forming a theoretically coherent whole, these justifications must be combined according to more or less complex formulae, with the same people being likely to switch between different forms of commitment from one situation to another. Our assumptions about the many dimensions of mobilizing worth and the complexity of staff reactions with respect to each dimension taken separately should be seen as related to this framework. Hence, rather than immediately presuming a shared basis of reactions, either within the framework of a common 'culture' (Hughes, 1989), or because the people holding them occupy identical positions in the organization (Peneff, 1992), the point of the situational approach, at least to begin with, is to be very attentive to those aspects of reactions to patients that stem from possibly differentiated or even fluctuating reactions, perhaps later and with caution looking at what might be likely to stabilize and align these reactions.

The field inquiry

To highlight the way in which the mobilizing worth of patients is built up during the course of the action, we have used ethnographic inquiry methods. We chose a monographic approach focusing on a medical emergency service in a French teaching hospital. This service has high patient flows: 17,134 consultations in 1993. The fieldwork was carried out between October 1992 and December 1993, in the form of direct observations of the work done in the service, and interviews (19) with staff: four with permanent consultants, four nurses, three supervisors, three residents, two social workers, one head of clinic, one clinic student and one nursing auxiliary – altogether 11 women and eight men. It is a genuine emergency service, not just a partial service delegated to deal with emergency cases, as in smaller hospitals. The permanent physicians in the service may be more insistent than others on the point that working in the emergency service calls for specialist skills, even if emergency medicine is not recognized as a separate medical specialty. In addition, as a teaching hospital, it has many very specialized services (neurology, cardiology, hematology . . .). Residents from those services, on duty in the emergency service, often refer – and here again perhaps more than elsewhere – to their determination to learn anything that has a bearing on their original speciality, up to and including the tensions that this may create in the course of their work in the emergency service. The importance of specialization also comes into play when patients are to be transferred from the emergency service into one of these specialized services. On the other hand, the hospital is located in a Paris neighbourhood which has quite a large proportion of inhabitants who are attracted first and foremost by the accessibility of the service (open 24 hours a day, no appointment needed, possibility of free treatment . . .). So, the service in which we carried out our fieldwork is an interesting area in which to view this dual movement of biomedical specialization of hospital services and their exposure to the effects of the social question.

Our study is based on the way in which personnel refer *explicitly*, by word and judgement, to what attracts their attention in patients. It does not aim to throw light on the silent influence of factors, only actual reference to these factors in the course of action, or retrospectively in comments or accounts. This provides a guarantee against misleading interpretations, but it is also a limitation, since it forces us to focus on the overt aspects of mobilization around patients, to the exclusion of anything that is not said or not conscious. We observed in turn the major points of the patients' trajectory: the actual reception; treatment dispensed by the service itself, which is dealt with in this article; and transfer to other services (Dodier and Camus, 1997). More precisely, we rely on three sources: observation *in situ* of a series of cases dealt with in the treatment cubicles (n = 60); observation of 'sketches', that is, comments or brief moments, in isolation from the actual cases but instructive for understanding the order of precedence (n = 23); interviews in which the actors deliver more comprehensive opinions about aspects of general arrangements (n = 16). After describing the general framework for establishing the order of precedence between patients in the service, we shall look one by one at the main dimensions of the mobilizing worth of patients.

Establishing orders of precedence

The general organization of the waiting list is closer to a 'distributed' than a 'planned' model of coordination. This means that no actor can be seen as a central authority with an overview of the whole process, and that this process results from a series of operations involving actors each engaged in initiatives which partly escape the others (Dodier, 1995b, Perrow, 1984; Star, 1989; Thévenot, 1993). In a typical day, it mobilizes, to varying degrees, three nurses, three nursing auxiliaries, three clinical students, two residents and one consultant. This organization hinges on two tools kept in one of the treatment cubicles: the chronological entry register and the file tray. In the entry register, a large ledger that is always on view on a table, we find a list of patients by name, in their chronological order of arrival, along with the following indications: date and time of entry, nurse's diagnosis on arrival, diagnosis when leaving the treatment cubicle, time at which the patient was transferred or left the hospital. From time to time, someone appears – a nurse, a nursing auxiliary or a consultant, sometimes a resident – and reviews the overall situation: Who is still waiting in the corridor? How long has this person been waiting? What are his/her symptoms? There is no codified procedure for choosing patients and chronological order is not necessarily important. It is even more distributed than the organization described by Hughes (1988, 1989): it is quite common for reception staff – by which we mean a nursing auxiliary or a nurse, not a clerical employee – to make an immediate technical judgement. Nurses write down in the register a specific form of diagnosis, the nurse's diagnosis, and any member of the staff can at any time bring a patient to the attention of one of the doctors.

The second tool is the file tray, in which files are placed one on top of the other by reception staff as they register a patient. There is no attempt at chronological order – the time of arrival is mentioned only in the file, on the labels. The patient's mobilizing worth, as evaluated by the doctor from information written in the file by reception staff, is of prime importance. From time to time, a doctor reaches into the tray, leafs through the files and decides to take a particular patient. The choice of patient is generally made in silence, without the doctor having to justify his or her decision. Hence, the information written in the file by the first person to see the patient on reception is vital.

> A female consultant mentions the following case: 'This case really made an impression on me. It was at night and we had a young woman of 27 who arrived with a high temperature after returning from a tropical country. Basically, when someone writes that down in the patient's file, you think "malaria". We were frantically busy on that particular ward. She had to wait an hour in the corridor. After an hour, I take all the papers, all the observations about patients to be seen and have a closer look. I see: "High temperature on return from a tropical country"; I say to myself: "Aha, it's probably a case of malaria, I'll go and see how she is", telling myself that if it's a serious bout, she's been waiting rather a long time already. I spy her on a stretcher, covered right up to here. . . . Then I start to panic: she's covered with purpura – obviously a meningococcal meningitis, an extreme medical emergency!'

An important factor is the verbal announcement made by reception staff. When placing a file in the basket, the nurse or nursing auxiliary makes a comment repeating the words written in it and indicating the degree of mobilization required by the case. The staff can also decide to put the file into the tray in silence, make a general announcement to the people present, who may be involved in other activities, or address a doctor directly to call his or her attention to the case. All these mini-procedures have an effect on the doctor's degree of mobilization. Fire brigade or SAMU staff, who bring patients directly into the department on stretchers, are obliged to present them to the treatment cubicles and have them entered in the current 'work lines', according to the usual process of negotiation in the hospital described more generally by Strauss et al. (1985), thereby bypassing the slower process of the register or the file tray. However, this verbal announcement does not necessarily mobilize doctors – it is simply a way of attracting their attention. Announcement of a new case can easily attract no response at all. Here again, the key element is the mobilizing worth of the patient as far as the doctor is concerned.

Another factor that comes into play is that of the reminders made to physicians concerning patients waiting to be seen. When personnel circulate in the corridor, they look around, depending on how preoccupied they are, to check the condition of waiting patients and any changes in their condition. They may even be reminded by patients themselves, who may complain about the length of time they have been waiting and the pain or discomfort they are feeling, or who express their anxiety. In some cases, patients or the people accompanying them may go to the treatment cubicles to remind staff of their presence. All these indicators may increase the patient's mobilizing worth for nurses or nursing auxiliaries, who may then pass on the information, if they consider it vital, to the doctors in the cubicles. Finally, consultants, nurses and nursing auxiliaries have access to pointers concerning the overall flow of patients: they estimate the number of people waiting in the corridor, they check the entry register in order to evaluate the patients waiting to be seen, the number of patients waiting and the different stages they have reached in the process. As a function of these observations, they call to order the doctors dispensing this treatment, particularly residents, to get them to expedite their current work or transfer their attention to another patient. The panoramic view enjoyed by the staff other than doctors is another reason, on top of those already identified by Hughes (1989), for them to feel authorized to intervene with the residents, who are involved in the actual clinical work on a case-by-case basis and are not concerned with fluctuations in flow[3].

Hence, establishing the order of precedence is a process distributed between numerous actors. It is the result of a whole series of micro-operations carried out by all personnel involved with a patient. Chronological order, as in the entry register, has a role to play, but it is a comparatively minor role compared with moments in which it is the patient's mobilizing worth that determines the degree to which staff concerned at that particular moment direct their efforts to ensuring that the patient moves further up the order of precedence. There is no specific procedure to be respected, but rather a series of individual initiatives based on the notes written in the file, quick evaluations of the state of waiting patients, and attempts by patients themselves to attract attention – this last initiative has a high failure rate. A person's 'rank' is not fixed once and for all, as it is in much more codified procedures of sequencing (Elster and Herpin, 1992). But it depends at all times on new arrivals in the service and changes in the state of existing patients. We look one by one at the aspects that are most frequently encountered. (See Appendix 1.)

Closeness to life-threatening emergency

In emergency manuals, as in spoken language, cases that are closest to the core of life-threatening emergencies are described as 'real emergencies'. Evaluations made within the emergency service put the proportion of real emergencies at 18 per cent of all the patients registered in the department. They are consistent with broader data on hospitals in France (Steg, 1989). The status of a particular case concerning the core of life-threatening emergencies has an effect on the quantity of resources mobilized: the number of persons, their professional capacity, the equipment employed. It also determines whether the case is serious enough to interrupt current work lines. At one extreme of mobilization, there is the patient for whom other patients are immediately removed from the resuscitation cubicle without anyone protesting and where all the people required to prevent the death of the patient immediately abandon the treatment on which they are currently engaged. The actual therapeutic gestures are not necessarily more rapid (Timmermans, 1995) but the different stages: waiting in the corridor, waiting for a cubicle to become free, even the diagnostic examination – since in general we are concerned with the therapeutic gestures implemented before an exact diagnosis can be made – are bypassed.

The further we depart from the life-threatening emergency and even from the 'real' emergency, the more likely we are to see the emergence of resistance to mobilization of resources. The patient has to wait longer and has more difficulty entering into the work lines. At an even lower degree of mobilization, questions will be voiced about the patient's rights in light of his or her condition: the person will be treated but will not be given an ambulance for the return home; staff will agree to give painkillers but will not extract a tooth in the middle of the night; staff will listen to the worried person's complaints but without paying great attention. At an even lower level of mobilization, the patient will be reproached for having applied to the emergency service. In this case, the patient is definitely a 'bad patient', who is assumed to have infringed a certain number of rules governing his/ her role (Jeffery, 1979).

> The cubicles are very calm. There are few patients. The reception nurse places a file in the tray. The clinical student takes it and goes off to see the patient in a cubicle. According to the file, this 19-year-old man has come to consult a doctor for 'vesiculate, pruriginous lesions in the right arm and left lumbar region'. The resident arrives in the cubicle. He asks the man: 'You don't have a temperature? How long has it been going on?'
> 'Since last week.'
> '*And you've only decided to come in now, when it's practically finished!* (to the clinical student) We'll give him some ointment. (to me) *He should never have come to the emergency service!*'

In this case, note that the reproach is based on the idea that only recent pain justifies recourse to the emergency service. If the pain is not recent, the patient's condition is not seen as a real emergency.[4]

Patients whose condition is well removed from this core of real emergencies also arouse recriminations during the actual treatment. There is a tangible atmosphere of dissatisfaction around cases not considered to be real emergencies, cases that should have been dealt with by a GP or in a hospital consultation, as shown by Roth and Douglas (1983: 84) in surveys carried out in the USA, the UK and Australia. In this manner, personnel express their belief that the patient could just as well have consulted a general practitioner or made an appointment in another hospital service rather than turning up at the emergency service: 'But why isn't she in the neurology service?' 'It would be better for your daughter to be seen by a GP'; 'That's exactly the sort of case that shouldn't be seen in the emergency service; He's come here for a nephrological check-up, what are we supposed to do?'

Two dimensions are evident in the words used by staff when expressing this attitude: the feeling of being useful and the concept of taking pleasure in one's work. This is particularly evident in the responses to questions we asked in interviews concerning the degree of interest in emergency cases.

> AC: What is your idea of an interesting case?
> Female consultant: My idea of an interesting case? *An interesting case is one where I have the feeling of being useful*, where we've arrived at a diagnosis and found a suitable treatment, that's an interesting case. (Interview notes enclosed)

> AC: Practically speaking, what's your idea of an interesting case?
> Male consultant: *First of all, a case where I feel useful*, where I can apply everything I've learned over the last few years. That's what I call an interesting case – a situation where I feel involved and useful. (Interview notes enclosed)

These excerpts refer to a general feeling on the part of doctors of being useful. But this feeling may also be related much more closely to a logic of specialization, as indicated by the following excerpt:

> What I have to offer is specific skills in the field of emergency medicine – *if it's not an emergency, anyone else could do it as well as me*, and maybe better, since that person would have more time and would feel more involved. (Interview notes enclosed)

Doctors feel they have done something useful when they have been able to mobilize a particular skill and not just the skills possessed by any doctor. This dimension provides a very strong basis for mobilization, combining a personal interest in the case, an awareness of possessing a rare skill (the doctor belongs to a small group of people who are alone capable of solving this type of problem) and the feeling of acting for the good of another person. Arguments stemming from both individual interest and the general interest are reconciled through the logic of hospital specialization. This feeling corresponds to a vision of work in the emergency service based on gestures of resuscitation.

> Say someone comes in with severe respiratory distress. I'll have to incubate and oxygenate the patient, hook her up to the machine, that's something I find interesting. Or say it's chest pain with an infarction, I will initiate a treatment, and if I don't do it, or some other doctor doesn't do it, then the patient will die. What I really like is to feel that the patient's life is in my hands – it makes me feel useful, as if I have a real mission in life. (Interview notes enclosed)

In this scheme of things, the patient's mobilizing worth for the doctor increases in line with his or her feeling of usefulness; that is, the extent to which the doctor can anticipate a visible improvement in the patient's state thanks to his or her expertise in an area of medical treatment not within the scope of an ordinary doctor. Hence, patients who consult the emergency service but are not considered real emergencies may succeed in obtaining immediate access to medical care – thanks to the emergency service's accessibility – but are then dependent on the doctor's decision either to avoid dealing with the case or to make it his or her business to treat the patient.

Social demands

In this category we have put patients who consult the emergency service because of their inability to obtain what they need elsewhere (Béland et al., 1990): difficulties in gaining access to medical care; difficulty in satisfying the minimum requirements of life (accommodation, protection against cold, food . . .). This category of patient arouses complex reactions, which can range from a very negative attitude to a deliberate mobilization around the problem, with differences or even conflicts arising between personnel about the right attitude to adopt. Negative reactions can fall into several different groupings. First come recriminations of the same type as we noted earlier, when it is suggested that it would be more appropriate for the case to be treated by a GP than in an emergency service: criticisms concerning the difference between the patient's actual case and a 'real' emergency, or even the absence of a genuine medical problem, anticipation of difficulties in placing the patient. The principle of a service open to all the spontaneous demands of users is accepted in terms of actual behaviour but is criticized verbally.

> The telephone rings in the cubicles and is answered by the consultant. He explains that it concerns a young man of 23, a drug addict, a 'social problem' with a huge dental abscess. 'I *can't refuse him*', he says, 'and I know there's no room for him in the relevant service, so . . .'

Apart from simple verbal recriminations, negative reactions may take the form of delayed or limited mobilization during treatment. For example, homeless people are often pushed further down the waiting list.

> We are in the cubicle where the entry register is kept. The resident for that afternoon is leafing through the book: 'I'll wait for a bit before I take that homeless fellow. I'm never in a hurry to see those people!' She adds: 'What's wrong with him?', then looks at the file and says: 'Nothing'. She looks at the fireman's sheet on which is written: 'Fit of faintness'. She comments: 'They feel faint all the time, they come here to be in the warm, that's all.'

These patients may also arouse suspicion as to the possibility that they are manipulating the emergency service to obtain certain advantages by simulating or exaggerating medical problems. As in many other medical contexts, the medical decision is at the same time a decision concerning allocation of rights, that influences how doctors deal with individual's complaints (Dodier, 1994).

> A homeless man is brought in by the fire brigade 'in an advanced state of drunkenness'. The residents tell me that in this sort of case, they 'do a dextro, look at the pupils and that's it.' Another resident says that he 'doesn't waste time giving them a complete check-up'. A nurse walks by: 'So who's going to see him?' No decision is made. A clinical student finally decides to examine the patient.

These reactions obviously delay treatment of such patients, who are often made to wait for quite a long time, until there are only a few people waiting to be seen.

The low mobilizing worth of these patients is also reflected in the way the interaction is initiated, with staff tending to take a moralizing tone: the person is reproached for having applied to the emergency service or for being drunk. The following case shows a whole range of negative reactions in the comments made, the speed of mobilization and the interaction with the patient, more or less transcended by attempts at humour or joking with the other doctors.

> This is the homeless person brought in by the fire brigade, the one referred to in the observation repeated above, whom the resident said she was in no hurry to see. I asked the resident if patients from the emergency department could easily be transferred to her department. She answered that she was 'a neurology resident and didn't like dealing with emergency patients,[5] the emergency service always has these social cases, there are always problems to do with discharging patients and the social problems compounded the medical problems. However,' she added, 'sometimes interesting things crop up and you have to be careful not to miss them. . . . In fact, the Clinical Director in Neurology comes down every morning to check out the emergency service.[6] He'll say: 'Okay, we'll take two, but only those two there. . .'. You have to be able to see whether there's something interesting going on'. Then she says: 'One thing that influences the quality of a hospital service is not having a whole lot of these emergency patients.'
>
> In a joking voice, this resident asks a consultant: 'So, what are we going to do with this homeless fellow? Chuck him out?' (that is, refuse to admit him to the emergency service). The consultant replies that 'we've had problems before, you have to see them.' The resident resigns herself, puts on some gloves and approaches the man whom she ushers into the cubicle. The resident is obviously disgusted by the homeless man, she pinches her nose when talking to him, looks past him at the others and makes faces, etc.
>
> She speaks roughly to him. She asks him to move his legs, stretch out his arms: 'Come on, come on, no messing about, do what I tell you, it's an order!' In the file she writes: 'breath impregnated ++++, no motor deficit, general feeling of weakness over the last three days.' When first questioned, the homeless man says he is really exhausted, that he wants to stay in the emergency service. At this point the resident replies 'it's understandable given the amount he puts away, but he can't stay here.' The homeless man replies 'Put me in detox.' She replied: 'The emergency service isn't a detox unit.'

She asks for a hemogram and blood electrolyte, sugar and alcohol tests. She tells the man 'we are going to check your blood sugar, you can stay a while in the corridor to rest up and then you have to go.' The man replies: 'So I don't have a choice.' The resident says: 'No, you don't have a choice.'

The resident's attitude in this sequence shows that her reaction to the patient is also governed by certain aspects – drunken behaviour and physical characteristics, particularly smell – that may be associated, in certain patients, with their 'social' demands, but which are not the same order.

Alongside this tendency to become demobilized when confronted with so-called social problems, we can also see efforts to remobilize, which can create conflicting and tense situations among staff. Some reminders made to doctors, notably residents, by nurses and nursing auxiliaries, which we mentioned earlier, can be seen in this light. We can even observe, in contrast with 'non-social' demands, moments of active mobilization when patients, even those whose problems should have been dealt with by consulting a GP or a specialist, find in the hospital emergency service a place that responds to their distress. Here, the patient's social problem gives him or her greater mobilizing worth than an ordinary patient suffering from a similar medical problem. These observations converge with what Strong (1979: 41–5) calls the 'charity format' in doctor/patient interaction. It is quite common for doctors to examine and treat without recrimination patients who are obviously using the emergency service as a place for free consultations, or for these doctors to call to order colleagues who overtly display a lack of willingness to treat this type of patient.

We will refer back to the case of the homeless man brought in by the fire brigade as mentioned above. I asked the consultant what he thought of the presence of such people in the emergency service. Should they be treated? He replied: 'You have to see these people. Because of the life they lead – living out of doors, wandering about, alcoholism – they often have conditions that require hospitalization. They can't consult a doctor because you have to pay before the visit, even in dispensaries they have to pay out 20 francs. There is this Paris-santé (health) card, but they have to be registered somewhere, they have to have an address, so the hospital is the only place that they can be seen and treated for free'. This consultant also believed that it was useful to hospitalize homeless people since hospitalization tended to improve their general condition.

In some cases, staff may even propose treatment or services which the person did not request. An example is a resident and a surgical consultant offering a homeless German woman the possibility of having her bandages checked in the emergency service – for free, they added, knowing that the woman had no money or medical insurance.

Some personnel explicitly refer to the hospital's 'social function', bringing up the historic tradition whereby the hospital is open to all types of demands. In this way, they justify responding positively to social demands that are rejected by others.

AC: Talking of all these social problems and so on: in your opinion, should they be dealt with in the emergency service? These people who . . . come here because they don't know where else to go . . .

Clinical student: Strictly speaking, given that this is an emergency service, no, they shouldn't be here. But where else can they go? The dispensaries aren't open – they are open at specific times but closed at night. . . . I don't know, I find it easier to accept some down-and-out coming here for treatment than some lady who comes in and says. 'I've had this pain for three weeks now, so I've come to the emergency service.' It bothers me less, I don't know why, it puts me out less. I believe this is one of the functions of the hospital, this social function. This idea of integration was one of the things behind the creation of hospitals, so I think it's quite logical to hold onto this idea of inclusion. (Interview)

In this excerpt, the clinical student highlights the principle of positive mobilization around social demands, where the emergency service performs a function appropriate to the hospital ('I believe this is one of the functions of the hospital, this social function'), even if it contradicts the strict definition of emergency ('given that this is an emergency service, no, they shouldn't be here').

The social demands made here on emergency services are not always a source of criticism or systematic lowering of mobilization, as work carried out in the UK and the USA have indicated (Jeffery, 1979; Roth and Douglas, 1983). They are highly variable and very much dependent on circumstances. On the one hand, as for all cases which diverge sharply from the core of genuine emergencies, the way in which the patient is treated will depend on the particular flow of patients at the time.

It's morning. The consultant is talking in the cubicles about a man in the corridor, lying on a stretcher, who wants to stay in the hospital because they're disinfecting the place where he lives and it triggers asthma attacks. The consultant explains to the male nurse that this man is staying in the corridor because he can't be hospitalized. The nurse suggests that he stay on the stretcher *as long as there aren't too many people* and that he leave afterwards. The consultant goes to explain to the man that he can't be hospitalized because that would take a bed from someone who was really sick, but that he can stay on the stretcher and that he should inform someone when he wants to leave.

The greater the flow of patients, the longer it will take for medical staff to mobilize around social demands or the more limited this mobilization will be.

In the absence of a stabilized and explicit arrangement, in other words a 'policy', treatment of social demands is also dependent on variations in individual response. We have already observed sharp contrasts between different personnel. It is also possible that a given individual's reaction to social demands may vary, in that this reaction can be dictated as much by temporary feelings (pity, mood) as by a set reaction to the problem (individual policy). In any case, this variability of reaction came to light in the interviews and discussions which we carried out. In the interview excerpt below, a resident makes the following point:

AC: And homeless people, those poor people who are rather . . . yes, what do you think of . . .?

Resident: It's completely open. . . .

AC: Yes, open, you mean. . . .?

Resident: You can't do anything . . . already, it depends a great deal on their attitude. If they inspire pity in people, it will be okay, they'll get a meal tray, they'll be dealt with . . . but if they're aggressive, if they stink, if they're drunk, no-one will have anything to do with them.

AC: Yes, I suppose that generally speaking, you have to see people who must be rather unpleasant to examine, physically speaking, because they smell bad, or, as we saw this morning, they have body lice. However, it seems to me that people do in fact agree to treat them. . . .

Resident: Okay, *they agree to treat them, but on a scale of zero to 100 per cent.* From time to time in the overnight stay section, you see homeless people hospitalized just so they can spend the night indoors. You might be better off paying a hotel room for them so they could watch TV . . . all because that night the head nurse was in a good mood or the resident felt sorry for them, so, they give them a bed in the overnight stay section even though there's nothing much wrong with them. So, they won't spend the night in the cold. They'll have a good sleep, they'll spend the night in the warm, but the next day they'll be thrown out like undesirables. *So it really depends a lot on the particular day.* (Interview with resident)

The intellectual interest of the case

What we mean here by intellectual interest is the extent to which a case presents a challenge in terms of the diagnosis. This dimension is close to what Dingwall and Murray call the 'rule of clinical priority': 'We would there characterize the doctors as working under what we have called a rule of clinical priority. What they want is a steady flow of interesting cases with sufficient time to savour each one' (1983: 143). They are cases that are difficult to solve, but where there is a hope of clarification, which excludes rather poorly differentiated conditions such as alterations in the general state of elderly people – unusual cases, cases that teach the doctor something. How do doctors actually express their reaction to the intellectual interest of a case? Intellectual interest generates a higher degree of mobilization in terms of treating the patient. The difference in treatment between an interesting condition and an uninteresting condition can be seen when choosing the next patient from the entry register or the file tray.

> A clinical student is standing in front of the register. He remarks: 'I'd like to have a look at that: epigastric pain, decompensation, very interesting!' He walks off into the corridor and sees an elderly woman lying on a stretcher: 'Ah! it must be her!'

An interesting condition can increase the doctor's level of commitment in terms of case follow-up and defending the case against other players, particularly since the patient will also be easier to transfer, given that the other people involved will also consider it to be interesting. (Dodier and Camus, 1997)

> The telephone rings for Doctor N, a resident. Someone goes to find her. She picks up the phone with a contented look. We hear only her half of the conversation: 'So, what was wrong with her? (. . .)[7] What? (. . .) But I thought there were one or two nodules. (. . .) But I thought that . . . (. . .) What? (. . .) *Interesting!* (. . .) She should come back, we'll hospitalize her here, I'm very pleased (. . .) but generally there is some arthralgia, isn't there? (. . .) Okay, so you'll send her back?'
> She speaks to the consultant, who has just arrived: '*I'm pleased, it's an erythema nodosum. Its not the first time I've seen that, but you usually get one big nodule, here's it's lots of small nodules!* They're going to send her back.'
> The consultant says: 'Why are they sending her back? Can't they hospitalize her over there? He's a big dumb, that dermatologist!' 'No, he's nice.' The resident calls the dermatologist back: 'It's the resident in the medical emergency service. I have a young woman with an erythema nodosum. Can you take her? *It's interesting, huh?* (. . .) Great!' A nurse goes past and asks whether the lady in question wants to be hospitalized. The doctor continues with her telephone conversation. 'I'll call you back. She's come to us from a medical consultation, I'm going to ask her if she agrees to be hospitalized.' She goes off in the cubicle alongside and asks, very excited, to be informed immediately the patient gets back.

In this example, we can see that the resident is so enthusiastic about hospitalizing this very interesting case that the nurse has to remind her discreetly that the lady may not in fact want to be hospitalized. Other examples of interest can be noted throughout the treatment procedure: the ease with which a doctor will move on to a new case, the energy and effort devoted to consulting books to find the information for an unusual diagnosis, the time it takes for other doctors to come and check out the case, the rank of the persons mobilized (a particularly interesting case will attract doctors high up in the hierarchy: chief residents, heads of service).

Another thing that enters into this category is any aspect of pedagogical interest for young doctors. Faced with an interesting case, clinical students and residents all examine the patient, dropping by one after the other to check out the symptoms for themselves. The case is then discussed in a staff meeting and commented on by the chief resident for the edification of all the doctors in the service. Conversely, uninteresting cases may trigger expressions of disappointment, grimaces, recriminations or even jokes about stratagems for getting rid of the case.

> A resident pulls a face when confronted with a patient brought in by the fire brigade and presented by them as epileptic whereas the patient himself believed he had asthma.

> A consultant comments on the files when coming on duty and stops at one that says: 'Very high transaminase count, no platelets.' He looks amazed: 'So what do

they expect me to do?' He asks the nurse: 'So what's he doing here?' The nurse replies that he was found lying in the subway. The consultant attending replies, ironically: '*How exciting!*' Nevertheless, he goes off to examine the man in a cubicle.

Here again, signs of lack of interest in a patient may be translated into action, but are also reflected in the words accompanying the different levels of action, even if the actual therapeutic gestures for treating the patient are not necessarily modified.

Intellectual interest can take a number of forms: in the short term, the immediate interest of a complicated case to be solved; in the longer term, the feeling of having acquired new knowledge through a case that added to the individual's personal 'log-book' of cases; in the even longer term, interest in terms of later publication. Here, concepts of intellectual pleasure, interest in knowledge and the search for credit or fame through publication are very closely related. They refer notably to the growing role of medical research in the activity of hospital doctors (Berg, 1995; Jamous, 1969; Löwy, 1996).

This said, the concept of 'an interesting case' has a complex status in the language of doctors. The idea itself is part of their spontaneous language. But at the same time, when we routinely asked the following question in interviews: 'What constitutes an interesting case for you?', we noted a reluctance to use the concept itself. The following example with a female resident is instructive:

AC: What, in your opinion, is an interesting case?
Resident: Don't go any further! I mean that's a personal judgement, there's no such thing as an interesting case.
AC: Be honest, there must be moments, there must be cases that you find more interesting than others . . .
Resident: Well actually, you really don't have the right . . .
AC: What?
Resident: Well, you're not supposed to think in those terms . . .
AC: Sure, you're not supposed to, but you can't help being human . . .
and doctors are more interested in some cases than in others, that's obvious.
Resident: Yes, I would say there are interesting shifts and less interesting shifts.

Degrees of mobilization according to the intellectual interest of the condition can generate a contradictory relationship between doctors and patients. This reason for mobilization exists, it can be observed and the doctors themselves admit it. At the same time, it contradicts the doctor's duty to act, first and foremost, in the patient's interests. The interests of the doctor, even if intellectual, should remain secondary. This general duty is sometimes mentioned – in our survey, primarily during the interviews – as a way of placing the intellectual interest of the case on a secondary plane.

Shifting responsibility to the emergency service

Some of the demands made on the emergency service correspond to the desire of other players – general practitioners, other hospital services, other hospitals (see Appendix 2) – to shift responsibility. These situations create a problem, which is that of the agreement or refusal of the emergency service to accept this transfer of responsibility for patients who have already been admitted but who are then caught between two medical authorities. From the point of view of the GP, the hospital emergency service can be used as a sort of buffer zone between the outside world and the hospital. It has the advantage of being accessible without the need to make preliminary arrangements. The task of transferring the patient to a particular place for hospitalization can then be carried out by the staff of the emergency service, which is seen as sufficiently non-specialist to avoid the doctor having to specify a particular specialty and give reasons for the transfer, which he may find difficult. Patients can be sent straight away without being allocated to any specific service. We will now look at emergency staff's reaction to this category of transfer to the emergency service. When these cases are not seen as belonging to the core of real emergencies, in the strict sense of the term, medical staff tend primarily to react by criticizing the doctor who sent the patient. However, the patient is there and has to be examined. Some criticisms merely comment on an error of judgement by a general practitioner as to the degree of urgency of the case.

> The consultant is on the telephone. She is seeking advice from the neurologist concerning a patient that she has just examined in a cubicle: '*I want to know if you can see a patient, not an emergency, but just to give your opinion.* He hasn't been able to grasp objects for three weeks. The neurological examination seems to be normal, but his doctor sent him to the emergency service (. . .) *Well, yes, as I said at the beginning, it's not an emergency.* I'll send him for a neurological consultation.' She hangs up and says to the nurse: 'I'm going to do a blood electrolyte to check his potassium level all the same.' Then she says to the man 'I spoke to the neurologist. There's nothing to be worried about. We'll make an appointment for you in the neurology service tomorrow.'

Other criticisms go further with suspicions of a deliberate intention behind the transfer. The doctor is suspected of taking advantage of the ease of gaining admittance to the emergency service in order to avoid all the organizational tasks involved in transferring a patient to the hospital or to some other place: making contact with the relevant service for a consultation or admittance, making contact with the technical services for additional examinations, as if emergency service personnel were there solely to take care of this type of work.

This is the case in the following interview excerpt, where a consultant talks about a diabetic patient suffering from migraines, who has been sent to the emergency service by his GP:

Consultant: It could be a perfectly ordinary migraine, but we should at least do a routine scan so we don't miss something important. But as you saw, I questioned him first, then examined him and afterwards asked for a scan. I didn't ask for a scan straight away.

AC: So here the scan is more to . . . more to define a condition more exactly, but there was also the idea of covering yourself against something . . .

Consultant: Oh, absolutely. It was to make sure – not from the medical-legal point of view, because that's not the point – but to make sure I hadn't missed something important. That's it really, because I'd be quite astonished if . . . finally, it's really so as not to miss something important . . . and then, one reason is that you can do that kind of thing in the emergency service. However, this is an atypical patient, this young man, *who in my opinion could easily have been dealt with through the normal medical channels*, and I was able to request a scan quickly. That said, he might have been able to get it quicker going through his doctor, than in . . .

AC: So, what happens when a patient goes through a GP and gets sent off to the hospital . . .

Consultant: *Ah no, that's because GPs unfortunately won't . . . don't want to take the trouble*, but a GP *who really wants to do the job properly* will question the patient like I did . . . he'll ask the same questions as me and will send him . . . he'll telephone a private diagnostic centre and within three hours his patient will have a scan. You can probably get a scan more quickly in the private sector than going through the public hospital. In my opinion, he'll have to wait several hours – he might not have his scan until 8 o'clock tonight.

AC: So it's strange that these GPs send patients to the emergency service, whereas . . .,

Consultant: *Because it's a lot easier for them to do this in Paris*. In Paris, people are only 10 minutes away from the nearest hospital, but when you're in the provinces, you can't just systematically send your patients off to the hospital – you have to take responsibility for things. In this case, the patient was not suffering from any serious distress.

AC: No, apparently not.

Consultant: Right, so . . . but the GP couldn't be bothered, *it's so much easier to just send the patient to the emergency service.*

In this interview, the criticism of general practitioners is reinforced by their error in believing that it is easier to gain access to technical services in the hospital: the emergency service is very accessible, but obtaining a scan in the hospital is apparently not as easy as getting one in a private laboratory. This situation further complicates the task of emergency service staff, since they have to deal with the problem arising for patients who arrive without an appointment but for whom they have to make an appointment with the hospital's technical services.

GPs who wish to allocate their patients to a specific service in the hospital must make some kind of prior diagnosis. In some cases, emergency service personnel suspect these doctors of not being willing or able to do this work and to be using the emergency service to do this preliminary spade-work on their behalf.

In one cubicle, a resident shows me a letter from a GP who has sent a women for a psychiatric problem. The letter is addressed to the psychiatrist, but the patient has been sent to the emergency service. According to the resident, the GP is trying to cover himself but doesn't want to be thought ridiculous by sending the patient directly to the psychiatrist. The GP no doubt believes the problem to be a psychiatric one, but is not completely certain, and wants the emergency service to do the preliminary spade-work for him.

Other recriminations reflect suspicions that the GP is dissociating him or herself from a patient with low mobilizing worth. Here the transfer is seen as a way of abandoning the patient. From the point of view of emergency staff, the doctor, by shrugging off responsibility, has not respected the minimal obligation to follow up the patient to which he had committed himself in practice. This criticism is formulated in terms such as: 'getting rid of the patient', 'palming a patient off', 'losing interest in a patient', 'abandoning a patient'. This is the exact counterpart, from the viewpoint of the emergency department, of the process for which residents are socialized in other services under the generic term of 'Getting Rid of the Patient' (Mizrahi, 1985).

> Morning visit on a Friday. A resident brings up the case of a woman sent in with a sudden rise in blood pressure. The doctors look at the letter accompanying this woman, who was sent by a retirement home.
> Resident: This lady is in a very excited state, she's been really putting on a show! She was on Catapressan when she arrived. This morning her blood pressure suddenly shot up to 24, I put her on Loxene.
> Assistant: *What's the point of sending someone to the emergency department for that!* She has high blood pressure which is not very well controlled. . . . *Why send her off here when the problem has been going on for days. The problem is she was overexcited and they couldn't deal with it anymore.*
> The doctors go to the patient's bedside. She confirms that she has sudden rises in blood pressure, complains of backache and says that 'it's horrible' back there (in the home). She would like to be someplace where she could be alone, because she feels very tired. She also mentions arthritis in her left arm. Back in the corridor, the assistant very strongly criticizes the treatment she was given at the retirement home and suggests a new treatment. He also suggests keeping her at the hospital where at least there are competent medical staff. Once again he criticizes this way of sending people to the emergency service. *According to him, 'she must have been "very excited" and they wanted to send her off to emergency so as to have a quiet weekend.'*

The situation of patients sent off to the emergency service when they are already being followed in another service is quite similar. Here again, the emergency service is seen as an easily accessible buffer zone, but the decision to send the patient is a little more specific than in the preceding case, in that the patient is already being followed in one of the services in the hospital, which justifies sending him or her to this particular hospital. There are fewer recriminations than in the preceding cases. In fact, some of the preliminary work of admittance has already been done and is therefore not the responsibility of the emergency service, even if the work of placing the patient will not necessarily correspond to the principle of follow-up. This type of case could include patients suffering from chronic conditions but subject to regular flare-ups, who are quite routinely treated by the emergency services before going back to the service which usually treats them. Here, the transfer formalities are fairly cut and dried.

Another channel concerns patients sent to the emergency service from a service in the same hospital. They may first of all be patients who should in fact be hospitalized or treated in a particular service, and who were sent to this service, but without any prior preparation for admittance. For lack of a bed, they are sent on to the emergency service. Here, the emergency service is used as a rallying point for remedying problems in transfers between the outside world and the hospital. Another category might concern patients who were already hospitalized in a hospital service, but whose condition has evolved in such a way that the service in question believes it no longer has the capacity to deal with the new problems that have arisen.

> For example, surgical emergency staff will visit the medical emergency service for a patient whose condition calls more for their particular specialty, but will make an arrangement with the medical emergency service to admit the patient to the medical section if there are no beds free in the surgical ward. In another case, the pneumology service sends a patient who needs an oxygen bottle if there is not one available in their service, or to have hormonal tests done.

The main criticism levelled against these services is the suspicion that they have abandoned a patient with little mobilizing worth and have reneged on their obligation to follow up the patient. The admitting specialty describe the patients as not being 'suitable' for the service, or claims that there are no resources available to treat them. Emergency personnel see these arguments as pretexts concealing a loss of interest in the patient, which the service in question is not able to admit overtly – and which is in any case difficult to admit given that the patient is already being treated by the service – and see this as getting rid of a person who is already 'its patient'. The criticism will be even sharper if the patient also has low mobilizing worth for the emergency service itself. A typical cause of conflict between hospital services is the arrival at the emergency service of people in terminal phase, already being treated in the hospital, but not accepted by their usual service. These patients have entered what Sudnow (1967) calls the phase of 'social death', which is primarily reflected in the lack of interest shown in them by the staff of this service.

> A man comes into the cubicle and says to the resident: 'I've brought you a little lady with a possible pleural problem, sent by R.' The resident goes to see the woman, who is lying on a stretcher and is 'much worse' than the woman with thoracic pain he was in the middle of examining in the cubicle. Since the

resuscitation cubicle is already taken, he decides to put her in cubicle M3. He tells me with a certain irony: '*If the lady is already in terminal phase, of course we'll be able to save her here! That's R's great specialty: palming their patients off on the emergency service!*' He says to the nurse: 'Do a blood electrolyte, anyway', then goes into cubicle M3. Here, several people with the SAMU initials on the back of their coats are busily dealing with the lady, who is extremely thin. They hook her up to an oxygen bottle. The lady asks for a cushion. According to the SAMU doctor, the GP indicated that the lady's heart had stopped, that he did a cardiac message and that it 'started up again'. He indicates that the tests done yesterday showed a sodium level at 128, potassium at 5 and calcium at 80. The resident explains that the reasoning behind the service not wanting to keep this woman who had come in to die was that '*it would take up a bed for nothing, so they think they might as well palm her off on the emergency service*'. He says that he's not going to leave her there, because 'it could last a quarter of an hour, or it could last several days'. He starts of towards the telephone. Walking in front of the scope, he sees that the woman is no longer breathing. The trace is flat. He feels her neck, fails to find a pulse and listens with his stethoscope. He tells the nurse that the scope is flat and that he can remove the drip. The nurse initiates the process of dealing with a dead person (closing the eyes, shutting the mouth, making a report, etc.).

Transferring patients who are close to death creates tensions between services. Such a transfer can be justified by the fact that the emergency service has resuscitation equipment. But this particular case concerned a patient whose death was pretty much inevitable. From the point of view of the oncology department, if there is a lack of beds, giving a bed to a patient for whom the treatment dispensed has little chance of being effective, is considered to be 'taking up a bed for nothing'. But at the same time, the service is exporting a difficult situation to emergency and breaching its commitment to 'its patient'.

The reference to 'an obligation of follow-up' is definitely inherent in criticisms of abandonment of patients. But the exact limits of this obligation raise many questions. The obligation to follow up a patient may be in contradiction with the concept of specialization. This is the case when a patient's problems evolve in such a way that they come within the scope of another specialty. Where does the obligation to follow up the patient give way to the need to redirect the case to the relevant specialty? At what point does the emergency service change from being a place equipped with specific resources enabling it to deal better than other services with patients in crisis, to a place to 'stock' patients not wanted or not placeable elsewhere? These are the terms of a recurrent debate that can make moments of transfer particularly difficult.

The reaction can go beyond verbal recriminations to a refusal to admit a patient when a transfer to emergency is requested.

We are in the office of the ward sister in the overnight stay section of the emergency service. The head nurse of another service rings up to ask if a patient can be admitted to emergency since her service is full. Pauline, the head sister in emergency, gives out the phone number of a clinic. She explains that she keeps a list of clinic numbers because 'unfortunately, they tend to transfer patients at the drop of a hat'. I ask why the person had requested a bed in the emergency service. Pauline explains that it was a patient who had been seen by a specialist resident on duty in the emergency service, who had asked the patient to consult his particular service. The patient did so, but it turned out there was no bed in this service and so the head nurse believes that the patient should be sent back to the emergency service. Pauline tells the supervisor that she should tell the resident: 'You accepted the patient, now you deal with him'.

In this example, the moral commitment made by the resident to the patient on duty in the emergency service was confirmed by his transferring the patient to his own service. Sending the patient back to emergency, with another transfer on the cards, is unacceptable from the ward sister's point of view. It is obviously easier to refuse by telephone than if the patient had already come back to the emergency service.

When we look at all these transfers of responsibility, we can see that the emergency service plays three major roles: (1) it is a place for absorbing cases that have not yet been placed in the hospital but which are directed to it (the hospital's 'front door'); (2) it is a holding area for mistaken referrals and for patients who are present but not wanted by the different departments; (3) and more generally, as an easily accessible service, the emergency service acts as a buffer zone for those difficult moments of transfer from one place to another. The latter function forces staff to take on the work involved in the transfer, which they accept without comment (26 per cent of the cases in our study), with recriminations (65 per cent of the cases) or may even refuse (9 per cent). In the event of disagreement (with or without a refusal), the dispute will centre on the fact that people are delegating to the emergency service tasks that are part of the duties incumbent on a doctor who accepts responsibility for a patient: organizing the patient's transfer to the hospital, ensuring treatment even when the case no longer has any mobilizing worth – in other words, they must not seek to 'get rid of patients' whose mobilizing worth has been lowered. Evaluation of the scope and limits of this obligation to follow up a case is the main cause of tensions between the protagonists.

Concluding remarks

In this chapter, we have identified the main actors that explicitly influence the differing degrees of mobilization of staff around the flow of demands to be dealt with in an emergency department: closeness to the core of real emergencies, social demands, the intellectual interest of the pathology, questions raised by transfers of responsibility. Other aspects also play a –

more secondary – role in our observations and we will mention them here for purposes of information: bodily contact, a dimension which has been analysed quite methodically in Peneff's study (1992); anticipation of failure in dealing with the patient; the degree to which the patient cooperates; specific questions around drunkenness; anticipation of difficulties in placing the patient; social category (Camus and Dodier, 1994). In this French example, our observations confirm that the logics of specialization and openness are both strongly present, simultaneously, within an emergency service. The three major categories (closeness to a real emergency, social demands, the intellectual interest of the case) are associated directly with one or other of them. The fact that budget criteria are not brought into play in judging patients, unlike what can be observed in other services (Dodier and Camus, 1997), is related to the fact that the emergency service budget is calculated on the number of patients treated, and is not modulated, as in other hospital services, by more precise considerations concerning the individual patient and, notably, the time of his/her stay. Our observations confirmed the existence of a whole range of mobilizing arguments that cannot be easily reduced to a dichotomy between good and bad patients. Work in the emergency service can be seen as the task of controlling a variable flow of patients, each of which has a different mobilizing worth. Systematic work on the different sources of this worth suggests three comments.

1. Reference to specialization of treatment raises not one, but two – very different – types of reaction: closeness to life-threatening emergency and the intellectual interest of the case. This distinction comes into play in terms of the degree of mobilization: it shows that patients whose case does not really fall into the category of an emergency – outpatient cases or GP cases – can be highly mobilizing to emergency staff if they are clinically interesting, a factor observed several times in earlier studies (e.g., Roth and Douglas, 1983: 95), but not systematically analysed there. This distinction also brings into play qualitatively different reactions: the concept of emergency is associated with what the doctor brings to the patient, and what the patient brings to him/her, in the present moment; the intellectual interest of the case is associated with the doctor's investment in the future, through what it teaches him, through the accumulation of medical-scientific observations and publications. As concerns the degree of urgency of the case, we observe that staff's reactions are straightforward and that they react as a unit: the closer the case is to a real emergency, the more the feeling of usefulness and spontaneous interest increases on the part of all staff. This is not so in terms of reference to other specialties, via the concept of the intellectual interest of the case. Here, reactions are much more complex. On the one hand, for doctors on duty in the emergency service, there is a tension between taking an interest in things related to their original specialty and things related to the different tasks of an

emergency service. But on the other hand, the intellectual interest in the case – as an interest in what the patient brings the doctor in terms of learning, publications, recognition by other doctors – is likely to come into contradiction with what the doctor gives the patient in terms of treatment.

2. Social demands arouse very mixed reactions: some refer to the concept of the emergency service as a specialized service and relegate social problems further down the order of precedence; conversely, others refer directly to the hospital's tradition of openness in order to defend the need to respond to these demands without pushing the patient down the waiting list. In this respect, the function of the emergency service is far from being fixed. The duality of the hospital, between specialization and openness, is a source of very different reactions on the part of its personnel. The position of the different players is important here: specialty residents tend to give social problems lesser importance, whereas certain nurses and nursing auxiliaries, and even non-specialist consultants, call their attention to this question. At the same time, we believe that in the absence of an explicit policy concerning the social question, personnel construct their own individual policies or express varying attitudes at different times. This variety of reactions means that people who apply to the emergency service because of its accessibility are exposed to great uncertainty as to the degree to which staff will mobilize around their case, either as a function of the flow of simultaneous demands, or because of the impossibility of predicting individual attitudes at a given time.

This complexity of reactions to social demands is a new finding with respect to earlier observations. This mixture of reactions seems to be much more a feature of the French example than observations concerning English or American hospitals, where the aspects that we identify as related to social demands are placed in the same category as 'bad patients' – the convergence between all these studies is quite striking. We might suggest two interpretations, which call for further and systematic comparative work. Either the difference is linked to analytical frameworks: in other words, the dichotomy between good and bad patients on which these works are based tends to flatten out complex reactions, and presupposition of a certain homogeneity tends to diminish the variety of these reactions, in which case, certain stances in favour of social demands would not have been picked up by these studies. Alternatively, there really do exist national differences, in that the mobilization of staff in emergency departments around the social question in France – more than in the USA and the UK – appears to have been more diffuse, more closely intermingled with everyday work, running counter to the spontaneous movement towards specialized selection of patients.

This taking into account of the social aspects of demands refers back to the social question, and must be clearly distinguished, analytically, from what Roth and Douglas (1983), in their extension to several earlier works on the hospital and more generally on relationships with a clientele, call judgements on the social worth of patients. It is rare to find any reference to patients' social worth in our body of cases, a point that is particularly obvious if we use a very circumscribed definition based on socio-professional category. Here again, and for lack of any complementary work, we might examine two quite different possibilities for interpreting this difference: either this categorization of patients plays a very negligible role in the everyday work of staff in the service which we studied, or indeed more generally, in French emergency services; or it belongs to that category of judgements, which, although having a genuine influence on activity, is not expressed and acts silently, in which case, given the way our study was organized, it remained outside our grasp.

3. Finally, there is another aspect of dealing with patients which earlier ethnographic studies have barely touched on: the question of transfer of patients between doctors. When looking at this question, these studies simply mentioned that patients sent on by doctors have greater legitimacy than patients arriving from other sources. Here, our observations highlight a more complex web of relationships built up between the people responsible for treatment. They are faced with the following question: to what extent is the transfer of a patient from one doctor to another justified by the division of tasks between specialties, and to what extent does it result from an advanced stage of demobilization, an abandonment of a patient with particularly low mobilizing worth? Here, the moral judgement no longer concerns the patient, but the agency responsible for his/her transfer to the emergency service. Our observations show the complexity of the work done by members of the emergency service to define, for each case, the responsibilities for following up their own patients incumbent on the other services. As Bosk and Frader (1990) suggest, the debate about how far doctors are obliged to go in dealing with patients in hospital is becoming more and more acute. Uncertainties here reflect questions about the way these questions are decided and the role of agencies outside the services themselves, notably hospital administration (see Green and Armstrong, 1993). We might think that certain important trends in contemporary hospitals tend to accentuate tensions between services around these questions. Under the influence of budget restrictions and the increasing emphasis on the scientific aspects of medicine, each hospital service tends to tighten up its patient profile around selective criteria. However, on this question, we can merely note the limitations of an inquiry strategy based on an ethnographic study of a service. The organizational repercussions of specialization tend to influence sociological methods. In a situation in which specialties are becoming increasingly interdependent, arrangements for ensuring circulation of patients between services take on capital importance. Studying them implies the need for transversal approaches – as well as ethnographic studies based on services – designed to recognize, right along the flow of patients, instances of solidarity and confrontation between the different actors making up together their access to treatment.

Appendix 1 *Factors explicitly influencing the mobilization of staff*

Total cases observed: 79 patients, or 113 items[8]

Breakdown of cases by source of mobilization	Number of cases
Degree of urgency of the case	33
Social demands	22
Intellectual interest of the case	13
Transfer of responsibility to the emergency service	13
Bodily contact	8
Anticipation of care failure	6
Patient's degree of cooperation	4
Drunkenness	4
Anticipation of placement difficulties	3
Other	5

Appendix 2 *Transfer by other doctors to the emergency service*

Total cases observed	34
Patients sent to the hospital by general practitioners but not expected in a department	14
Patients sent to the hospital by general practitioners, already followed by a service, but sent without previous contact being made with this service	7
Patients sent to the emergency service by another hospital service	13

Notes

1. For France, see particularly Castel (1995), Faure (1982), Foucault (1979), Imbert (1982), Maillard (1988).
2. See notably the research of Luc Boltanski and Laurent Thévenot on the ordinary sense of justice (Boltanski, 1990; Boltanski and Thévenot, 1991). For a presentation of the analytical framework thus created and its extension to other fields of investigation, see Dodier (1993, 1995a). Indications about the consequences in terms of ethnographic work may be found in Baszanger and Dodier (1997).
3. Nurses' injunctions to residents to work faster is described by Mizrahi (1985), although he does not suggest a link between the panoramic work of managing patient flows and clinical attention to individual cases.
4. For further remarks on antagonism between users and staff on this point at reception, with users finding it difficult to understand that a persistent pain can generate a refusal to admit them to the emergency service, see Camus and Dodier (1994). In English hospitals, this reference to the time when the symptoms first

appeared is used as a criterion of eligibility, in an even more codified manner, since it is explicitly mentioned at the entrance that injuries must not be more than 48 hours old (Hughes, 1989).

5. This is an example of a 'specialist' resident, assigned to services other than emergency, but who is nevertheless obliged to work shifts in the emergency service.

6. Patients can remain no longer than 24 hours in the service. After the morning visit, those who are to remain hospitalized must be placed in other services. Here, the clinical student is referring to the fact that during the daily morning visit in the emergency service, emergency doctors solicit the opinion of the chief resident in the neurology service.

7. The three dots between brackets (. . .) indicate the unheard part of the telephone call.

8. The same patient may simultaneously present several characteristics.

References

Baszanger, I. and N. Dodier (1997) 'Ethnography: relating the part to the whole', in D. Silverman (ed.), *Qualitative Analysis: Issues of Theory and Method*. London: Sage.

Béland, F., L. Philibert, J.P. Thouez and B. Maheux (1990) 'Socio-spatial perspectives on the utilization of emergency hospital services in two urban territories in Quebec', *Social Science and Medicine*, 30(1): 53–66.

Béland, F., A. Lemay, L. Philibert and B. Maheux (1991) 'Elderly patients' use of hospital-based emergency services', *Medical Care*, 29: 408–18.

Berg, M. (1995) 'Turning a practice into a science: redrawing the nature and flaws of postwar medical practice', *Social Studies of Science*, 25: 437–76.

Boltanski, L. (1990) *L'Amour et la Justice Comme Compétences. Trois Essais en Sociologie de l'Action*. Paris: Métailié.

Boltanski, L. and L. Thévenot (1991) *De la Justification. Les Économies de la Grandeur*. Paris: Gallimard.

Bosk, C. and J. Frader (1990) 'AIDS and its impact on medical work: the culture and politics of the shop floor', *The Milbank Quarterly*, 68(supp. 2): 257–79.

Callon, M. (ed.) (1989) *La Science et ses Réseaux*. Paris: La Découverte.

Camus, A. and N Dodier (1994) *L'Intérêt pour les Patients à l'Entrée de l'Hôpital. Enquête Sociologique dans un Service d'Urgences Médicales*. Paris: CERMES-GSPM.

Castel, R. (1995) *Les Métamorphoses de la Question Sociale. Une Chronique du Salariat*. Paris: Fayard.

Dingwall, R. and T. Murray (1983) 'Categorization in accident departments: "good" patients, "bad" patients and "children"', *Sociology of Health and Illness*, 5(2): 127–48.

Dodier, N. (1993) 'Acting as a combination of "common words"', *The Sociological Review*, 41(3): 556–71.

Dodier, N. (1994) 'Dealing with complaints in expert medical decision: a sociological analysis of judgment', *Sociology of Health and Illness*, 16(4): 489–514.

Dodier, N. (1995a) 'The conventional foundations of action: elements of a sociological pragmatics', *Réseaux. The French Journal of Communication*, 3(2): 147–66.

Dodier, N. (1995b) *Les Hommes et les Machines. La Conscience Collective dans les Sociétés Technicisées.* Paris: Métailié.

Dodier, N. and A. Camus (1997) 'L'admission des malades. Histoire et pragmatique de l'accueil à l'hôpital', *Annales. Histoire, Sciences Sociales,* 4: 733–63.

Elster, J. and N. Herpin (ed.) (1992) *Ethique des Choix Médicaux.* Poitiers: Actes Sud.

Faure, O. (1982) *Genèse de l'Hôpital Moderne: les Hospices Civils de Lyon de 1802 à 1845.* Lyon: Presses Universitaires de Lyon.

Foucault, M. (ed.) (1979) *Les Machines à Guérir.* Bruxelles. Pierre Mardaga.

Genell Andrén, K. and U. Rosenqvist (1987a) 'Heavy users of an emergency department – a two-year follow-up study'. *Social Science and Medicine,* 25(7): 825–31.

Genell Andrén, K. and U. Rosenqvist (1987b) 'An ecological study of the relationship between risk indicators for social disintegration and use of a somatic emergency department', *Social Science and Medicine,* 25(10): 1121–7

Green, J. and D. Armstrong (1993) 'Controlling the "bed state": negotiating hospital organisation', *Sociology of Health and Illness,* 15(3): 337–52.

Herzlich, C. (1973) 'Types de clientèle et fonctionnement de l'institution hospitalière', *Revue Française de Sociologie,* 14: 41–59.

Hughes, D. (1988) 'When nurses know best: some aspects of nurse/doctor interactions in a casualty department', *Sociology of Health and Illness,* 10(1): 1–22.

Hughes, D. (1989) 'Paper and people: the work of the casualty reception clerk', *Sociology of Health and Illness,* 11(4): 382–408.

Imbert, J. (ed.) (1982) *Histoire des Hôpitaux en France.* Toulouse: Privat.

Jamous, H. (1969) *Sociologie de la Décision. La Réforme des Études Médicales et des Structures Hospitalières.* Paris: Editions du CNRS.

Jeffery, R. (1979) 'Normal rubbish: deviant patients in casualty departments', *Sociology of Health and Illness,* 1(1): 90–107.

Latour, B. (1989) *La Science en Action.* Paris: La Découverte.

Lejonc, J.L., J. Amselem, G. Marchalot-Leclercq, A.-M. De Saxce, M.-N. Fleury and C. Marsault. (1993) 'L'Hôpital universitaire peut-il assurer sa mission d'hôpital général? L'expérience du service des urgences et de l'unité de médecine générale de l'hôpital Henri-Mondor (Créteil)', *Gestions Hospitalières,* 328: 489–93.

Löwy, I. (1996) *Between Bench and Bedside: Science, Healing and Interleukin-2 in a Cancer Ward.* Cambridge, MA and London: Harvard University Press.

Maillard, C. (1988) *Histoire de l'Hôpital de 1940 à nos Jours. Comment la Santé est Devenue une Affaire d'Etat.* Paris: Dunod.

Mannon, J. (1976) 'Defining and treating "problem patients" in a hospital emergency room', *Medical Care,* 14(12): 1004–13.

Mannon, J., L. Green, M. Levine, G. Gibson and H. Gurlay (1987) 'Using the emergency department as a screening site for high blood pressure', *Medical Care,* 25: 770–80.

Mizrahi, T. (1985) 'Getting rid of patients: contradictions in the socialisation of internists to the doctor–patient relationship', *Sociology of Health and Illness,* 7: 214–35.

Mol, A. and J. Law (1994) 'Regions, networks and fluids: anaemia and social topology', *Social Studies of Science,* 24: 641–71.

Peneff, J. (1992) *L'Hôpital en Urgence. Etude par Observation Participante.* Paris: Métailié.

Perrow, C. (1984) *Normal Accidents. Living with High Risk Technologies.* New York: Basic Books.

Roth, J. (1972a) 'Some contingencies of the moral evaluation and control of clientele: the case of the hospital emergency service', *American Journal of Sociology,* 77(5): 839–56.

Roth, J. (1972b) 'Staff and client control strategies in urban hospital emergency', *Urban Life and Culture,* 1: 139–60.

Roth, J. and D. Douglas (1983) *No Appointment Necessary. The Hospital Emergency Department in the Medical Services World.* New York: Irvington.

Star, S.L. (1989) 'The structure of ill-structured solutions: boundary objects and heterogeneous distributed problem solving', in L. Gasser and M. Huhns (eds), *Distributed Artificial Intelligence* (vol. 2). London: Pitman.

Steg, A. (1989) *Rapport Pour le Conseil Économique et Social sur la Situation des Services d'Urgences.* Paris: La Documentation Française.

Strauss, A., S. Fagerhaugh, B. Suczeck and C. Wiener (1985) *The Social Organization of Medical Work.* Chicago: University of Chicago Press.

Strong, P. (1979) *The Ceremonial Order of the Clinic.* London: Routledge and Kegan Paul.

Sudnow, D. (1967) *Passing On. The Social Organization of Dying.* Englewood Cliff, NJ: Prentice-Hall.

Thévenot, L. (1993) 'Les formes de savoir collectif selon les régimes pragmatiques: des compétences attribuées ou distribuées', in J.P. Dupuy, P. Livet and F. Reynaud (eds), *Limitations de la Rationalité et Constitution du Collectif.* Paris: La Découverte.

Timmermans, S. (1995) 'La déconstruction/reconstruction oles "soi" dans les techniques de réanimation', *Techniques et Culture,* 25–6, *Les Objets de la Médecine,* 245–61.

Vassy, C. and F. Renard (1992) 'Quels malades pour l'hôpital public? Deux stratégies de segmentation', *Annales des Mines,* coll. *Gérer et Comprendre,* June, 29–39.

Guided reading exercises

These exercises consist of questions to focus your attention on key features of the individual readings and to compare those in each section. You may want to use them to guide your personal reading and note-taking, or in seminar situations, as a basis for discussion.

Exercise on Chapter 1: *Bourgois*

1. Why did Bourgois select this particular population and locality to study?
2. What theory or explanation of social marginalization is he writing to challenge?
3. What role does he take as a reasearcher? How would you describe his relationship to the people he is studying and to the data he collects?
4. What kinds of evidence does he present? How did he obtain this? (*Note*: This may not be directly stated.)

Exercise on Chapter 2: *Maher and Dixon*

1. What practical effect is this research intended to have? Who are the authors seeking to persuade or influence?
2. What evidence is presented for the claims? How is this different from the evidence presented in the previous study? What reasons can you suggest for this difference?
3. To what extent can Maher and Dixon's findings be generalized to other situations?

Exercise comparing Chapters 1 and 2

These first two ethnographic studies are broadly similar in that both investigated illegal drug markets in urban areas. But there are also major differences.

1. In what respects are the writing styles different? Why do you think this is so?
2. What questions are the researchers seeking to answer in each case?

Exercise on Chapter 3: *Hey*

1. Although this is not a conventional educational study, it was conducted in schools. What practical steps did the researcher have to take to set up this project and obtain permission to conduct it?
2. How were the original plans for the study modified as she proceeded? (*Hints*: What problems did she have gaining access to the people she was interested in? What additional data did she gather?)

Exercise on Chapter 4: *Alexander*

1. How did Alexander select the group of young men that she studied?
2. What forms of data collection did she use in the study?
3. What is the relationship of this researcher to her research? In what ways are the research process and the findings affected by who she is?

Exercise comparing Chapters 3 and 4

The two readings in this section both consider the identities which people acquire and develop through their relationships.

1. What categories of identity is each researcher particularly interested in?
2. According to these readings, how far are individuals free to reject or modify these identities?

Exercise on Chapter 5: *Salzinger*

1. As you will notice from the title, Salzinger's study of a workplace is particularly concerned with workers as sexual subjects and objects. She is not, however, investigating 'sexual harassment' as this is usually understood (there is a definition in the fourth paragraph). In what way is the focus of this study different?
2. How did the researcher collect her data?
3. The essence of any empirical work, including ethnography, is that claims and interpretations are based on evidence. What kinds of evidence are used in this study? (*Hint*: These may not be described but only referred to indirectly.)

Exercise on Chapter 6: *Hutchins and Klausen*

1. Hutchins and Klausen study an airline cockpit as a *system*. According to this reading, what are the component parts which make up this system?
2. How did the researchers collect their data? (Notice that we are given a short transcript from a single occasion but the detailed explanation of events is obviously based on a more extended study.)
3. In this example the researchers use 'an ethnography of the setting to provide the interpretative bridge' between their data and their theory. This bridge consists of several layers or levels. What are these?
4. Unlike some of the other studies in the collection, this piece of ethnographic research has clear practical applications. Can you identify one training application and one application for equipment design?

Exercise comparing Chapters 5 and 6

1. Each of these studies is about processes involved in work and a workplace. A conventional way to study work might be to follow one individual worker but each of these research projects has a larger focus. What is the unit of analysis in each study?
2. What is the general problem which concerns the researcher(s)? (*Hint*: One way to identify this is to ask 'What is this study against? What does it want to prevent or change?)

Exercise on Chapter 7: *Edensor*

1. Why did Edensor choose to study the Taj Mahal?
2. What behaviours docs he study? What evidence of these does he collect and how does he collect it?
3. Edensor quotes directly from a number of the people he interviews. What is his purpose in doing this?

Exercise on Chapter 8: *Kraidy*

Overview

As a starting point, you may find it useful to mark the sections which cover the following points:

(a) the global (for example, as the level on which imperialism or international media operate) and the local (as the level of national or ethnic cultures);
(b) the concept of hybridity;
(b) the arguments against two extreme views of media outputs and their audiences.

1. Why does the author see Lebanon as a particularly appropriate case for the study of these issues?
2. What methods of data collection were used in the study and what was the connection between them?
3. Who are 'the interlocutors' he refers to?
4. What is a native ethnographer and why does the author define himself as one?
5. Which two discourses does Kraidy identify in the talk he analyses? Which other dualities or contrasting pairs of concepts does he discuss?

Exercise comparing Chapters 7 and 8

1. I have put these two readings together as examples of the consumption of cultural products. In each case, what is the culture being referred to? (*Note*: This may or may not be a widely recognized, named entity, like a national culture, for example Indian.)
2. To what extent is this culture stable and separate from other cultures?

3. What is the ethnographer's position in relation to this culture? (For example, insider? outsider? both?) How do their positions differ?
4. What advantages and disadvantages does the ethnographer's position have for the study?

Exercise on Chapter 9: *Griffiths*

Overview

Griffiths analyses talk from meetings in which teams of workers negotiate as part of a decision-making process. Check that you understand the following points:

(a) the (different) occupations of the team members and their relative status (in particular, note which people present in Team A and Team B have the highest status);
(b) the work of the team as a whole;
(c) the purpose of the meetings.

The data

The data are talk from the meetings.

1. What was the main method of data collection?
2. What other methods were used? (*Hint*: What other information is drawn on in the interpretation of the talk? How do you think the researcher gathered this?)
3. What information is included in the transcripts apart from the words spoken? (*Hint*: Try reading the transcript out loud. What are you told about who is speaking and how they speak? Look at the extra information in Note 2. Notice also how these transcripts differ from the one in Chapter 6 by Hutchins and Klausen.)

The analysis

4. Griffiths identifies two 'discourses' which provide two 'sense-making frameworks'. What are these?
5. As the title indicates, the chapter considers the function of 'humour' in the teams' talk. What aspects of the talk does this

term, 'humour' refer to? (In other words, what do the speakers do that is referred to as examples of humour?)

6. What is meant in this analysis by the term 'resistance'?

Exercise on Chapter 10: *Dodier and Camus*

1. A key premise in this study is that a hospital has a dual role. What is this? From what you are told in this chapter, would this be a general characteristic of hospitals or might it be specific to hospitals in this country (France)?

2. As part of their analysis, the researchers propose a new concept, 'mobilizing worth'. How do they define this?

3. The researchers are interested in how staff categorize patients in the emergency services. They reject the broad dichotomy identified in previous studies as oversimple. How many dimensions does their analysis of categorization consider?

4. What do they take as evidence of the factors which operate in the categorization process? What does this omit?

5. What do they draw on from previous studies? Where do they disagree with them? (*Note:* It will be useful to mark these points as you go through the reading.)

Exercise comparing Chapter 9 and 10

1. To what extent to these two studies have implications for:
   (a) similar medical services (community mental health care, hospital emergency services) outside the specific national contexts in which they were conducted? (*Hint:* What relevant features of the services would be different in other countries?)
   (b) non-medical contexts, such as interactions and decision-making within other kinds of organization, including in the private sector?

Index